Who's Who in Space

The First **25** Years

The joint U.S.-U.S.S.R. Apollo-Soyuz Test Project (ASTP) crew patch.

The ASTP official emblem chosen by NASA and the Soviet Academy of Sciences.

The ASTP Prime Crewmen: Standing (left to right), Stafford and Leonev; seated (left to right), Slayton, Brand, and Kubasov.

Who's Who in Space

The First **25** Years

MICHAEL CASSUTT

G.K. HALL & CO.
70 Lincoln Street, Boston, Mass.

G. K. Hall & Co.
70 Lincoln Street
Boston, MA 02111

87 88 89 90 / 4 3 2 1

Cassutt, Michael.
Who's who in space.

1. Manned space flight—History. 2. Astronauts—Biography. I. Title.
TL788.5.C37 1987 629.45'0092'2 86–26988
ISBN 0–8161–8801–7

Designed and produced by Carole Rollins.
Copyediting supervised by Michael Sims.
Set in 9½ / 11 Aster by R/TSI Typographic Co., Inc.

EASTFOTO: Farkas, Jaehn, Magyari, Remek; Gubarev and Remek.

Hughes Aircraft: Konrad.

Library of Congress: Alexandrov, Ivanov, Jankowski, Kohllner, Liem, Lopez-Falcon, Pelczak, Prunariu.

National Research Council Canada: Bondar, Maclean, Money, Thirsk, Trygvvason.

NOVOSTI from SOVFOTO: Komarov; Demin and Sarfinov.

PHOTO CNES: Clervoy, Deshays, Favier, Haignere, Patat, Tognini, Viso.

TASS from SOVFOTO: Al Fares, Andreyev, Anikeyev, Artyukhin, Belyayev, Beregovoy, Bykovsky, Chretien, Dediu, Dobrovolsky, Filatyev, Filipchenko, Ganzorig, Grechko, Gubarev, Gurragcha, Habib, Hermaszewski, Khrunov, Klimuk, Leonov, Makarov, Malhotra, Malyshev, Nelyubov, Popov, Popovich, Rafikov, Rozhdestvensky, Ryumin, Savinykh, Serebrov, Sevastyanov, Sharma, Tamayo-Mendez, Titov, Tuan, Volk, Zaikin, Zholobov, Zudov; and all photographs in the Soviet Space Travelers photoessay with the exception of Demin and Sarafinov, and Gubarev and Remek.

U.K. Ministry of Defence: Boyle.

USAF: Abrahamson, Adams, Aldridge, Armor, Bobko, Casserino, Crews, Crippen, Detroye, Engle, Finley, Fullerton, Gordon, Hamel, Hartsfield, Herres, Higbee, Holder, James, Jones, Joseph, Kincheloe, Knight, Lacomb, Lawrence, Lawyer, Lydon, Macleay, McKay, Neubeck, Odle, Overmyer, D. Peterson, F. Peterson, Puz, Rij, Roberts, Rogers, Rushworth, Sefchek, Sponalbe, Sundberg, Taylor, Thompson, Truly, Vidrine, Watterson, A. White, R. White, Wood, Wright, Yeakel.

VAAP: Aksenov, Alexandrov, Anokhin, Atkov, Berezovoy, Bondarenko, Demin, Dzhanibekov, Feoktistov, Gagarin, Glazkov, Gorbatko, Illiarionov, Ivanchenkov, Kizim, Kovalenok, Kubasov, Lazarev, Lebedev, Lyakhov, Nikolayev, Patsayev, Romanenko, Rukavishnikov, Sarafinov, Savitskaya, Shatalov, Shonin, Solovyov, Strekalov, Tereshkova, Vasyutin, A. Volkov, V. Volkov, Volynov, Yegorov, Yeliseyev.

All other photographs courtesy of NASA.

Who's Who in Space

The First **25** Years

Contents

Part 3 International Space Travelers

Acknowledgments

The author wishes to thank those who provided photographs, biographical materials, and other assistance:

Billie Deason, NASA Public Affairs, NASA Johnson Space Center, Houston, Texas; Lisa Vazquez of Media Services, Inc., at the NASA Johnson Space Center; Dr. T. C. Handley and Elizabeth Levack of the USAF Space Division History Office, El Segundo, California; Lt. Col. John Booth and Larry Hannon, Space Division Public Affairs; Cheryl Hortel at the History Office, Edwards Air Force Base, California; Victoria Edwards of Sovfoto, New York; Vladimir Tverdovsky of VAAP, Moscow; Elizabeth Hess of Hughes Aircraft, El Segundo, California; Jacqueline Charboneau of the National Research Council, Ottawa, Canada; Dr. Arthur Manfredi of the Congressional Research Service, US Library of Congress, Washington D.C.

In addition, special thanks are due space sleuths James Oberg, Alcestic Oberg, Rex Hall, David Shayler, Charles P. Vick, and G. Harry Stine, as well as journalist Henry Gris. Without them *Who's Who in Space* would not exist.

Final thanks to Cynthia Cassutt, my agent Richard Curtis, and my editor Meghan Robinson Wander.

M.C.

Acronyms and Abbreviations

AAC — United States Army Air Corps, forerunner of the US Air Force

AAP — Apollo Applications Program, the original name for proposed manned Apollo missions to follow the first lunar landing

AFB — air force base

ALT — Space Shuttle Approach and Landing Tests, a series of unpowered test flights conducted with the orbiter Enterprise at Edwards AFB in 1977

AMU — astronaut maneuvering unit, a rocket-powered backpack designed for Gemini and Apollo astronauts

ARPS — Aerospace Research Pilot School, an advanced course at the USAF Test Pilot School at Edwards AFB designed to train pilots for space flight

ASTP — Apollo-Soyuz Test Project, the American name for the joint US-USSR manned space program

ATDA — Augmented Target Docking Adaptor, a one-time replacement for failed Agena upper stages intended for use in manned Gemini missions

AWACS — Airborne Warning and Control System, specially equipped US Air Force planes carrying sophisticated electronic detection gear

BA — bachelor of arts degree

BS — bachelor of science degree

Cal — University of California at Berkeley

Capcom — originally a contraction for "capsule communicator," now refers to astronauts or cosmonauts serving in mission control as voice contacts with colleagues in space

CERN — Centre Europeen de Recherches Nucleaires, the European nuclear research center near Geneva

CFES — Continuous Flow Electrophoresis System, a space manufacturing project of McDonnell Douglas and the Johnson & Johnson company

CM — command module, the portion of a manned spacecraft that contains crew couches and controls, and which must return to Earth

CNES — Centre National d'Etudes Spatiales, the French national space agency

DDM — drop dynamics module, an experiment flown aboard Spacelab 3 in 1985

DFVLR — Deutsche Forschungs- und Versuchsanstalt fur Luft- und Rumfahrt, or the Federal German Aerospace Research Establishment, the West German national space agency

DOD — US Department of Defense

DOSAAF — Russian acronym for the Voluntary Society for Assistance to the Army, Air Force and Navy, a civil defense organization in the USSR that, among other activities, trains young people to be pilots and parachutists

DOSO — the Bulgarian equivalent of the USSR DOSAAF (which see)

DSCS — Defense Satellite Communication System, a series of American military communications satellites deployed in geosynchronous orbit

Dyna-Soar — contraction of "dynamic soaring," a phrase originally intended to describe the flight characteristics of delta-winged space vehicles

E — east

EDT — United States Eastern Daylight Time

EOM — Spacelab Earth Observation Mission, a series of proposed followups to Spacelab 1, using the same experiment package

EOS — Electrophoresis Operations in

	Space, designation for the advanced model of the McDonell Douglas CFES, originally scheduled to fly on the Shuttle in 1986
ESA	the European Space Agency
EST	US Eastern Standard Time
ET	Space Shuttle external tank
EVA	extra-vehicular activity or "space walk"
FAA	US Federal Aviation Administration
FAI	French Federation Aeronautique Internationale, the world aviation record-keeping body
FSL	flight simulation laboratory, an installation located in Downey, California, home of Rockwell, builders of the Space Shuttle, and used for, among other things, astronaut training
G	as in G-force, intended to refer to one Earth gravity (acceleration of 32 feet per second per second) and in this context used to measure the amount of stress placed on space travelers during launch and re-entry. For example, during a 3G launch, a person weighing 150 pounds on Earth will feel as though he weighed 450 pounds.
GIRD	Russian contraction for words meaning Gas Dynamics Laboratory and referring to the famed group of Russian rocket pioneers of the 1930s
HEAO	High Energy Astrophysical Observatory, a US scientific satellite program
HMCS	Her Majesty's Canadian Ship
HOTOL	Horizontal Takeoff and Landing project, a proposed British aerospace plane
IPS	instrument pointing system, part of the Spacelab 2 experiments
ISRO	Indian Space Research Organization, guiding force for the Indian space program
IUS	inertial upper stage, a Boeing rocket built for the US Air Force and designed to boost heavy satellites into geosynchronous orbit following deployment from the Shuttle
JSC	NASA Johnson Space Center, in Houston, Texas; until 1973 known as the Manned Spacecraft Center
KSC	NASA Kennedy Space Center on Merrit Island, Florida
LDEF	long duration exposure facility, an experiment package designed to be deployed from the Shuttle in space and retrieved at a later date
LGU	Leningrad University
LM	Apollo lunar module
LTA	Apollo lunar test article, a mockup of the lunar module
LTV Aerospace	Ling-Temco-Vought, US company
MA	master of arts degree
MAI	Sergo Ordzhonikidze Moscow Aviation School, one of the foremost Soviet aerospace colleges
MBA	master of business administration degree
McDAC	McDonnell Douglas Aerospace Corporation
MECO	main engine cutoff, the point in a Shuttle launch at which the three main engines cease firing, ideally about eight minutes into the flight
MIT	Massachusetts Institute of Technology, Cambridge
MMU	manned maneuvering unit, the rocket backpack used on Shuttle mission in 1984 and 1985
MOL	Manned Orbiting Laboratory, a US Air Force manned space project from 1965 to 1969
MS	master of science degree
MSE	manned spaceflight engineer, US Air Force Shuttle payload specialists
MT	Moscow Time
N	north
NACA	the National Advisory Committee on Aeronautics, a US government agency devoted to aviation; founded in 1915, its facilities and personnel were absorbed by NASA in 1958
NASA	the National Aeronautics and Space Administration, the US government civilian space and aviation agency
NASDA	National Space Development Agency, the Japanese national space agency
NBC	National Broadcasting Company
NE	northeast

NRL	the Naval Research Laboratory, a US Navy scientific installation in Washington, D.C.
NW	northwest
OFT	orbital flight tests, an early NASA designation for the first manned Shuttle flights
OSS	Office of Space Sciences, a NASA department that developed scientific experiments carried on early Shuttle missions
OSTA	Office of Space and Terrestrial Applications, a NASA department that developed Earth-sensing experiments carried on early Shuttle missions
PDT	US Pacific Daylight Time
PhD	doctor of philosophy degree
PST	US Pacific Standard Time
RAF	British Royal Air Force
REDCO	Resolution Engineering and Development Company, a firm founded by former astronaut Richard Gordon in 1978
RMS	the Shuttle remote manipulator system, formal name for the Canadian-built robot arm
S	south
SAIL	Shuttle Avionics Integration Laboratory, a facility at the NASA Johnson Space Center where Shuttle computer software is created and tested
SAS	space adaptation syndrome, formal name for the "space sickness" that afflicts about half of all space travelers
SDI, SDIO	US Strategic Defense Initiative Organization, the so-called "Star Wars" missile defense program
SE	southeast
SEAL	contraction of Sea/Land, refers to US Navy elite fighting force
SHEAL	Shuttle High-Energy Astrophysics Laboratory, a series of planned Spacelab missions
SL	originally an abbreviation for Skylab, later used for Spacelab
SLS	Spacelab Life Sciences missions, dedicated to medical studies
SMD III	Spacelab Mission Demonstration III
SMEAT	Skylab Medical Experiments Altitude Test, a 56-day simulation of a Skylab mission performed by astronauts Bobko, Crippen, and Thornton in 1970.
SPO	systems project officer, US Air Force officer who supervises the development of a military space system
SRB	the Shuttle solid rocket booster
STA	the Shuttle training aircraft, a Gulfstream II executive jet modified to give it landing characteristics similar to a Space Shuttle
STS	Space Transportation System, formal name for the Shuttle program
SVS	space vision system, a Canadian Shuttle experiment
SW	southwest
TDRS	Tracking and Data Relay Satellite, a series of communications satellites designed to permit constant contact between orbiting Shuttles and mission control
T-minus	T refers to scheduled launch time; T-minus is any time prior to that
T-pad	a jawlike device used by astronaut George Nelson during his attempted capture of the Solar Maximum Mission satellite in 1984
TWA	US airline
UFO	unidentified flying object
USAF	United States Air Force
USGS	United States Geological Survey
USN	United States Navy
USS	United States ship
W	west
Wright-Pat	shorthand for Wright-Patterson Air Force Base, Dayton, Ohio

Introduction

From the very beginning, it was a time for ceremonies and symbols.

Yuri Gagarin would write later that it was a beautiful spring morning on the usually arid steppes of Kazakhstan, this Wednesday, April 12, 1961. Flowers were in bloom and the air smelled rich and warm. Though it was still early, the sun reflected off the top of the huge rocket as the blue-and-white bus carrying Gagarin and his comrades arrived at the launch pad.

Wearing a white helmet and clad in the heavy pressure suit with its bright orange covering, Gagarin had trouble walking. He was helped out of the bus into a waiting group that included Sergei Korolev, the chief designer of the Vostok rocket and spacecraft. Farewells and expressions of good luck were exchanged, then Gagarin stepped up to a microphone. "Dear friends," he began, "you who are close to me, and you whom I do not know. Fellow Russians, and people of all countries and continents: In a few moments a powerful space vehicle will carry me into the distant realm of space. What can I tell you in these last minutes before the launch? My whole life now appears to me as one beautiful moment. . . ."

Two hours later, Gagarin became the world's first space traveler.

Another time and place, another ceremony.

It was an unusually cool, rainy, and cloudy morning on the Florida coast, this Saturday, February 1, 1986. Before another crowd, this one composed of American space officials and workers, astronaut Robert Overmyer read a poem by John Gillespie Magee, Jr., which ends, ". . . I slipped the surly bonds of earth to touch the face of God." At precisely 11:39 a wreath of white chrysanthemums adorned with seven red carnations was dropped into the ocean not far offshore. The words and the flowers commemorated seven space travelers—Francis Scobee, Michael Smith, Ellison Onizuka, Ronald McNair, Judith Resnik, Gregory Jarvis and Christa McAuliffe—who died days earlier when the Space Shuttle Challenger disintegrated during its ascent.

Between these two ceremonies are twenty-five years of triumph and tragedy, 116 successful manned launches and three launch failures. Fifty-eight Soviet citizens, 120 Americans, and 18 others from nations such as Czechoslovakia, Saudi Arabia and France have traveled in space—almost two hundred space travelers. Missions have lasted as little as fifteen minutes, or as long as ten months. Some of them ended in fatal explosions just ten miles high, others resulted in two men walking on the Moon.

Who's Who in Space: The First Twenty-five Years is a record of the people who took part in the first twenty-five years of manned spaceflight. When I began to work on it, my intention was to remind us all that human beings ride those rockets. When we see floating astronauts and cosmonauts on our televisions, we are seeing not superhumans, but fathers and mothers, people who have been high school and college students, who have worked as lathe operators or farmhands on their way to becoming scientists, engineers, and pilots. The events of January 1986 serve as a further reminder of the human involvement in the exploration of space.

Who's Who in Space is also a reference work in which students and scholars will find biographies of all those who have traveled in space, and most of those who trained with them. All entries are based on material received from official sources such as the National Aeronautics and Space Administration, the United States Air Force, the Soviet news agency TASS, and appropriate international organizations such as the European Space Agency, the Canadian National Research Council, and the British Ministry of Defence. The official information has been supplemented with stories obtained from published memoirs, newspaper articles, and numerous interviews.

Who's Who in Space does not attempt to provide a full history of manned space flight. For further details I refer you to David Baker's *The History of Manned Spaceflight* (1981) or *Jane's Spaceflight Directory* by Reginald Turnhill (1985). In addition, *Red Star in Orbit* by James E. Oberg (1981) is a unique and valuable look at the Soviet space program. A complete list of space records can be found in *Guinness Spaceflight: The Records* by Tim Furniss (1985). All of these were invaluable to me, as were works cited in the text.

Who's Who in Space is, however, the most

comprehensive biographical work dealing with manned space flight that has been published, consisting of essays, biographical profiles organized by nationality, a glossary, and three appendixes. The essays that precede the various sections give a historical view of the evolution of the various national manned space programs and place the biographical entries in context. The profiles give each subject's personal facts in the following sequence: name (and nickname, if any), notable achievement in space travel, date and place of birth, education, career, and family details. The glossary explains unfamiliar terms and names. The appendixes include a chronological list of the 199 space travelers of the first twenty-five years and a chart of all manned space flights of that period.

As I write these words the American space program is going through an agonizing period of doubt and re-evaluation following the Shuttle Challenger explosion, but the Shuttle will fly again. Meanwhile, CNES, the French space agency, is developing its Hermes manned spacecraft, while the British consider their HOTOL aerospace plane and the Japanese National Space Development Agency designs a prototype manned vehicle of its own. Most important, Soviet cosmonauts Leonid Kizim and Vladimir Solovyov, veterans of the world's longest space flight, are hard at work activating Mir, the first space vehicle intended for permanent manned occupation.

So perhaps this is a fitting place to pause . . . to remember . . . to commemorate the years when space was explored by test pilots and engineers, as we prepare for the time when it becomes home to teachers, writers, construction workers, and their families.

There will be hundreds and eventually thousands of new space travelers in the coming years. One day soon, sooner than we all think, a child will be born in Earth orbit, or on the Moon, or on the way to Mars, an event that will be an unmistakable sign that human beings are not limited to one world.

On that gray February morning, as the Challenger wreath settled on the waves, seven dolphins—harbingers of good fortune for travelers all through history—arced into the air, then disappeared with a splash. I would like to think they were bringing luck for space travelers still to come.

Michael Cassutt

Los Angeles

PART 1 *American Space Travelers*

NASA Astronauts

David J. Shayler

When the National Aeronautics and Space Administration began its activities in October 1958, one of its first tasks was to select a group of suitably qualified persons who, after a period of training, would complete the first manned orbits of the Earth in the small spacecraft then under initial stages of development.

At that time there was international interest in the exploration of space by unmanned automated space satellites and growing interest in America in manned exploration of space. A large number of scientific journals and books had been written on what could be expected by travelers in space, but no human had yet ventured beyond the atmosphere.

A great deal of experience in high altitude flying had been gathered by many years of manned balloon flights and by NASA's (and forerunner NACA) high-speed and high-altitude aeronautical research flights in rocket aircraft of the X series.

Initial requirements for the selection of astronaut applications for what eventually became Project Mercury had been worked out at NASA's Space Task Group at Langley Research Center, Virginia, during November 1958. It was decided to arrange a meeting between the NASA group and representatives from industry and the military services. The result would be a joint selection of a pool of some 150 men from which 36 candidates would be selected for physical and psychological testing. A group of 12 would be selected from this group to undergo a training and qualification program that would last nine months, upon the completion of which a final group of six would be selected to make the Mercury space flights.

It was decided that only males between the ages of 25 and 40 would be selected for the program, owing to the expected high physical stress a human body might endure in flight. Candidates were limited to a height of less than 5 feet, 11 inches, so that they could fit into the one-man Mercury capsule, whose size in turn was governed by the available booster rockets, the Redstone and Atlas ballistic missiles. All candidates must also hold at least a bachelor's degree to be considered.

In addition, candidates with three years' work in the physical or biological sciences could apply, as could those with similar experience in engineering or technical research. This meant that people such as pilots of aircraft or balloons, commanders of submarines, navigators and communications engineers, medical doctors, mountaineers, deepsea divers, race car drivers, parachutists, and Arctic explorers all would technically qualify as candidates for space flight.

But in December 1958 President Dwight Eisenhower declared that the first American astronauts would be selected from the hundreds of military test pilots, men who were used to risking their lives in the high-speed testing of modern performance jet aircraft, who already possessed security clearances, and who were used to the disciplines of military life. (This decision had a lasting effect on the nature of future American space travelers. Of the 157 career astronauts selected by NASA between April 1959 and May 1985, 95 were test pilots.)

On January 5, 1959, NASA finalized its selection criteria. Candidates must

- Be under the age of 40
- Be less than 5′11″

- Be in excellent physical condition
- Be a graduate of a test pilot school
- Be holder of a bachelor's degree or its equivalent
- Have 1500 hours of flight time (10 years of experience)
- Be a qualified jet pilot.

A screening of military personnel records produced 110 men who met these criteria, 58 from the US Air Force, 47 from the US Navy, and 5 from the US Marine Corps. Thirty-five of these men were invited to a meeting in Washington on February 2, 1959, and, following a briefing about Project Mercury and the man in space project, 24 of them volunteered. When an even higher percentage of the second group of candidates also volunteered, NASA realized it had more than enough qualified men and canceled the invitation to the rest of the original 110. At the same time the number of men to be selected, originally set at 12 because of an anticipated high dropout rate, was reduced to six.

A series of written tests, technical interviews, psychiatric examinations, and medical history reviews followed, and by March 32 men had been invited to the Lovelace Clinic in Albuquerque, New Mexico, for an extraordinarily detailed set of physical tests. They were subjected to seventeen different eye examinations; they had their brain waves measured; they were dunked in water to determine their bodies' specific gravity; they pedalled stationary bicycles against increasing loads; they had water dripped in their ears to study reactions to motion sickness; they were shocked, spun, prodded and punctured; their hearts and lungs were measured; and they were placed in chambers exposing them to extreme heat and extreme cold.

Only one candidate dropped out during this phase of testing. Another round of tests, this time psychological, was conducted at Wright-Patterson Air Force Base in Ohio, and a fourth round at Lovelace again. By the end of March the selection board reviewed the results of the exhaustive testing and evaluated each man's career and achievements and, failing to reduce them to six, on April 2 selected seven pilots as America's Mercury astronauts.

At 2 p.m. on April 9, 1959, Navy Lieutenant Malcolm Scott Carpenter, Air Force Captain Leroy Gordon Cooper, Jr., Marine Lieutenant Colonel John H. Glenn, Jr., Air Force Captain Virgil I. "Gus" Grissom, Navy Lieutenant Commander Walter M. Schirra, Jr., Navy Lieutenant Commander Alan B. Shepard, Jr., and Air Force Captain Donald K. "Deke" Slayton were introduced to the press.

Gemini and Apollo

Three years later, on April 18, 1962, following successful manned flights by Soviet cosmonauts Gagarin and Titov and Americans Shepard, Grissom and Glenn, NASA announced that it would accept applications for a second group of astronaut trainees. The agency planned to select between five and ten who, after an initial training period, would join Mercury astronauts in flying the two-man Gemini spacecraft in 1964 and who would probably crew early Apollo missions beginning in 1967.

The list of qualifications, which was modified to allow applications by civilians, demanded that candidates:

- Be experienced jet test pilots and preferably presently engaged in flying high-performance jet aircraft;
- Have attained experimental test pilot status through military service, the aircraft industry or NASA, or have graduated from a military test pilot school;
- Hold a degree in physical or biological sciences or in engineering;
- Be a citizen of the United States, under 35 years of age at the time of selection, and no taller than six feet in height. [The increase in allowable height was due to the slightly larger size of the Gemini spacecraft.]
- Be recommended by their parent organizations.

By June 1962 NASA had screened a total of 253 suitable candidates from those who applied. Following several weeks of medical tests and other examinations, nine men were selected: civilian Neil Armstrong, Air Force Major Frank Borman, Navy Lieutenant Charles Conrad, Navy Lieutenant Commander James Lovell, Air Force Captain James McDivitt, civilian Elliott See, Air Force Captains Thomas Stafford and Edward White, and Navy Lieutenant Commander John Young. They reported to the new Manned Spacecraft Center in Houston, Texas.

The "Original Nine," as they dubbed themselves, became the most experienced group of astronauts. Eight of its members would fly in space; two would die, one of them just prior to his first flight. Armstrong became the first person to walk on the Moon. Borman and Lovell were two of the first humans to orbit the Moon. White became the first American to walk in space. McDivitt commanded the first manned flight of the Apollo lunar module. Conrad commanded the first Skylab mission. Stafford commanded the joint US-Soviet mission. Young commanded the first flight of the Space Shuttle.

Even before the astronauts in the second group reported to NASA it was clear that a third selection would be needed. Several of the Mercury astronauts (Glenn, Carpenter, Slayton) were grounded or otherwise unavailable for future flights, and with ten manned Gemini missions scheduled to begin in late 1964, followed by an unknown number of Apollo missions, it was clear that NASA needed more than thirteen active astronauts.

In June 1963 NASA issued a call for its third astronaut group. The selection criteria this time required a candidate to

- Be a citizen of the United States
- Hold a bachelor's degree in engineering or the physical or biological sciences
- Have logged 1000 hours of flying time with the armed services, NASA or the aircraft industry
- Be 34 years of age or younger at the time of selection.

For the first time pilots without test flying experience were allowed to apply. It was hoped that the lower number of flying hours required might tempt applications from persons with scientific backgrounds as well. The age limit of 34 reflected NASA's belief that members of this group should plan on having long careers as astronauts.

By July 1, 1963, NASA had received 271 applications, 200 from civilians and 71 from military personnel, including two black pilots. Two women also applied. By the end of August 32 finalists had been selected, all of them white males, and these were invited to Brooks AFB, Texas, for medical examinations.

On October 17 the fourteen new astronauts were announced. Although some of the pilots (Bassett, Bean, Collins, Eisele, Freeman, Gordon, Scott and Williams) had testing backgrounds, many did not. Air Force Major Edwin Aldrin held a PhD from the Massachusetts Institute of Technology and civilians Walter Cunningham and Russell Schweickart were performing scientific research at the time of selection. Navy Lieutenant Roger Chaffee had flown reconaissance aircraft over Cuba during the October 1962 missile crisis.

Four of the new astronauts, Freeman, Bassett, Chaffee and Williams, would die in training or space-related accidents before they could fly in space. Two members of the class of 1963, Aldrin and Collins, would take part in the first lunar landing.

Even as military pilots were being recruited and trained as astronauts, NASA officials were concluding that professional scientists should also be selected for the manned space program. Trained geologists could explore the Moon, oceanographers could study the Earth from space, and astronomers could operate orbiting telescopes. Following a recommendation by the NASA Space Science Board in July 1962 that "scientist-astronauts" should be included in the astronaut group and assigned to the first lunar landing, and after months of internal debate over selection criteria, NASA and the National Academy of Sciences issued a call for astronaut candidates who were

- Born on or after August 1, 1930
- Citizens of the United States
- No taller than 6′
- Holders of a PhD or the equivalent in natural science, medicine or engineering.

Pilot experience was not required, though preference was given to applicants who had it. All selectees would be required to attend a year-long course at a US Air Force flight school to qualify them as jet pilots.

Coincidentally, the call was issued on October 19, 1964, just one week after the Soviet Union launched the first Voskhod spacecraft carrying a physician and an aerospace engineer, neither of whom were pilots.

By December 31, 1964, NASA had received a total of 1351 applications or letters of interest and by February 10, 1965, had forwarded the names of 400 applicants (including four women) to the National Academy of Sciences, which would judge their scientific credentials. The Academy was to select 10 to 15 candidates for final judging by NASA's astronaut selection board. Sixteen candidates were sent to NASA for medical and psychological testing, and six—only half the number NASA had originally intended to recruit—were announced on June 28, 1965.

The first group of scientist-astronauts consisted of an electrical engineer (Dr. Owen Garriott of Stanford University), two physicists (Dr. Edward Gibson of the Philco Corporation and Dr. Curtis Michel of Rice University), two physicians (Lieutenant Commander Joseph Kerwin of the US Navy and Dr. Duane Graveline of the NASA Manned Spacecraft Center), and a geologist (Dr. Harrison Schmitt of the US Geological Survey.) Kerwin and Michel were qualified jet pilots and reported for astronaut training on July 1, 1965. The others were sent to Williams Air Force Base in Arizona on July 29, 1965, to enter flight school. (Graveline resigned from the space program shortly thereafter, for personal reasons.)

The scientist-astronauts were never really welcomed by the test-pilot-dominated astronaut office and their selection was premature. Nevertheless, geologist Schmitt did walk on the Moon while physician Kerwin was included in the crew of America's first month-long space flight. Garriott and Gibson also went into space.

By September 1965 NASA had 30 active astronauts (including three scientist-astronauts attending flight school), a sufficient number to provide prime, backup and support crews for the remaining Gemini missions and the early Apollo mission, including the first lunar landing.

But the space agency also had plans for later manned flights, known successively as Apollo X, Apollo Extension System, and Apollo Applications Program. The AAP schedule called for as many as ten more lunar landings and three orbiting research laboratories, over forty manned Apollo flights beginning in late 1968. A team of thirty astronauts flying two or three missions each could not meet this schedule, and with attrition would be totally inadequate. So plans were made for a dramatic two-phase expansion in the astronaut team.

Phase one began on September 10, 1965, when NASA began to recruit a fifth group consisting of 15 astronauts. The selection criteria were similar to those of the 1963 group, though the age limit was raised to 36. By December 1, 351 applications had been received, including six from women pilots and one from a young US Navy officer, Lieutenant Frank E. Ellis, who had lost both his legs in a jet crash in July 1962. Ellis maintained that in spite of his handicap his flying ability was unimpaired, and that being able to run and jump was irrelevant to an astronaut. Ellis was not one of the 159 finalists, but NASA did nominate him for special work in the space program.

On April 4, 1966, NASA announced the selection of 19 new astronauts who would report to the Manned Spacecraft Center in May. All were experienced jet pilots. Air Force Captain Joe Engle already held astronaut wings for his work on the X-15 rocket plane. Dr. Don Lind, a NASA physicist, had a background that ultimately caused him to be considered a scientist-astronaut in spite of the fact that he had been a Navy jet pilot. He was one of four civilians in the group (the others were NASA's Fred Haise, Vance Brand of Lockheed, and Jack Swigert of Pratt-Whitney). The rest were from the Air Force, Navy and Marines. Most had graduated from test pilot schools. Two, Navy Lieutenant Commanders Ronald Evans and Paul Weitz, had flown combat missions in Southeast Asia.

Phase two was a second group of scientist-astronauts who would, it was hoped, represent the scientific community in the development of experiments for the Apollo Applications missions in addition to serving as potential crew members. On September 26, 1966, NASA and the National Academy of Sciences issued a joint news release announcing that a "limited number" of scientist-astronauts were being sought. Applicants must be

- US citizens as of March 15, 1967
- No taller than 6′
- Born on or after August 1, 1930
- Holders of a PhD in the natural sciences, medicine or engineering.

By January 8, 1967, 923 applications had been received for the 20 to 30 openings. Two months later the science academy forwarded 69 names to NASA for final screening and selection and on August 4, 1967, eleven new astronauts were announced.

The August 1967 group included the first naturalized citizens to be chosen for the astronaut group, Welsh-born Dr. John Anthony Llewellyn and Australian Dr. Philip K. Chapman. (Neither would fly in space.) Two of the new astronauts, Dr. Karl Henize of Northwestern University and Dr. William Thornton of the US Air Force were technically too old to qualify—Henize, at 40, is still the oldest person to be selected as a NASA astronaut. At the other extreme, Anthony England of MIT was just 25; he is still the youngest astronaut ever selected.

None of the new astronauts was a jet pilot and all were scheduled to attend undergraduate pilot training at either Williams Air Force Base or Vance Air Force Base in early 1968. The delay was caused by the Air Force's need to train more pilots for the Vietnam War. Llewellyn and Dr. Brian O'Leary dropped out of the group during flight school. Cuts in the budget of Apollo Applications (finally renamed Skylab) made it apparent to the remaining scientist-astronauts that their chances of flying in space were slim. Dr. Donald Holmquest left the space program in 1971 and Chapman and England followed in 1972. Others took leaves while awaiting the development of the Space Shuttle. The first members of this group to fly in space, Dr. Joseph Allen and Dr. William Lenoir, waited until November 1982, fifteen years after joining NASA. Henize and England (who returned to NASA later), the last to make initial flights, did so in July 1985.

There was a third, unanticipated addition to the astronaut team in this period. On August 14, 1969, NASA accepted seven more pilots into the program, though by then it was clear that these men would not be making flights in Apollo or Skylab, but would have to wait until the Space Shuttle was ready. All seven had transferred from the US Air Force Manned Orbiting Laboratory program, which had suddenly been canceled. (See the entry on MOL for details.) Fourteen pilots were still training with MOL at the time of cancellation. Those who came to NASA were not yet 36 years old, while those who remained on duty with the Air Force were all older, except for Lieutenant Colonel Albert H. Crews, Jr., who joined the flight crew directorate at the NASA Manned Spacecraft Center as a pilot.

The addition of the MOL pilots increased the number of active astronauts to more than 50 at a time when a maximum of eleven Apollo and Skylab flights were planned.

The Shuttle Era

The transfer of the seven former MOL pilots in 1969 was the last addition to the astronaut team for nearly nine years. By late 1977, with the Space Shuttle still in development and initial flights still two or more years in the future, the number of active NASA astronauts had dropped to 27.

During the Seventies it became clear to NASA that selection criteria for Shuttle astronauts could be substantially different from those applied to Mercury, Gemini and Apollo astronauts. Experienced pilots would still be needed to fly the vehicle, but scientists and engineers with no pilot training would perform such duties as satellite deployment, space walks, and operation of scientific experiments. And since the Shuttle would not subject its crew to loads greater than 3 Gs (compared with 8G loads some Apollo crews endured), the physical requirements could also be eased.

Two types of astronauts were needed then, with two sets of selection criteria: pilots would

- Have a BS in engineering, the physical sciences or mathematics
- Have at least 1000 hours of command pilot time with 2000 hours desirable; experience with high performance jet aircraft and in testing was also desirable
- Be able to pass a Class I physical examination and be between 5′4″ and 6′4″ in height.

These were not much different from requirements for the 1963 and 1966 pilot selections, except for the absence of an upper age limit and the increase in allowable height.

The other type of astronauts sought, called mission specialists, were required to

- Have a BS in engineering, biological or physical science or mathematics with an advanced degree or equivalent experience desirable
- Be able to pass a Class II physical examination (which has greater latitude for non-standard vision and hearing) and be between 5′0″ and 6′4″.

There was no age limit for mission specialists, either, and the size requirements were dictated by the design of Shuttle EVA spacesuits, not by the size of the spacecraft itself.

The initial announcement, on July 8, 1976, urged women and members of minority groups to apply.

By the end of June 1977, 659 pilots (147 military, 512 civilian) had applied as had 5680 hopeful mission specialists, including 1251 women and 338 minorities. The selection board reviewed all 8079 applications and found that only about half actually met the stated criteria. (Most military applicants had been screened and nominated by their service.) The selected half were reviewed again and 208 were ultimately invited to the NASA Johnson Space Center for a week of interviews and medical tests to be conducted in August and September of 1977. Of the 208, 149 were found to be medically qualified for the astronaut group and were still interested in participating.

On January 16, 1978, NASA announced the selection of 35 new astronauts, fifteen pilots and twenty mission specialists. Technically known as astronaut candidates, they were to report to the NASA Johnson Space Center in July 1978 to commence a two-year training and evaluation course. Dropouts, if any, would be offered jobs elsewhere in NASA. (It was soon discovered that the two-year training course could be completed in one year, and that there were no dropouts in the 1978 group or in later groups.) The civilian astronauts, who would be paid according to civil service scale, were expected to remain with NASA for at least five years. Military officers were considered to be on a seven-year (with possible extension) tour of duty governed by an understanding between NASA and the Department of Defense.

The 1978 group was, understandably, the largest and most diverse ever selected by NASA. There were six women: two physicians (Dr. Anna Fisher and Dr. Rhea Seddon), a biochemist (Dr. Shannon Lucid), a physicist (Dr. Sally Ride), a geophysicist (Dr. Kathryn Sullivan), and an engineer (Dr. Judith Resnik). There were three black Americans, Air Force Majors Guy Bluford and Frederick Gregory, and Hughes physicist Ronald McNair, and an Asian American, Air Force Captain Ellison Onizuka. Also selected was the first US Army officer, Major Robert Stewart. What was also significant was the number of Vietnam veterans: twenty of the new astronauts had combat experience.

Even though by the summer of 1979 the Shuttle program was encountering technical and financial difficulties that postponed the first flight until late 1980, and eventually to April 1981, NASA realized that following the initial series of two-man test flights Shuttle crew size could increase to six or seven astronauts per mission. With veteran astronauts expected to leave the program after completing one or two early Shuttle flights, and given the need to place astronauts in various support roles (such as capcom, payload support, and Shuttle Avionics Integration Laboratory personnel, where "crews" of astronauts worked three eight-hour shifts debugging vital Shuttle computer software), sixty astronauts would simply not be enough.

Therefore, on August 1, 1979, NASA announced that it would begin accepting applications for the astronaut group on a regular basis (ideally every year, though this proved too optimistic). Between October 1 and December 1, hopeful pilots and mission specialists could apply for a group to begin training in the summer of 1980.

Criteria for this ninth group of astronauts were generally the same as for the eighth group, except that pilot applicants could now have a degree in biology and their minimum flight time had to have been logged in jets. Mission specialists would be allowed to substitute an advanced degree for experience, although degrees in technology, aviation and psychology no longer qualified.

By December, 3278 people had applied for the 10 to 20 openings. Many had also applied in 1978, including all the military personnel, whose names were simply re-submitted by their services. During March and April 1980, 121 candidates were interviewed at the Johnson Space Center, on on May 19, 1980, 19 new astronaut-candidates were announced, to report to JSC on July 7. Eight were pilots and 11 were mission specialists. Two were women; one pilot was black and one mission specialist was Hispanic. Also among those selected was Dr. William Fisher, husband of 1978 astronaut Dr. Anna Fisher.

It was not until May 16, 1983, that NASA was able to intiate its annual selection of astronauts. Criteria were now standardized at those used for the 1980 group. Between October 1 and December 1, 1983, 4934 applications were received for six pilot and six mission specialist openings. In February and March 1984, 128 finalists were interviewed, and on May 23, 1984, 17 new candidates were announced. Three were women and one was Hispanic. Navy Commander Manley "Sonny" Carter, a former forward for the Atlanta Chiefs soccer team, became the first professional athlete to join the astronaut team.

It is interesting to note that of the five civilians chosen, four were current NASA employees (Marsha Ivins, Charles Veach and Dr. Ellen Shulman at JSC and George Low at the Jet Propulsion Laboratory) and one (Dr. Kathryn Thornton) worked at the US Army Foreign Science and Technology Center, meaning that all new astronauts were already employed by the US government. Low was also the first son of a NASA official to become an astronaut.

The apparent bias against "outside" applicants was even more notable in that no applications were solicited for the 1985 group. NASA simply re-examined applications for 1984 and invited 59 to JSC for interviews. Thirteen were announced on June 4, 1985 and again, all were either serving as military officers or NASA employees. There were no new astronauts from industry or academe.

1985 and Beyond

In 1985, anticipating the long-awaited full-scale operations of the Shuttle system and with 14 or more flights planned for 1986 and successive years, NASA announced that beginning on August 1, 1985, it would accept applications for the astronaut group from civilians on a continuing basis. Military astronaut applicants would be nominated by their services once a year. Selections would take place each spring with successful applicants reporting to JSC that summer. The exact number of candidates to be accepted would be determined by mission requirements and attrition rate in the current astronaut group.

Minimum qualifications for pilot would be:

- A BS from an accredited institution in engineering, physical science, biological science or mathematics
- 1000 hours pilot-in-command time in jet aircraft
- Ability to pass a NASA Class I flight physical
- Height between 5′4″ and 6′4″

Minimum qualifications for mission specialist would be:

- A BS from an accredited institution in engineering, physical science, biological science or mathematics
- Three years of related professional experience. Advanced degrees would be desirable and may be substituted for experience
- Ability to pass a NASA Class II flight physical
- Height between 5′0″ and 6′4″

The Shuttle Challenger disaster and the subsquent reduction in planned Shuttle flights, however, suspended regular astronaut recruitment including selections for a new group scheduled to be announced in June 1986.

NASA Mission Crew Patches

1 Gemini-Titan 5
Cooper and Conrad

2 Gemini-Titan 6-A
Schirra and Stafford

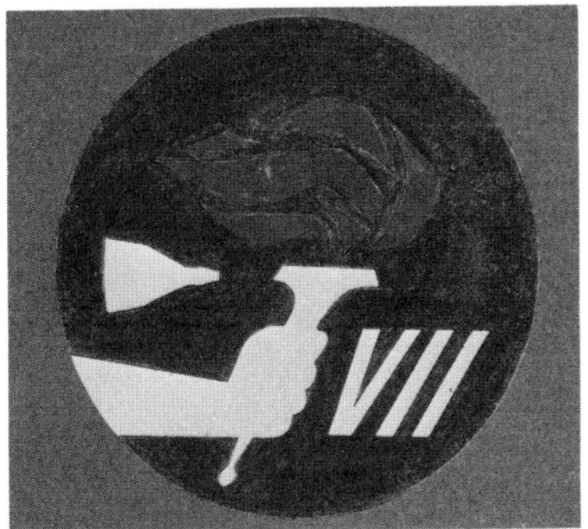

3 Gemini-Titan 7
Borman and Lovell

4 Gemini-Titan 8
Armstrong and Scott

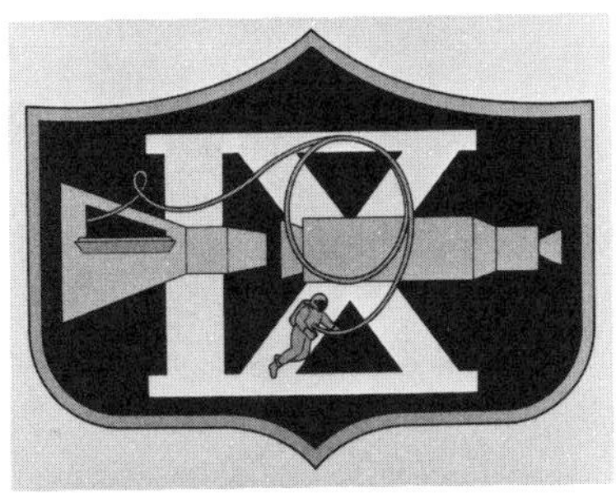

5 Gemini-Titan 9-A
Stafford and Cernan

6 Gemini-Titan 10
Young and Collins

7 Gemini-Titan 11
Conrad and Gordon

8 Gemini-Titan 12
Lovell and Aldrin

9 Apollo-Saturn 204
Grissom, White, and Chaffee

10 Apollo-Saturn 7
Schirra, Eisele, and Cunningham

11 Apollo-Saturn 8
Borman, Lovell, and Anders

12 Apollo-Saturn 9
McDivitt, Scott, and Schweikart

13. Apollo-Saturn 10
Stafford, Young, and Cernan

14 Apollo-Saturn 11
Armstrong, Collins, and Aldrin

15 Apollo-Saturn 12
Conrad, Gordon, and Bean

16 Apollo-Saturn 13
Lovell, Swigert, and Haise

17 Apollo-Saturn 14
Shepard, Roosa, and Mitchell

18 Apollo-Saturn 15
Scott, Worden, and Irwin

19 Apollo-Saturn 16
Young, Mattingly, and Duke

20 Apollo-Saturn 17
Cernan, Evans, and Schmitt

21 Skylab SL-2 (Skylab 1)
Conrad, Kerwin, and Weitz

22 Skylab SL-3 (Skylab 2)
Bean, Garriott, and Lousma

23 Skylab SL-4 (Skylab 3)
Carr, Gibson, and Pogue

24 Apollo-Soyuz M
See Frontispiece.

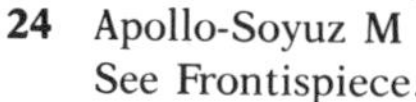

25 STS-1
Young and Crippen

26 STS-2
Engle and Truly

27 STS-3
Lousma and Fullerton

28 STS-4
Mattingly and Hartsfield

29 STS-5
Brand, Overmyer, Allen, and Lenoir

30 STS-6
Weitz, Bobko, Musgrave, and Peterson

31 STS-7
Crippen, Hauck, Fabian, Ride, and Thagard

32 STS-8
Truly, Brandenstein, Bluford, Gardner, and Thornton

33 STS-9
Young, Shaw, Garriott, Parker, Lichtenberg, and Merbold

34 41-B
Brand, Gibson, McNair, Stewart, and McCandless

35 41-C
Crippen, Scobee, Nelson, Hart, and Van Hoften

36 41-D
Hartsfield, Coats, Mullane, Hawley, Resnik, and Walker

37 41-G
Crippen, McBride, Leestma, Ride, Sullivan, Scully-Power, and Garneau

38 51-A
Hauck, Walker, Fisher, Gardner, Allen

39 51-C
Mattingly, Shriver, Onizuka, Buchli, and Payton

40 51-D Bobko, Williams, Seddon, Griggs, Hoffman, Walker, and Garn

41 51-B Overmyer, Gregory, Thornton, Thagard, Lind, van den Berg, and Wang

42 51-G Brandenstein, Creighton, Lucid, Nagel, Fabian, Baudry, and Al-Saud

43 51-F Fullerton, Bridges, Musgrave, England, Henize, Acton, and Bartoe

44 51-I
Engle, Covey, van Hoften, Lounge, and Fisher

45 51-J
Bobko, Grabe, Hilmers, Stewart, and Pailes

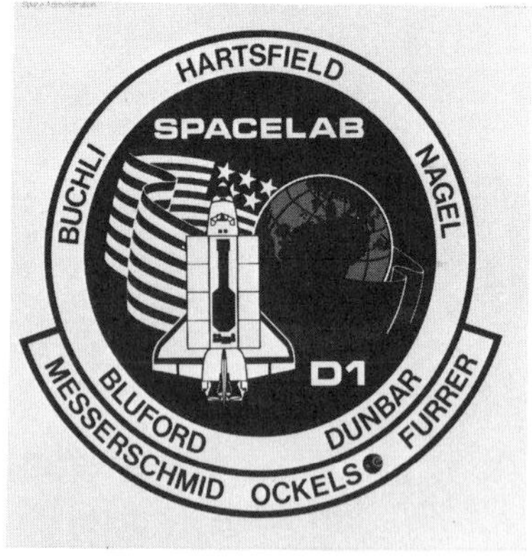

46 61-A Hartsfield, Nagel, Bluford, Buchli, Dunbar, Furrer, Messerschmid, and Ockels

47 61-B
Shaw, O'Connor, Ross, Cleave, Spring, Walker, and Neri Vela

48 61-C
Gibson, Bolden, Chang-Diaz, Hawley, Nelson, Cenker, and Nelson

49 51-L
Scobee, Smith, Onizuka, Resnik, McNair, Jarvis, and McAuliffe

NASA Astronaut Biographies

Adamson, James

Army Major James C. Adamson was selected as an astronaut candidate by NASA in May 1984 and in June 1985 completed a year-long training and evaluation course, making him eligible for assignment to future Shuttle crews as a mission specialist.

Adamson was born March 3, 1946, in Warsaw, New York, but grew up in Monarch, Montana. He graduated from high school in Geneseo, New York, in 1964, then attended the US Military Academy at West Point, receiving a BS in engineering in 1969. He earned an MS in aerospace engineering from Princeton University in 1977.

As an Army officer Adamson served in a Nike Hercules missile battery based in West Germany from 1969 to 1971, then became an Army aviator flying in the Air Cavalry in Vietnam. Returning to the US, he studied at Princeton and after completing his degree was a teacher at West Point. In 1980 he graduated from the US Navy Test Pilot School at Patuxent River, Maryland. At the time of his selection as an astronaut candidate Adamson was assigned to the NASA Johnson Space Center, where he had worked as a flight controller for several Shuttle missions, and as a research pilot and test pilot.

In December 1985 Adamson was assigned to a Shuttle crew for a Department of Defense mission then scheduled for the fall of 1986.

Adamson and his wife, Susan, have a son, Erik.

Aldrin, Edwin

Astronaut "Buzz" Aldrin, lunar module pilot of Apollo 11, was the second man to walk on the Moon.

It was just after three in the afternoon, Central Daylight Time, on Sunday, July 20, 1969, when the lunar module Eagle closed to within fifty thousand feet of the surface of the Moon. Its descent rocket fired and burned for twelve minutes, slowing the Eagle to a safe landing on the Sea of Tranquility. "Contact light?" Aldrin asked aloud, meaning that wire probes extending from the Eagle's landing pads had touched the lunar surface. "Okay," he went on, as the craft settled to the ground, "engine stop, ACA out of detent." Armstrong broke in to say, "Got it." Aldrin continued, "Mode controls both auto, descent engine command override off. Engine arm off. 413 is in." They were safely on the surface, engine shut down. Astronaut Charles Duke, the capcom in Houston, radioed, "We copy you down, Eagle." Armstrong answered, "Houston, Tranquility Base here. The Eagle has landed."

Seven hours later the two astronauts had donned pressure suits and backpacks and had depressurized the Eagle to allow them to exit. Armstrong was the first down the ladder to the lunar surface. Aldrin followed, uttering his first words, "Beautiful view." For the next two hours the astronauts collected samples of rock and soil and set up a scientific experiment package. They also erected an American flag, read a plaque mounted on the Eagle, and had a conversation with the president of the United States.

The two moonwalkers, together with Michael Collins, who had remained in lunar orbit aboard the command module Columbia, returned to Earth after an eight-day mission on July 24, 1969, to a three-week quarantine (because of fears that some unknown lunar microorganism could cause contamination), followed by a worldwide tour.

Apollo 11 was Aldrin's second space flight. In November 1966 he had served as pilot of Gemini 12, the last manned Gemini mission. During four days in space Aldrin performed the first effective spacewalks, spending a total of 5.5 hours in EVA. When the Gemini 12 rendezvous radar failed, Aldrin also had the opportunity to use handheld charts he had developed to perform the complex rendezvous calculations that usually required a computer.

Aldrin spent just over 12 days in space, including eight hours of orbital and lunar EVA.

Edwin Eugene Aldrin, Jr., was born January 30, 1930, in Montclair, New Jersey. His father, Gene, Sr., was an executive with Standard Oil and a pilot who had served as a colonel in the Army Air Corps. Buzz (a name given to him by his sister) graduated from Montclair High School at the age of seventeen and entered the US Military Academy at West Point. He received a BS in 1951. He later performed graduate work at the Masschusetts Institute of Technology, earning a PhD in astronautics in 1963. His thesis dealt with rendezvous between manned orbiting vehicles.

After graduating from West Point in 1951, Aldrin underwent pilot training at bases in Florida, Texas and Nevada. In December 1951 he was assigned to the 51st Fighter Wing in Seoul, Korea, and eventually flew 66 combat missions in the F-86, destroying two enemy MiGs. He returned to the US in December 1953 and became aide to the dean of faculty at the new US Air Force Academy, where he remained until June 1956. For the next three years he was an F-100 pilot with the 36th Fighter Day Wing at Bitburg, Germany.

As a pilot Aldrin eventually logged over 3500 hours of flying time, including 2900 hours in jets and 140 hours in helicopters. He also flew the NASA lunar landing training vehicle.

At the time he was selected as a NASA astronaut in October 1963, Aldrin was already working on Air Force experiments for the Gemini program at the Manned Spacecraft Center. (He had applied for the September 1962 group, asking that the requirement for test pilot experience be waived, but was turned down.) He underwent basic classroom and survival training and also became a member of the panel developing Gemini rendezvous techniques.

He served as capcom for Gemini 5 in August 1965 and for Gemini 10 in July 1966. In January 1966 he was named backup pilot for Gemini 10. Aldrin was disappointed by the assignment, since it would not lead to a later flight (he could expect to rotate to Gemini 13, except that the Gemini program ended with flight 12) and would keep him from joining an early Apollo crew.

But on February 28, 1966, astronauts Elliott See and Charles Bassett, the prime crew for Gemini 9, were killed in a plane crash at St. Louis. Their backups, Thomas Stafford and Eugene Cernan, became prime crewmen for the flight, while Aldrin and Lovell went from backing up Gemini 10 to backing up Gemini 9, thus freeing them to fly on the last Gemini. Without that Gemini flight experience Aldrin would not have been eligible for Apollo 11.

In fact, the composition of the first crew to land on the Moon was the result of a series of accidents and schedule changes, not some deliberate plan. Both Armstrong and Aldrin were assigned to "dead end" Gemini backup jobs when the first Apollo crews began training. The Apollo 1 fire on January 27, 1967, which caused an eighteen-month hiatus in flights, allowed both men to form, with James Lovell, the backup crew for what was then scheduled to be Apollo 9, the third manned Apollo.

But Apollo 9 and Apollo 8 switched places in the schedule, and the crews switched as well, putting Armstrong and Aldrin in line for the fifth Apollo rather than the sixth. By this time Lovell had replaced Michael Collins on the Apollo 8 prime crew. Collins would become eligible for flights again by late December 1968, so the "magic" decision made by NASA planners was simply assigning the next two astronauts in line, Armstrong and Aldrin, to the next available mission, and replacing Fred Haise (who had not flown in space) with Gemini veteran Collins, who had by then spent two years training as an Apollo command module pilot. It should also be noted that when the assignment was made in January 1969, there was no guarantee that Apollo 11 would be the first lunar landing. First there were two other missions (Apollo 9 and Apollo 10) which had to go perfectly.

When Aldrin was finally able to return to work after his publicity tour he became involved with early designs for the Space Shuttle. He also served as host for visiting Soviet cosmonauts Andrian Nikolayev and Vitaly Sevastyanov in October 1970.

He resigned from NASA in July 1971 to return to the Air Force as commander of the Test Pilot School at Edwards AFB, California, becoming the first astronaut to return to military service. But personal problems, culminating in a nervous breakdown, caused him to retire from the Air Force on March 1, 1972.

Aldrin wrote candidly about his personal crisis in an autobiography, *Return to Earth*, published in 1973. The book was filmed as a movie-for-television starring Cliff Robertson in 1976.

In 1972 Aldrin founded Research & Engineering Consultants, a firm he headed for many years. He also served as a consultant to Mutual of Omaha Insurance, the Inforex Computer Company, the Laser Video Corporation, and the Beverly Hills Oil Company. Since 1985 Dr. Aldrin has been a professor at the Center for Science, University of North Dakota in Grand Forks.

Among his current projects he is developing a science fiction story called *Encounter*.

Divorced from his second wife, Aldrin has three children, Michael, Janice and Andrew, from his first marriage.

Allen, Joseph

Dr. Joseph Allen took part in the first salvage mission in space history. As a mission specialist aboard Shuttle flight 51-A in November 1984, Allen and fellow astronaut Dale Gardner performed two spacewalks during which the errant satellites Palapa B-2 and Westar VI were retrieved and loaded aboard the shuttle Discovery for return to Earth. Allen used the manned maneuvering unit backpack in his capture of the Palapa, and found himself literally holding the weightless (but not inertialess) Palapa over his head for an entire orbit of the Earth while Gardner improvised a way to lock the satellite into the Shuttle's cargo bay.

Allen was also a mission specialist aboard the first operational Shuttle mission, STS-5 in November 1982 and supervised the first launching of a satellite, SBS C, from the Shuttle. A planned spacewalk by Allen and William Lenoir during that mission had to be canceled.

He logged 314 hours in space, including approximately 11 hours of EVA time.

Joseph Percival Allen IV was born June 27, 1937, in Crawfordsville, Indiana, where he graduated from high school. He attended DePauw University, receiving a BA in math-physics in 1959, then earned an MS and a PhD in physics from Yale University in 1961 and 1965.

Allen was a Fulbright Scholar in Germany in 1959 and 1960 and after earning his PhD from Yale was a staff physicist at the Nuclear Structure Laboratory there. When selected by NASA he was a research associate at the Nuclear Physics Laboratory at the University of Washington.

One of the 11 scientist-astronauts selected by NASA in 1967, Allen underwent jet pilot training at Vance Air Force Base in Oklahoma, where he earned the "outstanding flying" award. He served as mission scientist, support crewman and capcom for the Apollo 15 lunar landing in 1971. Between 1972 and 1978 he held several administrative positions while retaining his astronaut status: he was a consultant on science and technology to the President's Council on International Economic Policy in 1974, and from 1975 to 1978 was assistant administrator for legislative affairs at NASA Headquarters in Washington, D.C.

After returning to the Johnson Space Center, Allen was a member of the support crew and capcom for the first Shuttle mission, STS-1.

In July 1985 Allen resigned from NASA to become vice president of Space Industries, Inc., a Houston-based firm which plans to launch a free-flying space manufacturing platform from the Shuttle in the 1990s.

Allen is the co-author of a book, *Entering Space* (1984).

He and his wife, Bonnie, have two children, David and Elizabeth. They live in Houston.

Anders, William

William Anders was a member of the first crew of space travelers to leave the Earth and orbit the Moon. The time was December 1968 and the flight was Apollo 8. Anders, Frank Borman and James Lovell thundered into Earth orbit on the Saturn 5 rocket, the most powerful ever used for a manned space flight, then fired one of the Saturn's upper stages to send them into a trans-lunar trajectory. Three days later, on Christmas Eve 1968, they used the engine on their Apollo service module to slow them into lunar orbit. In the next twenty hours the astronauts circled the Moon ten times, becoming the first human beings to see the far side of the Moon with their own eyes. On Christmas morning, just prior to leaving the Moon, the astronauts read a passage from the Book of Genesis to a worldwide audience on television.

The triumph of Apollo 8 was the result of a daring and risky decision by NASA officials, notably George Low, to keep the Apollo program on target for a manned lunar landing in 1969. The essential first flight of the lunar module had been delayed until March 1969 and NASA was facing a five-month gap between missions. Sending Apollo 8, without a lunar module, to the Moon in late December, when lighting conditions were the same as those of the planned landing, would serve to qualify the Saturn 5 for manned flight while gathering data for later lunar missions, and might just beat the Russians, who were rumored to be planning a manned circumlunar flight of their own. It did all three. The three astronauts were chosen *Time* magazine's men of the year.

Apollo 8, which lasted 148 hours, was Bill Anders' only space flight.

William Alison Anders was born October 17, 1933, in Hong Kong, where his father, a naval officer, was stationed. Like his father, Anders entered the US Naval Academy at Annapolis, graduating with a BS in 1955. He later earned an MS in nuclear engineering from the Air Force

Institute of Technology in 1962. He also completed the advanced management program at Harvard Business School (1979).

Anders elected to serve in the US Air Force and underwent pilot training in Texas and Georgia, receiving his wings in December 1956. For the next three years he was a fighter pilot in all-weather interceptor squadrons of the Air Defense Command in California and Iceland, then attended the Air Force Institute of Technology at Wright-Patterson Air Force Base, Ohio. Upon completing his degree, he became a nuclear engineer and instructor pilot at the USAF Weapons Laboratory at Kirtland AFB, New Mexico.

As a pilot Anders eventually logged over 5000 hours of flying time.

Anders was one of the 14 astronauts selected by NASA in October 1963. Because of his scientific background he was assigned to work on spacecraft environmental systems and, in particular, to study the amount and type of radiation exposure astronauts might endure on a trip to the Moon. He served as capcom for Gemini 4 and Gemini 12, and was backup pilot for Gemini 11 prior to joining the Apollo crew commanded by Frank Borman in November 1966.

The Borman crew was originally scheduled to fly the third manned Apollo mission in 1969, riding a Saturn 5 to an altitude of 4000 miles in a rehearsal for a lunar landing mission. Borman and Anders would have tested a lunar module, and Anders spent months working on LM systems and learning to pilot helicopters and the lunar landing training vehicle in preparation. But when NASA officials developed the Apollo 8 lunar orbit project, they offered Borman and James McDivitt, commander of the second manned Apollo, a choice of missions. Borman elected to take Apollo 8, and lunar module pilot Anders went into space without a lunar module.

Following Apollo 8 Anders served as backup command module pilot for Michael Collins on Apollo 11, the first lunar landing mission. Astronaut chief Deke Slayton told Anders he could serve as command module pilot of a later Apollo mission, and then command a Skylab flight, but Anders had already elected to leave the astronaut group. In September 1969 he became executive secretary of the National Aeronautics and Space Council, which reported to the president and vice president concerning space research. He remained with the Council until August 1973, when he was appointed to the Atomic Energy Commission. He later served as first chairman of the Nuclear Regulatory Commission (1975) and US Ambassador to Norway (1976-77). During this time he remained a NASA astronaut, though he was classified as "unavailable for flight assignment."

Anders left the federal government in 1977 and, after a brief term as a fellow of the American Enterprise Institute, joined the General Electric Company in San Jose, California, as vice president and general manager of their nuclear products division. Since 1980 he has been general manager of GE's aircraft equipment division in Dewitt, New York. He is also a consultant and serves as a major general in the US Air Force Reserve.

Anders and his wife, Valerie, have six children, Alan, Glen, Gayle, Gregory, Eric and Diana.

Apt, Jerome

Dr. Jerome "Jay" Apt was selected by NASA as an astronaut candidate in June 1985 and in August of that year began a year-long training and evaluation course to qualify him as a mission specialist for Shuttle crews.

Apt was born April 28, 1949, in Springfield, Massachusetts. He graduated from Shady Side Academy in Pittsburgh in 1967, received a

BA in Physics (magna cum laude) from Harvard in 1971 and a PhD in Physics from the Massachusetts Institute of Technology in 1976.

From 1976 to 1980 Dr. Apt, a member of the Center for Earth & Planetary Physics at Harvard, was involved in the Pioneer Venus space probe project. He also made temperature maps of the planet Venus from Mt. Hopkins Observatory. In 1980 Apt joined NASA's Jet Propulsion Laboratory and continued his studies of the solar system. From 1981 to 1985 he was a flight controller for the Space Shuttle at the Johnson Space Center.

Apt is single.

Armstrong, Neil

Neil Armstrong will always be remembered as the first man to walk on the Moon. At 9:56 P.M., Houston time, Sunday, July 20, 1969, he stepped off the footpad of the lunar module Eagle, saying, "That's one small step for a man, one giant leap for mankind."

With every one of his early steps a theory about the lunar surface evaporated. The worry that an astronaut would sink in a deep coating of dust? Armstrong reported that his boots sank "maybe an eighth of an inch." Would an astronaut trying to walk in the unwieldy space suit and backpack simply fall over? "There seems to be no difficulty," he said. "It's even perhaps easier than the simulations at one-sixth G."

As millions watched on television, Armstrong dug a small "contingency" sample of lunar soil, in case the moon walk had to be cut short. Then, joined by Buzz Aldrin, he began to set up scientific experiments and searched for more comprehensive rock samples. He and Aldrin also set up an American flag and took a phone call from President Richard Nixon. They also read the words printed on a plaque mounted on the descent stage of the Eagle, which would remain forever on the Sea of Tranquility: "Here men from the planet Earth first set foot upon the Moon, July 1969 A.D. We came in peace for all mankind."

Just over two-and-a-half hours later Armstrong, Aldrin and the precious box containing the first Moon rocks were safely back inside the Eagle. At 12:55 P.M. the next day the Eagle lifted off from the Moon to rejoin the orbiting Columbia and its pilot, Michael Collins.

Apollo 11 ended with a successful splashdown in the Pacific and recovery by the carrier USS Hornet. Armstrong, Collins and Aldrin faced three weeks of quarantine, and months of public appearances.

Armstrong had commanded one previous space flight, Gemini 8 in March 1966. Gemini 8 accomplished the first docking between two spacecraft when it linked up with an unmanned Agena 6.5 hours after liftoff. It also became the first American space flight to be aborted. A thruster on the Gemini began to fire uncontrollably, sending the combined Gemini-Agena vehicle into a spin. Suspecting at first that the Agena was causing the problem, Armstrong and pilot David Scott separated from the unmanned craft, which only made matters worse. Forced to use re-entry thrusters to stabilize the Gemini, Armstrong and Scott then had to return to Earth. They splashed down 600 miles south of Yokosuka, Japan, and waited in the floating spacecraft for 45 minutes until divers could reach them from a C-54 rescue plane. It wasn't until three hours after splashdown that the weary, seasick astronauts were safe aboard the destroyer Leonard F. Mason. They had completed less than eleven hours of a planned three-day mission.

Armstrong spent a total of eight days and 14 hours in space, including two hours and 14 minutes walking on the Moon.

Neil Alden Armstrong was born August 5, 1930, at a farm six miles outside Wapakoneta, Ohio. His father was an auditor for the state of Ohio and so the family moved every year, though Neil graduated from high school in Wapakoneta. He built model airplanes and got his student pilot's license on his sixteenth birthday.

Armstrong wanted to go to college and study aeronautical engineering, but could not afford it without some sort of aid. He applied for a US Navy scholarship, got it, and enrolled at Purdue University in 1947. A year-and-a-half later the Navy called him to active duty. He entered flight school at Pensacola, Florida, and became a fighter pilot. Before he could return to Purdue, however, the Korean War broke out. Armstrong was assigned to Fighter Squadron 51 and served in Korea until the spring of 1952. He described his combat experience as "bridge breaking, train stopping, tank shooting and that sort of thing." In September 1951 he had to bail out of his F9F-2 jet when a wire stretched across a Korean valley tore the wing off his plane.

Out of the Navy, he returned to Purdue in the fall of 1952 and graduated with a BS in aeronautical engineering in January 1955. He would later receive an MS from the University of Southern California (1970).

Armstrong went to work for the National Advisory Committee on Aeronautics (NACA), the forerunner of NASA, at its Lewis Flight Propulsion Laboratory in Cleveland. He soon transferred to the NACA station at Edwards AFB, California, where he became an aeronautical research pilot. Among other vehicles, he flew the X-5, F-102A, F5D-1 Skylancer (making simulated X-20 Dyna-Soar launchings and landings in these two), the Paresev, and the X-15 rocket plane. He made six flights in the X-15 between December 1960 and July 1962, ultimately reaching an altitude of 207,000 feet.

Considered a shoo-in for the second group of NASA astronauts selected in 1962, Armstrong was one of the first two civilians chosen for the manned space program. He underwent survival training, then became involved in Gemini development. One of his jobs, beginning in 1964, was to supervise the work of the 14 new astronauts chosen in 1983, including Aldrin and Collins. Armstrong was assigned as backup commander for Gemini 5, the third manned Gemini mission, in early 1965. He served as capcom for Gemini 5 and for Gemini 9 as well, and also served as backup commander for Gemini 11.

Following Apollo 11 Armstrong served at NASA Headquarters in Washington, D.C., as deputy associate administrator for aeronautics, and became known as an advocate of research into computer control of high-performance aircraft.

He resigned from NASA in August 1971 to become professor of engineering at the University of Cincinnati. He remained there through 1979, when he joined the Cardwell International Corporation of Lebanon, Ohio, as chairman of the board. In 1984 he became chairman of the board of CTA, Inc., in Lebanon.

An intensely private person, Armstrong refrained from making public appearances for many years. However, in early 1984 he accepted an appointment to the National Commission on Space, a Presidential panel whose members included, in addition to Armstrong, astronaut Kathryn Sullivan, former test pilot Chuck Yeager, and former NASA administrator Thomas Paine. The NCOS was to develop goals for a national space program extending into the 21st century. Before its report could be delivered, however, the Shuttle Challenger exploded during launch on January 28, 1986. Armstrong was immediately named vice chairman of the committee investigating the disaster.

Armstrong and his wife, Jan, live in Lebanon, Ohio. They have two children, Eric and Mark. A daughter, Karen, died in infancy.

Bagian, James

Dr. James Bagian was one of the 19 astronauts selected by NASA in May 1980. In 1985 he was assigned to make his first Space Shuttle flight on a mission scheduled for 1986.

James Phillip Bagian was born February 22, 1952, in Philadelphia, Pennsylvania. He graduated from Central High School there in 1969, then attended Drexel University, receiving his BS in mechanical engineering in 1973. He later earned his MD from Thomas Jefferson University in 1977.

While studying to be a doctor, Bagian worked as a mechanical engineer at the US Naval Test Center at Patuxent River, Maryland. In 1978 he was a resident in surgery at Geisinger Medical Center in Danville, Pennsylvania, then went to work at the NASA Johnson Space Center as a flight surgeon and medical officer. He studied further at the USAF School of Aerospace Medicine in San Antonio, Texas, and at the University of Pennsylvania. Dr. Bagian is a private pilot with over 1000 hours time in propeller and jet airplanes, helicopters and gliders.

Dr. Bagian provided medical support for the first six Shuttle missions. After completing his astronaut training and evaluation course in August 1981 he also served as the astronaut office coordinator for Shuttle payload software and crew equipment. Prior to being assigned to a Shuttle mission in September 1985 Bagian worked for over a year on the Spacelab 4 mission.

He is married to the former Tandi Benson.

Baker, Michael

Lieutenant Commander Michael A. Baker, USN, is one of the 13 astronaut candidates selected by NASA in June 1985. In August 1985 he started a year-long training and evaluation course to qualify him as a pilot on future Space Shuttle crews.

Baker was born October 27, 1953, in Memphis, Tennessee, but grew up in Lemoore, California, graduating from high school there in 1971. He attended the University of Texas, earning his BS in aerospace engineering in 1975.

Baker entered the US Navy following graduation from Texas and earned his wings in 1977. After serving as a carrier pilot he attended the US Naval Test Pilot School at Patuxent River, Maryland. He was a test pilot at Patuxent River, then an instructor at the school. At the time he was selected by NASA, Baker was an exchange test pilot instructor at the Empire Test Pilots School in Boscombe Down, England.

He has logged over 2000 hours of flying time in 50 different types of airplanes.

Baker and his wife, Karen, have two daughters, Lesley and Jane.

Bassett, Charles

Major Charles A. Bassett, USAF, was killed in the crash of a T-38 jet in St. Louis, Missouri, on February 28, 1966. At the time of his death Bassett was assigned as the pilot of the Gemini 9 mission scheduled for June 1966. Killed with him in the crash was Gemini 9 commander Elliott See.

Charles Arthur Bassett II was born December 30, 1931, in Dayton, Ohio. He graduated from Bera High School in Dayton, then attended the University of Ohio in Athens. He left college without getting a degree and joined the US Air Force. He would later perform additional

study at the University of Southern California, and eventually earned his BS in electrical engineering from Texas Technical College in 1960.

As a pilot, Bassett was stationed in the Pacific and at bases in New York and Ohio. In 1961 he attended the USAF Test Pilot School at Edwards Air Force Base, California, and remained there as a student and test pilot until selected by NASA in October 1963.

As an astronaut Bassett served as a capcom for Gemini 7 and Gemini 6 in December 1965. He had been named as pilot for Gemini 9 in November 1965 and was training to perform a spacewalk on that mission.

Bassett was survived by his widow, Jean, and two children, Karin and Peter.

Bean, Alan

During the flight of Apollo 12, Alan Bean became the fourth person to walk on the Moon. On November 18, 1969, he and commander Charles Conrad landed the lunar module Intrepid in the Oceanus Procellarum just 200 yards from the unmanned Surveyor III probe, which had landed there three years earlier. During the next 31½ hours the astronauts conducted two walks on the Moon, setting up an experiment package and visiting the Surveyor. They and command module pilot Richard Gordon returned to Earth on November 24.

Bean's second space flight was as commander of Skylab 3, the second manned visit to the Skylab orbiting space station. For over 59 days, from July 28 to September 25, 1973, Bean and fellow astronauts Owen Garriott and Jack Lousma conducted medical experiments, observations of the Sun, and Earth resources photography while also performing necessary maintenance on Skylab, which had been badly damaged during its launch on May 14. The Skylab 3 mission came close to becoming the first manned flight to end with a rescue: problems with thrusters aboard the Apollo service module used to ferry the astronauts to Skylab forced NASA to prepare another Apollo, this one specially modified to carry five astronauts, as a standby. But the Skylab Rescue was not needed.

Bean logged approximately 69 days, 16 hours in space during his two flights, including 6 hours and 50 minutes walking on the Moon and 2 hours and 45 minutes in a Skylab EVA.

Alan LaVern Bean was born March 15, 1932, in Wheeler, Texas, but grew up in Fort Worth, where he graduated from Paschal High School in 1950. He spent a year as an electronics technician with the US Naval Reserve in Dallas, then entered the University of Texas at Austin, graduating with a BS in aeronautical engineering in 1955.

A Navy ROTC student at Texas, Bean was comissioned upon graduation and received pilot training in Florida and Texas. From 1956 to 1960 he was assigned to Attack Squadron 44 at the Jacksonville, Florida, Naval Air Station. He then attended the US Naval Test Pilot School at Patuxent River, Maryland, remaining at Pax River as a test pilot through 1962. When chosen by NASA he was stationed with Attack Squadron 172 at Cecil Field, Florida.

As a pilot Bean eventually logged approximately 5500 hours of flying time, 4900 in jets, in 27 different types of aircraft.

Bean was one of the 14 astronauts chosen by NASA in October 1963. His area of specialization was spacecraft recovery systems. He was a capcom for Gemini 7/6 and Gemini 11 and backup command pilot for Gemini 10. In September 1966 he was assigned as chief of the Apollo Applications Office (later Skylab), which effectively eliminated his chance of making a flight to the Moon, but when astronaut C. C.

Williams was killed in October 1967, Pax River classmate Charles Conrad asked Bean to replace him on his Apollo crew. Conrad, Gordon and Bean were backups for Apollo 9.

After his Skylab flight Bean served as backup commander for the Apollo-Soyuz Test Project. In August 1975 he was assigned to the Space Shuttle program. He retired from the Navy as a captain in October of that year, but remained a NASA astronaut. From May 1978 to June 1981 Bean was acting chief astronaut, replacing John Young, and supervised the training of the 1978 and 1980 astronaut candidates, including NASA's first women astronauts.

Although he was expected to be chosen to command the first Shuttle/Spacelab mission, Bean resigned from NASA on June 26, 1981, to pursue a career as a painter working in the style of famed space artist Robert McCall. (Bean had begun to study painting in 1962, and after an interruption caused by his activities in the Apollo program, resumed study in 1974.) His work has been displayed at the National Air and Space Museum, at the Meredith Long and Company Gallery in Houston, and is published in the book *The Planets* (1985).

Bean is the divorced father of two children, Clay and Amy. He lives in Houston, Texas.

Blaha, John

Colonel John Blaha, USAF, is one of the 19 astronauts selected by NASA in May 1980. At the time of the Shuttle Challenger disaster he was scheduled to pilot a Space Shuttle mission in July 1986.

John Elmer Blaha was born August 26, 1942, in San Antonio Texas. His father was an Air Force officer and Blaha grew up at bases all over the world. He graduated from Granby High School in Norfolk, Virginia, in 1960, then attended the US Air Force Academy in Colorado Springs, graduating with a BS in engineering science in 1965. He earned an MS in astronautical engineering from Purdue University in 1966.

Blaha earned his wings in 1967, then was assigned as a pilot in Vietnam, where he flew 361 combat missions. Returning to the US in 1971, he attended the USAF Aerospace Research Pilot School at Edwards Air Force Base, California, piloting an NF-104 research jet to an altitude of 104,000 feet. He was an instructor at the school, then in 1973 was assigned as an exchange test pilot with the Royal Air Force at Boscombe Down, England. He returned to the US in 1976 to attend the USAF Air Command and Staff College and was stationed at USAF Headquarters in the Pentagon when selected by NASA.

Blaha has logged over 3800 hours of flying time in 32 different aircraft.

After completing his year-long astronaut training and evaluation course in August 1981 Blaha was involved in Shuttle computer software and hardware development. From April 1983 to October 1984 he was a capcom on Shuttle missions.

Blaha and his wife, Brenda, have three children, James, Steven, and Carolyn.

Bluford, Guion

"Guy" Bluford became the first black American to go into space when he served as a mission specialist aboard STS-8 in August 1983. In addition to launching an Indian communications satellite and experimenting with the Canadian-built remote manipulator arm, STS-8 also

made the first nighttime launch and landing in the Shuttle program.

Bluford made a second space flight aboard Mission 61-A/Spacelab D1 in October and November 1985, one of eight astronauts aboard this scientific mission controlled by the Federal German Aerospace Research Establishment (DFVLR). With the completion of this second flight he has logged 314 hours in space.

Guion Stewart Bluford, Jr., was born on November 22, 1942, in Philadelphia, Pennsylvania. His father was a mechanical engineer and Bluford became interested in aviation as a result. He graduated from Overbrook Senior High School in Philadelphia in 1960 and attended Pennsylvania State University, where he received a BS in aerospace engineering in 1964. He later received an MS with distinction from the Air Force Institute of Technology in 1974, and a PhD in aerospace engineering with a minor in laser physics from the institute in 1978.

An ROTC student at Penn State, Bluford entered active duty with USAF upon graduation in 1964. He earned his pilot's wings in January 1965, then flew F-4Cs in 144 combat missions—65 of them over North Vietnam—in the next two years. Returning to the US, he served as an instructor pilot at Sheppard Air Force Base in Texas and attended Squadron Officers School. In August 1972 he entered the Air Force Institute of Technology at Wright-Patterson AFB, Ohio, and after completing his studies, remained there as a staff engineer. He has logged over 3500 hours of flying time in jets, including 1300 hours as an instructor. He has also published several scientific papers.

Bluford was selected as an astronaut candidate by NASA in January 1968. In August 1979 he completed the year-long training and evaluation period, and worked on the remote manipulator system, Spacelab 3 experiments, Shuttle systems, Shuttle Avionics Integration Laboratory, and other assignments until being chosen for the STS-8 crew in April 1982.

Colonel Bluford and his wife, Linda, an accountant, have two sons, Guion Stewart III and James Trevor. They live in Clear Lake, Texas.

Bobko, Karol

"Bo" Bobko has made three flights aboard the Space Shuttle, each one aboard a different orbiter.

He was pilot of STS-6, the maiden voyage of the orbiter Challenger, in April 1983, and commander of Mission 51-D on the orbiter Discovery in April 1985. In October 1985 he commanded the maiden voyage of the orbiter Atlantis. He has logged approximately 386 hours in space.

Bobko was born in New York City on December 23, 1937, and graduated from Brooklyn Technical High School in 1955. He was a member of the first graduating class of the US Air Force Academy, where he received his BS in 1959. In 1970 he received an MS in aerospace engineering from the University of Southern California.

As an Air Force officer, Bobko completed pilot training in 1960 and flew F-100 and F-105 aircraft at Cannon AFB in New Mexico and Seymore Johnson AFB in North Carolina until 1965. He attended the USAF Aerospace Research Pilots School at Edwards AFB, California, in 1965 and in 1966 was assigned to the USAF Manned Orbiting Laboratory program. When that program was canceled in 1969, Bobko transferred to NASA as an astronaut. He has logged over 6100 hours of flying time.

Bobko was a crew member for the Skylab Medical Experiments Altitude Test in 1970, a 56-day ground simulation of a Skylab mission, then a support crew member for Apollo-Soyuz Test Project from 1973-75. In 1976-77 he was a support crew member for the Space Shuttle Approach and Landing Test flights, working as capcom and chase pilot.

Colonel Bobko and his wife, Dianne, have two children, Michelle and Paul.

Bolden, Charles

Charles Bolden was pilot of Shuttle Mission 61-C, which suffered seven different launch delays before finally lifting off on January 12, 1986. Included in the crew were Florida Congressman Bill Nelson and RCA engineer Robert Cenker. During a 6-day flight the astronauts deployed the RCA Satcom Ku-1 satellite and conducted experiments in astrophysics and materials processing.

He has logged 146 hours in space.

Charles Frank Bolden, Jr., was born August 19, 1946, in Columbia, South Carolina, where he graduated from C. A. Johnson High School in 1964. He attended the US Naval Academy at Annapolis, earning a BS in electrical science in 1968. He received an MS in systems management from the University of Southern California in 1978.

Bolden elected to serve in the US Marine Corps and was commissioned in 1968. He underwent pilot training in Florida, Mississippi and Texas before earning his wings in May 1970. From 1970 to 1972 he was an A-6A pilot at Cherry Point, North Carolina, then was assigned to Nam Phong, Thailand, where he flew 100 combat missions over North and South Vietnam, Laos, and Cambodia. Returning to the US in June 1973, he spent two years as a Marine Corps recruiting officer in Los Angeles, then, from 1975 to 1978, was stationed at the Marine Corps Air Station in El Toro, California.

In 1978 Bolden entered the US Naval Test Pilot School at Patuxent River, Maryland, and following graduation served as a test pilot there until his selection by NASA.

As a pilot he has accumulated over 4000 hours of flying time.

Bolden was one of the 19 astronauts selected by NASA in May 1980. In August 1981 he completed a training and evaluation course that qualified him as a Shuttle pilot. He worked in the systems development group (which was involved with tile repair, the Shuttle solid rocket boosters, and launch debris), on Shuttle cockpit displays and controls, and on computer systems at the Shuttle Avionics Integration Laboratory. He has also been technical assistant to the director of flight crew operations.

He is currently assigned as pilot for the launch of the Hubble Space Telescope.

Colonel Bolden and his wife, Jackie, have two children, Anthony and Kelly.

Borman, Frank

Frank Borman commanded Apollo 8, which became the first manned spacecraft to orbit the Moon. In a memorable broadcast to the world from Apollo 8 on Christmas Eve 1968, Borman and fellow astronauts James Lovell and William Anders read passages from the book of Genesis. Their safe return to Earth after ten orbits of the Moon made the Apollo 11 lunar landing possible.

Borman's crew was originally scheduled to test the lunar module in a 4000-mile high Earth orbit in the third manned Apollo flight, but delays in the preparation of the LM and the fear that the Soviets would launch a manned circumlunar mission in December 1968 forced Apollo officials to consider a risky option: to send three astronauts around the Moon on the second Apollo flight, which would be the first launched aboard the huge Saturn 5 rocket. Given the choice of missions, Borman opted for the lunar flight while astronaut James McDivitt kept his crew on the LM flight.

It was a typically daring move by Borman, who had served on the review board which studied the tragic Apollo 1 fire that killed astronauts Grissom, White and Chaffee. Borman later headed the team that re-engineered the Apollo spacecraft. Astronaut Michael Collins would later write that Borman "made decisions faster than anyone I have ever known, with a high percentage of correct ones which would have been even higher if he'd slowed down."

Apollo 8 was Borman's second space flight. In December 1965 he was commander of Gemini 7, during which Borman and Lovell set an endurance record by spending fourteen days in space.

He logged approximately 19 days, 22 hours in space.

Frank Borman was born March 14, 1928, in Gary, Indiana, but grew up in Tucson, Arizona. He earned an appointment to the US Military Academy at West Point, graduating in 1950 with a bachelor of science degree. He later earned an MS in aeronautical engineering from the California Institute of Technology in Pasadena in 1957, and graduated from the Advanced Management Training Program at the Harvard Business School in 1970.

Borman entered the US Air Force after graduation from West Point and became a pilot in 1951. He was a fighter pilot with the 44th Fighter Bomber Squadron in the Philippines from 1951 to 1953, then a pilot and instructor with various fighter squadrons in the US. From 1957 to 1960 he taught thermodynamics and fluid mechanics at West Point, then attended the USAF Aerospace Research Pilot School at Edwards AFB, California. He was an instructor there when chosen by NASA.

As a pilot Borman logged over 6000 hours of flying time.

One of the 9 astronauts selected by NASA in September 1962, Borman quickly established himself as one of the senior members of the group. He was training as pilot of the first manned Gemini flight when his commander, Alan Shepard, was grounded for medical reasons. Given his own command, Borman served as backup to James McDivitt on Gemini 4 in 1965. After his flight on Gemini 7 he was named backup commander for the planned Apollo 2 mission with astronauts Stafford and Collins. In a major shuffling of crews and missions in November 1966, just three months prior to the Apollo fire, Borman was named to command the third manned Apollo.

The Apollo 1 fire on January 27, 1967 suspended all manned Apollo flights. Borman was named the astronaut representative on the panel investigating the accident.

After Apollo 8 Borman was the field director of the NASA Space Station Task Force. He retired from the Air Force and NASA in July 1970 to join Eastern Airlines, eventually becoming chairman of the board, president and chief executive officer of that company.

In addition to these activities, in 1966 and 1968 Borman served as a special presidential ambassador on trips to the Far East and Europe, and in 1970 made a worldwide tour to seek support for the release of American prisoners of war held in North Vietnam.

In June 1986 Borman resigned from Eastern. He currently lives in Las Cruces, New Mexico, where he is writing his autobiography.

Borman and his wife, Susan, have two sons, Frederick and Edwin.

Brand, Vance

Vance Brand made three space flights between 1975 and 1985, including the first international mission, Apollo-Soyuz, and the first operational flight of the Space Shuttle.

Brand was command module pilot for the Apollo-Soyuz Test Project, launched July 15, 1975, for a docking with the Soviet Soyuz 19. Brand and fellow astronauts Thomas Stafford and Deke Slayton spent two days docked with the Soviet vehicle crewed by cosmonauts Alexei Leonov and Valery Kubasov. During the Apollo splashdown on July 24, poisonous nitrogen tetroxide gas from a leaking thruster flooded the Apollo cabin. Brand was knocked unconscious, but revived when an oxygen mask was placed on his face. The astronauts suffered no lasting injury, but the incident was an embarrassment.

Brand's second trip into space was as commander of STS-5, the first operational flight of the Space Shuttle. During the November 1982 flight of Columbia and its crew of four astronauts, the largest crew sent into space at that time, two communications satellites were successfully deployed. STS-5 ended after five days with a landing at Edwards AFB, California.

In February 1984 Brand commanded Mission 41-B, during which astronaut Bruce McCandless became the first human to fly freely in space with the manned maneuvering unit backpack. Other elements of the mission didn't go as well: two communications satellites, though deployed safely from the Challenger, suffered engine problems and failed to reach their proper orbits. (Both were retrieved and returned to Earth later in 1984.)

Brand has logged approximately 531 hours in space on his three missions.

Vance DeVoe Brand was born May 9, 1931, in Longmont, Colorado, where he grew up, graduating from high school in 1949. He attended the University of Colorado, receving a BS in business in 1953. He later earned a BS in aeronautical engineering from Colorado in 1960, and an MBA from the University of California at Los Angeles in 1964.

He joined the US Marine Corps in 1953, serving as a jet pilot until 1957. (He would fly for the Marine Corps Reserve and Air National Guard until 1964.) After further schooling at Colorado, he went to work for the Lockheed Aircraft Corporation in 1960, first as a flight test engineer, later, after attending the US Naval Test Pilot School, as an experimental test pilot. He applied for the 1963 NASA astronaut group, but was not selected. When finally chosen, in 1966, he was working for Lockheed at the flight test center at Istres, France.

As a pilot he has logged over 8100 hours of flying time, including 7000 hours in jets, in 30 different types of aircraft.

Brand was one of 19 astronauts chosen by NASA in April 1966. In 1968 he and astronauts Joseph Kerwin and Joe Engle conducted vacuum chamber tests of the re-designed Apollo command and service modules. Brand later served on the support crews for Apollo 8 and Apollo 13. He served as backup command module pilot for Apollo 15 and would have flown around the Moon on Apollo 18, but the mission was canceled.

He served as backup commander for the last two Skylab missions, and when an opening occurred on the Apollo-Soyuz crew in late 1972, began training simultaneously for that mission. Following Apollo-Soyuz he worked on Space Shuttle development.

Since Mission 41-B Brand has been assigned as commander of two Shuttle/Spacelab missions which were canceled before they could fly, including the Spacelab Earth Observation Mission in 1986.

Brand and his wife, Beverly, have six children, Susan, Stephanie, Patrick, and Kevin from Brand's first marriage, and Erik and Dane.

Brandenstein, Daniel

Dan Brandenstein has made two Space Shuttle flights. He was pilot of the STS-8 Challenger mission in 1983, which performed the first night launch and landing in the Shuttle program. In 1985 he commanded the seven-astronaut crew of Mission 51-G, which included Saudi prince Sultan al-Saud and French pilot Patrick Baudry. Three communications satellites were launched from the Shuttle Discovery during 51-G.

Brandenstein has logged approximately 315 hours in space.

Daniel Charles Brandenstein was born January 17, 1943, in Watertown, Wisconsin, where he graduated from high school in 1961. He received a BS degree in mathematics and physics from the University of Wisconsin at River Falls in 1965.

After completing US Navy pilot training in 1967, Brandenstein served two combat tours in Vietnam on board the carriers USS Constellation and USS Ranger, flying 192 missions. Returning to the US, he tested weapons and tactics for A-6 aircraft and also attended the US Naval Test Pilot School at Patuxent River, Maryland. He was assigned to carrier duty aboard the USS Ranger again from 1975 to 1977, and was an A-6 instructor pilot when selected by NASA.

He has logged over 5000 hours of flying time in 24 different types of aircraft, and has made 400 carrier landings.

Brandenstein was one of the 35 astronaut candidates chosen by NASA in January 1978. In August 1979 he completed a training and evaluation course which qualified him as a pilot on Shuttle crews. He then served as capcom and support crew member for the first two Shuttle missions in 1981.

Captain Brandenstein and his wife, Jane, have a daughter, Adelle.

Bridges, Roy

Colonel Roy Bridges, USAF, was pilot of Space Shuttle Mission 51-F in July and August 1985. This eight-day Spacelab 2 mission was devoted to astronomy and was completed successfully, but not without several problems. For example, failures in the scientific Instrument Pointing System (IPS), a device intended to aim delicate sensors at distant objects, forced Bridges and commander Gordon Fullerton to perform dozens of extra maneuvers to ensure that Spacelab's telescopes were aimed properly.

In addition, Bridges and six other astronauts had to suffer through the second launch pad abort in the Shuttle program on July 12, and an unusual "abort-to-orbit" during launch on July 29, when one of the three Shuttle main engines quit. Because of the problem, the orbiter Challenger and its Spacelab 2 pallet were placed in a lower than desired orbit, which was eventually raised later in the flight. Mission specialist Anthony England, riding on the flight deck with Bridges and Fullerton, later recalled that Bridges, seeing the light warning of an engine failure, pointed to it and said, "You're a simulation. I don't believe you."

Roy Dunbard Bridges, Jr., was born July 19, 1943, in Atlanta, Georgia, but grew up in Gainesville, where he graduated from high school in 1961. He attended the US Air Force Academy, receiving a BS in engineering science in 1965, and Purdue, where he earned an MS in astronautics in 1966.

Following pilot training at Williams AFB, Arizona, in 1967, Bridges became an F-100 tactical fighter pilot. He flew 226 combat missions in Vietnam in 1968, then returned to the US, where he was an instructor and, in 1970, a student at the USAF Test Pilot School at Edwards AFB, California. After graduation in 1971 he spent four years there as a test pilot.

He attended the Air Command and Staff College in 1975, then was assigned to Headquarters USAF in the Pentagon, where he took part in the development of the F-15 and A-10 aircraft. He was stationed at Nellis AFB, Nevada, when chosen by NASA.

As a pilot Bridges has logged over 3800 hours of flying time in 20 different types of aircraft.

Bridges was one of the 19 astronauts selected by NASA in May 1980. In August 1981 he completed a training and evaluation course which qualified him to be a pilot on future Shuttle missions. From June 1982 to June 1983 he was a Shuttle capcom. He was named to replace David Griggs on the Spacelab 2 crew in September 1984. He was assigned as pilot of Mission 61-F, the launch of the Galileo space probe scheduled for May 1986, but that mission was postponed in the wake of the Shuttle Challenger disaster.

In May 1986 Bridges was recalled to Air Force duty and is currently commander of the 6510th Test Wing at Edwards Air Force Base, California.

Bridges and his wife, Benita, have two children, Tanya and Brian.

Brown, Mark

Mark N. Brown was one of the 17 astronaut candidates selected by NASA in May 1984. In June 1985 he completed a one-year training and evaluation course that qualified him as a mission specialist on future Shuttle crews and in November 1985 he was assigned to a Department of Defense mission then scheduled for 1986.

Brown was born November 18, 1951, in Valparaiso, Indiana, and graduated from high school there in 1969. He attended Purdue University, receiving his BS in aeronautical and astronautical engineering in 1973. He later earned an MS in astronautical engineering from the Air Force Institute of Technology in 1980.

An Air Force ROTC student, Brown entered the USAF upon graduation from Purdue and completed pilot training the next year. He flew T-38 and F-106 aircraft at Sawyer Air Force Base, Michigan, before being assigned to the Air Force Institute of Technology. From 1980 to 1984 he was an engineer at the NASA Johnson Space Center.

Major Brown and his wife, Lynne, have a daughter, Kristin.

Buchli, James

James Buchli was a mission specialist aboard two Shuttle missions launched in 1985. Mission 51-C, a flight dedicated to a classified Department of Defense payload, was launched January 24 after a delay of more than a year. Mission 61-A, a German Spacelab mission, was launched October 30. Buchli's duties on both missions involved supervision of Space Shuttle orbiter systems as flight engineer.

He has logged approximately 243 hours in space.

James Frederick Buchli was born June 20, 1945, in New Rockford, North Dakota, though he grew up in Fargo. He graduated from Fargo Central High School in 1963, then earned an appointment to the US Naval Academy in Annapolis, graduating with a BS in aeronautical engineering in 1967. He later earned his MS in aeronautical engineering systems from the University of West Florida in 1975.

Buchli was commissioned in the US Marine Corps following his graduation from Annapolis, and served as a platoon commander and company commander with Marine units in Vietnam. Returning to the US in 1969, he underwent naval flight officer training and from 1970 to 1974 served with Marine fighter/attack squadrons in Hawaii, Japan and Thailand. He was at the USN Test Pilot School at Patuxent River, Maryland, when selected by NASA. He has logged over 3000 hours of flying time, 2800 hours in jets.

A member of the January 1978 astronaut selection, Buchli completed a one-year training and evaluation period in August 1979. He was a member of the support crew for STS-1 and STS-2 and capcom for STS-2. He was assigned to STS-10, the scheduled Department of Defense mission, in November 1982, and was also assigned to the STS-19 crew (commanded by Joe Engle and flown as Mission 51-I in August 1985), but had to be replaced on the latter crew when his first mission was delayed.

Colonel Buchli and his wife, Jean, have two children, James and Jennifer.

Bull, John

Lieutenant Commander John Bull, US Navy, was a NASA astronaut until discovery of a rare pulmonary illness forced him to leave the space program and the Navy in July 1968.

John Sumter Bull was born September 25, 1934, in Memphis, Tennessee. He received a BS in mechanical engineering from Rice in 1957, an MS in 1971 and a PhD in 1973 in aeronautics and astronautics from Stanford.

From 1959 to 1963 Bull was a naval aviator flying F-3 Demons and F-4 Phantom IIs in Texas and California, and on three tours aboard the carriers Ranger, Hancock and Kitty Hawk in the Pacific. In February 1964 he graduated from the USN Test Pilot School at Patuxent River, Maryland (where he was named "outstanding student") and when selected as an astronaut in April 1966 was a project test pilot in the Carrier Suitability Branch there.

As an astronaut Bull trained as an Apollo lunar module pilot and was assigned to the support crew for what was then the third manned Apollo flight (later flown as Apollo-8 by astronauts Borman, Lovell and Anders) when he was stricken.

Since leaving the astronaut corps Bull has been employed by the NASA Ames Research Center at Moffet Field, California, where he is chief of the aircraft systems branch.

He and his wife, Nancy, have two children, Scott and Whitney, and live in Los Altos, California.

Cabana, Robert

Robert D. Cabana was one of the 13 astronaut candidates selected by NASA in June 1985. In August of that year he began a one-year training and evaluation course intended to qualify him as a pilot on Shuttle missions.

Cabana was born January 23, 1949, in Minneapolis, Minnesota, and graduated from Washburn High School there in 1967. He attended the US Naval Academy at Annapolis, receiving a BS in mathematics in 1971.

After graduation Cabana became a Marine bombardier and navigator for A-6 aircraft and was based in North Carolina and Japan. Returning to the US in 1975, he became a pilot. He attended the US Naval Test Pilot School at Patuxent River, Maryland, in 1981, and served as a test pilot there on a number of aircraft, including the X-29.

When selected by NASA Cabana was serving with Marine Aircraft Group 12 in Iwakuni, Japan.

He has logged over 2600 hours of flying time. Major Cabana and his wife, Nancy, have three children, Jeffrey, Christopher, and Sarah.

Cameron, Kenneth

Kenneth D. Cameron was one of the 17 astronauts selected by NASA in May 1984. In June 1985 he completed the year-long training and evaluation course qualifying him as a pilot on future Shuttle missions.

Cameron was born November 29, 1949, in Cleveland, Ohio, and graduated from Rocky River High School in Rocky River, Ohio, in 1967. He earned a BS and MS in aeronautics and astronautics from the Massachusetts Institute of Technology in 1978 and 1979.

Cameron joined the US Marine Corps at the age of 20 and served as an infantry platoon commander in Vietnam in 1970 and 1971. After returning to the US he attended flight school, winning his wings in 1973. As a pilot his duties took him to bases in Yuma, Arizona, and Iwakuni, Japan, and to the Pacific Missile Test Center in Hawaii. In 1982 he attended the US Naval Test Pilot School at Patuxent River, Maryland, and was a test pilot there when selected by NASA.

He has logged 2000 hours of flying time.

Major Cameron and his wife, Michele, have a son, Robert.

Carpenter, Scott

One of the original Mercury astronauts, Scott Carpenter made the second American orbital flight and also pioneered the exploration of the oceans, becoming the world's first astronaut/aquanaut.

Carpenter's only space flight, Mercury-Atlas 7 on May 24, 1962, lasted four hours and fifty-six minutes, during which the astronaut made three orbits of the Earth. John Glenn's flight three months earlier had proved that an astronaut could survive in space, so Carpenter's task was to see whether an astronaut could work in space. His flight plan was crowded with scientific experiments that included observations of flares fired on earth and the deployment of a tethered balloon.

Carpenter found John Glenn's mysterious "fireflies" when he rapped on the side of the spacecraft, raising a cloud of luminous particles. He tried to reproduce the disorientation reportedly suffered by Soviet cosmonaut Gherman Titov (later revealed to be the first case of space adaptation syndrome) and failed. And he radioed greetings—in Spanish—to ground controllers at Guaymas, Mexico.

Seemingly distracted and behind schedule throughout the flight, Carpenter used too much attitude control fuel and was forced to fire his retrorockets manually. He was successful, but late, and Aurora 7 splashed down over 200 miles off-course, far from the waiting recovery carrier. Carpenter climbed out of the floating spacecraft and into a life raft to wait for rescue swimmers and ships, which began arriving forty minutes later. The minutes of uncertainty about Carpenter's survival created a tense moment for the American space program. CBS newscaster Walter Cronkite stated on the air that he was afraid America "had lost an astronaut."

Carpenter's performance precluded future space missions. (It was rumored that flight director Christopher Kraft informed him that he would never fly again.) He was assigned to the development of the lunar module and also worked as executive assistant to the director of the Manned Spacecraft Center.

In the spring of 1965 the astronaut took a leave of absence from NASA to participate in the Navy's Man-in-the-Sea program and that summer spent 30 days living and working on the ocean floor in Sealab II. Carpenter was leader of two of the three teams that spent a total of 45 days at a depth of over 200 feet.

Returning to the space program, Carpenter was responsible for liaison with the Navy for underwater zero-G training when he suffered an elbow injury in a motorcyle accident in Bermuda. With his flight status even more questionable, Carpenter left the astronaut team for good on August 10, 1967.

Malcolm Scott Carpenter was born May 1, 1925, in Boulder, Colorado, and graduated from high school there. His parents separated when he was three years old and when his mother was institutionalized for treatment for tuberculosis, Carpenter was raised by a family friend. He would later describe himself as a "hell-raising" teenager.

After graduating from high school in 1943 Carpenter entered the Navy's V-5 flight training program, which was intended to give potential pilots advanced academic training at the same time they were given basic experience in aircraft. World War II ended before Carpenter could complete the program and after stays in Iowa and California he wound up as a student at the University of Colorado, majoring in aerospace engineering. He received a bachelor of science degree in 1962.

He returned to the Navy in 1949 and finally earned his wings, following training in Florida and Texas. Assigned to Patrol Squadron 6, he flew anti-submarine, ship surveillance and aerial mining missions in the Yellow Sea, the South China Sea and the Formosa Straits during the Korean War. Returning to the US in 1954, he attended the US Naval Test Pilot School at Patuxent River, Maryland, and remained at the Naval Test Center there until 1957. He attended the Navy General Line School and the Navy Air Intelligence School in 1957 and 1958 and was assigned as an intelligence officer aboard the carrier USS Hornet when chosen by NASA in April 1959.

As an astronaut Carpenter served as John Glenn's backup for Mercury-Atlas 6, and was named to MA-7, America's second manned orbital flight when Donald Slayton, the original pilot, was grounded.

As a pilot Carpenter logged over 3500 hours of flying time, including 700 hours in jets.

After leaving NASA he served as assistant for Aquanaut Operations for Sealab III until retiring from the US Navy with the rank of commander on July 1, 1969. Since then he has been an engineering consultant in addition to being involved in wasp-breeding.

Carpenter is married to the former Maria Roach (daughter of pioneering movie maker Hal Roach) and lives in New York. They have two sons, Matthew and Nicholas. Carpenter has four children from his first marriage, Marc, Robyn, Kristen and Candace.

Carr, Gerald

Gerald Carr commanded America's longest manned space flight, Skylab 4, from November 1973 to February 1974.

Carr, science pilot Edward Gibson, and pilot William Pogue spent 84 days in space aboard the Skylab orbiting workshop, the third crew to occupy the station. They carried out experiments in studies of the Earth, in the effects of weightlessness on human beings, and made extensive observations of the Sun while operating the Apollo Telescope

Mount attached to Skylab for 338 hours. Carr also logged almost 16 hours in spacewalks outside Skylab.

The mission also became notorious when the astronauts staged the first "strike" in space history, complaining of overwork and poor planning by ground controllers.

Skylab 4 was Carr's only space flight.

Gerald Paul Carr was born August 22, 1932, in Denver, Colorado, but grew up in Santa Ana, California, graduating from high school there. He attended the University of Southern California, receiving a BS in mechanical engineering in 1954, and later earned a second BS in aeronautical engineering from the US Naval Postgraduate School in 1961. He also earned an MS in aeronautical engineering from Princeton University in 1962.

Carr joined the US Navy immediately after high school and attended USC as a Naval ROTC student. Upon graduation in 1954 he was commissioned in the US Marine Corps and became a pilot. He was assigned to Marine All-Weather Fighter Squadron 114 flying F-9 and F-6A aircraft until entering graduate school, then flew with All-Weather Squadron 122 in the US and the Far East until 1965. His last assignment prior to becoming an astronaut was as a test director with Marine Air Control Squadron 3.

As a pilot Carr logged over 6100 hours of flying time, 5400 in jets.

He was one of 19 astronauts selected by NASA in April 1966. After basic astronaut training he specialized in Apollo lunar module systems and, later, the lunar roving vehicle. He served as capcom and support crew member for Apollo 8 and Apollo 12. In early 1970 he was tentatively assigned to be lunar module pilot for the planned Apollo 19 flight when NASA budget cuts forced its cancellation. He transferred to the Skylab program and was named commander of the third mission in January 1972.

After his Skylab flight Carr was named head of the astronaut office Shuttle design support group. He retired from the Marine Corps as a colonel in September 1975, and from NASA in June 1977 to become vice president of Bovay Engineers, Inc., Houston, Texas.

Since 1983 Carr has been a senior consultant to the president of Applied Research, Inc., a company based in Los Angeles and Houston. He has also served on the Citizen's Advisory Council on National Space Policy.

Carr has six children, including two sets of twins: Jennifer, Jamee and Jeffrey (an artist employed by NASA), John, Jessica and Joshua. He and his second wife, Dr. Patricia L. Musick, live in Houston.

Carter, Manley

Manley Lanier "Sonny" Carter, Jr., is the first ex-professional athlete to be selected for astronaut training. Carter played soccer for the Atlanta Chiefs of the North American Soccer League from 1970 to 1973 while he was a student in medical school. He was one of the 17 astronauts selected by NASA in May 1984.

Carter completed the one-year training and evaluation course in June 1985 and was assigned as a mission specialist for a Shuttle flight originally planned for the fall of 1986.

Sonny Carter was born August 15, 1947, in Macon, Georgia, but considers Warner Robins, Georgia, to be his hometown. He graduated from Lanier High School in Macon in 1965. He received a BA in chemistry from Emory University in Atlanta in 1969 and an MD from Emory in 1973.

After completing an internship in internal medicine at Grady Memorial Hospital in Atlanta in 1974, Carter entered the US Navy's flight surgeon school in Pensacola, Florida. He served in that capacity with the Marine Corps, then attended flight school, winning his wings in 1978. He has served as a Marine F4 fighter pilot and a Naval carrier pilot and graduated from the Navy's "Top Gun" school. He was a student at the US Naval Test Pilot school in Patuxent River, Maryland, when selected by NASA.

Carter has logged 1700 hours of flying time, including 160 carrier landings.

He and his wife, Dana, have two daughters.

Casper, John

Colonel John H. Casper, USAF, was one of the 17 astronauts selected by NASA in May 1984. In June 1985 he completed a one-year training and evaluation course which qualified him as pilot on future Shuttle missions.

Casper was born July 9, 1943, in Greenville, South Carolina, and graduated from Chamblee High School in Chamblee, Georgia, in 1961. He attended the US Air Force Academy in Colorado Springs, earning a BS in engineering science in 1966. In 1967 he earned an MS in astronautics from Purdue.

After completing pilot training, Casper served in Vietnam flying F-100s on 229 combat missions. From 1970 to 1974 he was based in Lakenheath, England, with the 48th Tactical Fighter Wing, then attended the US Air Force Test Pilot School at Edwards Air Force Base, California, where he remained as a test pilot and, later, commander of the test squadron, until 1980. At the time of his selection by NASA he was at USAF Headquarters in the Pentagon.

Casper has logged over 4200 hours of flying time. He and his wife, Christine, have two children, Robert and Stephanie.

Cernan, Eugene

Gene Cernan made three space flights, including Apollo 17 in December 1972, during which he became the last person to walk on the Moon in the first 25 years of manned space flight.

Cernan's crewmates on Apollo 17 were command module pilot Ronald Evans and lunar module pilot Dr. Harrison Schmitt, the only scientist to have visited the Moon during that period. Following a spectacular night-time launch from the Kennedy Space Center, the astronauts arrived in lunar orbit on December 10, 1972. While Evans remained in the command module America, Cernan and Schmitt landed the lunar module Challenger at Taurus-Littrow, on the edge of the Sea of Serenity. For the next three days they explored the rugged terrain there, collecting soil and rock samples and ranging far from their landing site in a lunar rover. Cernan and Schmitt spent more than 22 hours walking on the Moon. After Schmitt preceeded him into Challenger at the end of their last excursion, Cernan said, "As we leave the Moon at Taurus-Littrow, we leave as we came and, God willing, as we shall return, with peace and hope for all mankind. God speed the crew of Apollo 17."

Cernan had previously served as pilot of Gemini 9 in June 1966. He and commander Thomas Stafford had intended to dock their Gemini with an orbiting Augmented Target Docking Adaptor (ATDA), a replacement for a target Agena upper stage which had failed. When they made rendezvous with the ATDA, however, they noticed that the shroud covering the adaptor had failed to separate, leaving the vehicle looking,

Cernan said, "like an angry alligator." The docking was called off, but later in the mission Cernan made a record two-hour-and-ten-minute spacewalk. The spacewalk, unfortunately, only showed how little space officials knew about the rigors of extra-vehicular activity. Cernan was supposed to test an astronaut maneuvering unit (AMU) backpack, but found that because Gemini was not equipped with the proper restraints he could not even don the AMU. His suit also overheated, preventing him from completing most of his tasks.

His second flight came in May 1969, when he was lunar module pilot of Apollo 10. Cernan and commander Stafford flew the lunar module Snoopy to within ten miles of the surface of the Moon in a full-scale dress rehearsal for Apollo 11. (Snoopy could not land on the Moon because it was too heavy to take off again. This particular lunar module had been designed only for orbital tests.)

Cernan has logged over 566 hours in space, including almost 25 hours of EVA, and is one of three astronauts (the others are John Young and James Lovell) to have visited the Moon twice.

Eugene Andrew Cernan was born March 14, 1934, in Chicago, Illinois, and graduated from Proviso Township High School in suburban Maywood in 1952. He attended Purdue University, receiving a BS in electrical engineering in 1956. In 1964 he received an MS in aeronautical engineering from the US Naval Postgraduate School. He later attended a petroleum economics and managment seminar at Northwestern University (1978).

A Navy ROTC student at Purdue, Cernan went on active duty in 1956 and served aboard the USS Saipan prior to entering flight school in October of that year. Following training in Florida and Tennessee, he was designated a naval aviator in December 1957, then served as a fighter pilot with Attack Squadrons 26 and 113 at the Naval Air Station at Miramar, California. He entered the Postgraduate School in 1961 and was a student there when chosen by NASA.

As a pilot Cernan eventually logged over 5000 hours of flying time, 4800 hours in jets, including over 200 carrier landings.

Cernan was one of 14 astronauts selected by NASA in October 1963. He underwent basic academic and survival training, then worked on spacecraft propulsion systems, including booster rockets such as the Titan and Saturn. He served as a capcom for Gemini 7/6 and was training as backup pilot for Gemini 9 with Stafford when the prime crew, Elliott See and Charles Bassett, were killed in a plane crash on February 28, 1966. Stafford and Cernan took their places. Cernan later served as backup pilot for Gemini 12, backup lunar module pilot for Apollo 7, and backup commander for Apollo 14.

In January 1971 Cernan crashed a helicopter into the Banana River near the Kennedy Space Center. Fellow astronauts assumed that the accident had eliminated Cernan and his crew of Ronald Evans and Joe Engle from the Apollo 17 assignment, which was pending. Fueling this speculation was the knowledge that Apollo 17 was to be the last lunar landing, and that NASA was under pressure to fly astronaut-geologist Harrison Schmitt, a member of another crew, to the Moon. When the Apollo 17 crew was finally announced months later, however, it consisted of Cernan, Evans, and Schmitt. It was Joe Engle who lost out.

Following Apollo 17 Cernan became involved with the Apollo-Soyuz Test Project. He met Soviet cosmonauts Leonov, Kubasov, Filipchenko and Yeliseyev at the Paris Air Show in June 1973, and was soon appointed special assistant to the ASTP manager at the Johnson Space Center. During the next two years Cernan accompanied the astronaut crews on training visits to the Soviet Union.

He resigned from NASA and retired from the Navy (with the rank of captain) on July 1, 1976, to join Coral Petroleum, Inc., of Houston, as vice president. He left Coral in September 1981 to start his own company, The Cernan Corporation, an aerospace and energy management and consulting firm. He has also served as commentator and co-anchor on ABC-Television broadcasts of Shuttle missions.

Cernan is the divorced father of a daughter, Teresa. He lives in Houston.

Chaffee, Roger

Lieutenant Commander Roger Chaffee, USN, was one of three astronauts killed in a flash fire aboard the Apollo 1 spacecraft on January 27, 1967.

Chaffee, Virgil "Gus" Grissom and Edward White were training for a planned 16-day Apollo mission scheduled for launch on February 14, 1967. It would have been the first manned Apollo flight.

Roger Bruce Chaffee was born February 15, 1935, in Grand Rapids, Michigan, where he grew up, graduating from Central High there in 1953. He attended Purdue University and received a BS in aeronautical engineering in 1957. He later studied at the Air Force Institute of Technology.

A Navy ROTC student, Chaffee went on active duty in 1957 and after training in Florida and Texas became a pilot. In March 1960 he was assigned to Heavy Photographic Squadron 62 at the Naval Air Station in Jacksonville, Florida, and flew many photo-reconaissance missions over Cuba during the October 1962 missile crisis. In January 1963 he entered the Air Force Institute of Technology to work on a MS in engineering.

Chaffee was one of the 14 astronauts selected by NASA in October 1963. After completing basic astronaut training, he worked on deep space communications and Apollo spacecraft development. He was named to the Apollo 1 crew in March 1966.

At the time of his death Chaffee had logged approximately 2300 hours of flying time, including 2000 hours in jets.

. . .*On Course to the Stars*, a biography of Chaffee coauthored by his father, was published in 1968.

He was survived by his wife, Martha, and two children, Sheryl and Stephen.

Chang-Diaz, Franklin

Dr. Franklin Chang-Diaz was aboard Shuttle Mission 61-C, which set an unwanted record when its launch was delayed seven different times. Mission 61-C marked the return to service of the Shuttle Columbia, which had been undergoing an overhaul since its last flight in December 1983. When Columbia finally lifted off on January 12, 1986, its crew of seven, including Florida Congressman Bill Nelson, successfully deployed an RCA communications satellite, but found that a special photographic unit designed to observe Halley's Comet failed to operate. The return to Earth of 61-C also had to be delayed because of weather problems at Cape Canaveral, and was ultimately switched to Edwards Air Force Base in California.

It was the last Shuttle flight prior to the fatal Mission 51-L Challenger launch on January 28, 1986.

Chang-Diaz was the first Hispanic American astronaut, though Cuba's Arnaldo Tamayo Mendez was the first Hispanic in space and Mexico's Rudolfo Neri Vela made a Shuttle flight a month before Chang-Diaz did.

Franklin Ramon Chang-Diaz was born April 5, 1950, in San Jose, Costa Rica, and graduated from Colegio De La Salle there in November 1967. As a grade schooler inspired by the launch of Sputnik, he wrote to Dr. Werner von Braun asking how to become an astronaut. To Franklin's surprise, von Braun wrote back, advising him to come to the United States to study science. In 1967, then, Chang-Diaz, who spoke very little English, arrived in the US, staying with relatives in Hartford, Connecticut. He graduated from high school there in 1969, then attended the University of Connecticut, receiving a BS in mechanical engineering in 1973. He entered the Massachusetts Institute of Technology, earning a PhD in applied plasma physics in 1977.

As an undergraduate at Connecticut Chang-Diaz did research in high energy atomic physics, and at MIT became heavily involved in the development of fusion reactors. After earning his doctorate he continued to work on fusion projects at the Charles Stark Draper Laboratory in Cambridge, Massachusetts. Since joining NASA he has studied new concepts in rocket propulsion.

In addition to his research, Chang-Diaz worked as manager of a rehabilitation center for chronic mental patients and drug abusers.

Chang-Diaz was one of the 19 astronauts selected by NASA in May 1980. In August 1981 he completed a training and evaluation course which qualified him as a mission specialist on future Shuttle crews. He has worked at the Shuttle Avionics Integration Laboratory (SAIL) and as capcom and support crewman for STS-9/Spacelab 1.

He is the divorced father of two daughters, Jean and Sonia.

Chapman, Phillip

Phillip Chapman was one of the 11 scientist-astronauts selected by NASA in August 1967. He resigned from the space program in July 1972 without making a flight.

Chapman was one of the first two naturalized US citizens chosen for the space program. He was born March 5, 1935, in Melbourne, Australia, and became a US citizen in May 1967. He received a BS in physics from Sydney University in Australia in 1956 and an MS in aeronautics and astronautics from the Massachusetts Institute of Technology in 1964. He earned his PhD in physics from MIT in 1967.

From 1957 through 1959 Chapman was a physicist studying the Earth's aurora with the Antarctic Division of the External Affairs Department, Commonwealth of Australia. In 1958 he participated in the International Geophysical Year as a member of the Australia National Antarctic Research Expedition. In 1960 and 1961 he was a staff engineer with Canadian Aviation Electronics in Dorval, Quebec, and prior to joining NASA was a physicist at MIT's Experimental Astronomy Laboratory.

Chapman also served in the Royal Australian Air Force Reserve.

As an astronaut Chapman served on the support crew for Apollo 14 in 1971. After leaving NASA Chapman joined the AVCO Everett Research Laboratories in Everett, Massachusetts, and in 1977 became a supervisory staff associate with Arthur D. Little in Cambridge, Mass.

Chapman is the divorced father of two children, Peter and Kristan.

Cleave, Mary

Dr. Mary Cleave used the Shuttle Atlantis's remote manipulator arm to test space construction techniques during Mission 61-B in November and December 1985. Cleave, the mission specialist and flight engineer, worked with space walkers Jerry Ross and Woody Spring, who assembled a trusslike tower and pyramid during two EVAs, at one point moving the astronauts by remote control from one place to another.

The crew of seven aboard Mission 61-B, including Mexican engineer Rudolfo Neri Vela, also deployed three communications satellites during their seven-day flight.

Mary Louise Cleave was born February 5, 1947, in Southampton, New York, and grew up on Long Island, graduating from Great Neck North High School in 1965. She attended Colorado State University, receiving a BS in microbial ecology in 1969, and later earned an MS in that subject (1975) and a PhD in civil and environment engineering (1979) from Utah State University.

From September 1971 to June 1980 Cleave was a researcher at the Ecology Center and the Utah Water Research Laboratory at Utah State working on environmental projects. She has published several scientific papers.

Cleave was one of the 19 astronauts selected by NASA in May 1980. In August 1981 she completed a training and evaluation course which qualified her as a Shuttle mission specialist. She has worked at the Shuttle Avionics Integration Laboratory (SAIL) and served as capcom for Shuttle missions STS-5 through 41-B.

Cleave is unmarried.

Coats, Michael

Michael Coats was the pilot of the maiden voyage of the third Space Shuttle orbiter, the Discovery, on Mission 41-D in August and September 1984. During the week-long flight Coats and five other astronauts launched three satellites and conducted tests of a huge solar power wing.

Coats was also aboard the first launch pad abort in the Shuttle program, on June 26, 1984.

He has logged approximately 145 hours in space and was assigned as commander of a Shuttle mission scheduled originally for 1986.

Michael Loyd Coats was born January 16, 1946, in Sacramento, California, but grew up in Riverside, where he graduated from Ramona High School in 1964. He was appointed to the US Naval Academy at Annapolis, graduating in 1968 with a BS. He later earned an MS in the administration of science and technology from George Washington University in 1977, and an MS in aeronautical engineering from the US Naval Postgraduate School in 1979.

After pilot training Coats was assigned to the carrier Kitty Hawk and from 1970 to 1972 flew 315 combat missions over Vietnam. Returning to the US, he served as a flight instructor, then attended the US Naval Test Pilot School at Patuxent River, Maryland. He was a student, test pilot and instructor there until 1977. He was attending the USN Postgraduate School when selected by NASA.

Coats has logged over 4000 hours of flying time, including 400 carrier landings.

A member of the January 1978 astronaut group, Coats completed the training and evaluation course in August 1979. He was a support crew member for STS-4 and capcom for STS-4 and STS-5, and, following his flight on Mission 41-D, served as capcom again from May to November 1985.

He and his wife, Diane, have two children, Laura and Paul.

Collins, Michael

Michael Collins, a self-described underachiever, circled the Moon while astronauts Neil Armstrong and Edwin Aldrin made the first lunar landing. As pilot of the command module Columbia for the flight of Apollo 11, Collins spent 24 hours alone in lunar orbit while Armstrong and Aldrin landed the lunar module Eagle on the Sea of Tranquility. It was the culmination of the entire Apollo program, fulfilling a goal set by President John F. Kennedy in 1961, to "land a man on the Moon and return him safely to Earth in this decade."

Apollo 11 was Collins' second space flight. He had previously served as pilot of Gemini 10 in July 1966. During that three-day rendezvous and docking mission he made two space walks.

Collins spent just over 11 days in space, including one-and-a-half hours of EVA time.

Michael Collins was born October 31, 1930, in Rome, Italy. His was an Army family: his father James became a major general, another uncle was a brigadier general, his brother was a colonel, and his uncle, J. Lawton Collins, became Army chief of staff. It was no surprise then, that Collins, after graduating from St. Albans School in Washington, D.C., attended the US Military Academy at West Point, receiving a BS in 1952. He later attended the advanced management program at the Harvard Business School in 1974.

In spite of his Army heritage, Collins elected to serve in the new US Air Force. He underwent pilot training in Mississippi and Texas and won his wings in 1953. For the next four years he served with the 2lst Fighter Bomber Wing at Nellis Air Force Base, Nevada, and at bases in Europe. From 1957 to 1960 he was assigned to Chanute AFB, Illinois, as a maintenance officer and, later, training officer. He finally entered the USAF Test Pilot School at Edwards AFB in 1960, and remained there as a test pilot and student (he attended the Aerospace Research Pilot School in 1963) until being chosen by NASA.

As a pilot Collins eventually logged over 5000 hours of flying time.

He was one of 14 astronauts selected by NASA in October 1963. Reporting in January 1964, he underwent basic academic and survival training, then was assigned to assist in the development of spacesuits and techniques for walking in space. He became the first member of his class to join a flight crew when he was chosen as backup pilot for Gemini 7 in June 1965.

Following Gemini 10 Collins served as lunar module pilot for a crew commanded by Frank Borman with Thomas Stafford as command module pilot. In a shuffling of flights and astronaut assignments in November 1966, Collins found himself "promoted" to command module pilot for the Borman crew (Stafford was given his own crew) and, as he later said, lost his chance to land on the Moon at that point.

It still took a series of accidents to place Collins on the first lunar landing. In July 1968 he was diagnosed as having a bone spur on his neck and underwent surgery. Temporarily removed from flight status, he was replaced on Borman's crew by his backup, James Lovell. A change in the flight schedule at the same time (swapping the Apollo 8 and Apollo 9 crews) made Collins available for assignment to Apollo 11 at the same time as Armstrong and Aldrin, who were backups to Apollo 8. Collins served as capcom for Apollo 8.

Just prior to Apollo 11 astronaut boss Deke Slayton offered Collins a chance to be backup commander for Apollo 14, and almost certainly commander of Apollo 17. Collins told Slayton that if Apollo 11 went well he would prefer to spend more time with his family and planned to leave the space program.

Collins resigned from NASA in January 1970 to become Assistant Secretary of State for Public Affairs. Beginning in 1971 he worked at the Smithsonian Institution, first as director of the National Air and Space Museum and later as under secretary for the Smithsonian, remaining there until 1980. For the next four years he was vice president of the Vought Corporation in Arlington, Virginia, and is currently president of Michael Collins Associates in Washington, D.C.

He is the author of a popular and vivid memoir, *Carrying the Fire* (1973) and of a children's book, *Flying to the Moon and Other Strange Places* (1976).

Collins and his wife, Patricia, have three children, Kate (a television actress), Ann and Michael. They live near Washington, D.C.

Conrad, Charles

"Pete" Conrad had one of the most remarkable careers of any space traveler, making four space flights between 1965 and 1973, in which, among other accomplishments, he twice set endurance records, commanded the first successful space station mission, and became the third man to walk on the Moon.

His first flight was as pilot of Gemini 5 in August 1965. With commander Gordon Cooper, Conrad spent almost 191 hours in space, shattering the endurance record held by Soviet cosmonaut Valery Bykovsky. Just over a year later Conrad commanded Gemini 11, a three-day rendezvous and docking mission which also established a world altitude record of 850 miles.

In November 1969 Conrad became the third person to walk on the Moon when he commanded Apollo 12. He and Alan Bean landed the lunar module Intrepid on the Ocean of Storms while Richard Gordon orbited overhead in the command module Yankee Clipper. As he stepped onto the lunar surface, the five-foot, six-inch tall Conrad's first words were, "Whoopie! That may have been a small one for Neil, but it's a long one for me!" During two moon walks Conrad and Bean set up a package of scientific experiments and walked over to the Surveyor III unmanned probe, which had been on the lunar surface for three years. (In an amazing demonstration of Apollo guidance and navigation capabilities, Intrepid had landed within 200 yards of the Surveyor.)

Conrad's fourth flight was Skylab 2, the first manned visit to the Skylab space station, in May 1973. Skylab suffered a major malfunction during its launch on May 14, 1973, when a micrometeoroid shield tore loose, taking with it one of the station's solar power panels and damaging the other panel. Flight controllers delayed the Skylab 2 launch for ten days while repair procedures could be developed and rehearsed. In a series of space walks, Conrad, Joseph Kerwin and Paul Weitz were able to activate Skylab, eventually completing 46 of their original 55 scientific experiments and remaining in space for 28 days, as planned.

On the way to logging approximately 1180 hours in his four space flights, including over 14 hours in EVA, Conrad also survived a lightning strike (lightning hit Apollo 12 moments after its launch on November 14, 1969) and an emergency bailout from a T-38 jet in 1971.

Charles Conrad, Jr., was born June 2, 1930, in Philadelphia, Pennsylvania, and grew up in the suburb of Haverford where his father, a former World War I balloonist, was a stock broker. He graduated from the Darrow School in New Lebanon, New York, then attended Princeton University, receiving a BS in aeronautical engineering in 1953.

Entering active duty with the Navy following college, Conrad underwent pilot training at Pensacola, Florida, and then served at the Jacksonville Naval Air Station. There is a vivid description of his life there in the early chapters of Tom Wolfe's *The Right Stuff* (1979). In 1957 Conrad entered the Navy Test Pilot School at Patuxent River, Maryland, remaining there for several years as a test pilot in the armaments test division, a flight instructor, and a performance engineer. At the time he was selected by NASA he was safety officer for Fighter Squadron 96 at the Miramar, California, Naval Air Station.

As a pilot he eventually logged over 6500 hours of flying time, including more than 5000 hours in jets.

Conrad was one of the nine astronauts chosen by NASA in September 1962. He had been a candidate for the Mercury astronaut group, but rebelled at the endless medical testing, earning a rejection. It is ironic that on his first Gemini flight and on Skylab Conrad found himself at the mercy of NASA doctors.

During early astronaut training Conrad took part in the development of the Apollo lunar module (until December 1968 he was considered the astronaut most likely to be the first man on the Moon). He also served as backup commander for Gemini 8 and Apollo 9. In 1970 he was tentatively assigned to command Apollo 20, then scheduled to be the last of the lunar landing missions, but lost that flight when it was cancelled for budgetary reasons. He took over the Skylab branch of the astronaut office and was officially named commander of the first mission in January 1972.

In December 1973, Conrad resigned from NASA and retired from the Navy with the rank of captain. He accepted a position as vice president, operations, and chief operating officer of American Television and Communications Corporation, a Denver-based cable TV company. In March 1976 he left ATC to become a vice president for the McDonnell Douglas Corporation, and is currently senior vice president for marketing for its Douglas Aircraft division in Long Beach, California. He has served as a consultant for a number of space-related projects, including the Martin Marietta Hubble Space Telescope, and in September 1985 donned a space suit again to perform underwater simulations of space station assembly techniques for Space Structures International and McDonnell-Douglas.

Conrad and his wife, Jane, have four sons, Peter, Thomas, Andrew and Christopher. They live in California.

Cooper, Gordon

One of the original seven Mercury astronauts, Gordon Cooper set American endurance records on both of his two flights into space.

Cooper was pilot of Mercury-Atlas 9, the last Mercury mission, launched on May 15, 1963. For the next 34 hours and 20 minutes, he orbited the earth in the spacecraft he had named "Faith 7," logging more time in space than all five previous Mercury astronauts combined. Cooper's primary job was to manage his "consumable" supplies—oxygen, water and electricity—and to report on his physical condition. He was the first American astronaut to go to sleep in orbit, for example.

He also saw objects on the Earth's surface in such detail (he reported seeing the wake of a boat on a river in India and actual houses on the plains of Tibet) that, at first, most experts refused to believe him.

Cooper's second space flight came two years later, as command pilot of Gemini 5. Charles Conrad accompanied him on a mission designed specifically to prove that astronauts could survive in space for eight days—the time it took for a spacecraft to go from the Earth to the Moon and back again.

To honor Gemini 5's major goal, Cooper designed the first mission patch in what has since become a NASA tradition. The Gemini 5 patch depicted a Conestoga wagon with the slogan, "Eight Days or Bust." In what has also become a NASA tradition, NASA officials deleted the slogan, just in case Gemini 5 failed to reach its planned duration.

But Cooper and Conrad did spend eight days in space, though not without some anxious moments. Gemini 5 was the first manned spacecraft equipped with fuel cells, portable generators of electrical power that made it possible for flights to last longer than a few days (the lifetime of most battery systems.) The fuel cells behaved erratically, requiring flight controllers and the astronauts to nurse them through the whole mission. In fact, Cooper and Conrad spent the last days of their flight in a "powered-down" drift, to conserve electricity.

On August 29, 1965, their final day in space, the astronauts talked by radio with Scott Carpenter, who was in Sealab II at the time, 200 feet underwater off the coast of California. Gemini 5 set a world space record that lasted for less than four months.

The youngest of the original astronauts, Cooper once said, "I'm *planning* on getting to the Moon. I *think* I'll get to Mars." In July 1969 he was in line to be named commander of Apollo 13, a lunar landing mission scheduled for April 1970. But in a shuffle of assignments Cooper was replaced by fellow Mercury astronaut Alan Shepard, who had recently returned to flight status after a four-year hiatus. By then Cooper's involvement with auto and speedboat racing had caused him problems with NASA officials, who saw him as a maverick and a daredevil. Cooper found himself assigned as assistant to flight crew operations boss Deke Slayton for the Apollo Applications Program (later known as Skylab). He left NASA and the US Air Force on July 1, 1970, without getting to the Moon or Mars.

Leroy Gordon Cooper was born March 6, 1927, in Shawnee, Oklahoma. His father, a World War I pilot, was a district judge, and young Gordo learned to fly before he was 16 years old.

After graduating from high school in Murray, Kentucky, in 1945, Cooper joined the Marines, and wound up a member of the Presidential Honor Guard in Washington, D.C. He also managed to attend the US Naval Academy Prep School.

Discharged in August 1946, he entered the University of Hawaii in Honolulu, but left after three years to become an officer in the US Army. He quickly transferred that commission to the US Air Force and completed flight training in 1949. For the next four years Cooper flew with the 86th Fighter Bomber Group in Munich, Germany. Returning to the US in 1954, he attended the Air Force Institute of Technology, earning a BS in aeronautical engineering in 1956. He was then assigned to the USAF Experimental Flight Test School at Edwards AFB, California, and was an engineering test pilot there when selected by NASA in April 1959.

Cooper was a capcom for the orbital flights of John Glenn and Scott Carpenter, and was backup for Walter Schirra. In addition to his two flight assignments, he also served as backup commander for Gemini 12 in 1966 and Apollo 10 in 1969.

Upon leaving NASA Cooper formed Gordon Cooper & Associates, Inc., a consulting firm specializing in aviation and aerospace projects, and in hotel and land developments. He has been a member of the board for and a consultant to a number of companies in the aerospace, electronics and energy fields. In 1975 he was vice president for research and development for Walt Disney Enterprises. He currently heads X=L, Inc., a firm developing an alcohol-based aviation fuel.

Cooper and his wife, Susan, live in Los Angeles. He has two daughters, Camala and Janita, from a previous marriage.

Covey, Richard

Colonel Richard Covey, USAF, was pilot of Space Shuttle Mission 51-I in August and September 1985, during which the ailing Leasat 3 satellite was retrieved, repaired, and redeployed. The astronauts of Mission 51-I also launched three new communications satellites during its week-long flight.

Richard Oswalt Covey was born August 1, 1946, in Fayetteville, Arkansas, but grew up in Fort Walton Beach, Florida. He graduated from Choctawhatchee High School in nearby Shalimar in 1964. He attended the US Air Force Academy, receiving a BS in engineering sciences in 1968, and earned an MS in aeronautics and astronautics from Purdue University in 1969.

Covey became an Air Force pilot in 1970 and in the next four years flew 339 combat missions in Southeast Asia. He then attended the USAF Test Pilot School at Edwards AFB, California, where he was named outstanding graduate of his class, and spent the next three years at Edwards testing the F-15 Eagle.

He has logged over 3500 hours of flying time in 20 different types of aircraft.

Covey was one of the 35 astronauts selected by NASA in January 1978. In August 1979 he completed a training and evaluation course which qualified him as a pilot on Shuttle crews. He served as a T-38 chase pilot for STS-2 and STS-3 and as support crewman for STS-5. He was also a capcom for STS-5 and STS-6, and in December 1985 began another tour as Shuttle launch capcom.

Covey and his wife, Kathleen, have two daughters, Sarah and Amy.

Creighton, John

Captain John Creighton, USN, was pilot of Space Shuttle Mission 51-G in June 1985. The seven astronauts of the 51-G crew, including a Saudi prince and a French test pilot, deployed three communications satellites and a scientific satellite, and conducted a laser-tracking experiment for the Strategic Defense Initiative during their seven days in space.

John Oliver Creighton was born April 28, 1943, in Orange, Texas, but grew up in Seattle, Washington, where he graduated from high school in 1961. He attended the US Naval Academy at Annapolis, receiving a bachelor of science degree in 1965. He later earned an MS in administration of science and technology from George Washington University (1978).

Creighton completed pilot training in October 1967 and subsequently spent two years aboard the carrier USS Ranger flying 175 combat missions in Vietnam. Returning to the US in June 1970, he attended the US Naval Test Pilot School at Patuxent River, Maryland, and remained there as an F-14 test pilot until July 1973. From 1973 to 1977 he was a member of the first operational F-14 squadron. When chosen by NASA he was again stationed at the Naval Air Test Center.

As a pilot Creighton has logged over 4500 hours of flying time, including 500 carrier landings.

Creighton was one of the 35 astronauts selected by NASA in January 1978. In August 1979 he completed a training and evaluation course which qualified him as a pilot on future Shuttle crews. For the next four years he had a variety of technical assignments, including duty in the Shuttle Avionics Integration Laboratory (SAIL) until assigned to his first flight crew. He is currently deputy manager for operations integration for the Shuttle Program Office.

Creighton is married to the former Terry Stanford.

Crippen, Robert

Robert Crippen is the most experienced astronaut of the Space Shuttle era, having made four flights between April 1981 and October 1984, including the first Shuttle ever launched. He was chosen to command the first Shuttle launched from Vandenberg Air Force Base, California, but that flight, Mission 62-A, had to be postponed indefinitely in the aftermath of the Shuttle Challenger disaster.

On April 12, 1981, the twentieth anniversary of the flight of Yuri Gagarin, and after years of frustrating delay, Crippen and commander John Young rocketed into space aboard the Shuttle Columbia, landing two days later at Edwards Air Force Base in California, the first astronauts to pilot their spacecraft to a runway landing.

Crippen's second mission, STS-7 in June 1983, saw the flight of America's first woman in space, Sally Ride. (As commander Crippen had a voice in selecting his crew and asked for Ride.) Crippen's third flight, Mission 41-C in April 1984, was marked by the rescue of the troubled Solar Max satellite by astronauts George Nelson and James Van Hoften. Crippen's fourth mission, 41-G in October 1984, was notable for being the first manned space flight to carry seven astronauts, and for the first spacewalk by an American woman astronaut, Kathryn Sullivan.

In his four flights he has spent a total of 23 days and 14 hours in space.

Robert Laurel Crippen was born September 11, 1937, in Beaumont, Texas, and grew up there. He got interested in airplanes as a teenager and attended the University of Texas at Austin with the idea of becoming a pilot. He received a BS in aeronautical engineering in 1960 and entered the US Navy via ROTC.

After completing basic flight training in 1962, Crippen served as a carrier pilot in the Pacific aboard the USS Independence until being selected for the Aerospace Research Pilot School (commanded by Colonel Chuck Yeager) in 1964. Crippen was talented enough to remain at the school as an instructor following graduation. In 1966 he was selected for the USAF Manned Orbiting Laboratory Program and trained for military space flights in that program until its cancellation in June 1969.

As a pilot Crippen has logged over 6000 hours of flying time, including 5500 hours in jets.

Crippen was one of seven ex-MOL pilots who transferred to NASA in August 1969, knowing that any possibility of a flight into space was at least eight or more years away. Nevertheless, Crippen got involved in the Skylab program, serving as team leader for the Skylab Medical Evaluation Altitude Test, a 56-day simulation of a Skylab mission, with astronauts Karol Bobko and William Thornton. He was a member of the astronaut support crew for all three Skylab missions and for the Apollo-Soyuz Test Project, after which he transferred to Space Shuttle development. In March 1978 he was named pilot of the first manned STS flight. His commander, John Young, said of Crippen, "He knows more about the computers that make this thing (the Shuttle) fly than anyone has a right to."

In October 1984 Crippen was named associate director of flight crew operations for the NASA astronaut group, an administrative job parallel to that of chief astronaut John Young. He gave up that position a year later to concentrate on training for Mission 62-A. He also served as an adviser to the presidential commission investigating the Shuttle disaster.

In October 1986 he was named a deputy to new Shuttle program director Arnold Aldrich and moved to NASA Headquarters in Washington, D.C. He remains an active astronaut, however.

Crippen is the divorced father of three daughters.

Culbertson, Frank

Commander Frank L. Culbertson, Jr., USN, was one of the 17 astronauts selected by NASA in May 1984. In June 1985 he completed a training and evaluation course which qualified him as a pilot on future Shuttle missions.

Culbertson was born May 15, 1949, in Charleston, South Carolina. He graduated from high school in Holly Hill, South Carolina, in 1967, then attended the US Naval Academy at Annapolis, receiving a BS in aerospace engineering in 1971.

After graduation Culbertson served as an ensign aboard the USS Fox in the Gulf of Tonkin before reporting for pilot training. From 1974 to 1981 he served in a variety of posts as a Naval aviator, including two tours aboard aircraft carriers. In 1981 and 1982 he attended the US Naval Test Pilot School at Patuxent River, Maryland, and remained there until 1984. At the time of his selection by NASA, Culbertson was based at the Naval Air Station in Oceana, Virginia. He has logged over 2500 hours of flying time in 30 different types of aircraft, including 350 carrier landings.

Culbertson is the divorced father of three daughters, Wendy, Amanda, and Ashley.

Cunningham, Walter

Walter Cunningham was a member of the crew of Apollo 7, the first manned Apollo flight. In eleven days following launch on October 11, 1968, Cunningham and fellow astronauts Walter Schirra and Donn Eisele performed rendezvous exercises, propulsion tests and general spacecraft systems tests in qualifying the Apollo for later flights to the Moon.

The Apollo 7 astronauts also had the unfortunate distinction of being the first space travelers to catch colds, and were generally physically miserable for much of the flight. They were able to make the first effective TV transmissions from an American spacecraft, the "Wally, Walt and Donn Show," which won a special Emmy award from the Academy of Television Arts and Sciences.

Cunningham logged 260 hours in space during his only flight.

Ronnie Walter Cunningham was born March 16, 1932, in Creston, Iowa, but grew up in Venice, California. He decided at the age of ten that he wanted to be a Navy pilot. At the age of 19 he dropped out of Santa Monica Community College and joined the Navy. He didn't have the required two years of college necessary for flight school, but was able to pass an equivalency test, and earned his wings in 1953. For the next three years he served as Marine aviator at bases in the US and in Japan. In August 1956 he was detached from active duty. He would remain a Marine reservist until retiring with the rank of colonel in 1975.

As a pilot Cunningham logged over 4500 hours of flying time, including 3400 hours in jets.

On the G.I. Bill, Cunningham studied at the University of California at Los Angeles, earning a BA in physics in 1960 and an MA in physics in 1961. He worked on a PhD in physics while employed by the RAND Corporation as a scientist. His projects at RAND included studies of defense against submarine-launched ballistic missiles and the problems of the Earth's magnetosphere. His research in the latter led to an experiment which went into space aboard the first Orbiting Geophysical Satellite.

Cunningham was one of the 14 astronauts selected by NASA in October 1964. After a year-long general training course Cunningham was assigned to Apollo program development. He also served as a capcom for Gemini 4 and Gemini 8.

In September 1966 Cunningham was officially named to the crew for Apollo 2, then planned for the summer of 1967. (Cunningham, Schirra and Eisele had been training as a team since early 1966.) When that flight was canceled two months after the announcement, the Schirra crew became backups to the Apollo 1 astronauts, Grissom, White and Chaffee.

The deaths of Grissom, White and Chaffee in a fire on January 27, 1967, forced a re-evaluation of the entire Apollo program. It was five months before NASA was ready to proceed, and the Schirra crew was assigned to make the first flight.

After Apollo 7 Cunningham was assigned to the Apollo Applications Program (later Skylab) branch of the astronaut office, a job he held until succeeded by Charles Conrad in August 1970. Cunningham had been chosen to be backup commander for the first Skylab mission and might have commanded the third and last, but he resigned from NASA on August 1, 1971.

From 1971 to 1976 he was president of the Hydro-Tech Development Company in Houston, and vice president for operations of Century Development. From December 1976 to October 1979 he was vice president and director of engineering for the 3D International Corporation in Houston. He is currently the sole principal in The Capital Group, a private banking investment firm based in Houston.

Cunningham is the author of the most candid book written by an astronaut, *The All-American Boys*, published in 1977.

He and his wife, Lo, have two children, Brian and Kimberly.

Duffy, Brian

Major Brian Duffy, USAF, was one of the 13 astronauts selected by NASA in June 1985. In August of that year he commenced a training and evaluation course which would qualify him as a pilot on future Shuttle missions.

Duffy was born June 20, 1953, in Boston, Massachusetts, and graduated from high school in nearby Rockland in 1971. He attended the US Air Force Academy in Colorado Springs, graduating with a BS in mathematics in 1975, and later earned an MS in systems management from the University of Southern California in 1981.

Duffy completed pilot training in 1976 and flew F-15s at bases in Virginia and Okinawa until 1982, when he attended the US Air Force Test Pilot School at Edwards Air Force Base in California. When selected by NASA he was directing F-15 tests at Eglin Air Force Base,

Florida. He has logged over 1800 hours of flying time in 25 different types of aircraft.

Duffy and his wife, Janet, have two children, Shaun and Shannon.

Duke, Charles

Charles Duke became the tenth person to walk on the Moon when he was lunar module pilot of the Apollo 16 mission in April 1972. Duke and commander John Young landed the lunar module Orion on the Cayley Plains near the crater Descartes six hours later than scheduled because of problems with the main rocket engine of their command module, Casper. Concern over the engine would force them to shorten their flight by a day, but Duke and Young nevertheless spent almost three days on the Moon, including almost 21 hours outside "Orion." They used a lunar roving vehicle to reach distant geological sites and to drive up nearby Stone Mountain.

Duke logged over 11 days in space on this, his only flight.

Charles Moss Duke, Jr., was born October 3, 1935, in Charlotte, North Carolina. He attended the US Naval Academy, graduating in 1957 with a BS degree. In 1964 he earned an MS in aeronautics and astronautics from the Massachusetts Institute of Technology.

After pilot training Duke spent three years with the 526th Interceptor Squadron at Ramstein, Germany. He attended the USAF Aerospace Research Pilot School at Edwards AFB, California, in 1965, and was an instructor there when selected by NASA.

As a pilot Duke logged 4200 hours of flying time, including 3600 hours in jets.

Duke was one of the 19 astronauts selected by NASA in April 1966. He served as support crewman for Apollo 10, and was capcom during the first lunar landing by astronauts Neil Armstrong and Edwin Aldrin in July 1969. He later served as backup lunar module pilot for Apollo 13, and backup lunar module pilot for Apollo 17. For several years he worked on Space Shuttle development.

He resigned from NASA in December 1975 and from Air Force active duty on January 1, 1976, to become distributor for Coors Beer in San Antonio, Texas. He left that business in March 1978 to work elsewhere in San Antonio, and has since been a Christian lay minister. Most recently he has headed his own investment company and is president of Southwest Wilderness Art.

Duke is a brigadier general in the USAF Reserve. He and his wife, Dorothy, have two sons, Charles and Thomas, and live in New Braunfels, Texas.

Dunbar, Bonnie

Dr. Bonnie Dunbar was a scientific mission specialist aboard Shuttle Mission 61-A/Spacelab Dl in October and November 1985. During the week-long flight Dunbar and seven other astronauts performed scientific experiments designed and controlled by the Federal German Aerospace Research Establishment (DFVLR) and the European Space Agency (ESA).

Dunbar has logged 169 hours in space.

Bonnie Jeanne Dunbar was born March 3, 1949, in Sunnyside, Washington. She graduated from Sunnyside High School in 1967 and attended the University of Washington, where she received a BS and

MS in ceramic engineering in 1971 and 1975. She later earned her PhD in biomedical engineering from the University of Houston in 1983.

After graduating from college in 1971 Dunbar worked for two years for Boeing as a computer systems analyst, then began researching her master's thesis. In 1975 she was invited to be a visiting scientist at Harwell Laboratories in Oxford, England, then became a senior research engineer at Rockwell International Space Divison in Downey, California, where she worked on the development of the Space Shuttle thermal protection system. She became a payload officer and flight controller at NASA's Johnson Space Center in 1978, working as one of the guidance and navigation officers during the Skylab re-entry in 1979.

Dunbar was selected as an astronaut candidate in May 1980 and in August 1981 completed a one-year training and evaluation course. She worked in the Shuttle Avionics Integration Laboratory before being assigned to Spacelab Dl in 1983.

She is a private pilot with over 200 hours flying time and has also logged 300 hours as a T-38 jet co-pilot. In addition to her astronaut duties, she is an adjunct assistant professor of mechanical engineering at the University of Houston.

Dr. Dunbar is unmarried.

Eisele, Donn

Donn Eisele was the command module pilot of Apollo 7, the first manned Apollo flight, in October 1968. The 11-day mission by Eisele and astronauts Walter Schirra and Walter Cunningham qualified the Apollo spacecraft, which had been completely re-designed following the tragic fire that killed three astronauts, for future flights to the Moon.

The Apollo 7 astronauts were the first American astronauts to beam live television pictures to the ground. The "Wally, Walt and Donn Show" won a special Emmy award from the Academy of Television Arts and Sciences. They also had the bad luck to be the first astronauts to catch cold in space.

Apollo 7 was Eisele's only space flight.

Donn Fulton Eisele was born June 30, 1930, in Columbus, Ohio, where he graduated from West High School in 1948. His father was a printer. Eisele earned a competitive appointment to the US Naval Academy at Annapolis, graduating with a bachelor of science degree in 1952. He later earned an MS in astronautics from the Air Force Institute of Technology in 1960.

Because of a lifelong interest in flying, Eisele elected to serve in the US Air Force after graduation from Annapolis. He underwent pilot training in Texas, Arizona and Florida, winning his wings in 1954. Until 1958 he was an interceptor pilot stationed at Ellsworth AFB, South Dakota. In 1958 he became a student at the Air Force Institute of Technology, and remained there as a rocket propulsion and weapons engineer after graduation. In 1961 he attended the Aerospace Research Pilot School at Edwards AFB, California, and was an instructor there as well. When chosen by NASA, Eisele was a test pilot at the USAF Special Weapons Center at Kirtland AFB, New Mexico.

As a pilot Eisele logged over 4200 hours of flying time, including over 3600 hours in jets.

Eisele was one of the 14 astronauts selected by NASA in October 1963. He was assigned to Apollo projects early in training and helped test the pressure suit later used for walks on the Moon. In late 1965 he was assigned as pilot of the first manned Apollo crew commanded by Virgil Grissom, but suffered a shoulder injury during a weightless training flight and was replaced by Roger Chaffee. After recovering, Eisele joined the Schirra crew, then was assigned to the second manned Apollo flight.

After Apollo 7 Eisele served as backup command module pilot for Apollo 10. When he was not assigned to a second Apollo flight he left the astronaut office to become technical assistant for manned spaceflight at the NASA Langley Research Center in Hampton, Virginia. Colonel Eisele retired from NASA and the USAF in July 1972.

Since then, Eisele has been Director of the US Peace Corps in Thailand and, after returning to the US, sales manager for the Marion Power Shovel Company. He is currently an executive with the investment firm of Oppenheimer & Company in Fort Lauderdale, Florida.

Eisele was the first active astronaut to get divorced. He and his second wife, Susan, have two children, Kristen and Andrew. Eisele had four children from his first marriage: Melinda, Donn, Mathew (deceased), and Jon.

England, Anthony

Dr. Anthony England was a mission specialist aboard Spacelab 2/ Shuttle Mission 51-F in July 1985. For seven days England and six other astronauts aboard the Shuttle Challenger conducted experiments in solar physics, astronomy and studies of the earth. The flight was only partly successful because a Shuttle engine failure during launch initially placed Challenger in a lower orbit than planned. And the Instrument Pointing System (IPS), a sophisticated aiming device for astronomical sensors, did not become fully operational until the last days of the mission.

Mission 51-F returned to Earth on August 6, 1985. England has logged 188 hours in space.

Anthony Wayne England was born May 15, 1942, in Indianapolis, Indiana, but grew up in West Fargo, North Dakota. After graduation from high school he attended the Massachusetts Institute of Technology, where he earned BS and MS degrees in geology in 1965, and a PhD in geoscience in 1970.

From 1965 to 1967 England was a graduate fellow at MIT, performing geophysical studies of the Earth's magnetic field and the structure of glaciers in the western United States.

He was one of 11 scientist-astronauts selected by NASA in August 1967. At 25, England was and remains the youngest person ever selected for astronaut training by NASA. He completed six months of training and familiarization with the Apollo spacecraft, then reported to Laughlin AFB, Texas, for 53 weeks of training that qualified him as a jet pilot. (As a pilot, he would eventually log over 2700 hours of flying time.) From 1968 to 1972 he was involved in preparations for Apollo manned lunar landings, and served as a support crewman for Apollo 13 and Apollo 16.

Because NASA budget cuts eliminated future Apollo manned lunar landings, England left the astronaut group in August 1972 to join the US Geological Survey. In the next seven years England led two expeditions to Antarctica, studied glaciers in Alaska (where he served as a bush pilot), was associate editor for the *Journal of Geophysical Research*, and served on several national committees concerned with Antarctic policy, nuclear waste containment, and earth sciences.

In June 1979 England returned to the Johnson Space Center as a senior scientist-astronaut (mission specialist) and helped develop computer software for the Space Shuttle. In February 1983, more than 15 years after his original selection as an astronaut, England was assigned to Spacelab 2. He is currently training for another Spacelab mission.

England and his wife, Kathleen, have two daughters, Heidi and Heather.

Engle, Joe

Joe Engle, one of the most experienced aviators ever to become an astronaut, commanded Space Shuttle missions in 1981 and 1985. Prior to that he had earned an official astronaut rating from the US Air Force for a flight in the X-15 rocket plane, and had also flown approach and landing tests with the Shuttle Enterprise.

STS-2 in November 1981 was the first re-flight of the Shuttle Columbia. Despite the fact that the flight was shortened from five days to two by a fuel cell problem, STS-2 successfully demonstrated that a Shuttle could be re-flown and that the Canadian-built remote manipulator system (RMS) arm would function.

In August and September 1985 Engle was commander of Shuttle Mission 51-I, during which his crew of five astronauts deployed two communications satellites and repaired a third in orbit.

Engle has logged approximately 224 hours in space.

Joe Henry Engle was born in rural Dickinson Country, Kansas, near Abilene, on August 26, 1932. He attended the University of Kansas, earning a BS in aeronautical engineering in 1955.

An Air Force ROTC student, Engle went on active duty after graduation from college and completed pilot training in 1957. He served with the 474th Fighter Day Squadron and the 309th Tactical Fighter Squadron at George AFB, California, then was assigned to bases in Spain, Italy and Denmark. In 1961 he attended the USAF Experimental Flight Test Pilot School at Edwards AFB, California, and the following year, graduated from the new Aerospace Research Pilot School.

In June 1963 Engle was chosen to be an X-15 pilot, and in the next three years made 16 flights in the rocket-powered research craft. Three of those flights in 1965 reached altitudes greater than 50 miles, qualifying Captain Engle as a USAF astronaut.

Engle became one of the 19 astronauts selected by NASA in April 1966. In 1968 he was one of three astronauts who tested the re-designed Apollo command module in a vacuum chamber. He served as support crewman for Apollo 10 and was backup lunar module pilot for Apollo 14.

By early 1971 he had informally been assigned as prime lunar module pilot for Apollo 17 when NASA budget cuts made it clear that Apollo 17 would be the last manned lunar landing. Scientist-astronaut Harrison Schmitt, a trained geologist who was informally assigned to Apollo 18, was named to Apollo 17 in Engle's place and became one of the last pair of American astronauts to walk on the Moon. In 1972 Engle was offered the chance to join the crew of the Apollo-Soyuz Test Project, but declined in order to devote his time to Space Shuttle development.

Having worked with the Shuttle from the beginning and given his experience as an X-15 pilot, Engle was a natural choice to pilot the Enterprise on a series of approach and landing tests at Edwards AFB in 1977. Engle and pilot Richard Truly flew one of three "captive" flights (with the Enterprise attached to a specially modified Boeing 747) and two of the five "free" flights, during which the Shuttle was released from the 747 at an altitude of 25,000 feet, gliding to a landing two minutes later.

From March 1978 to April 1981 Engle and Truly served as backups for STS-1, the first manned Shuttle orbital test flight.

Following STS-2, from March to December 1982, Engle served as deputy associate administrator for manned space flight at NASA headquarters in Washington D.C. He returned to the Johnson Space Center in January 1983 and was assigned to his second Shuttle command later that year.

Described as a "natural stick-and-rudder" pilot, Engle has logged over 11,400 hours of flying time, over 8000 in jets, in 140 different types of aircraft. In November 1986 he resigned from NASA and retired from the Air Force.

He and his wife, Mary Catherine, have two children, Laurie and Jon.

Evans, Ronald

Ronald Evans was command module pilot on the last manned flight to the Moon, Apollo 17 in December 1972. Evans orbited the Moon for three days while astronauts Eugene Cernan and Jack Schmitt explored the Taurus-Littrow area. On the return to Earth, Evans performed an EVA lasting 1 hour and 6 minutes.

Evans logged approximately 12 days and 14 hours in space.

Ronald Ellwin Evans was born November 10, 1933, in St. Francis, Kansas. He received a BS in electrical engineering from the University of Kansas in 1956, and later earned an MS in aeronautical engineering from the US Naval Postgraduate School in 1964.

Evans entered the US Navy through ROTC and completed flight training in 1957. He became a carrier pilot on several overseas cruises and flew F8 aircraft on combat missions from the carrier USS Ticonderoga over Vietnam prior to joining NASA.

He was one of the 19 astronauts selected in April 1966. He served as a member of the support crew for the first scheduled Apollo mission, and for Apollo 7 and Apollo 11 as well. He was backup command module pilot for Apollo 14 and for the Apollo-Soyuz Test Project. He resigned from the Navy with the rank of captain in April 1976, and from NASA in March 1977. He was employed by the Western American Energy Corporation in Scottsdale, Arizona, until 1978, and has been an executive with Sperry Flight Systems in Phoenix since then.

Evans and his wife, Janet, have two children, Jaime and Jon.

Fabian, John

Dr. John Fabian was mission specialist aboard two Shuttle flights, STS-7 in June 1983 and Mission 51-G in June 1985. On both flights Fabian took part in the launching of communications satellites owned by countries such as Canada, Mexico, Indonesia and the Arab League, and in the deployment and retrieval of the scientific satellites SPAS-01 and Spartan.

On his two flights Fabian logged 317 hours in space.

John McCreary Fabian was born January 28, 1939, in Goosecreek, Texas, but grew up in Pullman, Washington, where he graduated from high school in 1957. He attended Washington State University, receiving a BS in mechanical engineering in 1962. He later earned an MS in aerospace engineering from the Air Force Institute of Technology in 1964, and a PhD in aeronautics and astronautics from the University of Washington in 1974.

Fabian joined the Air Force through ROTC in 1962 and after completing basic training and further schooling was assigned as an engineer at Kelly Air Force Base, Texas. He attended flight training at Williams Air Force Base, Arizona, and spent five years as a KC-135 pilot based at Wurtsmith AFB, Michigan. During this time he flew 90 combat missions in Vietnam. When selected by NASA in 1978 he was an instructor at the US Air Force Academy.

He has logged 4000 hours flying time, 3400 hours in jets.

Fabian qualified as an astronaut in August 1979 and for several years assisted in the development of satellite deployment and retrieval systems, and in the Canadian-built Remote Manipulator System (RMS). In April 1982 he was assigned to the STS-7 crew. In addition to his two flights, he trained for many months as a crewman for the Spacelab 4 mission (61-D), which was canceled in June 1985, and was assigned to Mission 61-G when he resigned from the space program in September 1985.

In January 1986 Colonel Fabian became Director of Space Programs at US Air Force Headquarters in the Pentagon.

Fabian and his wife, Donna, have two children, Michael and Amy.

Fisher, Anna

Dr. Anna Fisher operated the Shuttle Discovery's remote manipulator arm in assisting astronauts Joseph Allen and Dale Gardner in the retrieval of two errant satellites during Mission 51-A in November 1984. The retrieval of the Palapa B-2 and Westar VI was the first salvage mission in space history. Fisher also took part in the deployment of two new satellites.

She has spent 192 hours in space.

Ann Lee Tingle Fisher was born August 24, 1949, in St. Albans, New York, but grew up in San Pedro, California, where she graduated from high school in 1967. She attended the University of California at Los Angeles, receiving a BS in chemistry in 1971 and an MD in 1976. She completed her internship at Harbor General Hospital in Torrance, California, a year later.

After receiving her chemistry degree, Fisher spent a year doing research in x-ray crystallography, publishing three papers in the *Journal of Inorganic Chemistry*. She entered UCLA medical school in 1972 and was working as an emergency room physician in Los Angeles when selected by NASA.

As a child, Fisher decided she wanted to be an astronaut and became a doctor because she knew that physicians would be needed on future space station missions. In 1977, while going through the astronaut selection process, she married a fellow emergency room physician, William Fisher, who had also applied for the space program. Anna was selected in January 1978; William was not chosen until May 1980.

Fisher completed a training and evaluation course in August 1979, qualifying her as a mission specialist on future Shuttle crews. Her astronaut assignments include working on the development of the remote manipulator arm, testing emergency EVA procedures (including repair kits for the Shuttle's thermal tiles), verifying Shuttle computer software, and integrating payloads. She also served as a standby rescue physician for STS-1 through STS-4, and was a capcom for STS-9/Spacelab 1.

In 1983 Anna and William Fisher became the parents of a daughter, Kristin, making Dr. Anna Fisher the first mother to go into space.

Fisher, William

Dr. William Fisher made a "housecall" on an ailing satellite, the Hughes Syncom IV-3 (Leasat 3), during Shuttle Mission 51-I in August

1985. Leásat 3 had been launched from the Shuttle in April 1985, but had failed to activate. Fisher, a medical doctor by profession, and astronaut James van Hoften performed two long EVAs during which they retrieved, repaired, and re-launched the satellite, which reached its intended orbit and full operations in October 1985. The astronauts also launched three new communications satellites during their flight.

Fisher has logged 170 hours in space, including 13 hours of EVA.

William Frederick Fisher was born April 1, 1946, in Dallas, Texas. His father was an Air Force colonel and Fisher moved frequently, graduating from North Syracuse, New York, Central High School in 1964. He received a BA from Stanford in 1968 and an MD from the University of Florida in 1975. He later earned an MS in engineering from the University of Houston in 1980.

After completing medical school Fisher was a surgical resident at Harbor General Hospital in Torrance, California, then specialized in emergency medicine. He currently practices at Humana Hospital-Clear Lake in Webster, Texas.

He is also a private pilot with over 1200 hours of flying time.

While at Harbor General Hospital Fisher met another emergency room physician, Anna Tingle, whom he married. Both doctors applied for the 1978 astronaut group but only Anna Fisher was selected. Her husband added an engineering degree to his credentials and was then selected by NASA in May 1980, completing his one-year training and evaluation course in August 1981. Dr. Fisher's duties have included acting as support crew member for STS-8, capcom for STS-8 and STS-9, and B-57 scientific equipment operator for high altitude research. He is also a specialist in extravehicular activity.

At the time of the Challenger disaster Fisher was assigned to a Shuttle mission scheduled for the summer of 1986.

He and Anna Fisher are the parents of a daughter, Kristin.

Freeman, Theodore

Captain Theodore Cordy Freeman, USAF, was the first American astronaut to die in a training accident. He was killed in the crash of a T-38 jet while attempting to land at Ellington Air Force Base, near the NASA Manned Spacecraft Center in Houston, on October 31, 1964.

Freeman was born February 18, 1930, in Haverford, Pennsylvania, but graduated from high school in Lewes, Delaware, in 1948. He attended the University of Delaware for one year, then earned an appointment to the US Naval Academy at Annapolis, graduating in 1953 with a BS degree. In 1960 he earned an MS in aeronautical engineering from the University of Michigan

After training as a pilot, Freeman served in the Pacific and California. In 1960, following schooling at Michigan, he was assigned to Edwards Air Force Base, California, as an aerospace engineer. He later attended the Aerospace Research Pilot School there, where his classmates included future astronauts David Scott and James Irwin, and was an instructor at ARPS at the time he was chosen by NASA.

He was one of the 14 astronauts selected by NASA in October 1963 and was on the verge of completing a year of basic training and evaluation at the time of his death. Fellow astronaut Walter Cunningham wrote later that "Freeman was one of the better pilots I have known" and would have rated "near the top" of the 1963 astronaut group.

Freeman was survived by his wife, Faith, and a daughter.

Fullerton, Charles

Gordon Fullerton has made two flights aboard the Space Shuttle. He was pilot of STS-3 in March 1982, an eight-day orbital flight test of the Columbia, during which he and commander Jack Lousma operated the remote manipulator arm and the OSS-1 scientific pallet. STS-3 was extended one day because of weather problems at Edwards Air Force Base, California, its primary landing site, and is the only Shuttle mission to land at Northrup Strip at White Sands, New Mexico.

In July 1985 Fullerton served as commander of Mission 51-F, the flight of Spacelab 2. The seven-man crew overcame one launch pad abort, a second abort-to-orbit (one of the Shuttle Challenger's main engines shut down during launch) and numerous equipment problems during an eight-day scientific mission.

Fullerton has spent approximately 380 hours in space.

Charles Gordon Fullerton was born October 11, 1936, in Rochester, New York, but grew up in Oregon, graduating from US Grant High School in Portland. He attended the California Institute of Technology, receiving a BS (1957) and MS (1958) in mechanical engineering.

While working on his master's at Caltech, Fullerton was employed by Hughes Aircraft in Culver City, California, as a mechanical design engineer. Upon completion of the degree in July 1958 he joined the US Air Force, undergoing pilot training in Georgia, Texas and Kansas. From 1961 to 1964 he was a B-47 jet bomber pilot with the Strategic Air Command's 303rd Bomb Wing based at Davis-Monthan AFB, Arizona.

Fullerton attended the USAF Aerospace Research Pilot School at Edwards AFB, California, in 1965, then reported to Wright-Patterson AFB, Ohio, as a bomber test pilot. He was at Wright-Pat in June 1966 when he was selected for the Air Force's Manned Orbiting Laboratory program. Three years later, following the cancellation of MOL, he transferred to NASA as an astronaut.

As a pilot Fullerton has logged over 11,000 hours of flying time in 84 different types of aircraft, including gliders.

With NASA Fullerton served on the astronaut support crew for Apollo 14 and Apollo 17, and as capcom for Apollos 14 through 17. He was one of the first astronauts assigned to the Shuttle program, and in 1976 was named to one of the two two-man crews for the Shuttle Approach and Landing Tests (ALT). The following year Fullerton and commander Fred Haise flew two captive and three free flights of the Shuttle Enterprise, including the first. In March 1978 he joined the group of astronauts training for the Shuttle's orbital flight tests.

In 1986 Fullerton wrote a report critical of plans for NASA's Space Station program, and in October of that year left the astronaut group. He is currently a test pilot at NASA's Dryden Flight Research Facility at Edwards AFB, California.

Fullerton and his wife, Marie, have two children, Molly and Andrew.

Gardner, Dale

Dale Gardner has been a mission specialist aboard two Shuttle flights, STS-8 in 1983 and Mission 51-A in 1984. During 51-A he and Joseph Allen performed spacewalks using the manned maneuvering unit (MMU) backpack to retrieve two errant satellites for return to Earth. It was the first salvage operation in space history.

He has spent 337 hours in space, including 11.5 hours of EVA.

Dale Allan Gardner was born November 8, 1948, in Fairmont, Minnesota, but grew up in Sherburn, Minnesota, and Savanna, Illinois. He

graduated from high school in Savanna in 1966, then attended the University of Illinois, receiving a BS in engineering physics in 1970.

In July 1970, just after graduation from Illinois, Gardner joined the US Navy and underwent flight officer training in Florida and Georgia. He was immediately assigned to the US Naval Air Test Center at Patuxent River, Maryland, to work on navigation systems for the F-14A. Beginning in July 1973 he served as an F-14A flight officer aboard the carrier USS Enterprise during two tours in the Pacific. From December 1976 until his selection by NASA he was with the Air Test and Evaluation Squadron at Pt. Mugu, California.

Gardner was one of the 35 astronauts selected by NASA in January 1978. In August 1979 he completed a training and evaluation course which qualified him as a mission specialist on Shuttle crews. He served as support crewman for STS-4, and in April 1982 was assigned to the crew of STS-8.

In October 1984 he was named to the crew of Mission 62-A, the first Shuttle launch from Vandenberg Air Force Base, originally scheduled for July 1986 and postponed because of the explosion of the Shuttle Challenger in January 1986. He has since left the astronaut group and is assigned to the US Space Command in Colorado.

Commander Gardner and his wife, Sue, have two children, Lisa and Todd.

Gardner, Guy

Lieutenant Colonel Guy Gardner, USAF, is one of the 19 astronauts selected by NASA in May 1980. In August 1981 he completed a training and evaluation course to qualify him as a pilot on Shuttle crews.

In October 1984 he was named as pilot of Mission 62-A, the first planned launch from Vandenberg Air Force Base, California, which was postponed indefinitely in the wake of the Shuttle Challenger explosion.

Guy Spence Gardner was born January 6, 1948, in Alta Vista, Virginia, but grew up in Alexandria, where he graduated from George Washington High School in 1965. He attended the US Air Force Academy, receiving a BS in engineering sciences, astronautics and mathematics in 1969, and Purdue University, receiving an MS in astronautics in 1970.

Gardner underwent pilot training at Craig AFB, Alabama, and MacDill AFB, Florida, before being sent to Thailand, where he flew F-4s on 177 combat missions. Returning to the US, he attended the USAF Test Pilot School at Edwards AFB, California, later becoming a test pilot and instructor there. When selected by NASA in 1980 he was operations officer with the lst Test Squadron at Clark AFB, the Philippines.

As a pilot he has logged over 3000 hours of flying time.

Between June 1983 and April 1984 Gardner served as a Shuttle capcom. He also flew the lead chase plane for STS-4 in 1982.

He and his wife, Linda, have three children, Jennifer, Sarah and Jason.

Garriott, Owen

Dr. Owen Garriott, a physicist and electrical engineer, has done scientific research in space aboard Skylab and Spacelab.

Garriott was science pilot of Skylab 3, the second manned Skylab mission, launched July 28, 1973. Garriott, Alan Bean and Jack Lousma

occupied the orbiting laboratory for 59.5 days, returning to Earth on September 25. It was the longest manned flight to date, and the most scientifically productive, since the astronauts were able to devote over 300 man-hours to observations of the Sun and completed 333 medical experiments. They also continued to repair Skylab itself, which had been damaged during its launch in May 1973. NASA officials judged that the Skylab 3 crew accomplished 150 percent of its goals.

On his second space flight, Garriott served as mission specialist of STS-9/Spacelab 1, launched November 28, 1983. The crew of six included four scientists who worked 12-hour shifts in Spacelab operating over 70 different experiments in a variety of fields, from life sciences to materials processing to Earth observations. Garriott also managed to find time, during his off-hours, to talk with amateur radio hams around the world (including Jordan's King Hussein) as operator of "station" W5LFL.

Garriott has logged approximately 1675 hours, almost 70 days, in space, including 13 hours and 43 minutes in Skylab EVA.

Owen Kay Garriott was born November 22, 1930, in Enid, Oklahoma, where he grew up. He attended the University of Oklahoma, graduating in 1953 with a BS in electrical engineering. Following a tour of duty with the US Navy, he attended Stanford University, receiving an MS (1957) and a PhD (1960) in electrical engineering.

He served as an electronics officer in the US Navy from 1953 to 1956, aboard the destroyers USS Cowell and USS Allen M. Sumner. When he completed work on his doctorate he became an associate professor in the department of electrical engineering at Stanford and taught there until his selection by NASA.

Garriott was one of six scientist-astronauts selected by NASA in June 1965. Although he was already a licensed pilot, he underwent a 53-week jet pilot course at Williams Air Force Base, Arizona, and ultimately logged over 3200 hours of flying time, 2900 of it in jets and the rest in light aircraft and helicopters.

His first assignment as an astronaut was working on the design and development of the Apollo Applications Program (AAP), later known as Skylab. In 1968 he served, briefly, as the chief astronaut representative to AAP. He was also a capcom for Apollo 11, the first lunar landing. He was officially named as a Skylab crew member in January 1972.

Between the conclusion of the Skylab program in 1974 and the first Shuttle assignments in 1978, Garriott served as deputy director, later acting director, for science and applications at the Johnson Space Center. He took a year's sabbatical leave in 1976 to teach at Stanford, and, in fact, remains a consulting professor with the school.

Garriott and Robert Parker were named mission specialists for Spacelab 1 in August 1978, more than two years before its scheduled launch, and five years before the actual flight. Their training program took them all over the world, especially to Europe, where Spacelab was being built.

Since Spacelab 1 Garrriott has trained for two Spacelab Earth Observation Missions, which are intended to re-fly experiments from that first flight. Both EOM-1 (originally scheduled for May 1985) and EOM-2 (September 1986) were canceled before launch. In June 1986 he resigned from NASA and the astronaut group to become a consultant.

Garriott is the author or co-author of more than 40 scientific papers and a textbook, *Introduction to Ionospheric Physics* (1969).

He and his wife, Helen, have four grown children, Randall, Robert, Richard (a famous computer hacker), and Linda.

Gemar, Charles

Captain Charles D. "Sam" Gemar, US Army, was one of the 13 astronauts selected by NASA in June 1985. In August 1985 he began a yearlong training and evaluation course to qualify him as a mission specialist on future Shuttle crews.

Gemar was born August 4, 1955, in Yankton, South Dakota, and graduated from high school in Scotland, South Dakota, in 1973. He earned a BS in engineering from the US Military Academy at West Point in 1979.

He enlisted in the US Army and was training in the 18th Airborne Corps when he earned an appointment to West Point. After graduation from the academy he became a helicopter and transport pilot. From 1980 to 1985 he was stationed at Hunter Army Airfield, Ft. Stewart, Georgia, where in addition to being a flight operations officer and flight platoon leader he also completed the Army Parachutist Course and Ranger School.

Gemar and his wife, Charlene, live in Houston.

Gibson, Edward

Dr. Edward Gibson was the science pilot of Skylab 4, the longest American manned space flight, spending 84 days aboard the Skylab space station. During Skylab 4 Gibson and fellow astronauts Gerald Carr and William Pogue conducted extensive observations of the Sun and of Comet Kahoutek. Gibson also took part in three space walks lasting a total of almost 16 hours.

Edward George Gibson was born November 8, 1936, in Buffalo, New York, and graduated from Kenmore High School. He attended the University of Rochester, New York, earning a BS in engineering in 1959, and the California Institute of Technology, where he received an MS in engineering in 1960. He earned his PhD in engineering from Caltech in 1964.

While working on his doctorate at Caltech, Gibson was a research assistant in jet propulsion and atmospheric physics, publishing technical papers on lasers. He then joined the Philco Corporation's Applied Research Laboratory in Newport Beach, California, and was there when selected by NASA.

Gibson was one of the first six scientist-astronauts chosen by NASA in June 1965. He underwent jet pilot training at Williams Air Force Base, Arizona, until July 1966, then became involved in the Apollo program, working on plans for the Orbital Worskhop (later known as Skylab) and learning to fly helicopters for a possible lunar landing. (In 1969 a helicopter piloted by Gibson crashed, but he walked away unscathed.) He served as capcom and support crew member for the Apollo 12 lunar landing in November 1969, then, following budget cuts that eliminated any chance of a flight to the Moon, worked exclusively on Skylab.

As a pilot Gibson eventually logged over 4300 hours of flying time, including 2300 hours in jets.

Gibson resigned from NASA in November 1974 to join the Los Angeles-based Aerospace Corporation, where he did research in solar physics. From March 1976 to March 1977 he served as a consultant to ERNO Raumfahrttechnik GmbH, West Germany, a company working on the European Spacelab, then returned to NASA as an astronaut, becoming chief of the selection and training of new mission specialist astronauts.

In October 1980, Gibson, who had been assigned as launch capcom for STS-1, resigned from NASA a second time, joining TRW, Inc., in

Redondo Beach, California, where he currently works as advanced systems manager for the energy development group.

He is the author of a textbook on solar physics, *The Quiet Sun* (1973).

Gibson and his wife, Julie, have four children, Jannet, John, Julie and Joseph. They live in southern California.

Gibson, Robert

Robert "Hoot" Gibson commanded Shuttle Mission 61-C, which set an unwanted record for delays when its launch was postponed seven times. When 61-C finally lifted off on January 12, 1986, it was plagued by other problems, including an experiment package designed to observe Halley's Comet that would not work, and weather problems at the Kennedy Space Center landing site. The crew of seven, including Florida Congressman Bill Nelson, was able to successfully deploy an RCA communications satellite.

Ultimately Mission 61-C ended when the Shuttle Columbia landed at Edwards Air Force Base in California. The switch from Kennedy to Edwards added six days to the turnaround time needed to prepare Columbia for its next mission, scheduled for early March. When the very next Shuttle flight, 51-L, exploded on January 28, some NASA officials, including chief astronaut John Young, questioned whether 61-C should have been flown at all, since one of its primary payloads had been removed prior to launch and the RCA satellite could have been postponed.

Gibson's first Shuttle mission, as pilot of 41-B in February 1984, was also plagued by equipment failures. The crew of five deployed two different satellites whose rocket motors failed, sending them into useless orbits. (The satellites were later retrieved by another Shuttle crew and returned to Earth.) A balloon intended to serve as a rendezvous target exploded, and the Challenger's remote manipulator arm malfunctioned. Nevertheless, during 41-B two astronauts made the first tests of the manned maneuvering unit backpack, and Gibson and commander Vance Brand made the first Shuttle landing at Kennedy Space Center.

Gibson has spent approximately 337 hours in space during his two flights.

Robert Lee Gibson was born October 30, 1946, in Cooperstown, New York, and graduated from high school in Huntington, New York, in 1964. Nevertheless, he considers Lakewood, California, to be his hometown. He attended California Polytechnic University, receiving a BS in aeronautical engineering in 1969.

He joined the US Navy in 1969 and underwent pilot training in Florida, Mississippi, and Texas. From April 1972 to September 1975 he was assigned to the carriers USS Coral Sea and USS Enterprise, and flew 56 combat missions in Southeast Asia. Returning to the US, Gibson served as an F-14A instructor pilot, then attended the US Naval Test Pilot School at Patuxent River, Maryland. He was a test pilot there when chosen by NASA.

As a pilot Gibson has logged over 3300 hours of flying time in 35 different types of aircraft. He has held a pilot's license since he was 17.

Gibson was one of the 35 astronauts selected by NASA in January 1978. In August 1979 he completed a training and evaluation course that qualified him as a pilot on Shuttle crews. He worked in the Shuttle Avionics Integration Laboratory and as a chase pilot, and in February 1983 was assigned as pilot of STS-11, later known as Mission 41-B.

Commander Gibson is married to astronaut Dr. Rhea Seddon and they have a son, Paul. Gibson has a daughter, Julie, by a previous marriage.

Givens, Edward

Major Edward Givens, USAF, was one of the 19 astronauts selected by NASA in April 1966. A member of the support team for the first manned Apollo mission, he was killed in an off-duty automobile accident near Houston, Texas, on June 6, 1967.

Edward Galen Givens, Jr., was born January 5, 1930, in Quanah, Texas. He attended the US Naval Academy at Annapolis, graduating with a BS degree in 1952.

He elected to serve in the US Air Force and became a pilot in 1953. After assignments at a number of bases he attended the USAF Test Pilot School at Edwards AFB, California, in 1958, and later completed the Aerospace Research Pilot course there in 1963. His classmates in the latter course included future astronauts Michael Collins, Charles Bassett and Joe Engle. Givens was then assigned to the USAF Space Systems Division Office at the NASA Manned Spacecraft Center and was working there on designs for the astronaut maneuvering unit (AMU), the so-called "Buck Rogers" backpack, when chosen as an astronaut.

Givens was survived by his wife and two children.

Glenn, John

The first American to orbit the Earth, John Glenn became the most famous astronaut and a United States senator and presidential hopeful as well.

On February 20, 1962, after weeks of frustrating delays caused by technical and weather problems, Glenn, then a 40-year-old Marine lieutenant colonel, was rocketed into space in a Mercury capsule named Friendship 7. In the next five hours he circled the Earth three times, becoming the first American to experience more than a few minutes of weightlessness.

Soviet cosmonauts Yuri Gagarin and Gherman Titov had already orbited the Earth, and Alan Shepard and Gus Grissom, two of Glenn's fellow Mercury astronauts, had made suborbital flights, but Glenn's was the first space flight to capture the attention and imagination of an entire world, which followed it on radio and television. The citizens of Perth and several other coastal cities in Australia, for example, turned on their lights as a greeting to the orbiting American.

The flight of Friendship 7 was not without drama. At the beginning of Glenn's second orbit, flight controllers picked up warning signals from the spacecraft telling them that the heat shield was loose. If true, Glenn was doomed to a fiery death on his return to Earth. Controllers suspected that the signal was wrong, but nevertheless instructed Glenn not to jettison the capsule's retrorocket pack, which was strapped atop the shield. It was a nervewracking re-entry for Glenn, who could see chunks of burning metal flying past his window, not knowing if they came from the retro pack or his heat shield. But Friendship 7 survived, splashing down approximately 800 miles southeast of Cape Canaveral near Grand Turk Island in the Bahamas.

Glenn became the most celebrated national hero since Charles Lindbergh, and soon found a friend in President John F. Kennedy who, along with his brother Robert, saw the handsome, charistmatic Glenn as a possible political ally. They encouraged him to explore a run for the U.S. Senate seat from Ohio.

The assassination of President Kennedy on November 22, 1963, robbed Glenn of his sponsorship, but Glenn went ahead with plans to leave NASA. (In January 1963 Glenn was assigned to Project Apollo, but, unknown to him, President Kennedy had instructed NASA not to send Glenn into space a second time.) Saying that he did not want to be "the world's oldest permanently training astronaut," Glenn left the astronaut group on January 16, 1964, to campaign for the Senate.

But just weeks later, on February 26, 1964, Glenn suffered a head injury during a fall in a hotel bathroom. Constantly dizzy and nauseated, facing months of recuperation, he withdrew from the race. He had already announced his retirement from the Marines and, after promotion to colonel in October 1964, retired on January 1, 1965.

Though he was named a consultant to the NASA Administrator in February 1965 and remained based in Houston, for the next five years Glenn worked primarily as an executive for Royal Crown, a soft drink company based in Atlanta, Georgia. He also served on the board of several other corporations, and made investments in hotel developments. Successful investments made Glenn a millionaire, but he never gave up his political ambitions. He remained close to the Kennedy family (it was Glenn who broke the news of their father's death to Robert Kennedy's children).

Glenn's 1970 Senate campaign in Ohio was badly organized and underfunded, and he was defeated in the primary by businessman Howard Metzenbaum. Glenn learned from this defeat; his 1974 campaign against Senator Metzenbaum was more efficient, though Metzenbaum defeated himself when he criticized Glenn for "never having held a job." An outraged Glenn blasted Metzenbaum in a debate, pointing out that he had indeed held jobs, in the Marines and in the space program, "where it wasn't my checkbook that was on the line, it was my life." Glenn handily defeated Republican Ralph J. Perk in the general election in November 1974 and entered the United States Senate eleven years after announcing his original intention to run.

Freshman Senator Glenn earned high marks for his ability to win votes on his amendments in spite of the fact that he had few of the traditional political skills. He became friends with Republican Senator Jake Garn of Utah, also elected in 1974, when Garn's wife died. (Garn would later become the first U.S. senator to make a space flight as a Congressional observer.) He was also considered briefly as a vice-presidential running mate by then-candidate Jimmy Carter.

President Carter and Senator Glenn had a public clash over the SALT II treaty and were never close allies. That became clear when in 1980 Glenn won re-election to the Senate overwhelmingly while Carter failed to carry Ohio.

In 1983 Glenn announced his intention to gain the Democratic presidential nomination in 1984. But his campaign, like his 1970 Senate campaign, struck observers as inefficient and unfocused. Glenn dropped out of the race prior to the convention.

He continues to serve in the US Senate.

John Herschel Glenn was born July 18, 1921, in Cambridge, Ohio, but grew up in New Concord. His father was a plumber. Glenn graduated from high school in New Concord, and was attending Muskingum College there when World War II broke out. Glenn, who had already earned a private pilot's license, dropped out to enter the Naval Aviation Cadet Program and was eventually commissioned in the US Marine Corps. (Based on later study at the US Naval Test Pilot School and the University of Maryland, Glenn eventually received a BS in engineering from Muskingum.)

Following pilot training he was assigned to Marine Fighter Squadron 155 and spent the final year of World War II flying F4U fighters on 59 combat missions in the Marshall Islands.

After the war, Glenn was assigned to Fighter Squadron 218 in North China and on Guam. He returned to the US in June 1948 as an instructor at Corpus Christi, Texas.

In the Korean conflict Glenn flew 63 combat missions with Marine Fighter Squadron 311, where his fellow pilots included Boston Red Sox star Ted Williams. He also flew 27 missions as an exchange pilot with the US Air Force. During the last nine days of fighting in Korea, Glenn shot down three enemy MiGs near the Yalu River.

In 1954 Glenn attended the US Naval Test Pilot School at Patuxent River, Maryland, and remained there as a project officer for two years. Assigned to the Navy Bureau of Aeronautics in Washington, D.C., he conceived, planned and piloted a record-setting transcontinental jet flight, flying an F8U from Los Angeles to New York in just 3 hours, 23 minutes on July 16, 1957. This earned him guest spots on television's "I've Got a Secret" and on "Name That Tune," where he and his partner won $25,000.

When the National Advisory Committee on Aeronautics (NACA, NASA's predecessor) and the US Navy began studies on manned space flight after the launch of Sputnik in October 1957, Glenn volunteered as a test subject and found himself riding the high-speed centrifuge that would later simulate launch and re-entry stress for future astronauts.

Glenn was one of the original seven Mercury astronauts chosen in April 1959. Widely expected by journalists covering the space program to be the first American in space, Glenn was disappointed to see that honor go to Alan Shepard. Glenn served as backup to both Shepard and Gus Grissom on their 1961 Mercury suborbital flights before being named to Mercury-Atlas 6, the first American manned orbital flight, in November 1961.

As a pilot Glenn has logged over 5500 hours of flying time, including 1900 hours in jets.

Glenn contributed to the book *We Seven, by the Astronauts Themselves* (1962), which described their selection, early training and first flights. A more enlightening version is told in Tom Wolfe's *The Right Stuff* (1979). The film version of this book, released in November 1984, was widely expected to act as a "campaign" film for presidential candidate Glenn. Though it generally received good reviews, *The Right Stuff* was not a commercially successful film.

Glenn also published a collection of letters written to him, *P.S., We Listened to Your Heartbeat* (1964).

A biography, *Glenn: The Astronaut Who Would Be President*, was published in 1983.

Glenn and his wife, Anna, have two children, John David and Carolyn Ann.

Godwin, Linda

Dr. Linda M. Godwin was one of the 13 astronauts selected by NASA in June 1985. In August 1985 she commenced a year-long training and evaluation course to qualify her as a mission specialist on future Shuttle crews.

Godwin was born July 2, 1952, in Cape Girardeau, Missouri, and graduated from high school in Jackson, Missouri, in 1970. She attended Southeast Missouri State, receiving a BS in mathematics and physics in 1974, and later earned her MS and PhD in physics from the University of Missouri in 1976 and 1980.

While working on her doctorate at Missouri, Godwin taught physics and conducted research in labs there. In 1980 she joined NASA as a flight controller and payload officer and worked on several Shuttle missions.

She is single.

Gordon, Richard

Dick Gordon made space flights aboard Gemini and Apollo. As pilot of Gemini 11 in September 1966, Gordon and command pilot Charles Conrad set a world record, soaring to an altitude of 850 miles. Gordon also conducted two space walks.

As command module pilot of Apollo 12 in November 1969, Gordon orbited the Moon for a day and a half while Conrad and Alan Bean explored the lunar Ocean of Storms.

Gordon spent approximately 316 hours in space, including 2 hours and 44 minutes in EVA.

Richard Francis Gordon, Jr., was born October 5, 1929, in Seattle, Washington, and graduated from North Kitsap High School in nearby Poulsbo in 1947. He attended the University of Washington, receiving a BS in chemistry in 1951. He later did graduate work in operations analysis at the US Naval Postgraduate School.

Entering active duty with the US Navy following college, Gordon underwent pilot training, earning his wings in 1953. For the next four years he was an all-weather fighter pilot based in Jacksonville, Florida, then attended the Navy Test Pilot School at Patuxent River, Maryland. From 1957 to 1960 he was a test pilot at Pax River, serving as project pilot for the F4H Phantom II. He also became friends with fellow Navy test pilots Charles Conrad and Alan Bean. Following his tour as a test pilot, Gordon became a flight instructor at Miramar, California, taking part in the introduction of the F4H to the Atlantic and Pacific fleets. In May 1961 he won the Bendix Trophy for setting a new Los Angeles to New York speed record of 870 miles per hour, flying across the United States in 2 hours and 47 minutes.

As a pilot Gordon eventually logged over 4500 hours of flying time, including 3500 hours in jets.

Gordon was a student at the USN Postgraduate School in October 1963 when he became one of the 14 astronauts selected by NASA. (He had been a semi-finalist for the 1962 group.) One of his early assignments was to help design the cockpits for Gemini and Apollo spacecraft, and he ultimately became head of the astronaut office Apollo branch. In September 1965 he was named backup pilot for Gemini 8 and also served as a capcom for Gemini 9. Following his Gemini 11 flight he was backup command module pilot for Apollo 9.

In March 1970 Gordon, Vance Brand and scientist-astronaut Harrison Schmitt were named as backups for Apollo 15, then scheduled for October of that year, expecting to be chosen as the prime crew for the Apollo 18 lunar landing. But cuts in the NASA budget that spring eliminated Apollos 18 through 20, and Gordon lost his chance to become the thirteenth person to walk on the Moon. With the completion of his assignment on Apollo 15 in August 1971 Gordon served as chief of advanced programs for the astronaut office, working on the new Space Shuttle, resigning from NASA and retiring from the Navy as a captain on January 1, 1972.

Gordon was hired away from NASA by John W. Mecom, Jr., to become executive vice president of the Mecom-owned New Orleans Saints team in the National Football League. In April 1977 Gordon became general manager of Energy Developers Ltd., a chemical research company owned by Mecom. He left the Mecom organization in May 1978 to become president of Resolution Engineering and Development Company (REDCO), a firm specializing in oil well control and fire-fighting, remaining with that company in several positions through August 1981.

From September 1981 to February 1983 Gordon was director for Scott Science and Technology, Inc., in Los Angeles, an aerospace firm founded by former Apollo 15 commander David Scott. Gordon is currently president of Astro Sciences Corporation in Los Angeles.

In the summer of 1984 Gordon served as technical consultant to the producers of the CBS television miniseries *Space*, playing the role of Capcom onscreen as well.

Gordon and his wife, Linda, live in Manhattan Beach, California. He has five surviving children from a previous marriage, Carleen, Richard, Lawrence, Thomas and Diane.

Grabe, Ronald

Ronald Grabe was the pilot of Space Shuttle Mission 51-J in October 1985, a flight dedicated to a classified Department of Defense payload. Mission 51-J was also the first flight of the fourth Shuttle Orbiter, Atlantis.

He has logged 98 hours in space.

Ronald John Grabe was born June 13, 1945, in New York City. He graduated from Stuyvesant High School there in 1962 and entered the US Air Force Academy in Colorado Springs, where he received his BS in engineering science in 1966. In 1967 he studied aeronautics as a Fulbright Scholar at the Technische Hochschule in Darmstadt, West Germany.

After completing pilot training, Grabe flew F-100 aircraft from Cannon Air Force Base, New Mexico, then was assigned to Vietnam, where he took part in 200 combat missions. Upon his return to the US he attended the USAF Test Pilot School, graduating in 1975, and from 1976 to 1979 served as an exchange test pilot with the Royal Air Force at Boscombe Down, United Kingdom. Prior to becoming an astronaut he was a test pilot at Edwards AFB, California.

As a pilot Grabe has logged over 3000 hours of flying time, 2900 hours in jets.

Grabe was selected as an astronaut candidate in May 1980 and in August 1981 completed the one-year training and evaluation course. He fulfilled several technical assignments in the Astronaut Office prior to being named to the Department of Defense standby flight crew—which later became Mission 51-J—in October 1983. He was also assigned as pilot on a Shuttle mission originally scheduled for 1986.

Grabe and his wife, Marijo, have two daughters, Hilary and Alison.

Graveline, Duane

Dr. Duane Graveline was one of the first six scientist-astronauts chosen by NASA in June 1965. Graveline resigned from the program two months later for personal reasons.

Duane Edgar Graveline was born March 2, 1931, in Newport, Vermont. He received a BS from the University of Vermont in 1952 and an MD from the University of Vermont Medical School in 1955. He later earned an MS in public health from Johns Hopkins University in 1958. He also served in the US Air Force and was a civilian physician at the Manned Spacecraft Center when chosen by NASA.
Vermont Department of Health, and has since set up his own medical practice in Colchester, Vermont.

He is married and the father of five children.

Gregory, Frederick

Ten years to the day after Fred Gregory flew refugees out of the beseiged American embassy in Saigon, Vietnam, he was in orbit aboard Space Shuttle Mission 51-B, the Spacelab 3 flight.

Gregory, the third black American astronaut, was pilot of the seven-man crew which performed medical and materials processing experiments during the mission, which lasted from April 29 to May 6, 1985. Gregory lead the Silver team, including mission specialist Norman Thagard and payload specialist Lodewijk van den Berg, in its twelve-hour shifts aboard Spacelab.

Frederick Drew Gregory was born January 7, 1941, in Washington, D.C. and graduated from Anacostia High School there in 1958. He attended the US Air Force Academy, where he received a bachelor of science degree in 1964. He later earned an MS in information systems from George Washington University in 1977.

Upon graduation from the Air Force Academy Gregory underwent training as a helicopter pilot and spent three years as a rescue crew commander, including a tour in Vietnam. In 1969 he cross-trained to jet fighters, then entered the US Naval Test Pilot School at Patuxent River, Maryland. From 1971 to 1974 Gregory was a test pilot at Wright-Patterson AFB, Ohio, and from 1974 to 1978 for NASA at Langley Research Center, Virginia.

During the evacuation from Saigon in April 1975 Gregory, a veteran helicopter rescue pilot, flew refugees from the American embassy to carriers off-shore.

As a pilot he has logged over 5300 hours of flying time in more than 40 different types of aircraft, including helicopters, jet fighters, transports and gliders.

As a teenager Gregory always wanted to be an astronaut but since his military flying was primarily in helicopters, not high-performance jets, the Air Force was reluctant to submit him to NASA as a candidate in 1977. Gregory offered to resign from the service, submitted his own application, and was chosen as one of 35 astronaut candidates by NASA in January 1978. In August 1979 he completed a training and evaluation course which qualified him as pilot on Shuttle crews. He then worked in the Shuttle Avionics Integration Laboratory until being assigned to the Spacelab 3 mission in February 1983.

Following his flight, in October 1985, Gregory began serving as mission control capcom for Shuttle flights. He was in contact with the crew of the Shuttle Challenger during its tragic launch on January 28, 1986. He currently heads a new office devoted to flight safety at NASA Headquarters.

Gregory and his wife, Barbara, have two children, Frederick, Jr., and Heather.

Griggs, David

Dave Griggs took the first unscheduled and unrehearsed spacewalk in the American space program on April 16, 1985. Griggs was one of seven astronauts aboard Shuttle Mission 51-D, which deployed two communications satellites. One of the satellites, the Hughes Syncom IV-3 (also known as Leasat 3), failed to activate because an arming lever was not automatically closed during deployment, leaving Leasat 3 floating useless in orbit.

NASA and Hughes controllers, working with the astronauts, devised a makeshift cardboard-and-electrical tape "flyswatter" which, it was hoped, could be attached to the robot arm of the Shuttle Discovery and used to snag the switch on the satellite. Mission specialists Griggs and Jeffrey Hoffman performed the unique EVA, attaching the "flyswatter," but the attempt by astronaut Rhea Seddon to activate the satellite failed. (Leasat 3 was repaired on a later Shuttle mission, and finally reached its intended orbit in October 1985.)

These events overshadowed the successful deployment of the Canadian Anik 3C communications satellite, and the flight on 51-D of United States Senator Jake Garn as a payload specialist and observer.

Griggs logged 148 hours in space during 51-B, spending 3 hours and 40 minutes in EVA.

Stanley David Griggs was born September 7, 1939, in Portland, Oregon, where he grew up, graduating from Lincoln High School in 1957. He attended the US Naval Academy at Annapolis, where he earned a bachelor of science degree in 1962. He later earned an MS in administration from George Washington University in 1970.

After completing pilot training in 1964 Griggs was attached to Attack Squadron 74 and flew A-4 aircraft from the carriers USS Independence and USS Roosevelt in Southeast Asia and the Mediterranean. In 1967 he attended the US Naval Test Pilot School at Patuxent River, Maryland, and remained there as a test pilot until 1970, when he resigned from the Navy. He continues to fly with the Naval Reserve and is currently a captain, commanding officer for the Naval Reserve Space Command based in Dahlgren, Virginia.

He has logged over 7500 hours of flying time, including 6500 hours in jets.

Griggs joined NASA in July 1970 as a research pilot based at the Johnson Space Center. In 1974 he was assigned to the development of the Shuttle Training Aircraft (STA), a specially modified jet which would eventually train astronauts to make Shuttle landings. He was chief of STA Operations when he was selected as an astronaut in January 1978. In August 1979 he completed a training and evaluation course which qualified him as a pilot on Shuttle crews. He worked on the manned maneuvering unit and served as a capcom for STS-4.

While training as the pilot for the long-delayed Spacelab 2 mission, Griggs was also assigned to be mission specialist and flight engineer for Mission 41-F, commanded by Karol Bobko and scheduled for launch in August 1984. Problems with the Shuttle manifest forced the Bobko crew to eventually transfer to Mission 51-D. Griggs lost his pilot assignment on Spacelab 2, then was assigned as pilot on Spacelab 4, which was also canceled. He was later chosen to pilot the Spacelab Earth Observation Mission.

Griggs and his wife, Karen, have two daughters, Alison and Carre.

Grissom, Virgil

"Gus" Grissom, one of the original seven Mercury astronauts, died in the Apollo 1 fire at Cape Canaveral on January 27, 1967. Killed with him were Edward White, the first American to walk in space, and Roger Chaffee.

The three astronauts were training for the first manned Apollo flight, a 16-day mission scheduled for launch on February 21, 1967. On Friday, January 27, they were rehearsing launch procedures while strapped into their seats inside their Apollo command module atop its Saturn lB booster. At 6:31 in the evening, at T-10 minutes and holding (a communications problem had developed), a wire inside the Apollo gave off a spark which flared easily in the 16 pounds per square inch, 100 percent oxygen atmosphere, turning the cabin into an inferno. As Grissom, White and Chaffee struggled out of their couches and fought to open the hatch, they were overcome by heat and flame.

The subsequent board of inquiry criticized NASA and North American Aviation, builders of Apollo, for failing to correct potential fire hazards in the spacecraft. (The Apollo cabin contained flammable materials and had a hatch which could not be opened quickly in an emergency.) Apollo flights were suspended for 18 months while the spacecraft was re-designed.

Air Force Lieutenant Colonel Grissom and Navy Lieutenant Commander Chaffee were buried at Arlington National Cemetery. Lieutenant Colonel White was buried at West Point.

Virgil Ivan Grissom was born April 3, 1926, in Mitchell, Indiana, where he grew up, graduating from high school in 1944. He attended Purdue University from 1946 to 1950, receiving a BS in mechanical engineering, and later attended the Air Force Institute of Technology.

Grissom enlisted in the US Army Air Corps as an aviation cadet in 1944 and was undergoing pilot training at Sheppard Field in Texas when World War II ended. He left the AAC to attend college, then reenlisted upon graduation in February 1950, earning his wings at Randolph AFB, Texas, thirteen months later.

Assigned to the 75th Fighter Interceptor Squadron, Grissom flew 100 combat missions in Korea. He returned to the US in 1952 and served as an instructor pilot, then, in August 1955, entered the Air Force Institute of Technology at Wright-Patterson AFB, Ohio. A year later he was sent to the USAF Experimental Test Pilot School at Edwards AFB, California, and in May 1957 returned to Wright-Pat as a fighter test pilot.

Grissom logged 4600 hours as a pilot, including 3500 hours in jets.

He was selected by NASA as one of its first astronauts in April 1959 and helped develop spacecraft simulators.

With John Glenn and Alan Shepard, Grissom was one of three candidates for the Mercury-Redstone series of suborbital flights.

On July 21, 1961, Grissom was launched to an altitude of 126 miles aboard Liberty Bell 7. Mercury-Redstone 4, as it was officially known, repeated Alan Shepard's pioneering Mercury flight of May 5. After splashdown in the Atlantic, however, the hatch flew off Liberty Bell 7 and the spacecraft began to take on water. Grissom dived into the ocean, where he was rescued by a recovery helicopter, but Liberty Bell 7 sank.

It was the loss of Liberty Bell 7 that inspired Grissom to name his next spacecraft the Molly Brown, after the stage play *The Unsinkable Molly Brown*. Following his Mercury flight Grissom had begun to work on the development of the Mercury Mark II spacecraft, later known as Gemini, and in April 1964 was named commander of the first mission. Grissom and John Young orbited the Earth three times on March 23, 1965, becoming the first astronauts to maneuver their spacecraft in orbit. (Previous American and Soviet space travelers had been able to change the attitude of their spacecraft, but not its actual orbit.)

Grissom and Young served as backups for Gemini 6 in December 1965, and then Grissom was chosen to command the first Apollo. He would have been the first person to go into space three times, and the first to fly in three different spacecraft.

Grissom contributed to the book *We Seven* (1962) and completed work on *Gemini* (1968) just before his death. He is the subject of *Starfall* (1974) by Betty Grissom and Henry Still.

He was survived by his wife, Betty, and sons, Scott and Mark. A US Air Force Base in Indiana has been named for him.

Gutierrez, Sidney

Major Sidney M. Gutierrez, USAF, was one of the 17 astronauts selected by NASA in May 1984. In June 1985 he completed a training and evaluation course which qualified him as a pilot on future Shuttle crews.

Gutierrez was born June 27, 1951, in Albuquerque, New Mexico, and graduated from Valley High School there in 1969. He attended the US Air Force Academy at Colorado Springs, receiving a BS in aeronautical engineering in 1973, and later earned an MS in management from Webster College in 1977.

At the Air Force Academy Gutierrez became a master parachutist, making over 550 jumps as a member of the team which won a national championship. He earned his pilot's wings at Laughlin Air Force Base, Texas, in 1975 and remained there as an instructor through 1977. After an assignment as an F-15 pilot at Hollomon AFB, New Mexico, Gutierrez attended the US Air Force Test Pilot School at Edwards AFB, California, in 1981. He was testing F-16 aircraft there when selected by NASA.

As an astronaut Gutierrez has been assigned to the Shuttle Avionics Integration Laboratory, where the highly complex and constantly changing computer software needed to fly the Shuttle is verified.

Gutierrez and his wife, Marianne, have two children, Jennifer and David.

Haise, Fred

Fred Haise was one of three astronauts aboard the unlucky flight of Apollo 13 in April 1970. Haise and commander James Lovell were to have landed on the Moon in the lunar module Aquarius, but on April 13, 1970, two days after launch from the Kennedy Space Center, an explosion aboard the command module Odyssey forced the two would-be lunar explorers and fellow crewman Jack Swigert to use the Aquarius as a lifeboat. With limited power, limited oxygen, and no possibility of a quick return to Earth, the astronauts struggled for 86 hours—three and a half days—to survive the first deep space abort in history. They returned safely on April 16, 1970.

The story of this flight was told in *13: The Flight That Failed*, a 1972 book by Henry S. F. Cooper, Jr. Apollo 13 was also dramatized in a television movie, *Houston, We've Got a Problem*.

Haise logged approximately 143 hours in space during Apollo 13, his only flight.

Fred Wallace Haise, Jr., was born November 13, 1933, in Biloxi,

Mississippi. He attended the University of Oklahoma intending to become a newspaper reporter, but dropped out to join the Navy. He later earned a BS in aeronautical engineering in 1959.

From 1952 to 1954 Haise was a US Navy aviation cadet and instructor, though he ultimately transferred to the US Marine Corps as a fighter pilot. He left the Marines in 1957 to return to school at the University of Oklahoma, and while a student flew with the Oklahoma Air National Guard. After graduation he became a research pilot for NASA's Lewis Research Center in Cleveland, serving in 1961 and 1962 as an officer in the US Air Force. He attended the USAF Aerospace Research Pilot School at Edwards AFB, California, where he was awarded the A. B. Honts Trophy as outstanding graduate of the class of 1964. At the time he was chosen by NASA to be an astronaut he was a civilian pilot at the NASA Flight Research Center at Edwards AFB.

As a pilot Haise eventually logged over 8700 hours of flying time, including 5700 hours in jets.

Haise was one of the 19 astronauts selected by NASA in April 1966. He served as a support crewman for the first flight of the lunar module—eventually flown as Apollo 9—until promoted to the backup crew for the Apollo 8 flight. He was backup lunar module pilot for Edwin Aldrin on Apollo 11, man's first landing on the Moon. After his flight on Apollo 13, Haise was backup commander for Apollo 16 and would have commanded the Apollo 19 lunar landing, had it not been canceled.

In 1973, while piloting a replica of a Japanese World War II aircraft for the Confederate Air Force, a flying air museum, Haise crashed and was badly burned.

When he returned to work, Haise became deeply involved in the Space Shuttle program, primarily as commander of the first Shuttle Approach and Landing Test flight in August 1977. Haise and Gordon Fullerton piloted the Shuttle Enterprise to a dead stick landing on the dry lakebed at Edwards AFB after the Shuttle was carried aloft by a specially modified Boeing 747. Haise and Fullerton later conducted two more such tests.

The following year Haise was designated as commander of the third planned Shuttle orbital flight test, one which was scheduled to rendezvous with the Skylab space station, then in orbit. A special rocket system was to be attached to Skylab, boosting it into a higher, safer orbit by remote control. But technical problems delayed the first Shuttle flight past Skylab's re-entry and destruction. Haise himself resigned from NASA on June 29, 1979, to join the Grumman Aerospace Corporation in Bethpage, New York, where he is currently president of the technical services division.

Haise and his wife, Mary, have four children.

Hammond, Blaine

Major Lloyd Blaine Hammond, Jr., USAF, is one of the 17 astronauts selected by NASA in May 1984. In June 1985 he completed a training and evaluation course which qualified him as a pilot on future Shuttle crews.

Hammond was born January 16, 1952, in Savannah, Georgia. He graduated from high school in Kirkwood, Missouri, in 1969, then attended the US Air Force Academy, where he received a BS in engineering mechanics in 1973. He later earned an MS in engineering mechanics from the Georgia Institute of Technology in 1974.

After becoming a pilot in 1975 Hammond was assigned to posts in Germany, then Arizona, where he trained pilots from foreign countries. He attended the Empire Test Pilot School at Boscombe Down, England, in 1981, then was assigned to Edwards AFB, California, as a test pilot and instructor. He has logged over 2000 hours in 15 American and 10 Royal Air Force aircraft.

As an astronaut Hammond was assigned as a Shuttle capcom beginning with Mission 61-A in October 1985.

He is single.

Hart, Terry

T. J. Hart used the remote manipulator arm of the Shuttle Challenger to latch on to the ailing Solar Max satellite during Shuttle Mission 41-C in April 1984. Hart's "catch" allowed astronauts George Nelson and James van Hoften to make the first satellite repair in space history. Hart redeployed Solar Max in orbit following the repair. The crew of 41-C also deployed the Long Duration Exposure Facility (LDEF), the first satellite designed to be retrieved and returned to Earth at a later date.

Hart logged approximately 168 hours in space.

Terry Jonathan Hart was born October 27, 1946, in Pittsburgh, Pennsylvania, graduating from Mt. Lebanon High School there in 1964. He attended Lehigh University, receiving a BS in mechanical engineering in 1968, and the Massachusetts Institute of Technology, receiving an MS in mechanical engineering in 1969. He later earned an MS in electrical engineering from Rutgers University (1978).

From 1968 to 1978 Hart worked for Bell Telephone Laboratories, designing electronic power equipment for the Bell System and receiving two patents.

He joined the US Air Force Reserve in June 1969 and completed pilot training at Moody AFB, Georgia, in December 1970. For the next three years he was an F-106 interceptor pilot with the Air Defense Command at Tyndall AFB, Florida, Loring AFB, Maine, and Dover AFB, Delaware. He continues to fly with the Air National Guard and has logged over 3000 hours of flying time.

Hart was one of 35 astronauts selected by NASA in January 1978. In August 1979 he completed a training and evaluation course which qualified him as a mission specialist on Shuttle crews. He served on the support crews and as capcom for STS-1, STS-2, STS-3 and STS-7. He was named to the crew for Mission 41-C, then known as STS-13, in February 1983. The crew for the challenging Solar Max rescue was widely regarded as a model team, since it included the most experienced Shuttle commander (Crippen), one of the best pilots of the 1978 group (Scobee), the two best EVA specialists (Nelson and van Hoften) and Hart, who was judged to be highly skilled at using the Shuttle's remote manipulator arm.

On May 15, 1984, shortly after the conclusion of Mission 41-C, Hart resigned from NASA to return to Bell Labs in Whippany, New Jersey, where he is supervisor of the military and space applications group.

Hart and his wife, Wendy, have two daughters, Amy and Lori.

Hartsfield, Henry

Henry Hartsfield has made three flights on the Space Shuttle, two of them as mission commander.

He was pilot of the fourth and last Shuttle orbital test flight, STS-4, in June and July 1982, a mission which carried a Department of Defense payload. He commanded Mission 41-D, the first flight of the Shuttle Discovery in August 1984. An attempted launch on June 26, 1984, had to be aborted on the pad, the first abort in the Shuttle program. Hartsfield also commanded the Mission 61-A/Spacelab Dl flight in October and November 1985.

He has logged 483 hours in space.

Henry Warren Hartsfield, Jr., was born November 21, 1933, in Birmingham, Alabama, and graduated from West End High School there in 1950. He attended Auburn University, where he received a BS in physics in 1954, and later performed graduate work in physics at Duke University and in astronautics at the Air Force Institute of Technology. He received an MS in engineering science from the University of Tennessee in 1971.

An ROTC student at Auburn, Hartsfield began serving with the US Air Force in 1955. He became a pilot and was stationed in Bitburg, Germany, and later at the USAF Test Pilot School at Edwards AFB, California. He was an instructor at the school when assigned in 1966 to the USAF Manned Orbiting Laboratory program. He has logged over 6400 hours of flying time, 5700 in jets.

When the MOL program was canceled in June 1969 Hartsfield transferred to NASA. He was a member of the astronaut support crew for Apollo 16, and for all three Skylab missions. He worked for many years on Space Shuttle development, serving as backup pilot for STS-2 and STS-3. He resigned from the USAF in August 1977 with the rank of colonel.

He is currently assistant chief of the astronaut office.

Hartsfield and his wife, Judy, have two daughters, Judy Lynn and Keely Warren.

Hauck, Frederick

Rick Hauck commanded Shuttle Mission 51-A, the first salvage operation in space history, during which astronauts Joseph Allen and Dale Gardner retrieved two errant communications satellites and stowed them in the payload bay of the Shuttle Discovery for return to Earth. Hauck's crew of five also deployed two new satellites and operated a materials processing experiment. Their eight-day mission ended November 16, 1984, at the Kennedy Space Center.

Earlier, in June 1983, Hauck served as pilot of STS-7 aboard the Shuttle Challenger. STS-7 had the first crew of five in space history, including Sally Ride, America's first woman in space.

Hauck has logged a total of 339 hours in space.

Frederick Hamilton Hauck was born April 11, 1941, in Long Beach, California, but grew up in Winchester, Massachusetts, and Washington, D.C., where his father was a Navy officer. He graduated from St. Albans School in Washington, D.C., in 1958, then attended Tufts University, receiving a BS in physics in 1962. He later earned an MS in nuclear engineering from the Massachusetts Institute of Technology (1966).

Hauck was a Navy ROTC student at Tufts, and was commissioned after graduation, serving for twenty months aboard the destroyer USS Warrington as a communications officer. From 1964 to 1966 he attended the US Naval Postgraduate School, the Defense Language Institute, and MIT, then entered flight school. He received his wings in 1968 and served aboard the carrier USS Coral Sea in Southeast Asia, flying 114 combat and support missions in the A-6.

Returning to the US in 1970, Hauck became an instructor, then attended the US Naval Test Pilot School at Patuxent River, Maryland. He graduated in 1971 and spent three years at Pax River testing, among other things, automatic carrier landing systems for many Navy jets. From 1974 until his selection by NASA he was an operations officer and executive officer for several naval squadrons.

As a pilot Hauck has logged over 4200 hours of flying time.

He was one of the 35 astronauts chosen by NASA in January 1978, and in August 1979 completed a training and evaluation course which qualified him as a Shuttle pilot. He served on the support crew and as capcom for STS-1 and STS-2, and in April 1982 became the first pilot of the 1978 class to be assigned to a flight crew. At the time of the Challenger accident in January 1986, Hauk was assigned to command Mission 61-F, then scheduled for launch that May. When Shuttle launches were suspended, he was appointed associate administrator for external affairs at NASA headquarters in Washington, D.C.

Hauck and his wife, Dolly, have two children, Whitney and Stephen.

Hawley, Steven

Dr. Steven Hawley has made two Shuttle flights, Mission 41-D in 1984 and Mission 61-C in 1986, suffering through five launch delays and the first Shuttle launch pad abort on 41-D, and no less than seven delays on 61-C.

He served as mission specialist and flight engineer for 41-D, the maiden voyage of the Discovery, which was three seconds away from lifting off the pad at the Kennedy Space Center on June 26, 1984, when computers shut down the main engines. Hawley reportedly quipped to veteran commander Henry Hartsfield, "Gee, I thought we'd be higher than this at MECO (main engine cutoff)." Discovery finally lifted off on August 30 with a crew of six, including the first industrial payload specialist, Charles Walker of McDonnell-Douglas. During the seven-day flight the crew deployed three communications satellites and tested an experimental solar power wing. They also used the Shuttle's remote manipulator arm to chip ice off the side of the Discovery, earning themselves the title of "icebusters."

For the seventh attempt to launch Columbia on Mission 61-C on January 12, 1986, Hawley wore a Groucho Marx mask to the launch pad, hoping, he said, to fool Columbia into thinking a different crew was coming aboard. The trick worked; Columbia finally got off the ground, and the astronauts were able to deploy an RCA communications satellite. A special camera designed to observe Halley's Comet failed to work, however.

Hawley has spent 291 hours in space on his two flights.

Steven Alan Hawley was born December 12, 1951, in Ottawa, Kansas, but grew up in Salina, where his father is a minister. He graduated from Salina (Central) High School in 1969, then attended the University of Kansas, where he received a BS in physics and astronomy, with the highest distinction (1973). He received a PhD in astronomy and astrophysics from the University of California at Santa Cruz in 1977.

While completing his schooling Hawley worked summers as a research assistant at the US Naval Observatory in Washington, D.C. (1972), and the National Radio Observatory in Green Bank, Virginia (1973-74). When selected by NASA in 1978 Hawley was a research associate at the Cerro Tololo Inter-American Observatory in La Serena, Chile.

Hawley was one of the 35 astronauts chosen by NASA in January 1978. In August 1979 he completed a training and evaluation course which qualified him as a mission specialist on future Shuttle crews. As an astronaut he served as a simulator pilot for flight software in the Shuttle Avionics Integration Laboratory and as support crew member for STS-2, STS-3 and STS-4.

He has been assigned to be mission specialist for the launch of the Hubble Space Telescope and is also working as technical assistant to George Abbey, the director of flight crew operations.

Hawley is the author of several scientific papers published in astronomical journals and was the subject of an *Esquire* magazine profile in 1985. He is married to astronaut Dr. Sally Ride.

Henize, Karl

Dr. Karl Henize is the oldest person to make a space flight. He was 58 years, 8 months old at the launch of Shuttle Mission 51-F in July 1985.

During 51-F, the long-delayed Spacelab 2 mission, Henize and six other astronauts operated 13 different scientific experiments, most of them in the field of astronomy, Henize's own specialty. Though plagued by a number of problems, including a launch pad abort, Spacelab 2 got results from 12 of the experiments. NASA doctors reported no unusual medical problems for Henize during the seven-day mission, confirming that calendar age had no relevance to travelers on the Shuttle.

Karl Gordon Henize was born October 17, 1926, in Cincinnati, Ohio, graduating from high school in nearby Mariemont. He attended the University of Virginia, receiving a BA in mathematics (1947) and an MA in astronomy (1948). He earned his PhD in astronomy in 1954 from the University of Michigan.

His career as a professional astronomer began in 1948, when he worked as an observer for the University of Michigan at the Lamong-Hussey Observatory in Bloemfontein, Union of South Africa. He returned to the US in 1951, and in 1954 became a Carnegie post-doctoral fellow at Mount Wilson Observatory in Pasadena, California. Two years later he joined the Smithsonian Astrophysical Observatory and began his long involvement with space exploration, establishing a global network of 12 stations for the photographic tracking of artificial Earth satellites.

In 1959 Henize joined the faculty of Northwestern University, where he taught and conducted research on stars and planetary nebulae. He was a guest observer at Mt. Stromlo Observatory in Canberra, Australia, in 1961 and 1962, and developed an ultraviolet stellar spectra experiment which was flown on three manned Gemini flights.

Henize was one of the eleven scientist-astronauts selected by NASA in August 1967. He completed initial academic training, then, at the age of 41, underwent a 53-week jet pilot training program at Vance Air Force Base, Oklahoma. Eventually Henize would log over 2300 hours of flying time in jets.

By 1968 it was apparent to the 1967 class of astronauts that their chances of making space flights in the foreseeable future were slim. Five of them left the program by 1972, and during the long hiatus between the end of Apollo in 1975 and the start of Shuttle missions in 1981, several others took leaves of absence. Henize remained at the Johnson Space Center, however, serving on the astronaut support crew and as capcom for the Apollo 15 lunar landing, and for all three Skylab missions. Another of his scientific experiments was flown on Skylab.

Henize later headed groups developing ultraviolet telescopes for proposed Spacelab missions and, in 1977, served as a mission specialist for the ASSESS II Spacelab simulation. In February 1983 he was officially assigned to the Spacelab 2 crew.

He is the author or co-author of over 70 scientific papers and remains active in the International Astronomical Union.

In April 1986 he left the astronaut group to become a senior scientist in the Space Sciences branch at the NASA Johnson Space Center.

Henize and his wife, Caroline, have four children, Kurt, Marcia, Skye, and Vance.

Henricks, Terence

Major Tom Henricks, USAF, was one of the 13 astronauts selected by NASA in June 1985. In August 1985 he began a yearlong training and evaluation course to qualify him as a pilot on future Shuttle flights.

Terence Thomas Henricks was born July 5, 1952, in Bryan, Ohio, but grew up in Woodville. He graduated from Woodmore High School in Elmore, Ohio, in 1970, then attended the US Air Force Academy, where he received a BS in civil engineering in 1974. He later earned an MS in public administration from Golden Gate University in 1982.

At the Air Force Academy Henricks became a master parachutist, making over 740 jumps as a member of the team which won a national championship. He earned his wings in 1975 and served at bases in England, Iceland, and Nevada before attending the US Air Force Test Pilot School at Edwards AFB, California. He was a test pilot there when selected by NASA.

Henricks has logged over 2000 hours of flying time in 30 different types of aircraft. He also holds an FAA commercial pilot rating.

Henricks and his wife, Kathy, have two children, Katherine and Terence, Jr.

Hieb, Richard

Richard J. Hieb was one of the 13 astronauts selected by NASA in June 1985. In August 1985 he began a year-long training and evaluation course intended to qualify him as a mission specialist on future Shuttle crews.

Hieb was born September 21, 1955, in Jamestown, North Dakota, and graduated from high school there in 1973. He attended Northwest Nazarene College, earning a BA in math and physics in 1977, and the University of Colorado, earning an MS in aerospace engineering in 1979.

In 1979 Hieb joined NASA at the Johnson Space Center, working as a member of the mission control team for the first Shuttle flight, STS-1. He was also involved in satellite deployments on STS-5 and STS-6, and on rendezvous procedures for STS-7, 41-B, 41-C, 51-A and other flights.

Hieb and his wife, Jeannie, live in Houston.

Hilmers, David

David Hilmers was a mission specialist aboard the first flight of the orbiter Atlantis, Shuttle Mission 51-J, in October 1985, which launched two Department of Defense satellites.

He has logged approximately 98 hours in space.

David Carl Hilmers was born January 28, 1950, in Clinton, Iowa, but grew up in DeWitt, Iowa. He graduated from Central Community High in DeWitt in 1968, then attended Cornell College, where he received a BS in mathematics in 1972, graduating summa cum laude. He later studied at the US Naval Postgraduate School, where he received an MS in electrical engineering (with distinction) and the degree of electrical engineer in 1978.

Hilmers joined the US Marine Corps in 1972 and after completing basic training and flight school, was assigned to the Marine Corps Air Station at Cherry Point, North Carolina, then to the 6th Fleet in the Mediterranean, as an A-6 crewman. After graduating first in his class from the Naval Postgraduate School he was stationed in Iwakuni, Japan, where he also taught mathematics for the University of Maryland's overseas branch. Hilmers has co-authored several technical papers, and has logged over 1000 hours flight time in 15 different types of aircraft.

Hilmers was selected as an astronaut candidate by NASA in May 1980 and completed the one-year training and evaluation course in August 1981. He worked on Shuttle upper stages such as the Centaur, the Payload Assist Module, and the Interial Upper Stage, and as Astronaut Office coordinator for Department of Defense payloads. He served as capcom for Shuttle missions between October 1984 and April 1985.

Lieutenant Colonel Hilmers was assigned to Space Shuttle Mission 61-F, scheduled for launch in the summer of 1986 but canceled following the Shuttle Challenger disaster.

He and his wife, Teresa, have two sons, Matthew and Daniel.

Hoffman, Jeffrey

Dr. Jeffrey Hoffman took part in the first unscheduled and unrehearsed space walk in the American space program during Shuttle Mission 51-D in April 1985. Mission specialist Hoffman and fellow astronaut David Griggs donned space suits and left the cabin of the Shuttle Discovery in order to attach a makeshift "flyswatter" to the end of the remote manipulator arm. The flyswatter was later used in an unsuccessful attempt to activate the ailing Syncom IV-3 satellite, which had earlier been deployed from the Shuttle. Hoffman spent 148 hours in space, including 3 hours, 40 minutes in EVA.

Jeffrey Alan Hoffman was born November 2, 1944, in Brooklyn, New York, but grew up in Scarsdale, where he graduated from high school in 1962. He attended Amherst College, where he received a BS in astronomy (graduating summa cum laude) in 1966. He received his PhD in astrophysics from Harvard University in 1971.

As a post-doctoral fellow at Leicester University in England from 1972-75, Hoffman worked on scientific packages for three rocket payloads, all of them relating to X-ray astronomy, his field of study. He was also project scientist for an X-ray experiment flown on the European Space Agency's Exosat satellite.

Returning to the US in 1975, he joined the Center for Space Research at the Massachusetts Institute of Technology as project scientist for X-ray and gamma-ray experiments for the first High Energy Astronomical Observatory (HEAO-1) satellite launched in August 1977. He was at MIT when chosen by NASA.

Hoffman was one of 35 astronauts selected by NASA in January 1978. In August 1979 he completed a training and evaluation course which qualified him as a Shuttle mission specialist, then worked for the next two years on Shuttle guidance, navigation and control systems at the Flight Simulation Laboratory in Downey, California. He later served as support crewman for STS-5 and capcom for STS-8.

He trained as a mission specialist for the Astro 1 Spacelab scheduled to observe Halley's Comet in March 1986, but that flight was canceled following the explosion of the Shuttle Challenger.

Hoffman is the author or co-author of more than 20 papers on X-ray astronomy.

He and his wife, Barbara, have two children, Samuel and Orin.

Holmquest, Donald

Dr. Donald Holmquest was one of 11 scientist-astronauts chosen by NASA in August 1967. These astronauts arrived in Houston just as a series of Congressional budget cuts wiped out most of the planned Apollo Applications missions, the flights for which they were to train. They dubbed themselves the XS-11 (excess eleven) and only seven of the group ever flew in space.

Donald Lee Holmquest was born April 7, 1939, in Dallas, Texas. He received a BS degree in electrical engineering from Southern Methodist University in 1962 and an MD degree from Baylor College of Medicine just prior to his selection as an astronaut.

Holmquest was a research associate at the Massachusetts Institute of Technology from 1962 to 1966 and was serving an internship at Methodist Hospital in Dallas when selected for astronaut training. During his first months at NASA he completed work on a PhD in physiology. In 1968 he underwent pilot training at Williams AFB, Arizona, eventually logging 750 hours of flying time. He was then assigned to the Skylab program, where he worked on medical experiments and habitability systems.

He took a leave from NASA in May 1971 to become an associate professor of radiology and physiology at Baylor, and resigned from NASA in September 1973 to become associate dean of the medical school at Texas A&M. He currently practices at the Nuclear Medicine Laboratory in Navasota, Texas.

He is married to Dr. Ann Nixon James and has one child by a previous marriage.

Irwin, James

James Irwin spent almost three days on the Moon in 1971 as lunar module pilot of Apollo 15. While Alfred Worden orbited overhead in the command module Endeavour, Irwin and commander David Scott landed the LM Falcon at Hadley Rille near the lunar Apennines, becoming the seventh and eighth persons to walk on the Moon. They were the first astronauts to use the lunar rover, a specially designed electric car, which carried them a total of 18 miles during three excursions.

Irwin logged a total of 295 hours in space during the flight of Apollo 15, including 19 hours and 46 minutes of lunar EVA.

James Benson Irwin was born March 17, 1930, in Pittsburgh, Pennsylvania, but grew up in New Port, Richy and Orlando, Florida; Roseburg, Oregon; and Salt Lake City, Utah. He graduated from East High School in Salt Lake City, then attended the US Naval Academy at

Annapolis, where he received a BS in 1951. In 1957 he earned an MS in aeronautical engineering and instrumentation engineering from the University of Michigan.

He elected to serve in the US Air Force and received flight training at Hondo AFB and Reese AFB in Texas. He served as a fighter pilot and, following graduate school at Michigan, attended the USAF Experimental Flight Test School (1961) and the Aerospace Research Pilots School (1963) at Edwards AFB, California. He went on to test the F-12 aircraft, forerunner of the SR-71 Blackbird spy plane, at Edwards. At the time of his selection by NASA he was chief of the advanced requirements branch at Headquarters Air Defense Command in Colorado Springs.

Irwin applied to be an astronaut in 1963 but was not selected because he was still recovering from injuries received in a 1961 plane crash. He was one of 19 astronauts selected by NASA in April 1966. Following basic training, he specialized in Apollo lunar module systems, commanding the two-man Lunar Test Article (LTA)-8 team which tested the lunar module in June 1968. He served on the support crew for Apollo 10 and was backup lunar module pilot for Apollo 12.

In August 1971 Irwin, along with Worden and Scott, was assigned to backup Apollo 17, the last lunar landing mission. But an investigation into the sale of stamps and envelopes carried to the Moon by the Apollo 15 crew led to a NASA reprimand, and to their removal from active astronaut training in May 1972. Now an Air Force colonel, Irwin retired from the USAF and resigned from NASA on July 1, 1972, to found the High Flight Foundation, a non-profit organization which allows him to share his faith in God through speaking engagements, retreats and other activities.

Irwin has published an autobiography, *To Rule the Night*, (1973), which discusses his astronaut career and the spiritual revelation he experienced while walking on the Moon.

Among his activities with High Flight, Irwin has lead five expeditions to Mount Ararat in Turkey, searching for the remains of Noah's Ark.

Irwin and his wife, Mary Ellen, have five children, Joy, Jill, James, Jan and Joe. They live in Colorado Springs, Colorado.

Ivins, Marsha

Marsha S. Ivins was one of the 17 astronauts selected by NASA in May 1984. In June 1985 she completed a training and evaluation course that qualified her as a mission specialist on future Shuttle flights.

Ivins was born April 15, 1951, in Baltimore, Maryland, and graduated from Nether Providence High School in Wallingford, Pennsylvania, in 1969. She attended the University of Colorado, receiving a BS in aerospace engineering in 1973.

Ivins went to work for NASA at the Johnson Space Center in 1974, first as an engineer working on Space Shuttle orbiter cockpit displays, later as a flight simulation and test engineer aboard the specially modified Gulfstream I known as the Shuttle Training Aircraft. She has logged 1200 hours in the STA and, as the holder of a transport pilot license, single engine airplane, and glider ratings, 3200 hours as a private pilot.

After completing her astronaut training and evaluation course in June 1985 Ivins was assigned to the support crew for Shuttle orbiter checkout.

She is unmarried.

Jernigan, Tamara

Tamara E. Jernigan is one of the 13 astronauts selected by NASA in June 1985. In August 1985 she began a training and evaluation course intended to qualify her as a mission specialist on future Shuttle crews.

Jernigan was born May 7, 1959, in Chattanooga, Tennessee, but grew up in southern California, graduating from high school in Santa Fe Springs in 1977. She attended Stanford University, receiving a BS in physics (with honors) in 1981 and an MS in engineering science in 1983. She earned an MS in astronomy from the University of California at Berkeley in 1985.

From June 1981 until her selection as an astronaut, while continuing her studies at Stanford and Berkeley, Jernigan worked for the NASA Ames Research Center at Moffet Field, California. Her field of research there is astrophysics and she is pursuing a PhD at Berkeley in that area as well.

Jernigan is single.

Kerwin, Joseph

Dr. Joseph Kerwin was the first American physician to make a space flight, and the first doctor to perform in-orbit medical research during a long duration mission.

As science pilot of Skylab 2 (SL-2), Kerwin spent 28 days aboard Skylab as a member of the first crew to board the station. Kerwin and fellow astronauts Charles Conrad and Paul Weitz had to repair the station, which had been badly damaged during its launch on May 14, 1973, before they could begin their scientific work. In spite of the delay, the crew completed eighty percent of its original program. Dr. Kerwin, monitoring his physical condition and that of Conrad and Weitz, found no medical reason to prevent longer Skylab missions.

Kerwin logged approximately 673 hours in space during Skylab 2, his only flight, including 3.5 hours of EVA.

Joseph Peter Kerwin was born February 19, 1932, in Oak Park, Illinois, and graduated from Fenwick High School there in 1949. He attended the College of the Holy Cross in Worcester, Massachusetts, receiving a BA in philosophy, then entered Northwestern University Medical School in Chicago. He received his MD in 1957 and the following year completed his internship at the District of Columbia General Hospital in Washington, D.C. In December 1958 he graduated from the US Navy School of Aviation Medicine at Pensacola, Florida, and was designated a naval flight surgeon.

He served as a medical officer at the Marine Corps Air Station at Cherry Point, North Carolina, from 1959 to 1961, then underwent pilot training in Florida and Texas, winning his wings in 1962. At the time of his selection by NASA Kerwin was on the medical staff of Attack Carrier Wing 4 at Jacksonville, Florida.

As a pilot he has logged over 4200 hours of flying time, including 3000 hours in jets.

Kerwin was one of the first six scientist-astronauts selected by NASA in June 1965. Following preliminary academic and survival training he began working on the Apollo and Apollo Applications (later Skylab) programs. He was involved in the design and development of biological insulation garments to be worn by astronauts returning from flights to the Moon, and also worked on the lunar receiving laboratory at the space center. In June 1968 Kerwin commanded an eight-day simulated Apollo mission intended to qualify the re-designed command module for manned flights. He also served as capcom for Apollo 13 prior to being named to a Skylab crew in January 1972.

In January 1974, as Skylab was drawing to a close, Kerwin was named director of life sciences for the astronaut office, a position he held for three years. At the same time he became involved in the development of the Space Shuttle, concentrating on the design of the crew station, controls, and medical monitoring. He also participated in the study group which produced the *Outlook for Space: 1980-2000* report (1975).

Beginning in 1978, when new scientist-astronauts, now known as mission specialists, were accepted into the astronaut program, Kerwin took part in their selection and served as their first boss. He was also in charge of planning operational Shuttle missions, including astronaut duties in rendezvous, satellite deployment and retrieval, and operation of the remote manipulator arm. He was an early candidate to serve as mission specialist for the Solar Max rescue (Mission 41-C), but in April 1982, before the crew could be chosen, was named to be NASA's senior science representative in Australia. He returned to the Johnson Space Center in January 1984 and became director of space and life sciences. He is still an active astronaut and is a candidate for assignment to a future Shuttle crew.

Captain Kerwin and his wife, Shirley, have two daughters, Sharon and Kristina.

Lee, Mark

Major Mark C. Lee, USAF, is one of the 17 astronauts selected by NASA in May 1984. In June 1985 he completed a training and evaluation course that qualified him as a Shuttle mission specialist.

Mark Lee was born August 14, 1952, in Viroqua, Wisconsin, graduating from high school there in 1970. He attended the US Air Force Academy at Colorado Springs, earning a BS in civil engineering in 1974. He earned an MS in mechanical engineering from the Massachusetts Institute of Technology in 1980.

Lee underwent pilot training in Texas and Arizona, then spent two-and-a-half years flying F-4s on Okinawa. After further schooling at MIT in 1979 and 1980, he was assigned to the Airborne Warning and Control System (AWACS) program office at Hanscom AFB, Massachusetts. In 1982 he became an F-16 pilot and flight commander at Hill AFB, Utah, where he was stationed when selected by NASA.

He has logged over 1500 hours of flying time.

In June 1985 Lee, an EVA specialist, was assigned as mission specialist for a Shuttle flight originally scheduled for 1986.

Lee is married to the former Diedre Ann O'Brien.

Leestma, David

David Leestma, together with Kathryn Sullivan, America's first woman spacewalker, made a 3.5-hour EVA during Shuttle Mission 41-G in October 1984, demonstrating refueling techniques for satellites. The seven-person crew of 41-G, the largest sent into space at that time, also deployed a scientific satellite and conducted Earth observations during a 198-hour flight.

Leestma was later assigned as mission specialist for Spacelab Astro intended to observe Halley's Comet in March 1986. That mission, 61-E, was canceled following the explosion of the Shuttle Challenger. Leestma's third crew assignment, to a Department of Defense mission scheduled for September 1986, was also canceled.

David Cornell Leestma was born May 6, 1949, in Muskegon, Michigan, but graduated from high school in Tustin, California, in 1967. He attended the US Naval Academy, earning a BS in aeronautical engineering in 1971 and standing first in his class. He later received an MS in aeronautical engineering from the US Naval Postgraduate School (1972).

After a brief tour as an ensign aboard the USS Hepburn and further school at the Naval Posgraduate School, Leestma underwent pilot training, receiving his wings in October 1973. For the next three years he served with Squadron 32 in Virginia Beach, Virginia, making three deployments overseas aboard the carrier USS John F. Kennedy. In 1977 he was assigned to Air Test and Evaluation Squadron 4 at Point Mugu, California, where he tested new computer software for the F-14A.

As a pilot he has logged approximately 2000 hours of flying time.

Leestma was one of the 19 astronauts selected by NASA in May 1980. In August 1981 he completed a training and evaluation course qualifying him as a mission specialist on Shuttle crews. In August 1983 he became the first member of his astronaut group to be assigned to a flight crew.

Commander Leestma and his wife, Patti, have three children, Benjamin, Katie and Emily.

Lenoir, William

Dr. William Lenoir was a mission specialist on STS-5, the first operational Shuttle flight, in November 1982. Lenoir and fellow mission specialist Joseph Allen deployed two communications satellites from the Columbia in the first demonstration of the Shuttle's value as a "space truck." A planned spacewalk by Lenoir and Allen had to be scrubbed because of mechanical failures in their EVA pressure suits.

Lenoir logged 122 hours in space.

William Benjamin Lenoir was born March 14, 1939, in Miami, Florida, and grew up in Coral Gables. He attended the Massachusetts Institute of Technology, where he received a BS in electrical engineering in 1961, followed by his MS (1962) and PhD (1965) in electrical engineering.

While working on his doctorate, Lenoir was an instructor at MIT. In 1965 he became assistant professor of electrical engineering and developed experiments for satellites until chosen by NASA.

Lenoir was one of the 11 scientist-astronauts selected by NASA in August 1967. After several months of initial academic training, he completed a 53-week flight school at Laughlin AFB, Texas. Eventually he would log over 3200 hours of flying time in jet aircraft.

As an astronaut Lenoir worked on the design and development of Skylab. He served as backup science pilot for the Skylab 3 and Skylab 4 missions in 1973-74, and was capcom for Skylab 4, primarily for solar science observations. From September 1974 to July 1976 Lenoir devoted much of his time to the NASA Satellite Power Team, which was investigating the possibility of adapting space power systems for use on Earth. From 1976 on he was heavily involved in Shuttle development, especially in the area of payload deployment and retrieval and EVA.

After STS-5 Lenoir held a planning job until resigning from NASA in September 1984. He is employed by the management and technology consulting firm of Booz, Allen & Hamilton, Inc., in Arlington, Virginia.

Lenoir and his wife, Elizabeth, have two children, William Jr., and Samantha.

Lind, Don

Dr. Don Lind holds the unwanted record for the longest wait between commencing astronaut training and making a flight into space. Chosen by NASA as one of 19 astronauts in April 1966, Lind did not fly in space until April 1985, 19 years later.

During his first flight, Mission 51-B/Spacelab 3, Lind was part of a seven-man crew that performed experiments in materials processing and space medicine. Lind himself had developed one of the experiments aboard, a means of making three-dimensional recordings of the Earth's aurora. The Spacelab 3 mission was notable for problems with several monkeys that were carried aboard, and for the fact that three of its astronauts (Lind, Thornton and van den Berg) were over 50 years old.

Lind has logged approximately 177 hours in space.

Don Leslie Lind was born May 18, 1930, in Midvale, Utah, where he grew up. He graduated from Jordan High School in Sandy, Utah, then attended the University of Utah, receiving a BS (with high honors) in physics in 1953. He earned his PhD in high energy nuclear physics in 1964 from the University of California at Berkeley. He later performed post-doctoral work at the University of Alaska's Geophysical Institute in 1975-76.

Lind served with the US Navy from 1954 to 1957, earning his pilot's wings in 1955 and becoming a carrier pilot flying from the USS Hancock. From 1957 to 1964, while working on his doctorate, he was employed at the Lawrence Radiation Laboratory in Berkeley, and in the two years prior to his selection as an astronaut was employed by NASA's Goddard Space Flight Center in Maryland as a space physicist.

As an astronaut Lind trained initially as an Apollo lunar module pilot and might have made a landing on the Moon, but budget cuts canceled the later Apollo missions and in 1969 he was transferred to the Apollo Applications group, later known as Skylab. He served as backup pilot for Skylab 3 and Skylab 4, the second and third manned Skylab visits, and in 1973 trained briefly as pilot of a Skylab "rescue" crew. Following his leave of absence in 1975 and 1976, Lind returned to the astronaut office and assisted in the development of payloads for the first four Shuttle flights. He was assigned to Spacelab 3 in February 1983.

An inspirational biography of Lind, *Don Lind: Mormon Astronaut*, written by his wife, Kathleen, was published in 1985.

In 1986 Lind resigned from NASA to join the faculty of Utah State University.

Lind and his wife have seven children: Carol Ann (who designed the Spacelab 3 mission patch), David, Dawna, Douglas, Kimberly, Lisa and Daniel.

Llewellyn, John

Welsh-born Dr. John Anthony Llewellyn was one of the first naturalized American citizens to become an astronaut when he was selected in August 1967. Unfortunately, neither Llewellyn nor fellow immigrant Phillip Chapman flew in space. Llewellyn resigned from the space program in August 1968 because he was unable to become a qualified jet pilot.

Llewellyn was born April 22, 1933, in Cardiff, Wales, and received a BS in chemistry from University College there in 1955 and a doctorate

in chemistry from the same university in 1958. He became a United States citizen on February 17, 1966.

Llewellyn was a chemist at the National Research Council of Canada from 1958 to 1960, then an associate professor at Florida State University until joining NASA. Since leaving the space program Llewellyn has taught at Florida State (where one of his students was future Spacelab 3 backup payload specialist Mary Helen Johnston) and the University of South Florida, and is currently a professor of chemistry at the University of Florida in Tallahassee.

He and his wife, Valerie, have three children.

Lounge, John

Mike Lounge was one of five astronauts in the crew of Shuttle Mission 51-I in August and September 1985. During 51-I, Lounge served as mission specialist and flight engineer, deploying the Australian Aussat communications satellite and operating the Shuttle Discovery's remote manipulator arm to assist astronauts William Fisher and James van Hoften in the retrieval and repair of the Syncom IV-3 satellite.

He has logged approximately 170 hours in space.

John Michael Lounge was born June 28, 1946, in Denver, Colorado, but grew up in Burlington, where he graduated from high school in 1964. He attended the US Naval Academy, receiving a BS in physics and mathematics in 1969, and later earned an MS in astrogeophysics from the University of Colorado (1970).

Following graduation from Annapolis, Lounge underwent flight officer training at Pensacola, Florida, becoming a radar intercept officer in F-4J Phantoms. Assigned to the carrier USS Enterprise, he took part in 99 combat missions in Southeast Asia. He later did a tour of duty aboard the USS America in the Mediterranean.

Lounge returned to the US in 1974 and became an instructor in physics at the US Naval Academy. Two years later he transferred to the US Navy Space Project Office in Washington, D.C. He resigned from the Navy in 1978 to become a NASA engineer at the Johnson Space Center, working on payload integration.

A lieutenant colonel in the Air Force Reserve, he continues to fly in F-4C aircraft as a weapons systems operator.

Lounge was selected as an astronaut in May 1980 and completed a training and evaluation course in August 1981. While an astronaut he served as a member of the launch support team at the Kennedy Space Center for STS-1, STS-2 and STS-3. His main technical assignment has been the Shuttle's computer system. He was named to his first Shuttle crew in August 1983 and following that flight was assigned to Mission 61-F, the launch of the Galileo Jupiter probe, which had to be postponed following the explosion of the Shuttle Challenger in January 1986.

Lounge is married to Kathryn Anne Havens, a training engineer at the Johnson Space Center. They have three children, Shannon, Kenneth and Kathy.

Lousma, Jack

Jack Lousma commanded the third orbital test flight of the Space Shuttle Columbia, STS-3, in March 1982. He and pilot Gordon Fullerton spent eight days in space testing Shuttle systems and the remote manipulator arm. They were the first Shuttle astronauts to land at

White Sands Missile Range, New Mexico, thanks to a storm that soaked the so-called dry lakebed at their primary landing site, Edwards Air Force Base in California.

Lousma was also pilot of Skylab 3, the second manned Skylab mission, in July, August and September 1973, spending over 59 days aboard the orbiting laboratory performing medical experiments, Earth resources studies, and astronomical observations. He also made two space walks.

He has spent over 67 days in space, including over 11 hours of EVA time.

Jack Robert Lousma was born February 29, 1936, in Grand Rapids, Michigan, but grew up in Ann Arbor. He attended the University of Michigan, receiving a BS in aeronautical engineering in 1959. He later earned the degree of aeronautical engineer from the US Naval Postgraduate School in 1965.

He joined the US Marine Corps in 1959 and completed pilot training the following year. He served with the 22nd Marine Air Wing as an attack pilot, and with the lst Marine Air Wing at Iwakuni, Japan. At the time of his selection by NASA he was a reconaissance pilot with the 2nd Marine Air Wing at Cherry Point, North Carolina.

As a pilot he has logged almost 5000 hours of flying time, 4500 hours in jets and 240 hours in helicopters.

Lousma was one of the 19 astronauts selected by NASA in April 1966. During his early training he specialized in the Apollo lunar module and served on support crews for Apollo 9, Apollo 10 and Apollo 13. In early 1970 he was informally assigned as lunar module pilot for Apollo 20 when that mission was canceled because of NASA budget cuts. Lousma transferred to the Skylab program and was named pilot of the second mission in January 1972. He also served as backup pilot for the Apollo-Soyuz Test Project.

Assigned to Space Shuttle development in 1976, Lousma was first named pilot of STS-3 in March 1978, only to be promoted to commander the following August after the resignation of Fred Haise.

Colonel Lousma resigned from NASA on October 1, 1983, and retired from the Marine Corps on November 1 that same year. He was an unsuccessful candidate for the US Senate from Michigan in 1984, and is currently president of his own high technology consulting firm based in Ann Arbor, Michigan.

Lousma and his wife, the former Gratia Kay Smeltzer, have four children, Timothy, Matthew, Mary and Joseph.

Lovell, James

James Lovell was the first astronaut to make four space flights. In December 1965 he was pilot of Gemini 7, spending 14 days in space, a record at the time, and the following November commanded Gemini 12, the last Gemini mission. In December 1968 he was command module pilot of Apollo 8, man's first flight around the Moon, and in April 1970 commanded Apollo 13, a planned lunar landing that had to be aborted because of an explosion aboard the Apollo service module. Lovell and astronauts Swigert and Haise turned their lunar module into a lifeboat and returned safely to Earth.

Lovell has spent almost thirty days in space.

James Arthur Lovell, Jr., was born March 25, 1928, in Cleveland, Ohio. He attended the University of Wisconsin for two years, then entered the US Naval Academy at Annapolis, graduating in 1952 with a BS degree. He later attended Harvard Business School (1971).

Lovell received flight training following graduation from Annapolis and served at a number of navy bases until entering the US Naval Test Pilot School at Patuxent River, Maryland, in 1958. During a four-year tour of duty at Pax River, Lovell was program manager for the F-4H Phantom. He was safety engineer for Fighter Squadron 101 at the Naval Air Station in Oceana, Virginia, when selected by NASA.

As a pilot Lovell eventually logged over 5000 hours of flying time, 3500 hours in jet aircraft.

One of the nine NASA astronauts chosen in September 1962, Lovell was first assigned as backup pilot for Gemini 4. In January 1966, after returning from Gemini 7, he was named backup commander for Gemini 10, a job generally thought to be a dead end. Under the NASA rotation system, Lovell could have expected to command Gemini 13, but the Gemini program ended with flight number 12. Lovell's continued involvement with Gemini would keep him from being named to the early Apollo flights.

But on February 28, 1966, Gemini 9 astronauts Elliott See and Charles Bassett were killed in a plane crash at St. Louis. In the subsequent shuffle of crew assignments, Lovell and pilot Buzz Aldrin moved from the Gemini 10 backup job to Gemini 9, and were later assigned to Gemini 12. A year after Gemini 12, in the wake of the tragic Apollo fire, Lovell was assigned with Neil Armstrong and Aldrin to the backup crew for what eventually became Apollo 8. In July 1968 Lovell was promoted to the prime crew, replacing Michael Collins. This sequence of events made it possible for Lovell to become one of the first humans to fly around the Moon, but cost him his participation in the first lunar landing.

A similar mix of good and back luck placed Lovell on Apollo 13. As backup commander of Apollo 11 he was in line to command Apollo 14. But an attempt by flight crew chief Deke Slayton to name Mercury astronaut Alan Shepard, recently returned to flight status, to Apollo 13, was blocked by NASA management, who thought Shepard needed more training. In August 1969 Lovell was asked if he and his crew could be ready in time to fly Apollo 13 eight months later. Lovell said they could and got the job.

Following Apollo 13 and a leave to attend Harvard, Lovell was named deputy director for science and applications at the Johnson Space Center in May 1971. On March 1, 1973, he retired from the Navy as a captain and resigned from NASA to join the Bay-Houston Towing Company, eventually becoming president and chief executive officer of the company.

In January 1977 Lovell left Bay-Houston to become president of Fisk Telephone Systems in Houston, and since January 1981 he has been group vice president of the Centel Corporation's business communications group in Chicago, Ill.

Lovell and his wife, Marilyn, have four children, Barbara, James, Susan and Jeffrey.

Low, David

David Low is one of the 13 astronaut candidates selected by NASA in May 1984. In June 1985 he completed a training and evaluation course which qualified him as a mission specialist on future Shuttle crews.

George David Low was born February 19, 1956, in Cleveland, Ohio, but graduated from high school in Langley, Virginia, in 1974. His father, George Low, was a high-ranking NASA administrator for many years. David attended Washington & Lee University, receiving a BS in physics-engineering in 1978. He later earned a second BS, this one in mechanical engineering from Cornell University, in 1980, and an MS in aeronautics and astronautics from Stanford University in 1983.

From March 1980 until being chosen as an astronaut in 1984, Low worked at the NASA Jet Propulsion Laboratory in Pasadena, California, as a spacecraft systems engineer involved in the Galileo space probe and the Mars Geoscience/Climatology Observer project.

He is single.

Lucid, Shannon

Dr. Shannon Lucid was a mission specialist aboard Shuttle Mission 51-G in June 1985. On this flight of the Discovery the seven-astronaut crew, which included Prince Sultan Salman al-Saud of Saudi Arabia and Patrick Baudry of France, deployed three communications satellites and the Spartan scientific satellite, which was later retrieved.

Lucid has logged approximately 170 hours in space.

Shannon Wells Lucid was born January 14, 1943, in Shanghai, China, but grew up in Bethany, Oklahoma, where she graduated from high school in 1960. She received a BS in chemistry from the University of Oklahoma in 1963, and an MS and PhD in biochemistry from the same school in 1970 and 1973.

While working for her doctorate Lucid held a variety of jobs: teaching assistant at the University of Oklahoma Department of Chemistry (1963-64), senior lab technician at the Oklahoma Medical Research Foundation (1964-66), chemist at Kerr-McGee (1966-68), and graduate assistant at the University of Oklahoma Health Science Center's Department of Biochemistry and Molecular Biology (1969-73). When chosen by NASA she was a research associate with the Oklahoma Medical Research Foundation, a position she had held since 1974.

Lucid was one of the 35 astronauts selected by NASA in January 1978. In August 1979 she completed a training and evaluation course that qualified her as a mission specialist on future Shuttle crews. As an astronaut she worked in the Shuttle Avionics Integration Laboratory (SAIL) and in the testing of payloads. Since August 1985 she has been a mission control capcom for Shuttle flights.

Lucid and her husband, Michael, have three children, Kawai, Shandara, and Michael.

McBride, Jon

Jon McBride served as pilot for Shuttle Mission 41-G in October 1984, the first seven-person crew in space. During 41-G the Earth Radiation Budget Satellite was deployed, Earth observations were conducted with the Shuttle Imaging Radar, and spacewalking astronauts conducted a satellite refueling experiment.

McBride was scheduled to command a Spacelab flight intended to observe Halley's Comet in March 1986, but that mission, 61-E, was

canceled because of the explosion of the Shuttle Challenger on January 28, 1986. He is likely to command an early mission following resumption of Shuttle launches in 1988.

He has spent approximately 197 hours in space.

Jon Andrew McBride was born August 14, 1943, in Charleston, West Virginia, but grew up in Beckley, where he graduated from high school in 1960. He received a BS in aeronautical engineering from the US Naval Postgraduate School in 1971. He has also performed graduate work in human resources managment at Pepperdine University.

McBride joined the Navy in 1965 and underwent pilot training at Pensacola, Florida, winning his wings in 1966. He served with Fighter Squadron 101 in Oceana, Virginia, then with Fighter Squadron 41. He also flew 64 combat missions in Vietnam.

Following attendance at the Naval Postgraduate School and another tour as a fighter pilot, McBride entered the Air Force Test Pilot School at Edwards AFB, California, graduating with future astronauts Guy Gardner, Loren Shriver and Steven Nagel in class 75-A. He was a test pilot with Air Test and Development Squadron 4 at Pt. Mugu, California, when selected by NASA.

As a pilot McBride has logged over 4500 hours of flying time, including 4000 hours in jets, in over 40 types of military and civilian aircraft. Between 1976 and 1978 he also flew the Navy "Spirit of '76" Bicentennial-painted F-4J Phantom at various air shows.

McBride was one of the 35 astronauts chosen by NASA in January 1978. In August 1979 he completed a training and evaluation course which qualified him as a Shuttle pilot. He was lead chase pilot for the first landing of Columbia (STS-1) and served as capcom for STS-5, STS-6 and STS-7.

He is the divorced father of three children, Richard, Melissa, and Jon.

McCandless, Bruce

Bruce McCandless is the first person to make an untethered space walk. On February 8, 1984, he donned a manned maneuvering unit (MMU), the so-called Buck Rogers backpack he had helped develop, and, disconnecting his safety line, flew 320 feet away from the Shuttle Challenger. As he fired the MMU's thrusters and backed away from the Challenger, McCandless said, "That may have been one small step for Neil (Armstrong), but it's a heck of a big leap for me." (In July 1969 McCandless had been the astronaut capcom on duty during the first walk on the Moon.) For almost six hours McCandless and fellow astronaut Robert Stewart tested the MMU. Two days later they performed a second EVA, rehearsing techniques for retrieving and repairing satellites with the MMU.

The tests of the MMU by McCandless and Stewart were highlights of a Shuttle mission plagued by the failure of two satellite rocket motors (which left the Palapa B-2 and Westar VI satellites in useless orbits), and the explosion of a balloon deployed from the Challenger to serve as a rendezvous target. Mission 41-B was the first Shuttle to land at the Kennedy Space Center, becoming the first manned spacecraft to end a mission at its launch site.

McCandless has spent 191 hours in space, including over 12 hours of EVA time.

The son and grandson of Navy officers, Bruce McCandless II was born June 8, 1937, in Boston, Massachusetts. After graduating from Woodrow Wilson Senior High School in Long Beach, California, he entered the US Naval Academy at Annapolis, receiving a BS in science in 1958 and standing second in a class of 899. He later earned an MS in electrical engineering from Stanford University in 1965 and performed work toward a PhD in that subject.

McCandless underwent pilot training at Pensacola, Florida, and Kingsville, Texas, earning his wings in March 1960. For the next four years he served as an F-6A Skyray and F-4B Phantom II pilot aboard the carriers USS Forrestal and USS Enterprise. He took part in the Cuban blockade in October 1962. He later did a tour as a flight instructor at the naval air station in Oceana, Virginia, then reported to Stanford University for graduate school.

As a pilot McCandless has logged over 4500 hours of flying time, including almost 4000 hours in jets. In addition to Navy jets and the T-38A used by NASA, he has also flown helicopters.

McCandless was one of the 19 astronauts selected by NASA in April 1966. He served as capcom for Apollo 10, Apollo 11 and Apollo 14 and was also a member of the support crew for the latter. In 1971 he began to work on the Skylab program, becoming co-investigator for the M-509 astronaut maneuvering unit (AMU), an earlier version of the Shuttle MMU. He was backup pilot for Skylab 2 and capcom for Skylab 3.

Between 1974 and 1983 McCandless worked on projects relating to the Space Shuttle, including the inertial upper stage (IUS), the Space Telescope, and the Solar Maximum Repair mission, in addition to his involvement with the MMU. In February 1983, following a wait of almost 17 years, he was assigned to his first flight crew, STS-11, later known as Mission 41-B. Following 41-B he was named as a mission specialist for the launch of the Hubble Space Telescope, originally scheduled for September 1985, but postponed in the aftermath of the Challenger explosion.

Captain McCandless and his wife, Bernice, have two children, Bruce III and Tracy.

McCulley, Michael

Commander Michael J. McCulley, USN, is one of the 17 astronauts selected by NASA in May 1984. In June 1985 he completed a training and evaluation course which qualified him as a pilot on future Shuttle crews.

In November 1985 he was assigned as pilot for a Department of Defense Shuttle mission then scheduled for 1986.

McCulley was born August 4, 1943, in San Diego, California, but grew up in Livingston, Tennessee. He graduated from Livingston Academy in 1961. He earned a BS and MS in metallurgical engineering from Purdue University in 1970.

He joined the US Navy right out of high school and served aboard submarines. In 1965 he entered Purdue, earning his officer's commission in 1970, the same year he earned both college degrees. He became a pilot and flew A-4 and A-6 aircraft from carriers until being assigned to the Empire Test Pilot School at Farnborough, England. He was a test pilot at the Naval Air Test Center at Patuxent River, Maryland, for several years. When chosen by NASA he was operations officer for Attack Squadron 35 aboard the carrier USS Nimitz.

McCulley has logged over 4000 hours of flying time, including 400 carrier landings on six different carriers, in 40 different types of aircraft.

He and his wife, Jane, have four children.

McDivitt, James

James McDivitt was command pilot of Gemini 4, the second manned Gemini mission, during which pilot Edward White became the first American to walk in space. McDivitt kidded White during the 20-minute EVA ("You smeared up my windshield, you dirty dog!") and took the now-famous photographs of his fellow astronaut floating at the end of his gold tether. Gemini 4 also set an American space endurance record by remaining in orbit slightly over four days.

In March 1969 McDivitt commanded Apollo 9, the first manned test of the Apollo lunar module, whose development and construction he had helped oversee. It was a vital step toward the first manned lunar landing, accomplished four months later.

McDivitt logged approximately 339 hours in space.

James Alton McDivitt was born June 10, 1929, in Chicago, Illinois, but grew up in Kalamazoo, Michigan, where he graduated from high school. Following high school he worked for a year as a water boiler repairman and took classes at Jackson Junior College in Jackson, Michigan. He later attended the University of Michigan, earning a BS in aeronautical engineering in 1959 and graduating first in his class.

McDivitt joined the US Air Force in 1951 and, after pilot training, flew F-80s and F-86s on 145 combat missions in Korea. Returning to the US, he remained in the Air Force, attending the University of Michigan, the USAF Experimental Test Pilot School, and the USAF Aerospace Research Pilot School. When selected by NASA he was a test pilot at Edwards AFB.

Dr. Ron McNair was one of the seven space travelers killed in the explosion of the Shuttle Challenger on January 28, 1986. During the planned six-day flight, mission specialist McNair was to have operated
1962 and quickly established himself as a first class pilot and a thorough engineer. NASA managers obviously agreed: just two years after joining the space program, McDivitt was chosen to command the complex Gemini 4 mission. He is the only American astronaut to command a mission without ever having served an "apprenticeship" on a backup or support crew. In fact, except for several months in 1966, when he worked as backup to Gus Grissom for the first manned Apollo mission, McDivitt spent his astronaut career training as commander of a prime crew.

In May 1969 McDivitt became NASA manager of lunar landing operations, directing the final months of the effort to land a man on the Moon. Following the triumph of Apollo 11, in August 1969, McDivitt was named manager of the entire Apollo spacecraft program, a job he held until June 1972. He was also promoted to the rank of brigadier general, USAF.

McDivitt retired from the Air Force and resigned from NASA in August 1972 to join Consumers Power Company as vice president for corporate affairs. In March 1975 he joined Pullman, Inc., of Chicago, America's largest builder of railroad cars, as president.

Since January 1981 he has worked for Rockwell International Corporation, builders of the Space Shuttle, where he is currently executive vice president for Defense Electronics Operations.

McDivitt is the divorced father of four children, Michael, Ann, Patrick and Kathleen. He lives in Anaheim, California.

McNair, Ronald

Dr. Ron McNair was one of the seven space travelers killed in the explosion of the Shuttle Challenger on January 28, 1986. During the planned six-day flight, mission specialist McNair was to have operated

the Spartan scientific package during observations of Halley's Comet. The flight, known as Mission 51-L, would have been McNair's second.

McNair was mission specialist aboard Mission 41-B in February 1984. During that eight-day flight he took part in the deployment of two communications satellites, and also operated the Shuttle Challenger's remote manipulator arm during the first space walks to use the manned maneuvering unit.

Ronald Erwin McNair was born October 21, 1950, in Lake City, South Carolina, where he graduated from Carver High School in 1967. He attended North Carolina A&T University, receiving a BS in physics in 1971, then studied at the Massachusetts Institute of Technology, where he earned his PhD in physics in 1976.

McNair did research in laser physics while at MIT and at the Ecole D'été Theorique de Physique at Les Houches, France. In 1976 he joined the Hughes Research Laboratories in Malibu, California, and was a scientist there when chosen by NASA.

He was one of the 35 astronauts selected by NASA in January 1978. In August 1979 he completed a training and evaluation course that qualified him as a Shuttle mission specialist. He worked at the Shuttle Avionics Integration Laboratory, and was assigned to STS-11 (later Mission 41-B) in February 1983. He also served as a capcom for flights 41-G and 51-A in October and November 1984.

McNair was the author or co-author of several technical papers. He also held a black belt in karate and is probably the first person to have played a saxophone in orbit.

He was survived by his wife, Cheryl, and two children, Reginald and Joy.

Mattingly, Thomas

Ken Mattingly lost his first chance at a space flight when he was replaced on the Apollo 13 crew just days before launch in April 1970. The temporary grounding occurred because Mattingly, who had trained for months as command module pilot for the lunar landing mission, had been exposed to German measles. NASA officials feared he would become ill during the flight, and might be unable to operate the Apollo command module in lunar orbit. Mattingly watched from mission control as the Apollo 13 service module suffered an explosion that canceled the lunar landing and forced astronauts Lovell, Swigert and Haise to make an emergency return to Earth.

Mattingly never did come down with the German measles. He went on to make three space flights.

The first was Apollo 16, in April 1972, for which Mattingly served as pilot of the command module Casper while astronauts John Young and Charles Duke explored the Moon in the lunar module Orion. During the return flight to Earth Mattingly performed an EVA of 1 hour and 13 minutes.

In June and July 1982 Mattingly commanded STS-4, the fourth orbital flight test of the Space Shuttle Columbia, which carried a Department of Defense sensor package called Cirrus. STS-4 was the first of many scheduled DOD-dedicated Shuttle flights. Some conversations between astronauts Mattingly and Henry Hartsfield and ground controllers at the Johnson Space Center in Houston and the USAF Satellite Control Facility in Sunnyvale, California, were conducted in code.

Mattingly's third flight, Shuttle Mission 51-C, was another DOD mission and was conducted with even greater secrecy. The launch time was not disclosed until T-minus nine minutes and once the Shuttle Discovery reached orbit, none of the astronauts' transmissions could be heard by the public. There was a total blackout on the payload itself, though it was reported in the press as a National Security Agency electronic intelligence satellite called Aquacade. (The USAF did acknowledge that the classified payload was mounted on an intertial upper stage, and that the IUS performed as designed.) Even the mission duration was not disclosed in advance. Mattingly and his four-man crew, which included the first Air Force Manned Spaceflight Engineer, Major Gary Payton, returned to Earth on January 28, 1985. Weather problems apparently forced the crew to return a day early; cold weather had also postponed the launch by a day. In fact, 51-C was the coldest Shuttle until the tragic Challenger launch in January 1986.

During his three flights Mattingly logged approximately 509 hours in space.

Thomas Kenneth Mattingly II was born March 17, 1936, in Chicago, Illinois. His parents moved to Florida when he was very young and Mattingly graduated from Miami Edison High School in Miami. He attended Auburn University from 1954 to 1958, earning a BS in aeronautical engineering.

Mattingly entered the US Navy in 1958 and completed pilot training in 1960. From 1960 to 1963 he flew AlH attack aircraft aboard the carrier USS Saratoga, and for the next two years flew A3Bs from the carrier USS Franklin D. Roosevelt. In 1965 he was enrolled in the USAF Aerospace Research Pilot School at Edwards AFB, California, and was a student there when selected by NASA.

One of the 19 astronauts selected by NASA in April 1966, Mattingly specialized in the systems of the Apollo command module and took part in the development of the Apollo spacesuit and backpack. He served on the support crews for Apollo 8 and Apollo 11 and was named to the prime crew of Apollo 13 in August 1969.

Between January 1973 and April 1981 Mattingly held several administrative jobs in the astronaut office and Shuttle program, as head of the Shuttle support group, then technical assistant to Deke Slayton, who was managing the Shuttle orbital flight test program, and, finally, head of the ascent/entry group. Mattingly and Hartsfield served as backups for STS-2 and STS-3, the last backup or standby astronauts designated by NASA. (Future replacements for Shuttle crew members will come from the pool of experienced astronauts.)

In October 1982 Mattingly was named to command STS-10, the first Department of Defense Shuttle mission, but upper stage problems aboard STS-6 in April 1983 forced several postponements, until January 1985, by which time the flight had received a new designation.

Mattingly resigned from NASA in June 1985 to become commander of the US Navy Electronics Systems Command.

Rear Admiral Mattingly is separated from his second wife. He has a son from his first marriage, Thomas K. III.

Meade, Carl

Major Carl J. Meade, USAF, is one of the 13 astronauts selected by NASA in June 1985. In August 1985 he began a training and evaluation course intended to qualify him as a mission specialist on future Shuttle crews.

An Air Force brat, Meade was born November 16, 1950, at Chanute AFB, Illinois, and graduated from high school at Randolph AFB, Texas, in 1968. He attended the University of Texas, receiving a BS (with honors) in electronics engineering in 1973, and in 1975 earned an MS in electronics engineering from the California Institute of Technology.

Prior to joining the US Air Force, Meade worked as an electronics

design engineer with the Hughes Aircraft Company in Culver City, California. (While a graduate student at Caltech he had been a Hughes Fellow.) After becoming an Air Force pilot, Meade flew RF-4C reconaissance aircraft at Shaw AFB, South Carolina, then attended the USAF Test Pilot School at Edwards AFB, California, where he was the outstanding graduate of Class 80B. He remained at Edwards as a test pilot until his selection by NASA.

Meade has logged over 2300 hours of flying time in 25 different types of aircraft.

He and his wife, Cheryl, have a son, David.

Michel, Curtis

In June 1965 Dr. Curt Michel became one of the first scientist-astronauts chosen by NASA. He also was the first to publicly criticize the space agency's emphasis on engineering at the expense of pure science and resigned from the program before being assigned to a mission in September 1969.

Frank Curtis Michel was born June 5, 1934, in LaCrosse, Wisconsin, and graduated from the California Institute of Technology in Pasadena with a BS in physics in 1955. He received his PhD in physics from Caltech in 1962.

Michel worked as a junior engineer in the Corporal missile program for Firestone in Southgate, California, while attending Caltech in the USAF reserve officer's training program. He received pilot training in Arizona and Texas from 1955 to 1957. When selected as a NASA astronaut he was teaching at Rice University in Houston.

Upon leaving the space program Michel returned to Rice University where he has been a professor of physics, chairman of the space physics and astronomy program, and, most recently, Andrew Hays Buchanan professor of astrophysics.

He and his wife, Beverly, have two children.

Mitchell, Edgar

Dr. Ed Mitchell was the sixth person to walk on the Moon. As lunar module pilot of the Apollo 14 mission in February 1971 he and commander Alan Shepard spent over 33 hours on the surface of the Moon near the crater Fra Mauro. They set up an experiment package and pulled a two-wheel trolley to a crater over a mile from their landing site during two walks on the lunar surface.

Mitchell also became famous for his interest in ESP and psychic phenomena and conducted several informal ESP experiments during free moments of the flight.

He logged over nine days in space, including nine hours of EVA, during Apollo 14, his only space flight.

Edgar Dean Mitchell was born September 17, 1930, in Hereford, Texas, but grew up in Artesia, New Mexico. He attended the Carnegie Institute of Technology, receiving a BS in industrial management in 1952. He later earned a BS in aeronautical engineering from the US Naval Postgraduate School in 1961, and a PhD in aeronautics/astronautics from the Massachusetts Institute of Technology in 1964.

Mitchell joined the Navy in 1952 and in 1954 completed pilot training. He flew aircraft from bases in Okinawa and from carriers until 1958, when he became a research project officer with Air Development Squadron 5. Following schooling at MIT, he worked as a US Navy representative for the Manned Orbiting Laboratory and had just graduated first in his class from the USAF Aerospace Research Pilot School at Edwards AFB, California, when chosen by NASA.

As a pilot Mitchell eventually logged over 5000 hours of flying time, 2000 hours in jets.

Mitchell was one of 19 astronauts selected by NASA in April 1966. A specialist in the Apollo lunar module, he was a support crewman for the first flight of the LM on Apollo 9. He was backup lunar module pilot for Apollo 10 before being named to the Apollo 14 crew in August 1969. After Apollo 14 he served as backup lunar module pilot for Apollo 16. He retired from the Navy and resigned from NASA on October 1, 1972.

Since then Mitchell has founded the Institute for Noetic Sciences in Palo Alto, California. The Institute conducts research into the powers of the mind and Mitchell remains its chairman. He was president of the Edgar Mitchell Corporation in Palm Beach, Florida, from 1974 to 1978, and is currently chairman of the board of Forecast Systems, Inc., a company based in Provo, Utah and West Palm Beach.

He is also the co-author of a book, *Psychic Exploration: A Challenge for Science* (1974).

Mitchell and his wife, Anita, have five children, Karlyn, Elizabeth, Kimberly, Paul and Marybeth.

Mullane, Richard

Mike Mullane was mission specialist aboard the maiden voyage of the Shuttle Discovery in August and September 1984. The six-person Discovery crew deployed three communications satellites, erected an experimental solar power wing, and operated a number of scientific and technical experiments during Mission 41-D. The flight lasted six days.

Richard Michael Mullane was born September 10, 1945, in Wichita Falls, Texas, but grew up in Albuquerque, New Mexico, where he graduated from St. Pius X Catholic School in 1963. He went on to attend the US Military Academy at West Point, earning a BS in military engineering in 1967. He later received an MS in aeronautical engineering from the Air Force Institute of Technology (1975).

After graduation from West Point Mullane served in the US Air Force. He flew 150 combat missions in Vietnam as an RF-4C weapon system operator in 1969, then was stationed for four years at the Royal Air Force Base in Alconbury, England. In 1976 he completed the flight test engineer course at the USAF Test Pilot School at Edwards Air Force Base, California, and was assigned to test weapon systems at Eglin AFB, Florida.

Mullane was one of the 35 astronauts selected by NASA in January 1978. In August 1979 he completed a training and evaluation course which qualified him as a Shuttle mission specialist. He served on the support crew for STS-4 prior to being assigned to STS-12 (later known as Mission 41-D) in February 1983.

From November 1983 to October 1984 Mullane trained as mission specialist for a Shuttle crew assigned to a Department of Defense "standby" payload, then moved (presumably with the classified payload) to the crew training for 62-A, the first Vandenberg launch. He also served as capcom for Shuttle missions from January to July 1985.

Mullane and his wife, Donna, have three children, twins Patrick and Amy, and Laura.

Musgrave, Story

Dr. Story Musgrave served as mission specialist aboard two Shuttle flights, including STS-6, the maiden voyage of the Challenger in April 1983. During that four-day flight Musgrave and Donald Peterson made the first spacewalk from a Shuttle. He was also aboard Mission 51-F/ Spacelab 2 in July 1985, as a member of a seven-man crew that operated 13 different scientific experiments.

Musgrave has spent 312 hours in space, including 4 hours in EVA.

Franklin Story Musgrave was born August 19, 1935, in Boston, Massachusetts, but considers Lexington, Kentucky, to be his hometown. He attended St. Mark's School in Southborough, Massachusetts, graduating in 1953, then joined the Marine Corps. When he returned to school some years later he accumulated a staggering number of degrees: BS in mathematics and statistics from Syracuse University (1958); an MBA in operations analysis and computer programming from the University of California at Los Angeles (1959); a BA in chemistry from Marietta College (1960); an MD from Columbia University (1964); and an MS in physiology and biophysics from the University of Kentucky (1966). He has also worked toward a PhD in physiology.

As a Marine, Musgrave served as an aviation electrician and aircraft crew chief aboard the carrier USS Wasp on duty in the Far East. After returning to the US he also worked for the Eastman Kodak Company, Rochester, New York, as a mathematician. When selected by NASA in August 1967 he was a researcher in cardiovascular and exercise physiology at the University of Kentucky, where he had previously interned as a surgeon and worked as a US Air Force post-doctoral fellow.

He has logged over 15500 hours of flying time, including 6300 in jet aircraft, in 145 different types of aircraft, and holds instructor, instrument instructor, glider instructor and transport ratings. He is also a parachutist with more than 445 free falls to his credit, including 100 experimental descents.

Musgrave was one of the 11 scientist-astronauts chosen by NASA in August 1967. He underwent military jet pilot training, then worked on the design and development of the Skylab space station, serving as backup science pilot for the first Skylab mission, Skylab 2. He was also capcom for Skylab 3 and Skylab 4. From 1974 on he helped design EVA equipment, including space suits, for the Shuttle program, and served as mission specialist for two simulated Spacelab flights. From 1979 to 1982 he was assigned to the Shuttle Avionics Integration Laboratory (SAIL), testing Shuttle computer software.

He also continued to be a part-time surgeon at Denver General Hospital and a part-time professor of physiology and biophysics at the University of Kentucky Medical Center. He has published 44 scientific papers concerning aerospace medicine, exercise physiology, and clinical surgery.

Musgrave is the divorced father of five children, Lorelei, Bradley, Holly, Christopher and Jeffrey.

Nagel, Steven

Steven Nagel made two Space Shuttle flights within five months of each other in 1985, one of them as a mission specialist, the other as pilot.

His assignment as a mission specialist and flight engineer was aboard Mission 51-G in June 1985. This crew, commanded by Daniel Brandenstein, had originally been scheduled to fly in August 1984, but payload problems and changes in the Shuttle manifest caused the de-

lay. During the flight of 51-G Nagel took part in the launch of three communications satellites and in the deployment and retrieval of the Spartan scientific satellite.

As pilot of Spacelab Dl in October and November 1985 Nagel led one of the two three-astronaut teams which worked 12-hour shifts aboard the European-built laboratory. With the landing of Spacelab Dl Nagel has logged approximately 339 hours in space.

He also has flown with citizens of more different countries than any other astronaut: Saudi prince Sultan al-Saud and French test pilot Patrick Baudry were with Nagel on 51-G, while scientists Ernst Messerschmid and Rheinhard Furrer of West Germany and Wubbo Ockels of The Netherlands were aboard Spacelab Dl.

Steven Ray Nagel was born October 27, 1946, in Canton, Illinois, and graduated from Canton Senior High School in 1964. He received a BS in aeronautical and astronautical engineering (with high honors) from the University of Illinois in 1969, and later earned an MS in mechanical engineering from California State University at Fresno in 1978.

An Air Force ROTC student at Illinois, Nagel was commissioned in 1969 and earned his wings in 1970. He was based in Louisiana and Thailand prior to attending the USAF Test Pilot School at Edwards AFB, California, in 1975. When selected by NASA he was a test pilot there. He has logged 4900 hours of flying time, 3100 hours in jets.

Nagel was chosen to be an astronaut candidate in January 1978 and completed a year-long training and evaluation course in August 1979. He has been a chase pilot for STS-1 and support crewman and capcom for STS-2 and STS-3. He has also been assigned to the Shuttle Avionics Integration Laboratory (SAIL) and the Flight Simulation Laboratory (FSL).

He is married to the former Linda Penney.

Nelson, George

Dr. George "Pinky" Nelson has served as a mission specialist on two Shuttle crews, including the first satellite retrieval and repair.

He was one of five astronauts in the crew of Mission 41-C, launched April 6, 1984, for a rendezvous with the malfunctioning Solar Maximum Mission satellite. Using the manned maneuvering unit (MMU) backpack, Nelson left the Shuttle Challenger and flew over to the Solar Max, attempting to lock on to the satellite using a special unit known as the T-pad. The T-pad failed, however, and Nelson was called back to Challenger by commander Robert Crippen. It appeared that the Solar Max rescue had not worked, but the next morning mission specialist T. J. Hart was able to grab the satellite with the Shuttle's remote manipulator arm. Nelson and James van Hoften were then able to make a second space walk, repairing the satellite, which was then released into space.

Nelson later served as mission specialist for the seven-times postponed flight 61-C in January 1986. His primary job on that mission was to use a special camera to take pictures of Halley's Comet. Nelson saw the comet, but the camera didn't work.

On two flights Nelson has spent 314 hours in space, including 9 hours of EVA.

George Driver Nelson, dubbed "Pinky" because of his complexion, was born July 13, 1950, in Charles City, Iowa, but grew up in Willmar, Minnesota, and Clinton, Iowa. He graduated from Willmar Senior High School in 1968, attracting the attention of baseball scouts, then attended Harvey Mudd College, receiving a BS in physics in 1972. He earned an MS (1974) and a PhD (1978) in astronomy from the University of Washington.

Nelson has performed astronomical research at the Sacramento Peak Solar Observatory in Sunspot, New Mexico; the Astronomical Institute at Utrecht, the Netherlands; and the University of Gottingen Observatory, West Germany. When selected by NASA he was a postdoctoral researcher at the Joint Institute of Laboratory Astrophysics in Boulder, Colorado.

One of the 35 astronauts chosen in January 1978, Nelson completed a training and evaluation course in August 1979. He later flew as a scientific equipment operator on the NASA WB-57F earth resources aircraft, worked on the Shuttle EVA spacesuit, and was the photographer in the lead chase plane during the STS-1 landing. He also served as capcom and support crewman for STS-3 and STS-4.

In 1986 he commenced a year-long leave of absence to teach at the University of Washington.

Nelson and his wife, Susan, have two daughters, Aimee and Marti.

O'Connor, Bryan

Bryan O'Connor was pilot of Shuttle Mission 61-B in November and December 1985. The seven astronauts on this second flight of the Shuttle Atlantis deployed three communications satellites and tested space construction techniques during their seven-day mission.

Bryan Daniel O'Connor was born September 6, 1946, in Orange, California, though he considers Twentynine Palms, California, where his father served as an officer in the Marine Corps, to be his hometown. O'Connor graduated from high school in Twentynine Palms in 1964, then attended the US Naval Academy, receiving a BS in engineering in 1968. He earned an MS in aeronautical systems from the University of West Florida in 1970.

He elected to serve in the Marine Corps and, following basic officer training at Quantico, Virginia, entered flight school at Pensacola, Florida, winning his wings in June 1970. For the next five years he served as a pilot and instructor in California, Texas, North Carolina, Korea and Japan, and also did a Mediterranean tour aboard the carrier USS Guam. In 1976 he attended the US Navy Test Pilot School at Patuxent River, Maryland, and remained as a test pilot at the center there for over three years. He was involved in testing short-takeoff-and-landing aircraft such as the X-22 and the British Harrier, and when chosen by NASA was a Harrier officer at the Naval Air Systems Command.

As a pilot O'Connor has logged over 3300 hours of flying time, including 3000 hours in jets.

He was one of the 19 astronauts selected by NASA in May 1980, and in June 1981 completed a training and evaluation course, which qualified him as a Shuttle pilot. He served as T-38 chase plane pilot for STS-3, and as capcom for STS-6 through STS-9. In 1985 he was assigned as pilot of a second Shuttle mission scheduled for the summer of 1986, but saw it canceled following the Challenger explosion. He is currently head of a Shuttle flight safety panel at the NASA Johnson Space Center.

Colonel O'Connor and his wife, Susan, have two sons, Thomas and Kevin.

O'Leary, Brian T.

Dr. Brian O'Leary trained as a NASA scientist-astronaut for six months before resigning. His book, *The Making of an Ex-Astronaut* (1970), discusses his dislike of jet pilot training and his disillusionment with NASA's treatment of scientist-astronauts at the time.

O'Leary was born January 27, 1940, in Boston, Massachusetts. He received a BA in physics from Williams College in 1961, an MA in astronomy from Georgetown University in 1964, and his PhD in astronomy from the University of California at Berkeley in 1967. Prior to becoming an astronaut O'Leary was a NASA pre-doctoral trainee in the Space Sciences Laboratory, Department of Astronomy, at Berkeley.

Selected by NASA in August 1967 as one of eleven scientist-astronauts, O'Leary underwent six months of ground training concentrated on Apollo and Apollo Applications (later Skylab) systems. He reported to Williams Air Force Base in Arizona to begin pilot training in February 1968, but soon resigned.

Since leaving NASA O'Leary has held teaching and research positions at Cornell University, Hampshire College in Amherst, Mass., the University of Pennsylvania, the California Institute of Technology, and at Princeton University. He has also been a consultant for energy matters for the Committee on the Interior, U.S. House of Representatives. He is currently senior scientist at Science Applications, Inc., in Redondo Beach, California.

O'Leary has published many popular articles and scientific papers. In addition to *The Making of an Ex-Astronaut*, he is also the author of *The Fertile Stars* (1981), *The New Solar System* (1981), and *Project Space Station* (1983). He co-authored a novel, *Spaceship Titanic* (1983).

He and his wife, Dolores, live in Los Angeles with their two children.

Onizuka, Ellison

Ellison "El" Onizuka was killed in the explosion of the Space Shuttle Challenger on January 28, 1986. He had been scheduled to serve as mission specialist during the planned six-day flight 51-L, supervising the deployment of a Tracking and Data Relay Satellite.

Onizuka had made a previous space flight, aboard Mission 51-C, the first "classified" Shuttle flight, in January 1985. During 51-C Onizuka took part in the deployment of a secret Department of Defense satellite. The flight lasted three days.

He was the first Asian-American in space.

Ellison Shoji Onizuka was born June 24, 1946, in Kealakekua, Hawaii, where he graduated from Konawaena High School in 1964. He grew up, however, in nearby Kona. He became interested in space flight at the time of Walter Schirra's Mercury mission in 1962, and entered the University of Colorado at Boulder to study aerospace engineering. He received his BS and MS in aerospace engineering in 1969.

An ROTC student at Colorado, Onizuka entered active duty in January 1970. For the next four years he served as an aerospace flight test engineer at McClellan Air Force Base, California. In August 1974 he was enrolled in the USAF Test Pilot School at Edwards AFB, and remained at the school as an instructor and engineer after graduation. He eventually logged over 1700 hours of flying time as an engineer on 43 different types of aircraft.

Onizuka was one of 35 astronauts selected by NASA in January 1978. In August 1979 he completed a training and evaluation course which qualified him as a Shuttle mission specialist. His astronaut assignments included working at the Shuttle Avionics Integration Laboratory and serving on the launch support crew for STS-1 and STS-2. In November 1982 he was assigned to the crew of STS-10, scheduled to be the first Department of Defense Shuttle mission, but it was canceled. Ultimately the five-man crew was assigned to Mission 51-C.

Onizuka is survived by his wife, Lorna, and two children, Janelle and Darien. An asteroid has been named for him.

Oswald, Stephen

Stephen S. Oswald was one of the 13 astronauts selected by NASA in June 1985. In August 1985 he began a training and evaluation course intended to qualify him as a pilot on future Shuttle crews.

Oswald was born June 30, 1951, in Seattle, Washington, and graduated from Bellingham High School in Bellingham in 1969. He attended the US Naval Academy, receiving a BS in aerospace engineering in 1973.

After graduation from Annapolis, Oswald underwent pilot training in Texas, earning his wings in 1974. He flew Corsair IIs aboard the carrier USS Midway in the Pacific and Indian Oceans until 1977. In 1978 he attended the US Naval Test Pilot School at Patuxent River, Maryland, and remained there as a test pilot until 1981. Oswald resigned from the Navy in 1982 to join Westinghouse Electric Corporation as a civilian test pilot. In November 1984 he went to work for NASA as an aerospace engineer and instructor pilot at Ellington AFB, near the Johnson Space Center.

Oswald has logged over 3100 flying hours in 35 different types of aircraft. He is currently an A-7 pilot with the US Naval Reserve.

He and his wife, Diane, have two daughters, Monique and Janna.

Overmyer, Robert

Robert Overmyer made Shuttle flights in 1982 and 1985, first as pilot of STS-5, the first operational Shuttle mission, and then as commander of Mission 51-B/Spacelab 3. Spacelab 3 carried a crew of seven, including two scientific payload specialists, as well as 24 rats and a pair of squirrel monkeys, and was intended to permit research in space manufacturing and medicine. Though plagued by equipment problems and the challenge of caring for animals in weightlessness, the crew completed most of its tasks, returning to Earth after seven days.

Overmyer has logged approximately 290 hours in space.

Robert Franklyn Overmyer was born July 14, 1936, in Lorain, Ohio, but grew up in Westlake, where he graduated from high school in 1954. He attended Baldwin Wallace College, receiving a BS in physics in 1958, and later earned an MS in aeronautics from the US Naval Postgraduate School (1964).

Overmyer joined the US Marine Corps in January 1958 and underwent pilot training in Texas. Between 1959 and 1965 he served as a fighter pilot at bases in the US and Japan and was a student at the Naval Postgraduate School. In 1965 he attended the USAF Test Pilot School at Edwards Air Force Base, California, then was chosen as an astronaut for the Manned Orbiting Laboratory (MOL) program. When MOL was canceled in 1969, Overmyer transferred to NASA.

Overmyer has logged over 7200 hours of flying time, including over 6000 hours in jets.

As an astronaut Overmyer worked on the design and development of the Skylab orbiting space station, then served as support crewman and capcom for Apollo 17, the last manned lunar landing. From January 1973 to July 1975 he was a member of the support crew for the Apollo-Soyuz Test Project and was American capcom at Kaliningrad mission control near Moscow during the flight. He later served as chase plane pilot for the Shuttle Approach and Landing Tests, and as deputy vehicle manager for the Shuttle Columbia, supervising the final stages of manufacturing and tiling. He was assigned to be a Shuttle pilot as early as March 1978, and named to the STS-5 crew in March 1982.

Overmyer took part in the investigation of the Shuttle Challenger disaster in 1986, then announced in April that he would resign from the Marine Corps and from NASA in June to become a space consultant.

Colonel Overmyer and his wife, Katherine, have three children, Carolyn, Patricia and Robert.

Parker, Robert

Dr. Robert Parker, an astronomer, was a mission specialist aboard STS-9, the first flight of the European research module Spacelab. For ten days the crew of six astronauts, the largest sent into space aboard a single vehicle at that time, carried out scientific experiments in a variety of disciplines. For example, Parker participated in an experiment intended to prove or disprove a 1914 Nobel Prize-winning theory that hot or cold air blown into a person's ears would cause the subject to believe he was turning. Contrary to the theory, it did not. Parker also became famous for a testy public exchange with controllers at the Marshall Space Center when he felt he and payload specialist Ulf Merbold were being rushed to start one experiment before they could finish another.

Robert Alan Ridley Parker was born December 14, 1936, in New York City, but grew up in Shrewsbury, Massachusetts, where he graduated from high school. He attended Amherst College, receiving a BA in astronomy and physics in 1958, and earned a PhD in astronomy at the California Institute of Technology in 1962.

After receiving his doctorate, and until his selection by NASA, Parker was an associate professor of astronomy at the University of Wisconsin.

Parker was one of the eleven scientist-astronauts selected by NASA in August 1967. In March 1968 he reported to Williams Air Force Base, Arizona, for jet pilot training, which he completed a year later. He has since logged over 3000 hours of flying time in jets.

Immediately upon reporting to NASA in September 1967 the eleven new scientist-astronauts were told that budget cuts had made it likely they would face a long wait to fly in space, if they got the chance at all. Though several members of the Excess Eleven (XS-11, as they dubbed themselves) left the space program, Parker remained, serving on the astronaut support crew for Apollo 15 and Apollo 17, and as program scientist for all three Skylab flights. From 1974 to 1978 he worked on Space Shuttle development and on Spacelab, and in August 1978 was named to be mission specialist aboard the first Spacelab. Ultimately he waited over sixteen years for his chance to fly in space.

Parker was later assigned as mission specialist for Astro 1, a Spacelab scheduled for launch in March 1986 and intended to observe Halley's Comet. But Astro 1 was canceled following the Challenger explosion on January 28, 1986.

Parker is married to the former Judy Woodruff. They have two children, Kimberly and Brian, from Parker's previous marriage.

Peterson, Donald

Don Peterson was a mission specialist on STS-6, the first flight of the Space Shuttle Challenger, in April 1983. Peterson and three other astronauts conducted experiments in materials processing and deployed the first Tracking and Data Relay satellite using the Intertial Upper Stage. The IUS failed to operate as planned, though the TDRS eventually reached its intended orbit.

Peterson and astronaut Story Musgrave performed the first spacewalk of the Shuttle program, spending 4 hours and 15 minutes in the Challenger's payload bay.

STS-6 lasted approximately 120 hours.

Donald Herod Peterson was born October 22, 1933, in Winona, Mississippi, where he grew up. He earned an appointment to the US Military Academy at West Point, graduating with a BS degree in 1955. He later earned an MS in nuclear engineering from the Air Force Institute of Technology (1962) and performed further work toward a PhD at the University of Texas.

Peterson elected to serve in the US Air Force and, after pilot training, worked as an instructor with the Air Training Command until 1960. He has also been a nuclear systems analyst with the Air Force Systems Command, a pilot with the Tactical Air Command, and a student at the Aerospace Research Pilot School at Edwards AFB, California.

He was one of four pilots chosen for the USAF Manned Orbiting Laboratory program in June 1967. When MOL was canceled in June 1969, Peterson and six other pilots transferred to NASA as astronauts. Peterson served on the support crew for Apollo 16 in 1972, then was assigned to Space Shuttle development. He was named a mission specialist for STS-6 in March 1982.

Peterson retired from the Air Force with the rank of colonel in January 1980, though he remained at NASA in a civilian capacity. In 1985 he resigned from NASA to become an aerospace consultant.

Peterson and his wife, Bonnie, have three children, Donald Jr., Jean and Shari, and live in Houston.

Pogue, William

William Pogue was pilot of the longest American manned space flight, the 84-day Skylab 4 mission from November 1973 to Feburary 1974. During that flight Pogue and fellow astronauts Gerald Carr and Edward Gibson conducted extensive observations of the Sun in addition to experiments in space medicine and Earth resources.

The Skylab 4 astronauts also became notorious for staging the first "strike" in space. Tired and overworked in their sixth week aboard Skylab, they announced that they were taking some time off, and did. During their first days in space the crew had been reprimanded for covering up the fact that Pogue had become ill. From that point on, the relationship between the astronauts and mission control was often contentious, though engineers and scientists on the ground were later grateful for the astronauts' frankness.

Pogue logged 84 days, 1 hour and 16 minutes on Skylab 4, including over 13 hours of EVA.

William Reid Pogue was born January 23, 1930, in Okemah, Oklahoma. He attended Oklahoma Baptist University, receiving a BS in secondary education in 1951, and later earned an MS in mathematics from Oklahoma State University in 1960.

He joined the USAF in 1951 and after earning his wings, flew 43 combat missions in Korea as a member of the Fifth Air Force. From

1955 to 1957 he was a member of the USAF "Thunderbirds" air demonstration team, and later was a mathematics instructor at the Air Force Academy. He also attended the Empire Test Pilot School in Farnborough, England, and was an instructor at the USAF Aerospace Research Pilot School at Edwards AFB, California, when chosen by NASA.

He ultimately logged over 5000 hours of flying time, including 4200 hours in jets.

Pogue was one of the 19 astronauts selected in April 1966. He served as a support crewman for the first manned Apollo flight, and later for Apollos 11, 13 and 14. He was training as a command module pilot for the planned Apollo 19 lunar landing mission when that flight was canceled. He transferred to the Skylab program and was named pilot of the third mission, Skylab 4, in January 1972.

He resigned from NASA and retired from the Air Force on September 1, 1975, to become vice president of the High Flight Foundation, a religious organization founded by fellow astronaut James Irwin and based in Colorado Springs, Colorado. He returned to NASA in 1976 and 1977 as a consultant on programs to study the Earth from space. He currently works in Fayetteville, Arkansas, as a privately employed consultant to aerospace and energy corporations.

Pogue is also the author of two books, *How Do You Go to the Bathroom in Space?* (1985), and *Astronaut Primer* (1985).

He and his wife, Helen, have three children, William, Layna, and Thomas.

Resnik, Judith

Judith Resnik, the second American woman to go into space, was killed in the explosion of the Shuttle Challenger on January 28, 1986. The seven-person crew for the flight, known as Mission 51-L, included high school teacher Christa McAuliffe and was scheduled to last six days, during which Resnik would deploy and retrieve the Spartan scientific satellite for observations of Halley's Comet.

Resnik's first flight was aboard Mission 41-D, the maiden voyage of the Shuttle Discovery. The first attempt to launch Discovery on June 26, 1984, ended in a launch pad abort, with the Shuttle's main engines igniting, then shutting down just seconds before liftoff. The abort was caused by a hydrogen fuel leak near those main engines, and was corrected for a successful launch two months later, on August 30. In the next seven days Resnik and five fellow space travelers deployed three communications satellites and erected a 100-foot-long experimental solar panel in the Discovery payload bay.

Judith Arlene Resnik was born April 5, 1949, in Akron, Ohio. She graduated from Firestone High School in Akron in 1966, then attended Carnegie-Mellon University in Pittsburgh, earning a BS in electrical engineering in 1970. She later earned a PhD in electrical engineering from the University of Maryland in 1977.

After graduating from college, Resnik went to work as an engineer for RCA in Moorestown, New Jersey, and Springfield, Virginia, where her projects included designs for sophisticated radar systems and for telemetry from rockets. From 1974 to 1977 she was a biomedical engineer in the Laboratory of Neurophysiology at the National Institutes of Health in Bethesda, Maryland, and then spent a year as an engineer with the Xerox Corporation in El Segundo, California.

Resnik was one of the 35 astronauts selected by NASA in January 1978. In August 1979 she completed a training and evaluation course that qualified her as a mission specialist on Shuttle crews. She worked on the Remote Manipulator System (the Shuttle robot arm) and on

Shuttle computer software until being named to a flight crew in February 1983.

Resnik was not married. A crater on the planet Venus and an asteroid have been named for her.

Richards, Richard

Dick Richards was scheduled to be pilot aboard Shuttle Mission 61-E, the Spacelab Astro 1 intended to observe Halley's Comet in March 1986. But 61-E was canceled following the explosion of the Shuttle Challenger during launch on January 28, 1986.

Richard Noel Richards was born August 24, 1946, in Key West, Florida, but grew up in St. Louis, Missouri, where he graduated from Riverview Gardens High School in 1964. He attended the University of Missouri, receiving a BS in chemical engineering in 1969, and earned an MS in aeronautical systems from the University of West Florida in 1970.

He was commissioned in the US Navy after graduation from Missouri and underwent pilot training, winning his wings in August 1969. From 1970 to 1973 he was an A-4 Skyhawk and F-4 Phantom pilot with Tactical Electronic Warfare Squadron 33 in Norfolk, Virginia, then served aboard the carriers USS America and USS Saratoga with Fighter Squadron 103. In March 1976 he entered the US Navy Test Pilot School at Patuxent River, Maryland, and after graduation remained at Pax River as a test pilot until 1980, working on the first carrier catapults and landings of the F-18A Hornet. He was on his way to a new assignment with Fighter Squadron 33 in May 1980 when chosen by NASA.

As a pilot Richards has accumulated over 3300 hours of flying time in 15 different types of airplanes. He has also made more than 400 carrier landings.

Richards was one of the 19 astronauts selected by NASA in May 1980. In August 1981 he completed a training and evaluation course which qualified him as a Shuttle pilot. He worked as deputy chief of aircraft operations and also managed the inflight refueling of the Shuttle carrier aircraft in addition to serving as a Shuttle capcom from April 1984 to September 1985.

He is married to the former Lois Hollabaugh.

Ride, Sally

Dr. Sally Ride became the first American woman space traveler on June 27, 1983, when she was one of five astronauts launched aboard the Shuttle Challenger on STS-7. During the six-day STS-7 flight she served as flight engineer, took part in the deployment of two communications satellites and in the deployment and retrieval of the German-built Shuttle Pallet Satellite (SPAS-01).

She went into space a second time aboard Shuttle Mission 41-G in October 1984. On this mission she deployed the Earth Radiation Budget Satellite and took part in scientific observations of the Earth made with the OSTA-3 pallet and the Large Format Camera. It was during 41-G that Kathryn Sullivan, who had attended the same first grade class as Ride, became the first American woman to walk in space.

Ride has spent 14 days and 8 hours in space.

Sally Kristen Ride was born May 26, 1951, in Los Angeles, California. She attended Westlake High School in Los Angeles, where she was a nationally ranked tennis player, and graduated in 1968. She went on to attend Stanford University, earning a BA in English and a BS in physics in 1973, and an MS (1975) and PhD (1978) in physics.

She was a teaching assistant and researcher in laser physics at Stanford when selected by NASA as an astronaut in January 1978. In August 1979 she completed a training and evaluation course that qualified her as a Shuttle mission specialist. She worked at the Shuttle Avionics Integration Laboratory, and served as capcom for STS-2 and STS-3 prior to being assigned to the STS-7 crew in April 1982.

Prior to the explosion of the Shuttle Challenger and the suspension of all Shuttle flights, Ride was training for her third mission, 61-M, scheduled for the summer of 1986. Instead she served as the astronaut office representative to the presidential commission investigating the tragedy. She currently serves as assistant to NASA administrator James Fletcher at NASA headquarters in Washington, D.C.

She is the co-author of a book, *To Space and Back* (1986).

Ride is married to astronaut Dr. Steven Hawley.

Roosa, Stuart

Stuart Roosa was the command module pilot of Apollo 14, the first lunar landing mission to be flown after the near disaster of Apollo 13. Roosa orbited the Moon in the command module Kitty Hawk while astronauts Alan Shepard and Edgar Mitchell spent over 33 hours on the surface in the lunar module Antares. Apollo 14 was launched on January 31, 1971, and splashed down on February 9.

Roosa logged approximately nine days in space.

Stuart Allen Roosa was born August 16, 1933, in Durango, Colorado. He joined the USAF in 1953 and later attended the University of Colorado through the Air Force Institute of Technology program, receiving a BS in aeronautical engineering in 1960.

After earning an Air Force commission in the Aviation Cadet Program, Roosa was an F-84F and F-100 pilot at Langley AFB in Virginia. Following college he served in Japan and in Pennsylvania. He graduated from the Air Force Aerospace Research Pilot School at Edwards AFB, California, in 1965, and was assigned as a test pilot there when selected by NASA.

Roosa was one of the 19 astronauts selected by NASA in April 1966. He served as a support crewman for Apollo 9 in 1969, then was named as command module pilot of Apollo 14.

He later served as backup command module pilot for Apollo 16 and Apollo 17, and worked for several years on Space Shuttle development.

Roosa retired as an Air Force colonel and resigned from NASA on February 1, 1976, to become vice president for international affairs for the US Industries Middle East Development Company in Athens, Greece. In 1977 he returned to the US as president of Jet Industries in Austin, Texas. Since 1981 he has been president and owner of Gulf Coast Coors in Gulfport, Mississippi.

Roosa and his wife, Joan, have four children, Christopher, John, Stuart, and Rosemary.

Ross, Jerry

Jerry Ross made two six-hour spacewalks demonstrating space construction techniques during Shuttle Mission 61-B in November and December 1985. Ross and astronaut Woody Spring erected and tore

down two experimental structures called EASE and ACCESS while occasionally being moved from point to point by the Shuttle Atlantis' remote manipulator arm. They proved that a future space station could be assembled manually by astronauts from elements delivered to orbit in pieces.

Mission 61-B lasted a total of 165 hours and ended with a landing at Edwards Air Force Base, California.

Jerry Lynn Ross was born January 20, 1948, in Crown Point, Indiana, where he grew up, graduating from high school in 1966. He attended Purdue University and received a BS (1970) and MS (1972) in mechanical engineering.

Ross was an Air Force ROTC student at Purdue and was commissioned in 1970, though he did not enter active duty until 1972. His first assignment was at the Aero-Propulsion Laboratory at Wright-Patterson Air Force Base, Ohio, where he worked on ramjet engines and air-launched missiles. In 1975 he entered the USAF Test Pilot School at Edwards AFB, California, and was named oustanding flight test engineer graduate. He remained at Edwards until 1979, serving as project engineer for the B-1 bomber. In February 1979 he was assigned to the payload operations division at the NASA Johnson Space Center.

He holds a private pilot's license and has flown 21 different types of aircraft, accumulating more than 1300 hours of flying time.

Ross was one of 19 astronauts selected by NASA in May 1980. In August 1981 he completed a training and evaluation course which qualified him as a Shuttle mission specialist. As an astronaut he has worked on the remote manipulator arm and as a chase plane crewman, and became an EVA specialist. He served as support crewman for Shuttle missions 41-B, 41-C and 51-A, all of which involved extensive EVA work, and was capcom for those missions and flights 41-D and 51-D as well.

In October 1984 he was assigned to be a mission specialist for flight 62-A, the first Shuttle mission scheduled to be launched from Vandenberg Air Force Base, California.

Lieutenant Colonel Ross and his wife, Karen, have two children, Amy and Scott.

Schirra, Walter

Walter Schirra was the only one of the original seven American astronauts to go into space in Mercury, Gemini and Apollo spacecraft.

On October 3, 1962, Schirra piloted Mercury-Atlas 8, which he had named Sigma 7, on a six-orbit mission lasting 9 hours and 13 minutes, proving that an astronaut could carefully manage the limited amounts of electricity and maneuvering fuel necessary for longer, more complex flights. (The Mercury missions of Glenn and Carpenter, which preceeded Schirra's, had been plagued by fuel and control problems.) Schirra had chosen the name Sigma because it symbolized engineering precision, and a precisely engineered flight was the result, ending with a splashdown just five miles from the carrier Kearsarge in the Pacific Ocean. True to his Navy background, Schirra elected to remain aboard the capsule until it was lifted to the deck of the carrier.

Schirra's second flight, as command pilot of Gemini 6, was intended to peform the first rendezvous and docking between different spacecraft, a vital prerequisite for missions to the Moon. But the unmanned Agena target for Gemini 6 failed to reach orbit on October 25, 1965. Gemini 6 was removed from the pad and replaced by Gemini 7, which was launched on December 4 on a planned 14-day flight. Eight days later Schirra and fellow astronaut Thomas Stafford were in their Gemini spacecraft atop the Titan booster when it ignited, then shut down after only two seconds. Schirra had the option at that point of ejecting himself and Stafford, but chose to remain in the spacecraft while technicians confirmed that the booster was not going to explode. Two days later Schirra and Stafford finally got off the ground, and less than six hours into the flight were "station keeping" just a few feet from astronauts Frank Borman and James Lovell in Gemini 7, 170 miles above the Mariana Islands.

A day later, after the astronauts made a Christmas "UFO" sighting (which ended with Schirra playing the harmonica and singing "Jingle Bells"), Schirra and Stafford were back on Earth.

In October 1968 Schirra and astronauts Donn Eisele and Walter Cunningham made the first manned flight of the Apollo spacecraft, spending an uncomfortable 11 days (the astronauts all developed head colds) qualifying the redesigned Apollo for future flights to the Moon after the tragic fire that killed astronauts Grissom, White and Chaffee in January 1967.

Schirra logged over 12 and a half days in space on his three flights.

Walter Marty Schirra, Jr., was born March 12, 1923, in Hackensack, New Jersey, and graduated from Dwight Morrow High School in Englewood. His father was a World War I ace who later flew in air circuses. Schirra's mother did wing-walking stunts. Nevertheless, though he grew up around airplanes, Schirra did not solo until naval pilot training.

After high school he spent a year at the Newark College of Engineering, then attended the US Naval Academy at Annapolis, earning a bachelor of science degree in 1945. He later received honorary PhDs from Lafayette College, Pennsylvania, the Newark College of Engineering, and from the University of Southern California.

Schirra served in the surface Navy for a year, then underwent pilot training at Pensacola, Florida, earning his wings in 1948. He was a carrier pilot for three years, then flew 90 combat missions in Korea as an exchange pilot with the US Air Force, shooting down two MiGs. Returning to the United States, he helped develop the Sidewinder missile while stationed at the Naval Ordnance Training Station at China Lake, California. After a three-year tour with the 124th Fighter Squadron aboard the carrier Lexington, Schirra attended the US Naval Test Pilot School at Patuxent River, Maryland. He was a test pilot at Pax River when selected by NASA.

Schirra admitted later that he was reluctant to give up his Navy career for the space program, but nevertheless was one of the seven astronauts chosen by NASA in April 1959. A precise pilot and engineer, Schirra also became notorious for his practical jokes.

In addition to his three space flights he served as backup to Scott Carpenter in 1962, and as backup command pilot for Gemini 3, the first manned Gemini mission, in 1965. He and his Apollo crew were originally assigned to the second manned Apollo flight, but were made backups to the Apollo 1 astronauts in November 1966.

He retired from the Navy as a captain and resigned from NASA on July 1, 1969, to become president of Regency Investors, a financial company based in Denver, Colorado. He was later employed by the ECCO Corporation, by the Johns-Manville Corporation, and by the Goodwin Company. Since January 1979 he has headed his own firm, Schirra Enterprises, and works as a consultant. He is also a television commercial spokesman for Actifed, a cold remedy.

Schirra and his wife, Jo, have two children, Walter III and Suzanne. They live in San Diego, California.

Schmitt, Harrison

Harrison "Jack" Schmitt became the first geologist to land on the Moon when he was lunar module pilot of Apollo 17, the last Apollo lunar landing.

Schmitt, commander Eugene Cernan and command module pilot Ronald Evans were launched in the early morning hours of December 7, 1972, the fiery climb of their Saturn 5 lighting up the sky for hundreds of miles around. Reaching lunar orbit three days later Schmitt and Cernan left Evans in the command module Challenger and boarded the lunar module America, to descend to a region of the Sea of Serenity, near the crater Littrow and the surrounding Taurus Mountains. During the next three days the astronauts set up scientific experiment packages and drove to the nearby mountains in a lunar rover, collecting soil and rock samples. During these excursions, while mission controllers operated a television camera mounted on the rover, geologist Schmitt gave detailed descriptions of the various craters, boulders, and soil found in the Taurus-Littrow Valley. At one point Schmitt and Cernan found orange-colored soil, which probably came from a lunar volcano, indicating that the Moon was not a geologically "dead" body. The astronauts returned to Earth on December 19, 1972, with a record 249 pounds of lunar material, ending the first phase of man's exploration of the Moon.

Harrison Hagan Schmitt was born July 3, 1935, in Santa Rita, New Mexico, and graduated from Western High School in Silver City in 1953. His father was a geologist who studied the American Southwest. Schmitt attended the California Institute of Technology, receiving a BS in science in 1957, then studied at the University of Oslo in Norway as a Fulbright Fellow in 1957 and 1958. He received his PhD in geology from Harvard University in 1964.

Between 1957 and 1961 Schmitt worked as a geologist, primarily with the US Geological Survey, at sites in southeastern Alaska, western Norway, New Mexico and Montana. He taught a course in ore deposits at Harvard in 1961, then joined the US Geological Survey's Astrogeology Center at Flagstaff, Arizona, where he participated in photographic and telescopic mapping of the Moon. He was also one of the USGS scientists who acted as an instructor for NASA astronauts.

Schmitt was one of six scientist-astronauts selected in June 1965, the first Americans chosen for space training because of their scientific skills and not because of their flying abilities. Nevertheless, two of the new scientists were already qualified jet pilots, and the four who were not—including Schmitt—were required to complete flight training. Schmitt attended a 53-week flight school at Williams Air Force Base in Arizona. Eventually he would log over 2100 hours of flying time, including 1600 hours in jets.

In 1966 Schmitt began to train for a possible Apollo lunar flight while also assisting veteran astronauts, who would make up the first Apollo crews, in lunar navigation and geology. He also took part in the analysis of samples returned from the Moon.

In late 1969 Schmitt was assigned as backup lunar module pilot for Apollo 15, then planned for October 1970, which put him in line for Apollo 18. But the Apollo 13 accident in April 1970 and Congressional budget cuts delayed some missions and eliminated others, including Apollos 18, 19, and 20. As the first and only scientist-astronaut assigned to an Apollo crew, Schmitt had apparently lost his chance to go to the Moon. Astronaut chief Deke Slayton, holding to his long-standing crew rotation system, submitted the Apollo 14 backup crew, Cernan, Evans and lunar module pilot Joe Engle, to NASA headquarters as candidates for Apollo 17. But headquarters overruled Slayton and replaced Engle with Schmitt.

In July 1973, following Apollo 17, Schmitt was named a Sherman

Fairchild Distinguished Scholar at Caltech, an appointment that ran through July 1975. At the same time Schmitt served as chief of NASA scientist-astronauts (from February 1974) and, beginning in May 1974, as NASA Assistant Administrator for Energy Programs.

In August 1975 Schmitt resigned from NASA to return to his home state of New Mexico to enter the race for the US Senate. On November 2, 1976, Schmitt, a Republican, was elected with 57 percent of the votes cast. He served in the Senate from January 1977 to January 1983 as a member of committees dealing with commerce, science and space, banking, urban affairs and ethics. He was defeated in his campaign for re-election in November 1982.

Schmitt is currently a consultant based in Albuquerque, New Mexico. One of his projects involves plans for a proposed manned flight to Mars. He serves on the President's Foreign Intelligence Advisory Board and several other government committees. He is unmarried.

Schweickart, Russell

"Rusty" Schweickart's only space flight was Apollo 9, during which he took part in the first manned test of the Apollo lunar module and the first test of the pressure suit and backpack designed for walking on the Moon.

Schweickart's spacewalk on March 6, 1969, was originally scheduled to last over two hours, during which he would crawl from the front hatch of the lunar module Spider to the open hatch of the command module Gumdrop. But during the first three days of the mission Schweickart suffered from dizziness and nausea, what would later be called space adaptation syndrome (SAS). Mission controllers, worried about Schweickart's safety, should he become ill in his pressure suit, shortened the EVA and eliminated the transfer from one spacecraft to another. Schweickart spent 38 minutes on the front porch of Spider, confirming that the Apollo spacesuit and backpack worked well.

Two days later Schweickart and command pilot James McDivitt separated Spider from Gumdrop and flew off to a distance of 85 miles before returning.

Schweickart logged approximately 241 hours in space during Apollo 9, his only flight.

Russell Louis Schweickart was born October 25, 1935, in Neptune, New Jersey, and graduated from high school in Manasquan in 1952. He attended the Massachusetts Institute of Technology, receiving a BS in aeronautical engineering in 1956. He later earned an MS in aeronautics and astronautics in 1963 from MIT for a thesis concerning stratospheric radiance.

From 1956 to 1960 Schweickart was a pilot in the US Air Force. He returned to MIT in 1960 as a graduate student and researcher, though he was recalled to active duty for a year in 1961 and subsequently served with the Air National Guard. At the time of his selection by NASA he was a scientist at the Experimental Astronomy Laboratory at MIT, doing research in the physics of the upper atmosphere and in star tracking.

As a pilot Schweickart eventually logged over 4200 hours of flying time, including 3500 hours in jets.

He was one of the 14 astronauts selected by NASA in October 1963 and following preliminary training, worked on inflight scientific experiments for Gemini and Apollo missions. In January 1966 he was assigned as backup lunar module pilot for the first manned Apollo mission. Ultimately that crew, consisting of astronauts McDivitt, Scott and Schweickart, was assigned to the third manned Apollo mission, Apollo 9.

In April 1969, following Apollo 9, Schweickart was assigned to the Skylab program, then known as Apollo Applications, and trained for a long-duration Earth orbit mission. He also served as a willing subject for NASA doctors studying space adaptation syndrome.

Schweickart served as backup commander for Skylab 2, the first mission to Skylab. When the SL–2 launch was delayed because of problems aboard Skylab itself, Schweickart spent many hours in EVA simulations developing and testing the tools that astronauts Conrad, Weitz and Kerwin would use to repair the station. He also served as capcom for all three Skylab missions.

At the conclusion of the Skylab program in April 1974, Schweickart was transferred to NASA Headquarters in Washington, D.C., to serve as Director of User Affairs in the Office of Applications, where he was responsible for making NASA technology available to companies and individuals outside the space program. In November 1976 he returned to the Johnson Space Center to work on policies regarding Shuttle payloads, and the following summer took a leave to serve California Governor Edmund G. "Jerry" Brown, Jr., as assistant for science and technology.

Schweickart resigned from NASA in July 1979 to become chairman of the California Energy Commission.

Schweickart and his wife, Clare, have five children: Vicki, Randolph, Russell, Elin and Diana. They live in Sacramento, California.

Scobee, Francis

Commander of Shuttle Mission 51-L, Dick Scobee was killed along with six crew members in the explosion of the Challenger during launch on January 28, 1986. It was the worst disaster in the history of manned spaceflight and brought the American space program to a halt.

Scobee, pilot Michael Smith, mission specialists Judith Resnik, Ronald McNair and Ellison Onizuka, payload specialists Gregory Jarvis of Hughes Aircraft and teacher Christa McAuliffe, were to have spent six days in orbit. Among their tasks were the deployment of the TDRS-B communications satellite and observation of Halley's Comet with the Spartan satellite. McAuliffe, the first private citizen to be selected for a Shuttle flight, was to conduct two "lessons" to be televised live to schoolchildren all over America.

The launch of 51-L was delayed twice by technical and weather problems, and finally lifted off at 11:38 A.M., EDT, after a night in which temperatures at Cape Canaveral dropped below freezing, a night in which, unknown to the crew, engineers at Morton Thiokol (builders of the Shuttle's powerful solid rocket boosters) and the NASA Marshall Space Flight Center were engaged in a debate over the safety of a launch in such weather. Some engineers were concerned that the O-rings, the seals beween segments of the huge boosters, would lose their flexibility in the cold, allowing superhot gases to escape from the SRB.

As analysis of films taken of the launch showed, a plume of smoke escaped from the right SRB at liftoff. Moments later, unknown to the crew or NASA flight controllers in Houston, the smoke was replaced by a jet of flame with a temperature of over 6000 degrees F—a blowtorch aimed at the metal strut that joined the SRB to the huge external fuel tank. As the Challenger rocketed to an altitude of nine miles, to the point known as "max Q," where speed and aerodynamic pressure place maximum stress on the vehicle, the attach point burned through and the aft wall of the tank blew open. A sudden and violent thrust forward, caused by fuel escaping from the ruptured tank, slammed the errant SRB into the right wing of the Challenger, shearing it off. An instant later the whole ET vaporized. The Challenger, broke apart owing to the violent stress. Originally thought to have been killed in the first surge from the external tank or in the disintegration of the Challenger itself, the astronauts apparently survived the initial breakup only to perish from oxygen deprivation or from the impact of the crew cabin (which emerged intact from the cloud of debris) as it hit the Atlantic three minutes later.

The crew compartment, resting on the floor of the Atlantic at a depth of over 100 feet, was not discovered until early March, six weeks after the accident. Recovery of the astronaut remains from the site took several more weeks. Scobee was finally buried at Arlington National Cemetery.

Mission 51-L was to have been Scobee's second Shuttle flight. In April 1984 he served as pilot of Mission 41-C, maneuvering the Challenger into a rendezvous with the ailing Solar Max satellite, which was then retrieved, repaired, and redeployed.

He spent a total of seven days in space.

Francis Richard Scobee was born May 19, 1939, in Cle Elum, Washington, but grew up in Auburn, where he graduated from high school in 1957. He enlisted in the US Air Force in October 1957 and was trained as an aircraft mechanic. While stationed at Kelly Air Force Base in San Antonio, Texas, Scobee took classes in night school, eventually qualifying for the Airman's Education and Commissioning Program. In 1963 he was enrolled at the University of Arizona in Tucson, and graduated two years later with a BS in aerospace engineering.

Commissioned as a second lieutenant in September 1965, Scobee managed to avoid being sent back to aircraft maintenance by volunteering for flight school. He spent eleven months at Moody AFB in Valdosta, Georgia, qualifying as a pilot, then learned to fly transport and cargo planes in South Carolina and Oklahoma. In November 1967 he began a tour in Vietnam with the 535th Tactical Airlift Squadron, flying C-7A Caribou twin-engine cargo planes into and out of combat zones. Returning to the US in 1969, he was a C-141 pilot at Charleston when he received a form letter soliciting his application for the Aerospace Research Pilot School at Edwards AFB.

The ARPS, as it was known, was originally an off-shoot of the better-known Air Force Test Pilot School, serving as a sort of postgraduate course in 1962 and 1963, until the two were merged. The ARPS name was adopted for both until the early 1970s, when it, too, reverted. Name aside, the school accepted only the best pilots, especially those who were young (under 30) with experience in high-performance fighter planes, and who had Academy backgrounds which put them on a fast career track. Scobee, in 1971, was already 32 years old, a cargo pilot (a "heavy" in Air Force slang), and a former enlisted man. He didn't think he had a chance, but applied. Unknown to him, the Air Force was changing the entrance requirements to allow pilots with more diverse backgrounds to enter the school. (Just two years later the requirements were changed again to allow flight engineers, such as Ellison Onizuka, to enroll.) And out of the hundreds who applied for the school, Scobee was one of the dozen chosen for Class 71-B. He arrived at Edwards in July 1971.

Following graduation the next summer, Scobee remained at Edwards as a test pilot. He flew the C-5, the E-4 (a specially modified Boeing 747), the F-111 and, beginning in 1975, the X-24B lifting body, a precursor to the Shuttle.

When NASA announced that applications were being taken for a new group of astronauts, Scobee applied and was accepted.

As a pilot he logged over 6500 hours of flying time in 45 different types of aircraft.

He was one of the 35 astronauts selected in January 1978 and in August 1979 completed a training and evaluation course. He served on the support crew for STS-1 and also flew the NASA/Boeing 747 shuttle carrier airplane. He was assigned to the STS-13 crew (later known as 41-C) in February 1983.

Scobee is survived by his wife, June, and two children, Kathie and Richard.

Scott, David

David Scott made three space flights between 1966 and 1972, taking part in the first docking in space, the first flight of the Apollo lunar module, and the first use of the lunar rover.

As pilot of Gemini 8, launched March 16, 1966, Scott and commander Neil Armstrong maneuvered their spacecraft to a linkup with an unmanned Agena 6.5 hours after launch, fulfilling one of the main goals of the Gemini program. Gemini 8 also became the first American space flight to be aborted when a steering thruster malfunctioned, causing the linked vehicles to revolve once a second. In order to control this dangerous spin, Armstrong was forced to use fuel reserved for reentry maneuvers. Mission rules dictated a return to Earth at the first opportunity, and Gemini 8 landed in the Pacific Ocean less than 11 hours after launch, cutting short a planned three-day mission and cancelling Scott's two-hour space walk.

Scott's second flight came in March 1969, as command module pilot for Apollo 9. During this 10-day mission, Scott piloted the command module Gumdrop while fellow astronauts James McDivitt and Russell Schweickart tested the lunar module Spider in free flight.

In July 1971 Scott commanded Apollo 15, the fourth lunar landing mission, becoming the seventh person to walk on the Moon. Scott and James Irwin, aboard the lunar module Falcon, used a four-wheeled electric car to explore an area of the lunar Apenines known as the Hadley Rille.

Scott logged almost 545 hours during his three space flights, including 20 hours and 46 minutes of EVA.

David Randolph Scott was born June 6, 1932, in San Antonio, Texas. His father was an Air Force general. Scott attended the University of Michigan for one year, then was accepted at the US Military Academy at West Point, graduating with a BS in 1954 and ranking fifth in a class of 633. He later did graduate work at the Massachusetts Institute of Technology, earning an MS in aeronautics and astronautics for a thesis concerning interplanetary navigation (1962).

After Air Force pilot training in Arizona Scott served with the 32nd Tactical Fighter Squadron, based in the Netherlands. He was at MIT from 1960 to 1962, then attended the USAF Experimental Test Pilot School at Edwards AFB, California. He did test flying after graduation in 1963, then was enrolled in the new Aerospace Research Pilot School, a special course designed to prepare Air Force officers for NASA and Department of Defense space programs. He was at ARPS when selected by NASA.

Scott came close to death in August 1963 when the NF-104 jet he was piloting crashed while simulating X-15 landings. Fellow ARPS student, and future MOL and X-15 pilot Michael Adams, riding in the back seat, ejected safely. Scott elected to stay with the aircraft, making a crash landing. Investigation later showed that both men would have been killed had they made any other choice.

As a pilot Scott eventually logged over 5600 hours of flying time, most of it in jets.

He was one of the 14 astronauts chosen by NASA in October 1963, and during early training specialized in spacecraft guidance and navigation systems. He served as a capcom for Gemini 4, and, in September 1965, became the first of his group to be assigned to a flight crew when he was named to pilot Gemini 8.

Scott trained for much of 1966 as a member of the backup crew for the first manned Apollo. When Apollo assignments were shuffled, he found himself on the prime crew for the first flight involving a manned lunar module. He later served as backup commander for Apollo 12, and was training as backup commander for Apollo 17 when he was removed in July 1972.

His removal was the result of an official reprimand directed at the entire crew of Apollo 15. Scott, Worden and Irwin had carried approximately 630 first day covers, specially printed and stamped envelopes, to the Moon in their personal kits. Eventually some of these envelopes were sold by stamp dealers to collectors. When NASA officials heard of the sales, they conducted an investigation and determined since the crew had carried a large number of unauthorized envelopes (some of the covers were authorized and other astronauts had carried similar covers on flights), a reprimand was in order. Scott was transferred to a desk job as technical assistant for the remaining Apollo missions while Worden left the astronaut group to take a job at the NASA Ames Research Center. Irwin resigned altogether.

By early 1973 Scott, who had met with Soviet cosmonauts on two different occasions, was assisting in the training of crew for the Apollo-Soyuz Test Project. He visited the Soviet Union in June of that year. In August 1973 he became deputy director of the NASA Dryden Flight Research Center at Edwards AFB. Following retirement from the USAF with the rank of colonel in March 1975 Scott was named director of Dryden, a job he held until resigning from NASA in October 1977.

Initially Scott founded Scott-Preyss Associates, a technical firm, and is now president of Scott Science and Technology in Los Angeles and Lancaster, California. One of his current projects is the development of an orbital transfer module for use with the Space Shuttle.

Scott and his wife, Lurton, have two children, Tracy and Douglas.

Seddon, Rhea

Dr. Rhea Seddon took part in an improvised and unsuccessful satellite rescue as a member of the crew of Shuttle Mission 51-D in April 1985.

Seddon deployed a Hughes Navy communications satellite, Leasat IV-3, from the Shuttle Discovery on April 13, only to have it fail to activate. Astronauts aboard the Discovery, including US senator Jake Garn, observed that an arming switch on the side of the Leasat had failed to close. Working with ground controllers, Seddon and the other astronauts built a makeshift "fly swatter," which was attached to the end of the Shuttle's robot arm by astronauts David Griggs and Jeffrey Hoffman. Seddon used the fly swatter to snag the arm on the Leasat, but the satellite remained adrift. (It was later retrieved, repaired and redeployed during another Shuttle mission.)

Seddon has spent 148 hours in space.

Margaret Rhea Seddon was born November 8, 1947, in Murfreesboro, Tennessee, and graduated from high school there in 1965. She attended the University of California at Berkeley, receiving a BA in physiology in 1970, and earned an MD degree from the University of Tennessee College of Medicine in 1973.

She completed a surgical internship and spent three years as a general surgical resident in Memphis, Tennessee. One of her areas of specialization was surgical nutrition; she also served as an emergency room physician. She continues to perform emergency room service in the Houston area.

Seddon was one of 35 astronauts selected by NASA in January 1978. In August 1979 she completed a training and evaluation course that qualified her as a mission specialist on Shuttle crews. She worked on computer software at the Shuttle Avionics Integration Laboratory and on the Shuttle medical kit and served as support crew for STS-6.

In August 1983 Seddon was assigned to a Shuttle crew scheduled to fly in July 1984. Because of various technical problems, she and her crewmates saw two different missions canceled prior to their launch on 51-D. In the meantime Seddon was assigned to Spacelab 4, a life sciences mission scheduled for January 1986. That, too, was canceled. She is currently training for another Spacelab life sciences flight.

Seddon is married to astronaut Robert Gibson. They have a son, Paul.

See, Elliott

Elliott See was training to be commander of Gemini 9 when he was killed in a plane crash in St. Louis, Missouri, on February 28, 1966. Killed with him was Major Charles Bassett, USAF, scheduled to be the pilot of Gemini 9.

Elliott McKay See, Jr., was born July 23, 1927, in Dallas, Texas. He received a BS from the US Merchant Marine Academy in 1949, then joined the General Electric Company, becoming a test pilot. From 1953 to 1956 he served on active duty as a US Navy pilot, then returned to GE. As a test pilot he was involved in the initial flights of the F-4H aircraft. He later earned an MS in engineering from the University of California at Los Angeles in 1962.

See was one of nine astronauts chosen by NASA in September 1962. He served as backup pilot for Gemini 5 prior to being named commander of Gemini 9 in September 1965.

He was survived by his wife, Marilyn, and three children, Sally, Carolyn, and David.

Shaw, Brewster

Brewster Shaw made two Shuttle flights, as pilot of STS-9/Spacelab 1 in 1983, and as commander of Mission 61-B in 1985. Spacelab 1 was crewed by six astronauts, the largest to fly aboard a single spacecraft, and carried a variety of scientific experiments which were operated around-the-clock for ten days. Mission 61-B saw the first demonstration of space construction techniques.

Shaw has logged approximately 389 hours in space.

Brewster Hopkinson Shaw, Jr., was born May 16, 1945, in Cass City, Michigan, and graduated from high school there in 1963. He attended the University of Wisconsin at Madison, receiving BS and MS degrees in engineering mechanics in 1968 and 1969.

After graduation from Wisconsin, Shaw joined the US Air Force and completed pilot training at Craig AFB, Alabama, in 1970. He received advanced training as an F-100 pilot at Luke AFB, Arizona, then was assigned to the 352nd Tactical Fighter Squadron at Phan Rang Air Base in Vietnam. For most of the next two years Shaw flew combat missions in Vietnam and Thailand, earning two "Top Gun" awards. Returning to the US, he served as an F-4 instructor pilot at George AFB, California, then attended the US Air Force Test Pilot School at Edwards AFB. He served as a test pilot at Edwards, and in 1978 was an instructor at the school there when selected by NASA.

He has logged over 4200 hours of flying time, including 644 hours of combat, in over 30 different types of aircraft.

Shaw was one of 35 astronauts chosen by NASA in January 1978. In August 1979 he completed a training and evaluation course which qualified him as a pilot on Shuttle crews. In 1982 he served as capcom for STS-3 and STS-4. In April 1982 he was named to the STS-9 crew.

In November 1985 Shaw was named to command a Department of Defense Shuttle mission then scheduled for late 1986.

Shaw and his wife, Kathleen, have three children, Brewster III, Jessica and Brandon.

Shepard, Alan

Alan Shepard became the first American in space on May 5, 1961, when he rode the Mercury-Redstone 3 spacecraft he had named Freedom 7 on a 15-minute flight, reaching an altitude of 116 miles and landing in the Atlantic 302 miles downrange from Cape Canaveral.

Shepard later commanded Apollo 14, the third manned lunar landing, in 1971, spending two days on the Moon. He and fellow astronaut Ed Mitchell used a two-wheel trolley to haul experiments and samples to sites near the crater Fra Mauro. Shepard also fulfilled a ten-year-old dream by becoming the first person to golf on the Moon.

He logged a total of nine days in space, including nine hours and 22 minutes of lunar EVA. He was the only one of the original seven Mercury astronauts to make a flight to the Moon.

Alan Bartlett Shepard, Jr., was born November 18, 1923, in East Derry, New Hampshire. His father was a career Army officer who had attended West Point. Following graduation from Pinkerton Academy in Derry, Shepard spent a year at Admiral Farragut Academy in New Jersey before attending the US Naval Academy, where he earned a BS in 1944.

During the final year of World War II Shepard served aboard the destroyer Cogswell in the Pacific. Upon his return to the US, he underwent pilot training at Corpus Christi, Texas, and Pensacola, Florida, receiving his wings in 1947. For the next three years he served with Fighter Squadron 42 at bases in Virginia and Florida, and aboard aircraft carriers in the Mediterranean. Between 1953 and 1956 he served as operations officer of Fighter Squadron 193, making two tours in the Pacific aboard the carrier USS Oriskany.

Shepard attended the US Navy Test Pilot School at Patuxent River, Maryland, in 1950, and served as a test pilot and instructor at Pax River from 1951 to 1953, and from 1956 to 1958. During his second tour there he graduated from the Naval War College. When selected by NASA for the Mercury program in 1959 he was on the staff of the commander in chief of the Atlantic Fleet, preparing to become commander of his own carrier squadron.

He would eventually log over 8000 hours of flying time, including 3700 hours in jets.

As an astronaut, Shepard quickly established himself as a first-rate pilot and engineer, and in January 1961 was chosen by NASA officials and by a vote of his fellow astronauts to make the first Mercury flight.

He served as capcom for the flights of Gus Grissom and John Glenn, and was backup to Gordon Cooper on the last Mercury flight.

Shepard and some NASA engineers lobbied for an additional Mercury flight, MA-10, a planned three-day flight to take place late in 1963. But senior NASA officials decided that priority should go to the new Gemini program. Shepard and astronaut Frank Borman were training as the crew for the first manned Gemini mission in early 1964 when Shepard contracted Meniere's syndrome, an inner ear ailment that caused the Navy to forbid him to fly solo in jet planes, and forced NASA to ground him. Shepard became chief of the astronaut office—in effect, boss of all the other astronauts, except Deke Slayton, who had already taken an administrative job.

According to astronaut memoirs, Shepard ran the office "like an admiral," with authority tempered occasionally by humor: Shepard's imitation of comedian Bill Dana's character "Jose Jimenez" became legendary. Unable to take part in active astronaut training, Shepard devoted his free time to investments, and by 1970 had become a millionaire.

In early 1969 Shepard underwent experimental surgery that corrected the inner ear problem; he was restored to full flight status that May and assigned to command Apollo 14 that August. Promoted to the rank of rear admiral, he resumed his position as chief astronaut in June 1971 and remained there until his retirement from NASA and the Navy on August 1, 1974.

Since leaving NASA Shepard has been partner and chairman of the Marathon Construction Company in Houston, Texas, and until recently was president of the Windward Coors Company in nearby Deer Park. He has also been a commercial spokesman.

In 1971 Shepard served as a delegate to the 26th United Nations General Assembly.

He contributed to the book *We Seven* (1962) and is featured in the book and movie *The Right Stuff*.

Shepard and his wife, Louise, have two children, Laura and Julie. They live near Houston.

Shepherd, William

Commander William M. Shepherd, USN, is one of the 17 astronauts selected by NASA in May 1984. In June 1985 he completed a training and evaluation course which qualified him as a mission specialist on future Shuttle flights.

Shepherd was born July 26, 1949, in Oak Ridge, Tennessee, but graduated from Arcadia High School in Scottsdale, Arizona, in 1967. He earned an appointment to the US Naval Academy at Annapolis, graduating with a BS in aerospace engineering in 1971. He later earned an MS in mechanical engineering and an MS in ocean engineering from the Masschusetts Institute of Technology in 1978.

After graduating from Annapolis, Shepherd served with a Navy underwater demolition team, and with the elite SEAL units. At the time of his selection by NASA he was the commanding officer of Special Boat Unit 20 at the Naval Amphibious Base at Little Creek, Virginia.

Shepherd is single.

Shriver, Loren

Loren Shriver was the pilot of Shuttle Mission 51-C in January 1985, the first Shuttle flight to be dedicated to a Department of Defense payload, and the first time an American space flight was carried out in relative secrecy. Launch and landing times were not disclosed in advance, all communications between the astronauts and mission control were encrypted, and no films or videotapes of activities aboard the Shuttle Challenger were ever released. The payload itself was classified, though press reports described it as a large National Security Agency electronic spy satellite which was placed in a synchronous orbit by an inertial upper stage.

Shriver logged slightly more than three days in space.

Loren James Shriver was born September 23, 1944, in Jefferson, Iowa, but grew up in Paton, Iowa, graduating from Consolidated High School there in 1962. A year later he entered the US Air Force Academy, earning a BS in aeronautical engineering in 1967. In 1968 he earned an MS in astronautical engineering from Purdue.

Following pilot training, Shriver was stationed at Vance Air Force Base, Oklahoma, as a T-38 instructor until 1973. He completed F-4 combat training in Florida, then was stationed in Thailand until October 1974. Returning to the US, he attended the USAF Test Pilot School at Edwards AFB, California, remaining at Edwards as a test pilot until his selection by NASA.

Shriver was one of 35 astronauts selected by NASA in January 1978. In August 1979 he completed a training and evaluation course that qualified him as a pilot on future Shuttle crews. He was a member of the support crew for STS-1 and STS-2. In October 1982 he was assigned to STS-10, then scheduled to be the first Department of Defense Shuttle mission, but it was canceled.

Following his flight on Mission 51-C Shriver was named to command Mission 61-M, then scheduled for 1986.

Colonel Shriver and his wife, Susan, have four children, Camilla, Melinda, Jered, and Rebecca.

Shulman, Ellen

Dr. Ellen M. Shulman is one of the 17 astronauts selected by NASA in May 1984. In June 1985 she completed a training and evaluation course which qualified her as a mission specialist on future Shuttle flights.

Shulman was born April 27, 1953, in Fayetteville, North Carolina, but attended Bayside High School in New York City, graduating in 1970. She received a BA in geology from the State University of New York at Buffalo in 1974, and an MD from Cornell University in 1978.

After completing medical school, Shulman spent three years training in internal medicine at the University of Texas Health Science Center in San Antonio. In 1981 she joined NASA as a medical officer at the Johnson Space Center. She was also graduated with honors from the Air Force Aerospace Medicine Course at Brooks Air Force Base in San Antonio. When selected as an astronaut Shulman was a physician in the Johnson Space Center flight medicine clinic.

Shulman and her husband, Kenneth Baker live in Houston.

Slayton, Donald

Donald "Deke" Slayton was one of the original seven Mercury astronauts chosen by NASA in 1959. Grounded because of a heart problem

in 1962, he supervised the training and selection of all Gemini and Apollo astronaut crews until he was restored to flight status in 1972. He eventually went into space in the Apollo-Soyuz Test Project in July 1975.

During the two-and-a-half years preceeding the launch, Slayton and the other American astronauts assigned to the prime and backup crews studied Russian and trained for weeks at Star Town, the cosmonaut center near Moscow.

The flight of ASTP had worldwide attention at its launch on July 15, 1975. Two days later Apollo docked with Soyuz 19 over Europe. Slayton and fellow astronauts Stafford and Brand swapped places with cosmonauts Leonov and Kubasov during the two days the ships remained linked. After five more days, Apollo returned to Earth. A fuel leak during splashdown seared the astronauts' lungs, a fortuitous accident for Slayton, since the detailed medical examination that followed showed that he had an undetected lung tumor, which was then removed.

Slayton logged approximately nine days in space.

Donald Kent Slayton was born March 1, 1924, in Sparta, Wisconsin, and grew up on a farm there. At the age of 18 he enlisted in the US Army Air Corps and earned his pilot's wings a year later. As a B-25 bomber pilot he flew 56 combat missions over Southern Europe and 7 over Japan. (In her 1966 book, *If the Sun Dies,* Italian journalist Oriana Fallaci recounts her discovery, during her meeting with Slayton, that he was one of the pilots of Allied planes that bombed her village.)

Returning to the US, Slayton entered the University of Minnesota, receiving a BS in aeronautical engineering in 1949. He later received an honorary PhD in engineering from Michigan Technological University in 1965.

From 1949 to 1951 Slayton was an aeronautical engineer with the Boeing Company in Seattle, Washington. Recalled to active duty during the Korean War, he was first assigned to 12th Air Force Headquarters, then, in 1955, to the Air Force Flight Test Pilot School at Edwards Air Force Base, California. From 1956 to 1959 Slayton was a test pilot there.

Selected as one of the original Mercury astronauts, Slayton was intended to be the first American to orbit the Earth. Astronauts Alan Shepard, Gus Grissom and John Glenn were assigned to make suborbital flights, but following the flights of Shepard and Grissom's, Glenn's was canceled. He was given the first orbital Mercury flight and Slayton, in November 1961, was assigned to the second.

In March 1962, however, just three weeks after Glenn's successful flight, NASA physicians grounded Slayton because of concerns over a long-standing heart condition. Slayton was replaced on the Mercury-Atlas 7 flight by Scott Carpenter.

Slayton remained with NASA as an astronaut, resigning his commission as a major in the USAF in November 1963, and taking on the additional duties of Director, Flight Crew Operations. In this job Slayton controlled astronaut flight assignments, making his own selections which were then forwarded to NASA headquarters for approval. He was not overruled until he assigned fellow Mercury astronaut Shepard to command Apollo 13. Shepard had been grounded for physical reasons from 1963 to 1969 and Slayton's bosses decided that the first American in space needed more training. (Shepard was assigned ultimately to Apollo 14).

Slayton never gave up in his quest to return to flight status. He continued to attend training sessions in Gemini and Apollo, and in 1966 came close to being confirmed as commander of the Apollo 2 crew. But it was not until 1972 that he was judged physically able to fly in space. Slayton won assignment to the Apollo-Soyuz Project in January

1973 and resigned as Director of Flight Crew Operations in February 1974.

As a pilot Slayton has logged over 7000 hours of flying time, most of it in jet aircraft.

Following his space flight Slayton managed the Approach and Landing Tests of the Space Shuttle Enterprise, and the orbital flight test program for the first four Shuttle missions. He retired from NASA in February 1981 (though he served as a consultant to the space agency for another year) to become vice chairman of the board of Space Services, Inc., a Texas-based private space firm that successfully launched its Conestoga rocket in 1983, and which later offered to send human ashes into permanent orbital repose.

Slayton was a contributor to *We Seven* (1962) and was profiled in Tom Wolfe's *The Right Stuff* (1979). He and his wife, Bobbi, live in Houston, Texas. Slayton has a son from a previous marriage.

Smith, Michael

Michael Smith was the pilot of the Shuttle Challenger for Mission 51-L, which exploded 74 seconds after launch on January 28, 1986, killing Smith and six other astronauts, including teacher Sharon Christa McAuliffe. Mission 51-L would have been Smith's first space flight.

Michael John Smith was born April 30, 1945, in Beaufort, North Carolina, where he graduated from high school in 1963. Always interested in aviation, he entered the US Naval Academy, planning to become a navy pilot. He graduated in 1967 with a BS in naval science, and a year later earned an MS in aeronautical engineering from the US Naval Postgraduate School.

After completing pilot training at Kingsville, Texas, in May 1969, Smith was assigned to the Advanced Jet Training Command, where he served as an instructor until March 1971. During the next two years he piloted A-6 Intruders from the carrier USS Kitty Hawk on combat missions over Vietnam.

Returning to the US in 1973, he attended the US Navy Test Pilot School at Patuxent River, Maryland, then spent two years as a test pilot and another 18 months as an instructor at Pax River. He was then assigned as maintenance and operations officer of Attack Squadron 75 aboard the carrier USS Saratoga.

As a pilot Smith had logged over 4500 hours of flying time, including over 4200 hours in jets, in 28 different types of aircraft.

He was one of the 19 astronauts selected by NASA in May 1980. In August 1981 he completed a training and evaluation course that qualified him as a pilot on future Shuttle crews. For the next three years he worked at a variety of assignments, including commander in the Shuttle Avionics Integration Laboratory, chief of the Aircraft Operations Division, technical assistant to the director of Flight Operations, and chase plane pilot for STS-5. Smith was originally assigned as pilot of Shuttle Mission 51-K, the Spacelab Earth Observation Mission 1, scheduled for the summer of 1985, but was transferred to Mission 51-L in January 1985 when EOM-1 was canceled.

Commander Smith is survived by his wife, Jane, and three children, Scott, Alison and Erin.

He is buried in Arlington National Cemetery.

Spring, Sherwood

Woody Spring took part in the first EVA involving space construction during Shuttle Mission 61-B in November and December 1985.

Spring and fellow mission specialist Jerry Ross took two space walks totalling over 12 hours. On EVA-1, November 29, Spring and Ross, who billed themselves as the "Ace Construction Company," assembled and then disassembled a 45-foot triangular truss called ACCESS and a 12-foot tetrahedron called EASE while working in the payload bay of the Shuttle Atlantis. Both structures were prototypes for elements of future space station construction. During EVA-2 on December 1, the astronauts practiced assembling the structures while perched at the end of the Shuttle's robot arm. Spring and Ross found that they were able to work quickly in microgravity, but also discovered after the EVAs that their hands got stiff and numb, and that they were extremely tired.

The crew of Mission 61-B also deployed three communications satellites and carried a McDonnell-Douglas pharmaceutical experiment.

Spring has logged 165 hours in space, including 12 hours and 14 minutes of EVA time.

Sherwood Clark Spring was born September 3, 1944, in Hartford, Connecticut, but considers Harmony, Rhode Island, to be his hometown. He graduated from Ponagansett High School in Chepachet, Rhode Island, in 1963, then attended the US Military Academy at West Point, earning a BS in general engineering in 1967. He later earned an MS in aerospace engineering from the University of Arizona in 1974.

After spending a year at airborne, ranger and microwave communication schools, Spring did a tour of duty in Vietnam with the 101st Airborne Division. He returned to the US in 1969 for training as a helicopter pilot at Fort Wolters, Texas, then went back to Vietnam for another tour with the lst Air Cavalry.

After his second tour in Vietnam, Spring received jet pilot training at Ft. Stewart, Georgia, and Ft. Rucker, Alabama, then attended the University of Arizona for two years. During the next five years he was stationed at the Army's flight test center at Edwards Air Force Base, California, and at the US Navy Test Pilot School at Patuxent River, Maryland, as a student and test pilot. When selected by NASA in 1980 he was operations officer for the 19th Aviation Battalion in Pyontaek, Korea.

As a pilot Spring has logged over 3000 hours of flying time in 25 different types of airplanes and helicopters.

Spring was one of the 19 astronauts chosen by NASA in May 1980. In August 1981 he completed a training and evaluation course that qualified him as a mission specialist on Shuttle crews. As an astronaut he worked on computer software at the Shuttle Avionics Integration Laboratory and the Flight Simulation Laboratory, and on the payloads for STS-5, 6, 7, 8, and 9.

Colonel Spring and his wife, Collette, have two children, Sarah and Justin.

Springer, Robert

Robert Springer was one of the 19 astronauts selected by NASA in May 1980. In June 1981 he completed a training and evaluation course that qualified him as a mission specialist on Shuttle crews. He was assigned to one Shuttle/Spacelab mission, 51-K, which was canceled before it could be flown. Prior to the Challenger accident in January 1986 he was assigned to Mission 61-H, scheduled for the summer of that year.

Robert Clyde Springer was born May 21, 1942, in St. Louis, Mis-

souri, but grew up in Ashland, Ohio, where he graduated from high school in 1960. He attended the US Naval Academy, where he received a BS in naval science in 1964. He later earned an MS in operations research and systems analysis from the US Naval Postgraduate School in 1971.

Springer elected to serve in the US Marine Corps and was commissioned upon graduation from Annapolis. He underwent basic training at Quantico, Virginia, then attended flight school at Pensacola, Florida, and Beeville, Texas, earning his wings in August 1966. He was stationed at the Marine Corps Air Station in Cherry Point, North Carolina, then transferred to Chu Lai, Vietnam, where he flew 300 combat missions. Beginning in June 1968 Springer served as an advisor to the marine corps of the Republic of Korea and flew 75 further combat missions in 01 Bird Dogs and UHl Huey helicopters.

Returning to the US, Springer attended the Naval Postgraduate School, then served in a variety of assignments at El Toro and Camp Pendleton, California; Okinawa; and Beaufort, South Carolina. He attended the Navy Fighter Weapons School in San Diego, also known as the "Top Gun" school, and, in 1975, the US Navy Test Pilot School at Patuxent River, Maryland, remaining there as a helicopter test pilot until 1977. He later attended the Armed Forces Staff College, and at the time of his selection by NASA was serving as aide-de-camp to the Commanding General, Fleet Marine Force, Atlantic.

As a pilot Springer has logged over 3200 hours flying time, including 2400 hours in jets.

As an astronaut Spring has worked on development studies for a Space Operations Center (later known as the Space Station), the remote manipulator arm, Get-Away-Special payloads, and other satellites. From October 1984 to October 1985 he was a Shuttle capcom at mission control.

Colonel Springer and his wife, Mary, have three children, Chad, Kira and Derek.

Stafford, Thomas

Thomas Stafford made four space flights between 1965 and 1975, two in Gemini and two in Apollo, taking part in a number of space firsts, including the first rendezvous and the first international flight.

Stafford was pilot of the Gemini 6 mission launched December 15, 1965, after a series of delays, including the first launch pad abort of a manned spacecraft on December 13. Stafford and command pilot Walter Schirra were originally scheduled to go into space in October 1965 on a three-day flight during which they would rendezvous with a previously launched Agena and dock with it. But the Agena failed to reach orbit, and Gemini 6 was taken off the pad and replaced by Gemini 7, launched December 4, 1965, on a two-week endurance flight with astronauts Borman and Lovell. The first attempt to launch Stafford and Schirra for a rendezvous ended less than two seconds after ignition of the Titan II first stage, but by choosing not to eject the astronauts allowed the Titan, and Gemini 6, one more chance, and on December 16 they met up with Gemini 7 in orbit.

Stafford was command pilot of Gemini 9, launched just six months later. He was originally backup commander, but prime crew astronauts See and Bassett were killed and backups Stafford and Eugene Cernan took their places. Once again, Stafford's "Agena jinx" was working, as the Gemini 9 target Agena failed. This time NASA had an alternative, a smaller Augmented Target Docking Adaptor, which reached orbit but failed to shed its protective shroud, preventing a docking. The rendezvous was successful and Stafford later supervised Cernan's difficult and unsuccessful two-hour spacewalk.

In May 1969 Stafford commanded Apollo 10, the final, full-scale dress rehearsal for a manned lunar landing. While John Young orbited the Moon in the command module Charlie Brown, Stafford and Cernan took the lunar module Snoopy to within 50,000 feet of the lunar surface to test the LM's propulsion and navigation systems. (That particular LM was too heavy to survive a lunar landing and liftoff, or Stafford might have become the first man to walk on the Moon.)

In July 1975 Brigadier General Stafford, the first general to make a space flight, commanded the American half of the Apollo-Soyuz Test Project. In orbit over Europe, Stafford, Vance Brand and Deke Slayton rendezvoused and docked their Apollo to Soyuz 19, crewed by Alexei Leonov and Valery Kubasov. Two days of joint activities followed, then each vehicle returned to Earth. During Apollo's splashdown a fuel leak caused problems for the astronauts.

During his four flights Stafford logged over 21 days in space.

Thomas Patten Stafford was born September 17, 1930, in Weatherford, Oklahoma, where he grew up. He earned an appointment to the US Naval Academy at Annapolis, graduating in 1952 with a bachelor of science degree.

Stafford elected to serve in the US Air Force and underwent pilot training in Texas, earning his wings in 1953. From 1953 to 1958 he served as an interceptor pilot at Ellsworth AFB, South Dakota, and Hahn AFB, Germany. Returning to the US, he attended the USAF Experimental Flight Test Pilot School at Edwards AFB, California, and on graduation in April 1959 received the A. B. Honts award as outstanding student. He remained at Edwards as an instructor, co-authoring *The Pilot's Handbook for Performance Flight Testing* and *The Aerodynamics Handbook for Performance Flight Testing.*

He eventually logged over 7100 flying hours in 110 different types of aircraft.

Stafford was one of the 9 astronauts selected by NASA in September 1962. He served as backup pilot for Gemini 3, the first manned Gemini flight, in 1965, and was variously backup command module pilot for Apollo 2, then backup commander for Apollo 7, in addition to his four space flights.

In June 1969 Stafford succeeded Alan Shepard as the chief of the astronaut office and played a major role in the selection of astronaut crews for Apollo and Skylab missions. In June 1971 he became deputy director of flight crew operations at the Manned Spacecraft Center until being named, in January 1973, to Apollo-Soyuz.

Major General Stafford left NASA in November 1975 to assume command of the USAF Flight Test Center at Edwards AFB. Promoted to lieutenant general in March 1978, he became deputy chief of staff for research development and acquisition at USAF Headquarters in Washington. He retired from the Air Force on November 1, 1979.

Stafford is currently vice president of Gibraltar Exploration, Ltd., in Oklahoma City, Oklahoma.

He and his wife, Faye, have two daughters, Dianne and Karin.

Stewart, Robert

During his two flights aboard the Space Shuttle Bob Stewart became one of the first astronauts to make an untethered space walk. Stewart was a mission specialist aboard Shuttle Mission 41-B in February 1984 and took part in two test flights of the self-contained Manned Maneuvering Unit, the so-called Buck Rogers rocket pack which allows astro-

nauts to fly freely in space away from the Shuttle. Mission 41-B also launched two communications satellites. Both satellites suffered propulsion failures and were retrieved and returned to Earth in November 1984.

In October 1985 Stewart was a mission specialist aboard 51-J, the first flight of the orbiter Atlantis, which carried two Department of Defense communications satellites into space.

Stewart has logged approximately 290 hours in space, including 12 hours in EVA.

Robert Lee Stewart was born August 13, 1942, in Washington, D.C., but grew up in El Lago, Texas. He graduated from high school in Hattiesburg, Mississippi, in 1960, and attended the University of Southern Mississippi, earning a BS in mathematics in 1964. He later earned an MS in aerospace engineering from the University of Texas in 1974.

Stewart joined the US Army in 1964 and served initially as an air defense artillery director at Gunter Air Force Base, Alabama. He became a helicopter pilot in 1966 and logged over 1000 hours in combat missions in Vietnam. Upon his return to the US he was an instructor pilot, then attended the US Naval Test Pilot School at Patuxent River, Maryland, graduating in 1974 and being assigned to the Army's helicopter test pilot group at Edwards Air Force Base, California. He has logged over 5400 hours of flying time in 38 different types of military and civilian aircraft.

Selected as an astronaut candidate by NASA in January 1978, Stewart completed the yearlong training and evaluation course in August 1979. Among his technical assignments he has served as support crewman for STS-4 and capcom for STS-5. In September 1985 he was assigned as mission specialist aboard the Spacelab Earth Observation Mission originally scheduled for 1986. When shuttle launches were suspended following the Challenger disaster, Stewart left NASA and was reassigned to the US Space Command in Colorado Springs, Colorado.

Colonel Stewart and his wife, Mary Jane, have two daughters, Ragon and Jennifer.

Sullivan, Kathryn

Dr. Kathryn Sullivan became the first American woman to walk in space when she spent three-and-a-half hours outside the Shuttle Challenger on October 11, 1984. Sullivan and astronaut David Leestma successfully conducted a satellite re-fueling test. In addition, the seven astronauts of Mission 41-G, the largest crew sent into space in a single spacecraft to that date, deployed the Earth Radiation Budget Satellite and conducted observations of the Earth's surface.

Sullivan has logged approximately 198 hours in space.

Kathryn Dwyer Sullivan was born October 3, 1951, in Paterson, New Jersey, but grew up in Woodland Hills, California. She and future astronaut Sally Ride were briefly classmates in the same elementary school. Sullivan graduated from Taft High School in Woodland Hills in 1969 and went on to attend the University of California at Santa Cruz, where she received a BS in earth sciences in 1973. She later earned her PhD in geology from Dalhousie University in Halifax, Nova Scotia, in 1978.

As a graduate student at Dalhousie Sullivan took part in a number of oceanographic expeditions by the US Geological Survey, visiting the Mid-Atlantic Ridge, the Newfoundland Basin, and fault zones off the coast of Southern California. She also taught at Dalhousie and worked for Geological Survey of Canada. In 1985 Sullivan became an adjunct professor of geology at Rice University in Houston, Texas.

Sullivan was one of the 35 astronauts selected by NASA in January 1978. In August 1979 she completed a training and evaluation course which qualifed her as a mission specialist on future Shuttle crews. She worked on the support crews of STS-3 through STS-8, and has also continued her research in geoscience by making high-altitude flights in the NASA WB-57F aircraft and being co-investigator of the Shuttle Imaging Radar system flown on Mission 41-G.

She was also assigned as a mission specialist on the launch of the Hubble Space Telescope, originally scheduled for 1986. In March 1985 President Reagan appointed her to the National Commission on Space, a year-long study to determine goals for US civilian space programs for the next 25 years.

Sullivan is unmarried and lives in Houston.

Swigert, John

Jack Swigert became the first astronaut to step into a flight crew on short notice when he replaced Thomas Mattingly as command module pilot of Apollo 13 on April 8, 1970, just three days before launch. When Apollo 13 suffered an explosion that forced the cancellation of its lunar landing, Swigert joined James Lovell and Fred Haise in using the lunar module Aquarius as a "lifeboat"—a procedure, ironically, for which Swigert had written the manual.

For three harrowing days the astronauts improvised, using Aquarius's rockets to maneuver the huge command and service module complex, rigging makeshift air filters, and keeping close track of their limited supplies of oxygen, electricity and water. They also tried to keep warm, since the temperature in the powerless command module Odyssey dropped to freezing. The astronauts returned to Earth on April 17, 1970, splashing down safely in the Pacific near the carrier USS Iwo Jima.

The unusual change occurred in the first place because all six prime and backup crewmen had been mistakenly exposed to German measles. Mattingly had never had the illness in childhood and NASA officials feared that should he become sick during the mission (he would be orbiting alone around the Moon for two days) he would be unable to function. Swigert was asked to step in, though he had to pass a grueling session in the flight simulator to prove to NASA officials that he was ready. (Because of the complexity of the lunar landing missions and the limited availability of simulators, backup crewmen were never trained as thoroughly as were members of the prime crew.) Swigert was ready to fly Apollo 13, but in the confusion of those three days he neglected one item of personal business: he forgot to file his income tax return and had to ask for an extension from space.

Apollo 13 was Swigert's only space flight.

John Leonard Swigert, Jr., was born August 30, 1931, in Denver, Colorado. His father was a physician. Swigert attended Regis and East High Schools in Denver, then went on to the University of Colorado, where he received a BS in mechanical engineering in 1953. He would later earn an MS in aerospace science from Rensselaer Polytechnic Institute in 1965 and an MBA from the University of Hartford in 1967.

Swigert joined the US Air Force upon graduation from Colorado and served as a jet fighter pilot in Japan and Korea until 1956. Leaving active duty, he flew with the Massachusetts Air National Guard until 1960, and with the Connecticut Air National Guard from 1960 to 1965. He became a pilot for Pratt and Whitney, builders of jet engines, and applied for the 1963 astronaut group. Rejected because of lack of test pilot experience or advanced schooling, Swigert enrolled at Rensselaer to work on a master's degree and also tested the inflatable Rogallo wing, a dart-shaped parasail that was intended to "fly" returning spacecraft to landing sites.

As a pilot Swigert would eventually log over 8000 hours of flying time, including more than 6500 hours in jets.

Swigert was one of the 19 astronauts selected by NASA in April 1966. He became a specialist in the Apollo command module and served on the support crew for Apollo 7, the first manned Apollo mission, and for Apollo 11, the first manned lunar landing. He was a capcom for Apollo 7 as well. In August 1969 he joined John Young and Charles Duke on the backup crew for Apollo 13.

Following Apollo 13 Swigert trained for the Apollo-Soyuz Test Project and had been informally assigned to the mission with Thomas Stafford and Deke Slayton when NASA began investigating the Apollo 15 envelope scandal. Other Apollo astronauts who had signed envelopes (which were later sold to collectors) were asked to disclose it. Swigert denied signing them, but later admitted that he had. His failure to make the disclosure when asked cost him the seat on ASTP.

Shortly thereafter, in April 1973, Swigert left the astronaut office to become executive director of the Committee on Science and Technology of the US House of Representatives, a position he held until August 31, 1977.

Swigert had the option of returning to the astronaut office as a Shuttle pilot in 1977 and considered it, but resigned instead to run for the US Senate from Colorado. His 1978 campaign was unsuccessful. From 1979 to 1981 Swigert was vice president for technology development of the BDM Corporation in Denver, and in 1981 and 1982 served as vice president for financial and corporate affairs for International Gold and Minerals, Ltd.

In February 1982 Swigert announced his candidacy for the US House of Representatives seat for the Colorado Sixth Congressional District. On November 2, 1982, Swigert was elected Republican Congressman with 64 percent of the popular vote.

During the campaign, however, it was learned that Swigert was suffering from bone cancer. He died in Washington, D.C., on December 27, 1982, just one week before he was to take his Congressional seat. He was the first American space traveler to die of natural causes.

Swigert was unmarried.

Thagard, Norman

Dr. Norman Thagard served as mission specialist aboard two Shuttle flights, STS-7 in 1983 and Spacelab 3 in 1985.

Originally trained as a physician, Thagard was added to the crew of four astronauts (which included Sally Ride, America's first woman in space) already assigned to STS-7 primarily to study space adaptation syndrome (SAS), so-called "space sickness" that affected about half of all the astronauts who had flown on the Shuttle until then. During the six-day STS-7 mission Thagard conducted physical tests and collected data on the crew members' adaptation to space. The astronauts also deployed two communications satellites and deployed and retrieved a third.

Thagard went into space a second time on Shuttle Mission 51-B carrying Spacelab 3, a mission dedicated to space manufacturing and medicine. In addition to its crew of seven astronauts and payload specialists, Spacelab 3 carried 24 experimental rats and a pair of squirrel monkeys. Caring for the monkeys, one of whom got sick, proved frustrating and time-consuming; nevertheless, 14 of the 15 scientific experiments carried on Spacelab 3 provided data to experimenters.

On his two flights Thagard logged just over 13 days in space.

Norman Earl Thagard was born July 3, 1943, in Marianna, Florida, but grew up in Jacksonville, where he graduated from Paxon Senior High School in 1961. He attended Florida State University, receiving BS and MS degrees in engineering science in 1965 and 1966 while also taking courses in pre-med. He received his MD from the University of Texas Southwestern Medical School in 1977.

On active duty with the Marine Corps Reserve beginning in September 1966, Captain Thagard underwent pilot training, earning his wings in 1968. He flew F-4 Phantoms at the Marine Corps Air Station in Beaufort, South Carolina, then was assigned to duty in Vietnam, flying 163 combat missions in 1969 and 1970. Returning to the US, he was an aviation weapons division officer at Beaufort until leaving the service in 1971. He then resumed his medical education while also continuing to study electrical engineering. At the time of his selection as an astronaut he was an intern at the Medical University of South Carolina.

Having learned of NASA's search for new astronauts through his wife, who saw the announcement, Thagard applied and in January 1978 was one of 35 new astronauts who was selected. In August 1979 he completed a training and evaluation course, becoming qualified as a Shuttle mission specialist. He worked in the Shuttle Avionics Integration Laboratory and also with the payloads for STS-7. He was already training for the Spacelab 3 mission in December 1982 when he was added to the STS-7 crew, whose members had been selected the previous April.

Thagard was assigned to the crew of Mission 61-H, scheduled for June 1986, then transferred to Mission 61-G upon the resignation of astronaut John Fabian, only to have the new mission canceled in the wake of the Challenger explosion.

Thagard and his wife, the former Rex Kirby Johnson, have three sons, Norman, James and Daniel.

Thorne, Stephen

Lieutenant Commander Stephen D. Thorne, USN, was one of the 13 astronauts selected by NASA in June 1985. In August he commenced a training and evaluation course that would have qualified him as a pilot on future Shuttle missions.

However, on May 24, 1986, Thorne was killed in an off-duty accident. He was a passenger in a Pitts 2-A sports plane piloted by NASA flight controller Jim Simons when it went out of control and crashed south of Houston.

Thorne was born February 11, 1953, in Frankfurt-on-Main, West Germany, and graduated from T. L. Hanna High School in Anderson, South Carolina, in 1971. He attended the US Naval Academy, where he received a BS in systems engineering in 1975.

After graduation from Annapolis, Thorne became a pilot, earning his wings in 1976. He flew F-4 Phantoms aboard the carrier USS Ranger in the Pacific, then, in 1981, attended the US Naval Test Pilot School at Patuxent River, Maryland. He was a test pilot there until 1984, and was an F-18 pilot aboard the carrier USS Coral Sea when selected by NASA.

Thorne had logged over 2500 hours of flying time, including 200 carrier landings, in 30 different types of aircraft.

He was survived by his wife, Sue.

Thornton, Kathryn

Dr. Kathryn C. Thornton is one of the 17 astronauts selected by NASA in May 1984. In July 1985 she completed a training and evaluation course qualifying her as a mission specialist on future Shuttle crews.

Thornton was born August 17, 1952, in Montgomery, Alabama, and graduated from Sidney Lanier High School there in 1970. She attended Auburn University, receiving a BS in physics in 1974, and earned her MS (1977) and PhD (1979) in physics from the University of Virginia.

While a graduate student at Virginia, Thornton took part in nuclear research programs at Oak Ridge National Laboratory, Brookhaven National Laboratory, the Indiana University Cyclotron Facility, and the Space Radiation Effects Laboratory. In 1979 she was awarded a NATO postdoctoral fellowship that enabled her to study at the Max Planck Institute for Nuclear Physics in Heidelberg, West Germany. Returning to the US in 1980, she went to work at the US Army Foreign Science and Technology Center in Charlottesville, Virginia.

Thornton and her husband Stephen have three children, two from his previous marriage, and a daughter, Carol.

Thornton, William

William Thornton waited sixteen years for his first space flight, STS-8 in August and September 1983, becoming, at age 54, the oldest person to fly in space at that time.

Technically assigned as a mission specialist, Thornton, like astronaut Norman Thagard on STS-7, had been added to the crew just months prior to launch in order to make a firsthand study of space adaptation syndrome (SAS), the so-called "space sickness" that affects approximately half of all space travelers. Thornton was well known as the astronaut office's resident SAS expert, and during the six-day STS-8 flight he did get sick. By the time he returned to Earth he claimed he had moved "years ahead" in the study of SAS.

Thornton had further opportunity to study SAS when he served as mission specialist aboard Spacelab 3 in April 1985. Spacelab 3, Shuttle Mission 51-B, was dedicated to life sciences and in addition to the crew of seven astronauts carried a crew of experimental rats and monkeys. Problems with the monkey cages caused Thornton and other astronauts to spend an unfortunate amount of time cleaning up after their passengers, but Thornton was still able to continue gathering data on his pet subject. He was also able to use a special exercise treadmill he had originally designed for Skylab flights and which had become standard equipment aboard all Shuttle flights. Thornton used the treadmill for ninety minutes one day, the amount of time it takes a Shuttle to circle the Earth—in effect, taking a "walk around the world."

Thornton has logged approximately 13 days in space.

William Edgar Thornton was born April 14, 1929, in Faison, North Carolina, where his father was a farmer. He attended schools in Faison and also ran a radio repair shop to support his family after the death of his father. He attended the University of North Carolina as an Air Force ROTC student, graduating in 1952 with a BS in physics. He earned his MD from North Carolina in 1963.

On active duty with the US Air Force, Thornton served at the Flight Air Test Proving Ground, where he developed a scoring system for pilots delivering missiles and bombs to targets. Leaving the Air Force in 1955, Thornton worked as an electronics engineer, eventually becoming chief engineer of the electronics division of Del Mar Engineering Laboratories in Los Angeles. He also organized and headed Del Mar's avionics research division.

From 1959 to 1963 Thornton attended medical school at North Carolina. He completed his internship in 1964 at Wilford Hall Air Force Hospital at Lackland AFB, Texas, then returned to active duty. At the Aerospace Medical Division at Brooks AFB, Texas, Thornton became involved in the study of human adaptation to spaceflight. He worked on a program of exercise for the Manned Orbiting Laboratory with Dr. Kenneth Cooper, later known as the "father" of aerobic fitness.

Thornton was one of eleven scientist-astronauts selected by NASA in August 1967, at a time when NASA expected to make several Apollo flights both to the Moon and in Earth orbit well into the 1970s. Shortly after the new scientist-astronauts reported, however, NASA's budget was cut and it was soon apparent that most of the 1967 group would have to wait years for a flight, if they got one at all. They dubbed themselves the XS-11, "Excess Eleven." By 1972 four of them would leave NASA without going into space.

Thornton was one of those who stayed, completing Air Force flight training at Reese AFB, Texas, in 1968, to become, at 39, a jet pilot. He would eventually log over 2600 hours of flying time.

He was involved in the development of the Skylab orbital workshop, joining astronauts Robert Crippen and Karol Bobko for the Skylab Medical Experiments Altitude Test (SMEAT), a 56-day simulation of a Skylab mission, in 1970. And he served as member of the support crew and capcom for all three Skylab missions in 1973-74.

After Skylab, in 1976, Thornton took a year's leave from NASA to study internal medicine at the University of Texas Medical School at Galveston, where he would eventually become a clinical instructor. Returning to the astronaut office, he took part in SMD III, a simulation of a Spacelab life sciences mission, and developed SAS experiments for STS-4, STS-5, STS-6 and STS-7. He had already been assigned as mission specialist aboard Spacelab 3 when in December 1982 he was added to the crew of the earlier STS-8.

An inventor as well as a scientist and astronaut, Thornton holds 35 patents.

He and his wife, Elizabeth, have two sons, William and James.

Thuot, Pierre

Lieutenant Commander Pierre J. Thuot, USN, was one of the 13 astronauts selected by NASA in June 1985. In August 1985 he began a training and evaluation course to qualify him as a mission specialist on future Shuttle flights.

Thuot was born May 19, 1955, in Groton, Connecticut, and graduated from high school in Fairfax, Virginia, in 1973. He attended the US Naval Academy, receiving a BS in physics in 1977, and later earned an MS in systems management from the University of Southern California in 1985.

After graduation from Annapolis, Thuot was trained as a naval flight officer. From 1978 through 1981 he flew aboard F-14s based on the carriers USS John F. Kennedy and USS Independence in the Mediterranean and Caribbean Seas. He graduated from the US Naval Test Pilot School at Patuxent River, Maryland, in 1982, and was an instructor there when chosen by NASA.

Thuot has logged over 1800 hours of flying time in 40 different aircraft, making over 270 carrier landings.

He is married to the former Cheryl Ann Mattingly of Leonardtown, Maryland.

Truly, Richard

Richard Truly made two Space Shuttle flights, as pilot of STS-2 in November 1981, and as commander of STS-8 in August and September 1983. During STS-2 Truly and commander Joe Engle became the first astronauts to go into space aboard a "used" spacecraft, the Shuttle Columbia, which had made its first trip into orbit the previous April. Truly and Engle's flight, launched on November 12, 1981, Truly's 44th birthday, was the first to test the Canadian-built Remote Manipulator System (RMS), the robot arm. The flight had to be cut from five days to two by a faulty fuel cell.

Truly later commanded STS-8, the first nighttime Shuttle launch and landing. The crew for this 6-day flight included America's first black astronaut, Lieutenant Colonel Guy Bluford, and 54-year-old physician William Thornton. The astronauts deployed a satellite for India and conducted tests of the ability of the RMS to move heavy payloads. Unknown at the time, one of the STS-8 solid rocket boosters came close to burning through its casing, which could have resulted in a catastrophe like that which would later destroy Challenger and claim the lives of the seven crewmen of Mission 51-L. In February 1986, in the wake of that disaster, Truly was named head of the entire Space Shuttle program.

On his two space flights Truly logged approximately eight days and eight hours.

Richard Harrison Truly was born November 12, 1937, in Fayette, Mississippi, and attended schools in Fayette and Meridien, Mississippi. A Navy ROTC student, he graduated from the Georgia Institute of Technology with a BS in aeronautical engineering in 1959.

Truly completed flight training at Beeville, Texas, in 1960, then was assigned to Fighter Squadron 33, serving aboard the carriers USS Intrepid and USS Enterprise, making more than 300 carrier landings. In 1963 and 1964 he attended the USAF Aerospace Research Pilot School at Edwards AFB, California, and upon graduation became an instructor there.

In November 1965 Lieutenant Truly was one of eight astronauts selected for the USAF Manned Orbiting Laboratory program. He remained with the MOL program until its termination, and in September 1969 was one of seven MOL pilots who transferred to NASA as astronauts.

As a pilot Truly has logged almost 7000 hours of flying time in many different types of aircraft.

At NASA Truly worked on the Skylab program, eventually serving on the support crew and as capcom for all three manned missions. He was also a capcom and member of the support crew for the Apollo-Soyuz Test Project.

At the end of 1975 Truly was teamed with Joe Engle as one of the astronaut crews for the Approach and Landing Tests of the Shuttle Enterprise. Between June and October 1977 Truly and Engle took part in captive flights, in which the Enterprise remained attached to its Boeing 747 carrier, and in two of the five free flights, when the Enterprise was released from its carrier plane to glide to landing at Edwards AFB. In March 1978 Engle and Truly were chosen as backups for STS-1, and in April 1981 were named to fly STS-2.

In October 1983 Truly left NASA to head the US Navy Space Command at Dahlgren, Virginia. He returned to NASA in February 1986 as associate administrator for space transportation systems.

Rear Admiral Truly and his wife, Colleen, have three children, Richard, Daniel and Lee.

Van Hoften, James

Dr. James van Hoften, better known to his fellow astronauts as "Ox" because of his size, took part in two different spacewalks repairing damaged satellites.

Van Hoften was a mission specialist aboard Shuttle Mission 41-C, launched April 6, 1984, and intended to retrieve, repair and redeploy the ailing Solar Maximum Mission satellite, which had been in space for four years. The first attempt to grab the satellite, by astronaut George Nelson using the manned maneuvering unit backpack, failed, but the next day astronaut Terry Hart succeeded, using the Shuttle's remote manipulator arm to haul Solar Max into the payload bay of the Challenger. Van Hoften did the major repairs on the satellite during a seven-hour EVA.

On van Hoften's second flight, Mission 51-I in August and September 1985, he also had the chance to demonstrate his satellite repair skills. The Hughes Leasat 3 had failed to launch itself into a higher orbit after being deployed by the Mission 51-D astronauts in April. During a record-breaking seven-hour, eight-minute spacewalk on August 31, 1985, van Hoften grabbed the drum-shaped, 7.5 ton satellite and attached a specially designed capture bar to it, so it could be lowered to the Shuttle Discovery payload bay for repairs. The process was complicated by problems with the Shuttle's robot arm, which limited its movements. Astronaut William Fisher did most of the repair work, "hot wiring" the satellite so its rockets would fire on command. During a second spacewalk on September 1, van Hoften, perched on the end of the robot arm, literally pushed the satellite into a three revolutions-per-minute spin, then shoved it into space.

By the end of October, Leasat 3 was on station in its geosynchronous orbit and operating as designed.

Van Hoften has logged approximately 14 days in space, including 22 hours of EVA.

James Dougal Adrianus van Hoften was born June 11, 1944, in Fresno, California, but grew up in Burlingame. He graduated from Mills High School in nearby Milbrae in 1962, then attended the University of California at Berkeley, where he received a BS in civil engineering in 1966. He went on to earn an MS and PhD in hydraulic engineering from Colorado State University in 1968 and 1976.

After completing work on his master's, van Hoften entered the US Navy, completing jet pilot training in 1970. He was stationed at Miramar Naval Air Station, California, then flew F-4 Phantoms on 60 combat missions from the carrier USS Ranger in Southeast Asia. He left the Navy in 1974 and resumed his academic studies. In September 1976 he became assistant professor of civil engineering at the University of Houston, teaching fluid mechanics and performing research on valves for artificial hearts. He also sold swimming pools.

Van Hoften has logged over 3300 hours of flying time, most of it in jet aircraft. He is currently a lieutenant colonel in the US Air Force Reserve.

Van Hoften was one of the 35 astronauts selected by NASA in January 1978. At 6 feet 4 inches and 200 pounds he was at the upper limit of NASA's newly relaxed astronaut physical requirements, hence the nickname "Ox." He completed a year-long training and evaluation course in August 1979, then worked at the Flight Systems Laboratory in Downey, California, on Shuttle computer software. He also led the astronaut support team at the Kennedy Space Center from 1981 to 1982, until being named to his first flight crew.

In July 1985 he was assigned to a third Shuttle mission scheduled for launch in 1986. When that mission was canceled, he resigned from NASA to join the Bechtel Corporation in San Francisco, California.

Van Hoften and his wife, Vallarie, have three daughters, Jennifer, Jamie and Victoria.

Veach, Charles

Lacy Veach was one of the 17 astronauts selected by NASA in May 1984. In August 1985 he completed a one-year training and evaluation course that made him eligible for assignment to Space Shuttle flights as a mission specialist.

Charles Lacy Veach was born September 18, 1944, in Chicago, but grew up in Honolulu. He graduated from Punahou School there in 1962, then entered the US Air Force Academy in Colorado Springs, graduating with a BS in engineering management in 1966.

After earning his pilot's wings, Veach was assigned to duty in Vietnam, flying 275 combat missions in the F-100 aircraft. He later served in England, Thailand, and Nevada, and in 1976 and 1977 was a member of the US Air Force air demonstration team, the "Thunderbirds." Veach left active duty in 1981 though he remains a pilot in the USAF Reserve. He has logged over 4000 flying hours.

Veach joined NASA in January 1982 as an engineer and research pilot based at the Johnson Space Center, where he was an instructor for the Shuttle Training Aircraft. As an astronaut he has served as a capcom for Shuttle flights beginning with Mission 61-A in October 1985.

Veach and his wife, Alice, have two children.

Walker, David

David Walker was pilot aboard Space Shuttle Mission 51-A in November 1984, during which astronauts Joseph Allen and Dale Gardner performed the first "space salvage" operation, collecting two malfunctioning satellites and stowing them in the Shuttle Discovery payload bay for return to Earth. The 51-A crew also launched two new satellites.

Walker has logged almost eight days in space.

David Mathieson Walker was born May 20, 1944, in Columbus, Georgia, but grew up in Eustis, Florida, where he graduated from high school in 1962. He attended the US Naval Academy at Annapolis, receiving a bachelor of science degree in 1966.

Walker underwent flight training in Florida, Mississippi and Texas, and, after becoming a naval aviator in 1967, served two combat tours in Vietnam as an F-4 pilot flying from the carriers USS Enterprise and USS America. After returning to the US in 1970 he attended the US Air Force Aerospace Research Pilot School at Edwards AFB, California, then was assigned to the Navy's Air Test Center at Patuxent River, Maryland, as a test pilot. He later became an F-14 pilot aboard the carrier USS America in the Mediterranean and was based at the Naval Air Station in Oceana, Virginia, when chosen by NASA.

Walker was one of the 35 astronauts selected by NASA in January 1978. In August 1979 he completed a training and evaluation course which qualified him as a pilot on Shuttle missions. As an astronaut he has served as a chase plane pilot for STS-1 and has worked on Shuttle computer software at the Shuttle Avionics Integration Laboratory (SAIL).

He was in training to command Shuttle Mission 61-G, scheduled for May 1986 when the Challenger accident forced NASA to suspend all Shuttle flights.

Captain Walker and his wife, Stacy, have two sons, Michael and Matt from Walter's first marriage.

Weitz, Paul

Paul Weitz commanded STS-6, the first flight of the Space Shuttle Challenger, in April 1983. The Challenger, the second Shuttle in the NASA fleet, was scheduled to make its maiden voyage in January 1983, but engine problems kept it grounded for three more months. When it was finally launched on April 4, 1983, it performed flawlessly during five days in orbit. In addition to qualifying the Challenger for future flights, Weitz and fellow astronauts Karol Bobko, Donald Peterson and Story Musgrave were to deploy the first Tracking and Data Relay Satellite, part of a planned system which would allow future Shuttle missions to remain in almost constant communication with mission control. The US Air Force inertial upper stage (IUS), which was supposed to boost TDRS-A into its synchronous orbit 22,500 miles above the Earth, suffered a malfunction, placing the satellite in a useless, looping orbit. Ground controllers, firing tiny maneuvering rockets aboard TDRS, were eventually able to steer the satellite to its proper station, but only after weeks. The IUS problem forced the cancellation of at least three subsequent Shuttle missions.

STS-6 was Weitz's second space flight. Ten years earlier he was the pilot of Skylab 2, the first manned visit to America's orbiting laboratory. The SL-2 crew of Weitz, Charles Conrad and Joseph Kerwin almost had their flight canceled when Skylab was severely damaged during its ride to orbit on May 14, 1973. One of the station's two huge solar panels was torn off along with a vital sun shield designed to wrap around the station, providing needed insulation and temperature control. Skylab appeared to be dead. But ground controllers postponed the SL-2 launch and quickly developed a makeshift sunshield which could be deployed by the astronaut crew.

SL-2 was launched on May 25, 1973, and rendezvoused with Skylab. As commander Charles Conrad maneuvered the Apollo-Skylab command and service module close to the huge station, Weitz leaned out the hatch of the CSM and tried to free the remaining solar panel, which was stuck in a closed position. Before Weitz could free the panel, however, darkness fell and he had to give up. The astronauts then docked with Skylab, after several harrowing attempts, and the next day entered the station, where the temperature was over 100 degrees F. Conrad and Kerwin managed to raise the makeshift sunshield—called the "parasol"—and freed the jammed solar panel during a spacewalk. Weitz later joined Conrad in another EVA. Eventually Skylab was restored to use and the astronauts completed the planned 28-day mission, a record at the time.

Weitz has logged over 33 days in space, including 2 hours and 11 minutes of EVA.

Paul Joseph Weitz was born July 25, 1932, in Erie, Pennsylvania, and graduated from high school in nearby Harborcreek in 1950. He attended Pennsylvania State University as a Naval ROTC student, graduating with a BS in aeronautical engineering in 1954. He later earned an MS in aeronautical engineering from the US Naval Postgraduate School in 1964.

Weitz entered active duty with the US Navy in 1954 and served first in destroyers. He completed flight school in 1956 and was assigned to the Naval Air Station in Jacksonville, Florida, as an instructor in tactics. In 1960 he was transferred to the Naval Weapons Center at China Lake, California, where he served as project officer for several different tests of air-to-ground delivery systems. Following further schooling at the USN Postgraduate School, Weitz flew combat missions in Vietnam. He was a detachment officer-in-charge at the Naval Air Station in Whidbey, Washington, when selected by NASA.

Chosen as one of 19 astronauts in April 1966, Weitz specialized in the Apollo command and service module system. He served as capcom for Apollo 12 and had been informally selected as backup command module pilot for Apollo 17 (putting him in line for a flight to the Moon on Apollo 20) when Congressional budget cuts eliminated that mission. In 1970 he began to work on the Apollo Applications Program Saturn Workshop, later known as Skylab, and was officially selected as pilot of Skylab 2 in January 1972.

On June 1, 1976, while working on Space Shuttle development, Captain Weitz retired from the Navy, though he remained with NASA as a civilian astronaut. He was assigned to command STS-6 in March 1982.

Since his Shuttle flight Weitz has worked as assistant to chief astronaut John Young, and frequently flew the Shuttle Training Aircraft during Shuttle launches from the Kennedy Space Center. In 1986 he left the astronaut group to become assistant to Johnson Space Center director.

Weitz and his wife, Suzanne, have two children, Matthew and Cynthia.

Wetherbee, James

Lieutenant Commander James Wetherbee, USN, was one of the 17 astronauts selected by NASA in May 1984. In June 1985 he completed a training and evaluation course that qualified him as a pilot on future Shuttle missions.

James D. Wetherbee was born November 27, 1952, in Flushing, New York, and graduated from Holy Family Diocesan High School in South Huntington, New York, in 1970. He attended Notre Dame, where he received a BS in aerospace engineering in 1974.

In 1975 Wetherbee joined the US Navy, becoming a pilot in 1976. From 1977 to 1980 he served as an A-7E pilot aboard the carrier John F. Kennedy. He then attended the US Naval Test Pilot School at Patuxent River, Maryland, and was a test pilot based at the naval air station in Lemoore, California, when chosen by NASA.

He has logged over 2000 hours of flying time in 20 different types of aircraft and has made 345 carrier landings.

As an astronaut Wetherbee has served as a capcom for Shuttle flights beginning with Mission 51-G in May 1985.

Wetherbee is married to the former Robin DeVore Platt of Jacksonville, Florida.

White, Edward

Edward White was the first American astronaut to take a walk in space. On June 3, 1965, White opened the hatch of the Gemini 4 spacecraft and, clad only in a special pressure suit and attached to the Gemini by a lifeline, floated free for 22 minutes, propelling himself with a small maneuvering gun that fired jets of gas while commander James McDivitt photographed him. Pictures of White floating in space became probably the most familiar of all space shots.

White and McDivitt returned to Earth on June 7 after spending four days in space, an American record at the time.

In March 1966 White was chosen to be senior pilot of the first

manned Apollo mission, scheduled for the first months of 1967. On January 27, 1967, White and astronauts Virgil Grissom and Roger Chaffee were killed in a flash fire inside their Apollo 1 spacecraft during testing on the launch pad at the Kennedy Space Center. White was buried at West Point.

Edward Higgins White II was born November 14, 1930, in San Antonio, Texas. His father was a pilot who later became an Air Force general. White attended the US Military Academy at West Point, earning a bachelor of science degree in 1952. He later received a master of science degree in aeronautical engineering from the University of Michigan in 1959.

After graduation from West Point, White underwent Air Force pilot training in Florida and Texas, earning his wings in 1953. For almost four years he was an F-86 and F-100 fighter pilot based in Germany, until returning to the US for further schooling. In 1959 he attended the US Air Force Test Pilot School at Edwards AFB, California, and was then assigned to Wright-Patterson AFB, Ohio, as a test pilot, when chosen by NASA.

At the time of his death he had logged over 4200 hours of flying time, including 3000 hours in jets.

White was one of the nine astronauts selected by NASA in September. In addition to assignments on Gemini 4 and Apollo 1 he was backup commander for Gemini 7.

He was survived by his wife, Pat, and two children, Edward and Bonnie.

Williams, Clifton

Major Clifton "C.C." Williams, USMC, was killed in the crash of his T-38 jet aircraft on October 5, 1967, near Tallahassee, Florida. At the time of his death he was training as the lunar module pilot of an Apollo crew commanded by Charles Conrad. Had he lived he would have been the fourth man to walk on the Moon.

Clifton Curtis Williams, Jr., was born September 26, 1932, in Mobile, Alabama. He graduated from Murphy High School in Mobile in 1949 and attended Spring Hill College. He received his BS in mechanical engineering from Auburn in 1954, then joined the US Marine Corps. After serving as a Marine aviator he attended the US Naval Test Pilot School at Patuxent River, Maryland, and was stationed there as a test pilot for three years. Prior to becoming an astronaut he was a student at the Marine Corps Intermediate Staff and Command School at Quantico, Virginia.

As a pilot he had logged 2600 hours of flying time, 2200 in jets.

Williams was one of fourteen astronauts selected by NASA in October 1963. He was a capcom for Gemini 4 and Gemini 11 and backup pilot for Gemini 10. The mission patch for Apollo 12, the lunar landing flight eventually made by Conrad's crew, contains four stars, the extra one as a tribute to Williams.

He was survived by his wife, Beth, and two children.

Williams, Donald

Captain Donald Williams, USN, was the pilot of Shuttle Mission 51-D in April 1985. The seven-astronaut crew of 51-D included United States Senator Jake Garn of Utah, who was acting as a congressional observer and payload specialist. The Senator observed the successful deployment of Canada's Anik C-1 communications satellite, and the troubled deployment of the Hughes Syncom IV-3 (Leasat 3), which suffered a

mechanical failure shortly after being jettisoned from the payload bay of the Discovery. Williams and commander Karol Bobko performed an unscheduled re-rendezvous with the ailing satellite so that David Griggs and Jeffrey Hoffman could attempt to repair it in an equally unscheduled and unrehearsed EVA.

Their attempt failed, but a later visit from the Mission 51-I astronauts in August successfully repaired Leasat 3, and by November 1985 it had reached its proper orbit.

Williams logged almost 7 days in space.

Donald Edward Williams was born February 13, 1942, in Lafayette, Indiana, graduating from high school in nearby Otterbein in 1960. He attended Purdue University in Lafayette, receiving a BS in mechanical engineering in 1964. Williams was a Navy ROTC student at Purdue and entered the service after graduation. He underwent pilot training in Florida, Mississippi and Texas, earning his wings in 1966, and for the next seven years was a pilot, flying 330 combat missions in Vietnam from the carrier USS Enterprise and serving as an instructor. In 1973 he attended the Armed Forces Staff College, then went to the US Naval Test Pilot School at Patuxent River, Maryland, where he remained until 1977. At the time of his selection as an astronaut Williams was an A-7 pilot with Attack Squadron 94.

Williams has logged over 4700 hours of flying time, 4500 hours in jets, including 745 carrier landings.

He was one of the 35 astronauts chosen by NASA in January 1978. In August 1979 he completed the training and evaluation course which qualified him as a Shuttle pilot. He has worked in the Shuttle Avionics Integration Laboratory (SAIL) and at the Kennedy Space Center in orbiter test, checkout, launch and landing operations. From September 1982 to July 1983 he was deputy manager for operations integration of the Shuttle program at the Johnson Space Center.

In September 1985 he was named to command a Shuttle mission originally scheduled for 1986, but postponed following the Challenger disaster.

Williams and his wife, Linda Jo, have two children, Jonathan and Barbara.

Worden, Alfred

Al Worden was the command module pilot of Apollo 15 and spent three days orbiting the moon alone in the command module Endeavour while fellow astronauts David Scott and James Irwin explored the lunar surface. On the return voyage to Earth, Worden performed the first "deep space" spacewalk, retrieving an experiment package attached to the Apollo service module.

Worden logged approximately 295 hours in space, including 38 minutes of EVA.

Alfred Merrill Worden was born February 7, 1932, in Jackson, Michigan. He attended the US Military Academy at West Point, graduating in 1955 with a BS, and in 1963 earned an MS in astronautical/aeronautical engineering and instrumentation from the University of Michigan.

Commissioned in the US Air Force after his graduation from West Point, Worden completed flight training in Texas and Florida, then served as a pilot and armament officer with the 95th Fighter Interceptor Squadron at Andrews AFB, Maryland. In 1965 he attended the Empire Test Pilot School in Farnborough, England and the USAF Aerospace Research Pilot School at Edwards AFB, California. He was an instructor at the aerospace school when chosen by NASA.

Worden was one of the 19 astronauts selected by NASA in April 1966. He was a member of the Apollo 9 support crew, then backup command module pilot for Apollo 12. After his flight on Apollo 15 he served briefly as backup command module pilot for Apollo 17, until he and fellow astronauts Scott and Irwin were removed for disciplinary reasons because of improprieties involving the sale of Apollo 15 souvenir stamps. (In 1983, following a NASA decision to allow the sale of commemorative stamps carried aboard the Space Shuttle, Worden sued the agency and, in a settlement, won back the materials he had lost in 1971.)

In September 1972 Worden was assigned to NASA's Ames Research Center at Moffet Field, California, serving as senior aerospace scientist, then as chief of the systems studies division. He resigned from NASA and retired from the US Air Force as a lieutenant colonel on September 1, 1975.

Since 1975 Worden has been involved in High Flight, the Colorado-based ministry founded by fellow astronaut James Irwin, and has worked as director of energy management for the Northwood Institute, Palm Beach, Florida. He is currently president of his own firm, Alfred M. Worden, Inc., in Palm Beach Gardens, Florida.

He has also published a book of poems, *Hello, Earth: Greetings from Endeavour* (1974), and, for children, *A Flight to the Moon* (1974).

The father of three, Worden is divorced from his second wife.

Young, John

John Young is the world's most experienced space traveler, having made six different flights involving four different types of manned vehicles. Among his accomplishments are two trips to the Moon and command of the first flight of the Space Shuttle, the world's first reusable spacecraft.

Young's first trip into space came on March 23, 1965, as pilot of Gemini 3. This three-orbit mission was the first manned Gemini flight, the first two-person American flight, and the first manned spacecraft to maneuver in orbit. It is also memorable as the flight in which Young, never a fan of astronaut food, smuggled a sandwich aboard, offering his surprised commander Gus Grissom a bite. That action also resulted in the first astronaut reprimand, which had little effect on Young's career.

He flew as commander on his second flight, Gemini 10 in July 1966. Young and pilot Michael Collins used their Gemini to rendezvous with two different Agena spacecraft and set a record by reaching an altitude of 475 miles.

In May 1969 Young served as command module pilot for Apollo 10, a full dress rehearsal for a manned lunar landing conducted in lunar orbit. Astronauts Thomas Stafford and Eugene Cernan took the lunar module Snoopy to within ten miles of the surface of the Moon while Young waited in the command module Charlie Brown.

The next time Young got close to the Moon, in April 1972, he landed on it. As commander of Apollo 16, he and Charles Duke set the lunar module Orion down in the highlands near the crater Descartes. For three days they remained on the Moon, setting up scientific experiments, collecting over 200 pounds of Moon rocks, and driving 17 miles in a lunar rover.

Young's fifth flight was STS-1, the first flight in the Space Shuttle program. On April 12, 1981, the twentieth anniversary of the flight of Yuri Gagarin, and following years of delay, the Shuttle Columbia carrying Young and pilot Robert Crippen roared off Pad 39A at the Kennedy Space Center. It was the first time men had been launched with dangerous solid rocket boosters—indeed, the first time the Shuttle configuration had been tested at all. Columbia performed well during its 54.5-hour maiden voyage, and returned to Earth on April 14, gliding to a landing on the dry lakebed at Edwards Air Force Base, California, the first controlled landing ever by a manned spacecraft.

In November and December 1983, Young commanded a second Shuttle mission, STS-9, which carried a record crew of six. STS-9 was the first flight of the European-built Spacelab, a scientific module crammed with experiments and carried in the Shuttle's payload bay. During the ten-day mission the crew worked 12-hour shifts and reached all of its goals, performing more than 70 experiments in a variety of fields. Computer problems delayed the landing by several hours, but Columbia returned safely to Edwards.

Young has spent 835 hours in space.

Though STS-9 was widely thought to be his last mission, Young was named in September 1985 to command the Shuttle launch of the Hubble Space Telescope. That flight, originally set for September 1986, had to be postponed indefinitely following the explosion of the Shuttle Challenger and the deaths of seven crew members.

Young became the center of a controversy during the investigation of the Challenger disaster. Memos he had written (before and after the accident) complaining of compromises in flight crew safety found their way to the press. During testimony before the Presidential commission investigating the disaster he admitted that he considered 1985, when nine Shuttle missions were launched, "a good year for the Shuttle program," and did not see how 15 missions, the number scheduled for 1986, could have been accomplished safely. Some unnamed astronauts complained that Young himself had been ineffective in raising safety issues with NASA management.

John Watts Young was born September 24, 1930, in San Francisco, California, but grew up in Orlando, Florida, where he graduated from high school. He attended the Georgia Institute of Technology, receiving a BS in aeronautical engineering (with the highest honors) in 1952. A Navy ROTC student, Young began active duty after graduation from Georgia Tech. He served aboard the destroyer USS Laws for a year, then underwent pilot training. From 1955 to 1959 he served with Fighter Squadron 103.

He attended the US Navy Test Pilot School at Patuxent River, Maryland, in 1959, then remained at the Naval Air Test Center for the next three years. In 1962 he set world time-to-climb records in the F-4 Phantom. At the time of his selection by NASA he was maintenance officer with Fighter Squadron 143 at Miramar, California.

As a pilot he has logged over 9500 hours of flying time.

Young was one of nine astronauts chosen by NASA in October 1962. He became the first of that group, which included Charles Conrad, Frank Borman and Neil Armstrong, to be assigned to a space flight when he was named pilot of Gemini 3 in April 1964. He was assigned to flight crews almost continuously for the next nine years: in addition to flights on Gemini 3, Gemini 10, Apollo 10 and Apollo 16, he was backup pilot for Gemini 6, backup command module pilot for Apollo 7, and backup commander for Apollo 13 and Apollo 17.

In January 1973 Young went to work on development of the Space Shuttle. A year later he was also made acting chief astronaut, and in January 1975, permanent chief, a job he holds today, supervising the activities of 100 astronauts. He stepped aside from March 1978 to April 1981 (and was replaced by Alan Bean) to concentrate on the long and arduous training program for STS-1.

Young is married to the former Susie Feldman of St. Louis, Missouri. He has two children, Sandy and John, from a previous marriage.

Civilian Shuttle Payload Specialists

From the beginning of the Space Shuttle program in 1972 NASA proclaimed that the size of Shuttle crews (from two to seven people) and the relatively comfortable environment (space travelers would not be subjected to physical stresses comparable to those inflicted on Mercury, Gemini and Apollo astronauts, for example) made it possible for non-astronauts to go into space to perform specific scientific experiments or other work, or to simply act as passengers.

In fact, NASA's physical criteria for the selection of Shuttle payload specialists required only that candidates have

- Vision correctable to 20/40 in one eye
- Hearing that can detect a whisper at three feet
- Blood pressure lower than 160/100
- Pulse rates of 176 to 190 after 12 to 15 minutes on a treadmill
- Absence of tuberculosis, glaucoma, pacemaker, anemia, ulcers; no kidney stones for at least two years.

There is no age limit; pilot experience is irrelevant. It was even suggested that a handicapped person could qualify.

The most important step in the selection of all payload specialists is approval by the Shuttle customer, whether it is the European Space Agency, the McDonnell-Douglas Corporation, the US Air Force (see the following section) or NASA itself. Foreign countries are allowed to select their own payload specialists, as long as those chosen can meet these minimal requirements.

Scientists

The first Shuttle payload specialists to be selected were professional scientists. The payload was the European Space Agency's Spacelab 1 scientific module, then scheduled to be carried aboard a Shuttle in 1981. ESA selected three finalists while NASA, through its Marshall Space Flight Center, coordinated the selection of American payload specialists. The scientists who had designed the principal experiments for Spacelab 1 were allowed to nominate two candidates each. Forty people were nominated, interviewed and tested (the physical requirements were originally somewhat stricter). In May 1978, two scientists, Lampton and Lichtenberg, were selected.

Spacelab 2, unlike Spacelab 1, which was open to a variety of scientific experiments, was dedicated to solar physics, which cut the number of experiments from over 70 (Spacelab 1) to 13 (Spacelab 2), and lowered the number of potential payload specialists as well. Only 16 candidates were nominated and four finalists, Acton, Bartoe, Prinz and Simon, were chosen in September 1978.

For Spacelab 3, a dedicated materials processing mission, only seven semifinalists were interviewed. Four scientists, Johnston, Trinh, van den Berg, and Wang, were selected in June 1983. Four more scientists, all of them with medical backgrounds, Fulford, Gaffney, Phillips, and Williams, were selected for life sciences Spacelab 4 (later known as SLS) and its followup in January 1984. Three astronomers, Durrance, Nordsieck, and Parise, were chosen in June 1984 to fly on three different Spacelab Astro (astronomy) missions.

It became obvious that, given the years of training the scientific payload specialists ultimately received, that it was best to recycle the backups on followup missions. In the summer of 1984, Byron Lichtenberg, who had flown aboard Spacelab 1, and his backup, Michael Lampton, were named to fly aboard the Earth Observation Mission, a Spacelab 1 followup. Another American scientist, Rick Chappell (who had headed the original Spacelab 1 selection committee at NASA Marshall) and ESA's Dirk Friemont, were chosen late in 1985 to work on EOM as well. They can be expected to fly aboard Spacelab in the future.

The explosion of the Shuttle Challenger in January 1986 effectively put a halt to the selection of future science payload specialists. The first mission to be canceled following the disaster was Spacelab Astro 1, scheduled for March 1986. The Life Sciences Spacelab and Earth Observation Mission were postponed.

Once Shuttle flights resume, and pending replacement of the Challenger in 1989 with a new orbiter, there should be new selections of scientists for the International Microgravity Laboratory (originally Spacelab 8), SHEAL (the Shuttle High-Energy Astrophysics Laboratory), and Sunlab, in addition to the West German and Japanese Spacelabs.

Commercial Payload Specialists

At the time Shuttle flights were suspended in January 1986, two commercial payload specialists had gone into space. Charles Walker, an engineer employed by McDonnell-Douglas Astronautics, actually made three Shuttle flights, one in 1984 and two in 1985, operating his company's pharmaceutical manufacturing unit. Robert Cenker, a satellite engineer with RCA, accompanied RCA's Satcom Ku-1 into space in January 1986.

A third commercial payload specialist, Gregory Jarvis of Hughes Aircraft, was killed in the Challenger explosion.

Commercial payload specialists are given approximately 160 hours of Shuttle training, much of it in workbooks rather than the familiar simulations. It is assumed that their companies will train them to operate their payloads. During a Shuttle flight they are primarily expected to keep out of the way, something Walker of McDonnell-Douglas managed quite well.

Jarvis was one of four Hughes employees who were selected in July 1984 to accompany Syncom (or Leasat) satellites into space. It is expected that at least one of the others, including John Konrad and backups William Butterworth and Steven Cunningham, will eventually go into space.

A second McDonnell-Douglas engineer, Robert Wood, was chosen in 1985 for a future Shuttle flight. American Satellite Communications was in the process of selecting a prime and backup payload specialist for a 1986 Shuttle mission when launches were suspended. Future commercial payload specialists might also be selected by the 3M Corporation and by the John Deere Company, in addition to satellite manufacturers such as Ford Aerospace.

Observers

The first observer to become a Shuttle payload specialist was a civilian employee of the US Navy, Paul Scully-Power, an oceanographer who was added to the crew of Mission 41-G just four months prior to launch.

In August 1984, President Reagan announced that the first "ordinary citizen" observer would be a primary or secondary school teacher. That choice was largely greeted with approval, except by some journalists who had expected that the first ordinary citizen would be one of them.

While the teacher-in-space was being selected, however, NASA created a real controversy. In November 1984, then-NASA Administrator James Beggs invited Utah Senator Jake Garn, chairman of the Senate Committee that oversees NASA's budget, to fly on the Shuttle. Garn, a former Navy pilot, underwent approximately 100 hours of training over the next five months, and went into space aboard Mission 51-D, months ahead of the scheduled flight of the teacher.

Some critics charged that NASA was trying to curry favor with politicans. NASA responded, somewhat lamely, that it had always planned to offer opportunities for passengers, either VIPs or ordinary citizens, to fly. Stung by the criticism, some NASA officials declared that no more politicans would fly in space. But in September 1985, Florida Congressman Bill Nelson, Garn's counterpart in the House of Representatives, received an invitation. He, too, flew before the teacher, in January 1986.

Civilian Shuttle Payload Specialist Sponsors

Hughes Aircraft
- William Butterworth
- Steven Cunningham
- Gregory Jarvis
- John Konrad

McDonnell Douglas
- Charles Walker
- Robert Wood

RCA Astrosystems
- Robert Cenker
- Gerard Magilton

US Navy
- Paul Scully-Power

The selection of observers for Shuttle missions was re-evaluated following the Challenger disaster. The ongoing selections for a journalist-observer were suspended.

President Reagan, acting NASA Administrator Graham and new NASA Administrator Fletcher all stated in the spring of 1986 that flights by observers would continue, but it is likely to be 1989 at the earliest before a teacher or journalist flies, if then.

Civilian Shuttle Payload Specialist Biographies

Acton, Loren

Dr. Loren Acton spent 9 days in space aboard Spacelab 2 in July and August 1985. The flight, Shuttle Mission 51-F, overcame a launch pad abort and several equipment failures before producing a record amount of data on the Sun.

Acton, a solar physicist employed by the Lockheed Corporation, was one of two payload specialists aboard Mission 51-F who operated 13 different experiments, including a solar optical telescope which in just three days of operation returned more images of the Sun than did telescopes aboard Skylab in 171 days of operation in 1973-74.

Loren W. Acton was born March 7, 1936 in Lewistown, Montana. He received a BA from Montana State University in 1959 and a PhD from the University of Colorado in 1965. A senior staff scientist with Lockheed's Space Sciences Laboratory in Palo Alto, California, Acton was chosen to be a Spacelab 2 payload specialist in 1978.

He and his wife, Evelyn, have two children, Cheryll Anne and Stanley Scott. They live in Palo Alto, California.

Bartoe, John-David

Dr. John-David Bartoe spent almost eight days in space as payload specialist aboard the Space Shuttle Challenger during Mission 51-F/ Spacelab 2. Bartoe operated a number of astronomical experiments, including the solar ultraviolet telescope, which he had designed.

John-David Francis Bartoe was born November 17, 1944, in Abington, Pennsylvania. He received a BS from Lehigh University in 1966, an MS and PhD from Georgetown University in 1974 and 1976.

Since 1966 Bartoe has been a researcher at the US Naval Research Laboratory in Washington, D.C. His speciality is the study of the Sun, and his experiments have been carried on sounding rockets, satellites, and on Apollo and Skylab missions in addition to Shuttle flights. Currently he is a supervisory astrophysicist at the NRL.

He was selected as a Spacelab 2 payload specialist in 1978.

Bartoe and his wife, Phyllis, and their three children, David, Kevin, and Joelle, live in Washington.

Butterworth, William

Bill Butterworth is the Hughes Aircraft satellite engineer who served as backup payload specialist to Gregory Jarvis on Shuttle Mission 51-L. Jarvis and the other crew members of that mission were killed in the explosion of the Shuttle Challenger during launch on January 28, 1986.

Louis William Butterworth was born July 17, 1948, in Casper, Wyo-

ming, but grew up in Hinsdale, Illinois, where he graduated from high school in 1966. He received a BS in engineering (1970) and an MS in mechanical engineering (1971) from the California Institute of Technology.

Butterworth worked at the NASA Jet Propulsion Laboratory while he was a Caltech student. In 1972 he joined Hughes Aircraft and began working on designs for communications satellites. In 1974 he transferred to a group working on the Pioneer Venus space probe, and after the completion of that project, took part in the design and development of the Galileo Jupiter Probe. He is currently assistant program manager for Galileo.

He and his wife, Jennifer, live in Los Angeles.

Cenker, Robert

RCA satellite engineer Bob Cenker served as payload specialist aboard Shuttle Mission 61-C in January 1986. During this six-day Shuttle flight, whose launch was delayed a record seven times, Cenker supervised the successful deployment of the RCA Satcom Ku-1 satellite.

Robert J. Cenker was born November 5, 1948, in Uniontown, Pennsylvania. He graduated from high school there in 1965, then attended St. Fidelis College and Seminary in Herman, Pennsylvania. He received his BS and MS in aerospace engineering from Penn State University, and also has an MS in electrical engineering from Rutgers University.

Cenker joined the RCA Astro-Electronics Division in East Windsor, New Jersey, in 1972, working on stabilization and control systems for RCA communications satellites, including Satcoms 1 and 2, the GTE Spacenet, and the US Navy Nova. Prior to 1972 he was a research assistant at Penn State and worked at the Westinghouse Bettis Atomic Power Laboratory in West Mifflin, Pennsylvania.

He and his wife, Barbara, have three children, Daniel, Brian and Laura. They live in East Windsor, New Jersey.

Chappell, Charles

Dr. Rick Chappell has been chosen as backup payload specialist for the Spacelab Earth Observation Mission, which was originally scheduled to fly in the summer of 1986. Following the explosion of the Shuttle Challenger in January 1986 all Shuttle missions were suspended. Spacelab EOM is not likely to be launched until 1989.

Charles Richard Chappell was born in 1943 in Greenville, South Carolina, but grew up in Montgomery, Alabama, where he graduated from Sidney Lanier High School in 1961. He attended Vanderbilt University, receiving a BS in physics (magna cum laude) in 1965, and earned his PhD in space science from Rice University in 1968.

From 1968 to 1974 Chappell worked for Lockheed at its Palo Alto, California, Research Laboratory, as a staff scientist. His research involved investigations of the Earth's plasmasphere and magnetosphere. In 1974 he joined the staff of the NASA Marshall Space Flight Center in Huntsville, Alabama, where he soon became mission scientist for Spacelab 1, work that culminated in a ten-day multidisciplinary scientific space flight in November and December 1983. During Spacelab 1 Chappell coordinated the efforts of more than seventy scientific investigators at Marshall's Payload Operations Center. He was also the "voice" of Spacelab 1.

When NASA and the European Space Agency decided to refly some

Spacelab 1 experiments on a new mission, Spacelab EOM, Chappell was chosen as one of the payload specialists.

Chappell is currently chief of the solar terrestrial division of the space science laboratory at NASA Marshall. He is the author of over 100 scientific papers and has been principal investigator on instruments flown on several American spacecraft.

He and his wife, Barbara, have a son and live in Huntsville.

Cunningham, Steven

Dr. Steven Cunningham was scheduled to be backup payload specialist to Dr. John Konrad, the second Hughes Aircraft satellite engineer to fly aboard the Space Shuttle. But the explosion of the Shuttle Challenger on January 28, 1986, which killed seven crewmembers including Hughes engineer Gregory Jarvis, forced NASA to suspend all future Shuttle launches.

Steven Lee Cunningham was born September 10, 1945, in Renton, Washington, but grew up in Englewood, Colorado, where he graduated from Cherry Creek High School in 1963. He attended the University of Denver, receiving a BS in physics in 1967, and earned an MS (1969) and PhD (1971) in physics from the University of Nebraska.

From 1971 to 1974 Cunningham was a research assistant at the University of California at Irvine, then he spent another year as a visiting associate at the California Institute of Technology. He joined the staff of Caltech in 1975 and remained there as a research chemist until 1977, when he went to work for Hughes as a senior staff physicist. Following a year during which he was involved with the Landsat 3 satellite, Cunningham has worked on military projects for Hughes.

He and his wife, Mary Anne, have three children, Nancy, Beth Anne, and Thomas.

Durrance, Samuel

Dr. Samuel T. Durrance was scheduled to be payload specialist for the Spacelab Astro-1 Shuttle Mission in March 1986. This flight was intended to observe Halley's Comet during a week of astronomical studies, but the explosion of the Shuttle Challenger on January 28, 1986, forced the cancellation of all Shuttle launches. Durrance is expected to be reassigned to another Spacelab Astro mission.

Durrance was born September 17, 1943, in Tallahassee, Florida. He attended California State University in Los Angeles, receiving a BS (1972) and MS (1974) in physics. He earned a PhD in astrogeophysics from the University of Colorado in 1980.

An associate research scientist in the physics and astronomy department at Johns Hopkins University in Baltimore, Durrance was assistant project scientist for the Hopkins Ultraviolet Telescope, one of the instruments scheduled to fly aboard Astro 1. He has also used instruments aboard Explorer and Pioneer space probes to study Venus, Mars, Jupiter, Io, Saturn, and Uranus. His main field of interest is the origin and evolution of the solar system and of other planetary systems, and the origin and evolution of life in the universe.

Durrance and his wife, Rebecca, have a son, Benjamin.

Fulford, Millie

Dr. Millie Hughes Wiley Fulford is the backup payload specialist in training for the Spacelab Life Sciences mission originally scheduled for 1987. Following the explosion of the Shuttle Challenger in January 1986 and the suspension of all Shuttle launches, SLS was postponed until 1989.

Fulford was born in 1946 in Mineral Wells, Texas, and attended Tarleton State University, receiving a BS in chemistry and biology in 1968. She earned her PhD in chemistry from Texas Women's University in 1972.

Since 1973 she has been an assistant professor of biochemistry at the Veteran's Administration Hospital in San Francisco. She is also a private pilot and a captain in the US Army Reserve.

Fulford is a fan of the science fiction series *Star Trek* and applied for the January 1978 NASA astronaut group, but was not selected. She was named as a payload specialist for the Spacelab Life Sciences mission in January 1984.

She and her husband have one child and make their home in Mill Valley, California.

Gaffney, Andrew

Dr. Drew Gaffney is one of the prime payload specialists training for the Spacelab Life Sciences mission now scheduled for 1989.

Francis Andrew Gaffney was born in 1944 and attended the University of California at Berkeley, receiving a BA in 1968. He recived his MD from the University of New Mexico in 1972. His area of specialization is cardiology.

Gaffney has interned at Cleveland Metropolitan General Hospital in Cleveland and been a cardiology fellow at the University of Texas Health Science Center, Southwestern Medical School, in Dallas. At the time he was selected as a Spacelab payload specialist in January 1984 he was director of echocardiography there.

Gaffney is the author of 47 medical papers. He is also a pilot with ratings for single and multi-engine planes.

In January 1985 he and Dr. Robert Phillips were named prime payload specialists for Shuttle Mission 61-D/Spacelab 4, scheduled for January 1986. When that mission was later canceled, Gaffney continued to train for the second life sciences Spacelab.

Gaffney is married, with two children.

Garn, Jake

Utah Senator Jake Garn, the Republican chairman of the Senate appropriations subcommittee that oversees the NASA budget, became the first politican in space when he flew aboard Shuttle Mission 51-D in April 1985.

Garn was invited to fly in space in November 1984 by NASA Administrator James Beggs, who said, "Given your NASA oversight responsibilities, we think it appropriate that you consider making an inspection tour and flight aboard the Shuttle." The invitation was controversial. Some critics charged that NASA was trying to curry favor with the powerful Senator, who had been critical in the past of both NASA's Shuttle pricing policies, and of some aspects of the proposed Space Station program. One of the principal Shuttle contractors, Morton Thiokol Inc., which builds the Shuttle's solid rocket boosters, was

also based in Utah. NASA responded that this was no different from inviting an elected official to take a ride in a military aircraft, a common practice.

During his seven days aboard the Discovery, Garn served as a test subject for space sickness experiments (becoming famous in the comic strip *Doonesbury* as "Barfin' Jake Garn"), and also observed an unscheduled rescue attempt of the failed Leasat 3 satellite, including an unrehearsed spacewalk by astronauts David Griggs and Jeffrey Hoffman.

Edwin Jacob Garn was born October 12, 1932, in Richfield, Utah. He attended the University of Utah, receiving a BS in business and finance and worked as an insurance executive for many years.

Garn served as a US Navy jet pilot from 1956 to 1960 and also served in the Utah Air National Guard, retiring with the rank of colonel in 1969. He has logged over 10,000 hours of flying time in military and civilian aircraft, more than any NASA astronaut except Joe Engle at the time of Mission 51-D.

As a businessman in Salt Lake City, Garn served on the city commission for four years, then, in 1971, was elected mayor. In November 1974 he was elected to the US Senate, and was re-elected in November 1980, winning 74 percent of the vote. In addition to his duties on the Senate Appropriations Committee, Garn is chairman of the Banking, Housing and Urban Affairs Committee and serves on three other subcommittees.

Garn married the late Hazel Thompson in 1957; they had four children: Jake Jr., Susan, Ellen and Jeffrey. In April 1977 Garn married Kathleen Brewerton, who has a son, Brook. Senator and Mrs. Garn have a son, Matthew, and a daughter, Jennifer, and a grandson, Ryan.

Jarvis, Gregory

Gregory Jarvis was the Hughes Aircraft satellite engineer who died in the explosion of the Shuttle Challenger on January 28, 1986. He was serving as payload specialist of Shuttle Mission 51-L, a planned six-day flight, during which he was to supervise the operation of a fluid dynamics experiment.

Jarvis's presence on 51-L was ironic, since he had been bumped off two previous Shuttle missions that carried satellites he had helped design. On both occasions he was replaced by politicans. He had only begun training for 51-L that month.

Gregory Bruce Jarvis was born August 24, 1944, in Detroit, Michigan, but grew up in Mohawk, New York, where he graduated from high school in 1962. He attended the State University of New York at Buffalo, where he received a BS in electrical engineering in 1967. He earned an MS in electrical engineering from Northeastern University in Boston in 1969, and completed work on a master's in management science at West Coast University in Los Angeles. That degree was to have been awarded during the flight of Mission 51-L.

An ROTC student at SUNY-Buffalo, Jarvis entered active duty with the US Air Force in July 1969. He was assigned to Space Division in El Segundo, California, and worked there for four years on military communications satellites such as the FLTSATCOM. Discharged as a captain in 1973, he joined Hughes Aircraft, and for the next 12 years worked on a variety of satellite programs, including Marisat and Syncom (also known as Leasat). In June 1984, when he was selected to accompany a Leasat into space, Jarvis was the test and integration manager for the program. At the time of his death he was working on advanced satellites.

Jarvis is survived by his wife, Marcia.

Johnston, Mary Helen

Dr. Mary Helen Johnston served as the backup payload specialist to Dr. Lodewijk van den Berg on the Spacelab 3 mission flown in April and May 1985. She acted as communicator and science support crewman from the Payload Operations Center at NASA's Johnson Space Center during the seven-day flight.

Johnston was born in 1945 in West Palm Beach, Florida, and graduated from Dan McCarty High School in Fort Pierce, Florida, in 1962. She entered Florida State University in Tallahassee and earned a BS and MS in engineering science while working part time at the NASA Marshall Space Flight Center in Huntsville, Alabama. She earned her PhD in metallurgical engineering from the University of Florida at Gainesville in 1973. One of her professors was former scientist-astronaut J. Anthony Llewellyn, who gave her some guidance about a possible career in space research.

Johnston has been a full-time scientist at the Marshall Space Flight Center since 1973 working on experiments and hardware for manned space flights. In 1974 she was a member of an all-woman crew that made a five-day simulated Spacelab flight. She applied in 1977 for the astronaut program but was not selected. Nevertheless, her work on Spacelab 3 materials processing experiments qualified her for selection as a Spacelab payload specialist in June 1983. She continues to train for a future Spacelab mission.

Johnston is married and lives in Huntsville, Alabama.

Konrad, John

Dr. John Konrad is a Hughes Aircraft satellite engineer who is scheduled to be a payload specialist on a future Shuttle flight. Konrad, who along with Gregory Jarvis was one of two prime Hughes payload specialists chosen in June 1984, was originally to have flown on Mission 51-I in the summer of 1985. NASA kept postponing the flight of Jarvis (who was to be the first Hughes engineer to go into space) until January 1986, and when he was killed in the explosion of the Shuttle Challenger, all future Shuttle flights, including Konrad's, were suspended.

John Harrison Konrad was born March 12, 1949, in Pontiac, Illinois, and graduated from high school in Burns Flat, Oklahoma, in 1967. He attended Oklahoma State University, receiving a BS in aeronautical and astronautical engineering in 1971, and later received a PhD in fluid mechanics from the California Institute of Technology (1976).

Konrad joined Hughes Aircraft in 1976 and worked as an engineer on the Anik and SBS communications satellite which were deployed on STS-5, the first operational Shuttle mission. He is currently assistant system engineering manager for the Telstar III and Intelsat VI satellites.

He and his wife, Connie, have two sons, James and John. They live in El Segundo, California.

Lampton, Michael

Dr. Michael L. Lampton served as a backup payload specialist for the Spacelab 1/STS–9 mission in October and November 1983, working as a communicator with the scientists aboard. He had been chosen to fly in space as a payload specialist aboard the Spacelab Earth Observation Mission originally scheduled for 1986.

Lampton was born March 1, 1941, in Williamsport, Pennsylvania. He attended the California Institute of Technology in Pasadena, graduating with a BS in physics in 1962. He earned his PhD in physics from the University of California at Berkeley in 1967.

In 1978 Lampton was a research physicist at the Space Science Laboratory at the University of California when he was selected to train for Spacelab 1. He continued his association with the Laboratory while training for Spacelab missions at the Johnson Space Center and the Marshall Space Flight Center.

He and his wife, Susan, have a daughter, Jennifer.

Lichtenberg, Byron

Byron Lichtenberg became the first non-professional American space traveler when he served as a Spacelab 1 payload specialist in October and November 1983.

The Spacelab l/STS-9 mission was the first flight of the reusable Spacelab module built by the European Space Agency. Lichtenberg and fellow payload specialist Ulf Merbold joined four NASA astronauts in carrying out 70 different experiments in a variety of fields, from space medicine to astronomy. Later Spacelab flights would be "dedicated" to certain types of experiments.

Lichtenberg logged almost 11 days in space during his first flight. He was later chosen to be a payload specialist aboard the Spacelab Earth Observation Mission originally scheduled for the summer of 1986, but postponed following the Shuttle Challenger disaster.

Byron Kurt Lichtenberg was born February 19, 1948, in Stroudsburg, Pennsylvania, and graduated from high school there in 1965. When he was a teenager he decided to become an astronaut and with that in mind studied aerospace engineering at Brown University in Providence, Rhode Island, earning his BS in 1969.

He then served in the US Air Force as a pilot, flying combat missions in Vietnam and earning two Distinguished Flying Crosses. He left active duty in 1973 and returned to college, earning an MS in mechanical engineering from the Massachusetts Institute of Technology in 1975 and a doctorate in biomedical engineering in 1979.

In 1977 he applied for the NASA astronaut group but was not chosen. In 1978, however, he was selected as a Spacelab payload specialist—a professional scientist who would be trained to survive in space aboard the Shuttle, but whose primary profession is the operation of scientific experiments.

Lichtenberg continues his association with MIT while training for Spacelab missions. He is also a fighter pilot with the Massachusetts Air National Guard. In 1983 *Esquire* magazine named him as one of its notable Americans under the age of 40.

Lichtenberg and his wife, Lee, have two daughters, Kristin and Kimberly.

McAuliffe, Christa

Christa McAuliffe was chosen from 10,463 applicants to be the first private citizen to go into space. Tragically, she was killed with six other space travelers during the launch of the Shuttle Challenger on January 28, 1986.

A high school social studies teacher from Concord, New Hamp-

shire, McAuliffe was scheduled to deliver two live TV "lessons" to schoolchildren all over America during her six-day trip. In the time between being chosen as the first teacher-in-space in July 1985 and the launch she had become famous—the first space traveler who was not a test pilot or a scientist or an engineer—and her sudden death in a vehicle most Americans viewed as being as safe as an airliner came as a tremendous shock.

Sharon Christa Corrigan McAuliffe was born September 2, 1948, in Boston, Massachusetts. She grew up in nearby Framingham and graduated from Marian High School there in 1966. She received a BA from Framingham State College in 1970 and an MA in education from Bowie State College in Maryland in 1978.

McAuliffe began her teaching career at Benjamin Foulois Junior High School in Morningside, Maryland, in 1970. She taught civics, American history, and English at several schools in Maryland and New Hampshire before arriving at Concord Senior High in 1982. There she taught economics, law, American history and a course she developed called "The American Woman" to 10th, 11th and 12th graders. She was considered a creative and dynamic teacher who was particularly fond of taking her classes on field trips to courtrooms, prisons, and police stations.

When President Reagan announced on August 27, 1984, that a schoolteacher would be the first private citizen in space (rather than the journalist most observers expected), McAuliffe was eager to apply. She wrote in her application essay, "I cannot join the space program and restart my life as an astronaut, but this opportunity to connect my abilities as an educator with my interests in history and space is a unique opportunity to fulfill my early fantasies. I watched the space program being born and would like to participate."

She proposed to keep a three-part journal of her experiences, the first part dealing with training, the second with the flight itself, and the third with the aftermath. She also planned to keep a video record of her activities on this "ultimate field trip."

Out of the thousands of applicants, 114 were invited to Washington, D. C., in late June for interviews with a panel that included four former astronauts, several university presidents, actress Pam Dawber, artifical heart inventor Robert Jarvik, and former pro basketball star Wes Unseld. Ten finalists were chosen and these were brought to the NASA Johnson Space Center in Houston for more interviews and tests beginning July 1. After a stop at the NASA Marshall Space Flight Center in Huntsville, Alabama, the finalists ended up in Washington, where Vice President Bush announced in a White House ceremony that McAuliffe was the choice.

Bob Hohler, a reporter from McAuliffe's hometown newspaper, *The Concord Monitor*, wrote a series of articles describing the teacher's adaptation to payload specialist training and to being a celebrity. Eventually these articles will form a book, to be published in late 1986. A film of McAuliffe's life is also planned.

She was survived by her husband, Steven, and two children, Scott and Caroline.

Magilton, Gerard

Jerry Magilton is the RCA engineer who served as backup payload specialist to RCA's Bob Cenker on Shuttle Mission 61-C. The RCA Satcom Ku-1 communications satellite was deployed from the Shuttle Columbia during the six-day flight of 61-C in January 1986.

Gerard E. Magilton was born May 7, 1942, Philadelphia, Pennsylva-

nia, where he attended Father Judge High School. He received a BS in electrical engineering from Drexel University in 1965.

He joined Philco Ford Defense Electronics in Willow Grove, Pennsylvania, after graduation from Drexel, but in 1967 went to work for RCA in East Windsor, New Jersey. His primary responsibility at RCA was the TIROS weather satellite. He is currently manager of integration and test for the astro-electronics division, responsible for the final assembly of all RCA's Series 3000 spacecraft, such as the Spacenet, GSTAR, and Satcom Ku.

He also served in the US Army Reserve from 1960 to 1968, including a six-month tour as a Nike missile crewman at Fort Bliss, Texas.

Magilton and his wife, Anna May, have four children, Gerard Jr., Suzanne, Monica and Nicholas. They live in Langhorne, Pennsylvania.

Morgan, Barbara

Barbara Radding Morgan was the alternate teacher-in space participant for Shuttle Mission 51-L. Following the explosion of the Shuttle Challenger during the 51-L launch, and the deaths of the astronauts and teacher Christa McAuliffe, the whole space flight participant program (a selection for a journalist-in-space was going on at the time) came into question. Nevertheless, in February 1986, just weeks after the disaster, acting NASA Administrator William Graham announced that private citizens would continue to be included in Shuttle crews, and Barbara Morgan accepted his invitation to fly in space when Shuttle launches resume.

Morgan was born November 38, 1951, in Fresno, California, where she graduated from Hoover High School in 1969. She attended Stanford University, receiving a BA with distinction in human biology. She earned her teaching credential from the College of Notre Dame in Belmont, California, in 1974.

Morgan first taught remedial reading and math at the Arlee Elementary School on the Flathead Indian Reservation in Montana. Since 1975 she has been an elementary school teacher at McCall-Donnell School in McCall, Idaho, except for one year spent at the Colegio Americano in Quito, Ecuador.

In addition to her teaching, Morgan is a member and acting director of the McCall Chamber Orchestra and the McCall Chorale and is a musician for local drama productions.

She was announced as runner-up to Christa McAuliffe at a White House ceremony on July 19, 1985.

Morgan is married to Clay McCall, a novelist.

Nelson, Bill

Florida congressman Bill Nelson, the Democratic chairman of the House Space Science and Applications Subcommittee, became the second politican to make a space flight when he served as a payload specialist aboard Shuttle Mission 61-C in January 1986. During the six-day flight of the Shuttle Columbia Nelson served as a subject for space sickness experiments devised by NASA doctors. He also operated a protein growth experiment sponsored by the University of Alabama at Birmingham.

Mission 61-C became best known for having its liftoff delayed seven times by weather problems or technical glitches. Nelson himself will be remembered as the first lawyer in space.

C. William Nelson, Jr., was born September 29, 1942, in Miami, Florida. He is a fifth generation Floridian whose family homesteaded the area that is now the Kennedy Space Center in 1917. Nelson grew up in Brevard County and graduated from high school in Melbourne, Florida, in 1960. He attended Yale University, earning a BA in 1965, and received a law degree from the University of Virginia in 1968. He was admitted to the Florida bar that same year.

Nelson joined the US Army Reserve after graduation from Yale in 1965 and served until 1971, including two years on active duty following completion of law school. Returning to Florida in 1970, he practiced law and, in 1972, won election to the Florida House of Representatives. He was elected to the US House in 1978. His Congressional District includes the Kennedy Space Center.

Nelson is married to the former Grace Calvert. They have two children, Billy and Nan Ellen.

Nordsieck, Kenneth

Dr. Kenneth Nordsieck was scheduled to serve as backup payload specialist to fellow scientists Samuel Durrance and Ronald Parise for Shuttle Mission 61-E, Spacelab Astro 1, in March 1986. The explosion of the Shuttle Challenger on January 28, 1986, caused NASA to cancel Mission 61-E. Nordsieck, Durrance and Parise continue to train for the future Spacelab Astro missions.

Nordsieck was born February 19, 1946, in New York City. He received a BS in astronomy from the California Institute of Technology in 1967, and a PhD from the University of California at San Diego in 1972.

Nordsieck is an associate professor at Washburn Observatory at the University of Wisconsin in Madison. It was his work as co-investigator for the Wisconsin Ultraviolet Photopolarimetry experiment that made him eligible for selection as an Astro payload specialist in June 1984. His field of research includes the structure of spiral galaxies and extragalactic objects.

He is single.

Parise, Ronald

Dr. Ronald A. Parise was scheduled to be a payload specialist aboard Shuttle Mission 61-E, the Spacelab Astro 1 designed to observe Halley's Comet during a seven-day flight in March 1986. The explosion of the Shuttle Challenger just six weeks earlier forced the cancellation of 61-E, however. Parise is likely to be assigned to one of the two remaining Astro missions.

Parise was born May 24, 1951, in Warren, Ohio, where he grew up. He attended Youngstown State University in Ohio, earning a BS in physics in 1973. He received an MS (1977) and PhD (1979) in astronomy from the University of Florida.

Parise is manager of the advanced astronomy programs section of the Computer Sciences Corporation in Silver Spring, Maryland. One of his projects is the design of the ultraviolet imaging telescope to be flown on Spacelab Astro missions. He has also done research with the International Ultraviolet Explorer satellite.

He and his wife, Cecelia, have a son, Nicholas.

Phillips, Robert

Dr. Robert Ward Phillips is a veterinarian training as a prime payload specialist for the Spacelab Life Sciences mission originally scheduled for 1987, but postponed to 1989 following the Shuttle Challenger disaster.

Phillips was born in 1934 and served in the US Army prior to attending Colorado State University, from which he received a BS and a doctorate in veterinary medicine in 1961. He earned his PhD in 1964 at the University of California at Davis.

At the time of his selection as a payload specialist in January 1984, Phillips was professor of physiology at the College of Veterinary Medicine and Biomedical Science at Colorado State University, Fort Collins.

In January 1985 Phillips and Dr. Drew Gaffney were named to fly aboard Spacelab Life Sciences 1 (also known as Spacelab 4), scheduled for January 1986, but that flight was later canceled.

Phillips is married with four children.

Prinz, Dianne

Dianne Prinz was the backup payload specialist to John-David Bartoe on the Spacelab 2/Mission 51-F shuttle flight in July 1985. She served as scientific capcom and provided mission support from the payload operations center at the NASA Johnson Space Center.

She is a candidate for a future Spacelab mission.

Dianne Kasnic Prinz was born September 29, 1938, in Economy, Pennsylvania. She received a BS from the University of Pittsburgh in 1960 and a PhD from Johns Hopkins University in 1967.

Dr. Prinz is a research physicist with the US Naval Research Laboratory in Washington, D.C. She and Dr. Bartoe had both designed optics and computer software for Spacelab 2 experiments, and were chosen as candidate payload specialists in 1978.

Dr. Prinz is married.

Scully-Power, Paul

Dr. Paul Scully-Power, a professional oceanographer, was a payload specialist aboard Shuttle Mission 41-G in October 1984. During this eight-day flight, which was devoted to a number of different Earth-oriented experiments, Scully-Power was able to make observations of three-fourths of the world's oceans. "When you look down from this field of view you can easily see not just one eddy but a whole series of them," he said at one point in the mission. Scully-Power's work was scientific in nature, but it also had some strategic value to the US Navy, which was concerned about its ability to hide submarines from the cameras of orbiting satellites. In March 1985 Admiral James D. Watkins admitted that Scully-Power had "found some fantastically important new phenomenology that will be vital to us in trying to understand the ocean depths."

Paul Desmond Scully-Power was born May 28, 1944, in Sydney, Australia. He attended primary and secondary schools there and in London, England, and graduated with a BS degree (including honors in education and applied mathematics) from the University of Sydney in 1966.

After graduation from college Scully-Power was asked by the Royal Australian Navy to set up its first oceanographic group. He did so, earning an appointment as scientific officer in January 1967, and remaining with the group as its head until July 1972, when he went to the US to serve as an exchange scientist with the US Navy at its Underwater Systems Center in New London, Connecticut. During this time he assisted the Earth observations team on Skylab, and since then has taken part in briefings before and debriefings after each Shuttle flight.

In March 1974 Scully-Power returned to Australia, where he planned and executed project ANZUS EDDY, a combined Australian-New Zealand-American year-long oceanographic study. He was a principal investigator on an experiment flown on the NASA Heat Capacity Mapping Mission satellite in 1976, and in October 1977 emigrated to the US to take a permanent position with the Naval Underwater Systems Center. He is currently a senior scientist there.

He was added to the crew of Shuttle Mission 41-G in June 1984, just four months prior to its scheduled launch, when deletion of a satellite from the payload allowed NASA and the Navy space oceanographic committee to add another payload specialist to the crew, taking advantage of Mission 41-G's 57-degree inclination. (Most Shuttle missions are flown at a 28-degree inclination to the equator and thus "see" only half as much of the Earth's surface. The few Shuttle missions which are flown at 57 degrees are usually Spacelab missions, which already have crews of seven or eight.) Scully-Power was actually the Navy's alternate choice, but veteran oceanographer Robert Stevenson of the Scripps Institute was unavailable for personal reasons.

Scully-Power has also taken part in twenty-four scientific cruises and is a qualified Navy diver. He has published over 60 scientific articles as well.

He and his wife, Frances, have six children, Adam, Lincoln, Holly, Victoria, William and Tara, and live in Mystic, Connecticut.

Simon, George

Dr. George W. Simon was a backup payload specialist for the Spacelab 2 mission flown in July 1985. During the eight-day flight, Shuttle Mission 51-F, which was dedicated to astronomical experiments, Simon served as a communicator to the astronaut crew from the Payload Operations Center at the NASA Johnson Space Center.

Simon was born April 22, 1934, in Frankfurt, Germany, but came to the US as a boy. He graduated from Grinnell College in 1955 with a BA degree, then earned an MS from the California Institute of Technology in 1961, a PhD from Caltech in 1963, and an MBA from the University of Utah in 1976.

Simon is a senior scientist at the US Air Force Geophysics Laboratory stationed at the National Solar Observatory in Sunspot, New Mexico. He developed the Solar Optical Universe Polarimeter, one of the Spacelab 2 experiments, which made him elegible to be a payload specialist aboard the flight. He was chosen as one of the finalists in 1978.

Simon is married with three children.

Trinh, Eugene

Dr. Eugene H. Trinh was a backup payload specialist for Space Shuttle Mission 51-B/Spacelab 3 in April and May 1985, supporting the scientific work aboard the lab from the Payload Operations Center at NASA's Johnson Space Center.

Trinh was born September 14, 1950, in Saigon, South Vietnam. He came to the US to attend school, earning a BS in engineering science from Columbia University in 1972, and an MS in applied physics in 1974, an MPh in applied physics in 1976, and a PhD in applied physics in 1978, from Yale University.

After a year-and-a-half as a post-doctoral fellow at Yale, Trinh joined the staff of the Jet Propulsion Laboratory in Pasadena, California, where his research involved fluid mechanics and acoustics. His work involved dozens of flights aboard the NASA KC-135 aircraft flying "low-G" parabolas, simulating weightlessness for short periods of time. He also holds three patents.

Trinh worked in a group headed by Dr. Taylor Wang preparing a Drop Dynamics Module experiment for Spacelab 3. When Wang was selected in June 1983 to fly aboard Spacelab 3, Trinh was chosen as his backup. He is likely to go into space himself on a later Spacelab mission.

Trinh is married and lives in California.

van den Berg, Lodewijk

Dr. Lodewijk van den Berg was a payload specialist aboard the Space Shuttle Mission 51-B/Spacelab 3 flight in April and May 1985. During that flight van den Berg, a chemical engineer, and six other astronauts conducted experiments in space medicine and manufacturing.

Van den Berg was born March 24, 1932, in Sluiskil, the Netherlands. He received an MS in chemical engineering from Technical University at Delft in the Netherlands in 1961, and later earned an MS and PhD in applied science from the University of Delaware in 1972 and 1975. From 1961 to 1971 he was employed as a chemical engineer.

Since receiving his doctorate van den Berg has been a scientist with the EG&G Corporation in Goleta, California, specializing in the growth of crystals for scientific and industrial uses. One of the results of this work has been the publication of over 15 articles in scientific journals.

He took part in the design and development of the Spacelab 3 vapor crystal growth system experiment and in June 1983 was selected to supervise its operation, and the operation of other space manufacturing experiments, on the flight of Spacelab 3.

Van den Berg is married with two children and lives in Goleta, California.

Walker, Charles

Charles Walker became the first commercial space traveler when he served as payload specialist on Shuttle Mission 41-D in August and September 1984. An employee of the McDonnell Douglas Corporation, which paid NASA $80,000 to cover the costs of his training, Walker operated his company's electrophoresis unit, a machine designed to manufacture drugs in space, not only on 41-D, but on Shuttle missions 51-D (April 1985) and 61-B (November/December 1985) as well.

Walker was actually the first space passenger, a paying one at that. Non-astronauts Byron Lichtenberg and Ulf Merbold had gone into space before Walker, but both men were scientists whose qualifications were much like those of professional astronauts. Walker's space training consisted of only 125 hours of workbook instruction with some hands-on study in contrast to Lichtenberg and Merbold's five years of work on Spacelab.

The electrophoresis project, technically known as the Continuous Flow Electrophoresis System (CFES), is a joint venture of McDonnell Douglas and the Ortho Pharmaceutical Division of Johnson & Johnson intended to produce a medical hormone. Under an agreement between the companies and NASA, the CFES unit flies on the Shuttle for free, until the companies begin to sell the hormone, at which time McDonnell Douglas becomes a paying customer. Electrophoresis is a process in which an electric charge is used to separate biological materials. The process works most efficiently in microgravity; in fact, in orbit the CFES can process 463 times as much material as it can on Earth.

Earlier versions of CFES were flown on STS-4, STS-6, STS-7, and STS-8 and operated by astronauts, but a full scale machine, which would run during an entire week long mission, required the presence of an onboard engineer. Walker, who had worked on the CFES since 1978 and also trained the astronauts who used the earlier model, was the only candidate considered by McDonnell Douglas. His assignment to the crew of STS-12, later known as Mission 41-D, was made in June 1983.

Sure enough, Walker had to perform on-the-spot repairs to the CFES unit during the first flight. The drugs were also contaminated. During his second flight, however, Walker reported that hardware and contamination problems had been overcome and on the third flight Walker actually produced some of the hormone, paving the way for flights by a still more advanced machine called EOS on future Shuttle missions.

Walker logged 458 hours in space during his three flights.

Charles David Walker was born August 29, 1948, in Bedford, Indiana, where he grew up interested in space flight. (He flew model rockets and skipped school in the seventh grade in order to watch John Glenn's launch.) He attended Purdue University, receiving a BS in aeronautical and astronautical engineering in 1971.

In 1972 he went to work for the Bendix Aerospace Company as a design engineer, and was later employed in the same capacity by the Naval Sea Systems Command Engineering Center in Crane, Indiana. He joined McDonnell Douglas in 1977. During that same year he applied for the NASA astronaut program and was not selected. Ironically, he flew in space before many members of that group.

Walker and his wife, Melissa, live in St. Louis, Missouri.

Wang, Taylor

Dr. Taylor G. Wang, a payload specialist aboard Spacelab 3, was one of the first scientists to go into space with a scientific experiment he had designed and built on Earth. During his spaceflight, Mission 51-B using the orbiter Challenger in April and May 1985, Wang also became the first scientist to repair his malfunctioning device.

Wang's Drop Dynamics Module, a machine in which drops of water, glycerine and silicon oil can be manipulated and mixed by sound waves, was an experiment designed to demonstrate one of the basic elements of space manufacturing: "containerless processing." The DDM failed on its first day in space, forcing Wang and ground controllers to spend two days diagnosing the problem. Once they did that, Wang repaired the machine in three hours and exposed 15,000 feet of film before the DDM broke down permanently.

Wang and the six other astronauts, two squirrel monkeys and 24 experimental rats aboard Spacelab 3 also conducted experiments in space medicine and atmospheric physics during the eight-day flight.

Taylor G. Wang was born in Shanghai, China, on June 16, 1940. His father was a businessman there who was forced to leave the country with his family when the Communist regime came to power in 1949. Wang grew up in Taiwan, then came to the United States, attending the University of California at Los Angeles, receiving his BS (1967), MS (1968) and PhD (1971) in physics. He also became a US citizen.

Wang joined the Jet Propulsion Laboratory at the California Institute of Technology in 1972 as a senior scientist. Eventually he became program manager for experiments devoted to materials processing in space. His experiments were flown on other Shuttle missions and on high-altitude aircraft and rocket flights. He holds ten patents.

Wang was selected as a Spacelab 3 payload specialist in June 1983 and spent the next two years training at JPL and at NASA's Marshall Space Flight Center in Huntsville, Alabama. He is likely to go into space a second time aboard a later Spacelab mission.

Wang is married, with two children.

Williams, Bill

Dr. Bill Alvin Williams trained for one year as a potential payload specialist for Spacelab 4 (also known as Spacelab Life Sciences) until resigning for personal reasons.

Williams was born in 1941 and received a BS in physiology from the University of California at Berkeley in 1963, an MA and PhD in biophysics and physiology from the University of Illinois in 1968.

From 1969 to 1983 he served as a researcher and scientist for both the National Academy of Sciences and NASA at the Ames Research Center in Palo Alto, California. He is the author of over 88 scientific papers, many of them concerning the physiology of animals.

Williams was a finalist in the 1980 astronaut selection. At the time he was named a Spacelab 4 payload specialist in January 1984 Williams was a scientist with the US Environmental Protection Agency in Corvallis, Oregon.

Wood, Robert

Robert Wood is an engineer employed by the McDonnell Douglas Astronautics Company who will operate a McDAC/Johnson & Johnson space manufacturing unit aboard a future Shuttle flight.

This unit, the electrophoresis operations in space (EOS), takes advantage of the space environment to separate and purify biological materials in the manufacture of unique drugs. An earlier version was operated by fellow McDAC engineer Charles Walker on three Shuttle missions.

Robert Jackson Wood was born June 26, 1957, in Fitchburg, Massachusetts, but graduated from high school in Wilton, New Hampshire, in 1975. He attended Ohio University, earning a BS in physics (summa cum laude) in 1978, and later earned an MS in physics from the Massachusetts Institute of Technology in 1980.

Wood has worked as a research assistant at MIT's Bates Linear Accelerator, and as a senior research scientist with the Fisher Scientific Company, developing automated laboratory instruments. In 1983 he went to work for McDonnell Douglas Astronautics in Houston, designing computer software for the EOS unit and supporting its previous flights from mission control. He was designated as the second industrial payload specialist in March 1985 and served as backup to Walker on Shuttle Mission 61-B in 1985.

Wood and his wife, Alicia, have a son, Lucas.

Military Shuttle Payload Specialists

Long before the launch of the first Shuttle in 1981, the US Air Force announced that it would train payload specialists to accompany Department of Defense satellites on "dedicated" missions, those devoted solely to military activities.

Most DOD Shuttle payload specialists would come from the new Manned Spaceflight Engineer program, which was begun as an experiment in 1979. Applications were solicited from USAF, USN and US Army officers who were required to have a BA in science or engineering and four years of experience in flying or space-related work. From 222 applications, 14 officers (12 Air Force, 2 Navy) were selected. One of the Navy officers declined the job in favor of a post at the US Naval Academy and was not replaced. An Air Force officer also declined and was replaced by an alternate. Thirteen MSEs began work at the Space Division in February 1980, though several men still had duties elsewhere and were forced to commute.

In the summer of 1982 announcements were circulated at Air Force bases and placed in Air Force publications soliciting applications for a second MSE group, this one limited to USAF personnel. From a pool of 63, 14 officers were selected, including two women (Captain Katherine Roberts and lst Lieutenant Maureen Lacomb) and one black (Captain Livingston Holder). Training began in January 1983.

A third group of five officers was to be selected in spring of 1986.

The USAF originally asked NASA to develop a training schedule only to have NASA decline. Consequently the members of the first MSE cadre developed their own training program, which gave them more extensive involvement with the Shuttle than other payload specialists. For example, MSEs donned suits and performed EVA simulations in the pool at Marshall Spaceflight Center.

Most MSE time was devoted to management and acquisitions relating to DOD payloads. Several MSEs were assigned to each payload office, some to more than one, working together with USAF SPOs (systems project officers). Approximately one year prior to planned DOD Shuttle missions prime and backup candidates—not necessarily from the payload group—were chosen.

The program was conducted in relative secrecy until late 1982, though it was not until October 1985 that the names of all active MSEs were released. By that time all of the members of the first cadre had been reassigned, or had resigned, and five members of the second cadre were working elsewhere at the Air Force Space Division.

In addition to MSEs, the Department of Defense had other sources for possible Shuttle payload specialists. In August 1985, Undersecretary of the Air Force Edward "Pete" Aldridge was assigned to the crew of Mission 62-A, the first scheduled Vandenberg Shuttle launch. Prior to that, in 1983, General Lawrence Skantze of the Air Force Systems Command was considered for a similar assignment. The Air Force also hopes to fly a meteorologist (much as NASA and the Navy flew oceanographer Paul Scully-Power) on a future Shuttle mission.

A Department of Defense Spacelab, to be devoted to experiments for the Strategic Defense Initiative Organization (SDIO), will also require at least two DOD payload specialists, who may be from the MSE cadre or from Air Force installations (such as the Weapons Laboratory at Kirtland AFB, New Mexico) who are engaged in SDI research.

Military Shuttle Payload Specialist Biographies

Aldridge, Edward

Edward "Pete" Aldridge, then undersecretary of the United States Air Force, was chosen as a payload specialist for Shuttle Mission 62-A, the first Shuttle scheduled to be launched from Vandenberg Air Force Base, California. The July 1986 launch, already postponed several times, was delayed indefinitely by the explosion of the Shuttle Challenger on January 28, 1986.

Aldridge, who has been the head of all Air Force space programs, played a major role in re-evaluating military use of the Shuttle following the Challenger disaster. Named as secretary of the Air Force later in 1986, he removed himself from the 62-A crew.

Edward C. Aldridge, Jr., was born August 18, 1938, in Houston, Texas, but grew up in Shreveport, Louisiana. He attended Texas A & M University, receiving a BS in aeronautical engineering in 1960, and earned an MS in aeronautical engineering (1962) from the Georgia Institute of Technology.

Aldridge has held a number of jobs in the aerospace industry and in the federal government. From 1962 to 1967 he was with Douglas Aircraft in St. Louis, Missouri, as manager of their missile and space division, and he later worked for LTV Aerospace in Dallas. From 1977 to 1981 he was vice president of the Strategic Systems Corporation.

He was named undersecretary of the Air Force for the US Department of Defense in 1981, and announced as a Shuttle payload specialist in September 1985.

Aldridge is married to the former Joanne Knotts, and they have four children.

Armor, James

Major James B. Armor, Jr., US Air Force, was a member of the second group of Department of Defense manned spaceflight engineers chosen in January 1983.

Armor was born September 25, 1950, and joined the Air Force in 1972. He has received a BS in electrical engineering and an MS in electro-optics. He also served as a missile crew commander and a project officer for military Shuttle payloads. Armor left the MSE group in 1985 and is currently working at USAF Headquarters in the Pentagon, Washington, D.C. He remains eligible for assignment to a future Shuttle crew.

Booen, Michael

Captain Michael W. Booen, US Air Force, served as backup payload specialist for Shuttle Mission 51-J in October 1985. Two Department of Defense communications satellites were placed in geosynchronous orbit during that flight.

Booen was born May 30, 1957, and graduated from the US Air Force Academy in 1979. He holds a master's degree, and was selected for the second group of DOD manned spaceflight engineers in January 1983.

Casserino, Frank

Air Force Captain Frank J. Casserino was one of the first 13 Department of Defense manned spaceflight engineers who began training as possible Shuttle payload specialists in February 1980.

He was born July 21, 1955 (making him, at 24, the youngest American to be a candidate for a spaceflight) and graduated from the US Air Force Academy in 1977. He is reported to have trained for a canceled DOD Shuttle mission scheduled for 1984. Although he left the MSE program in 1985, he remains at Space Division in Los Angeles and is a candidate for a future Shuttle flight.

Detroye, Jeffrey

Air Force Captain Jeffrey E. Detroye was a member of the first group of Department of Defense manned spaceflight engineers who began training as potential Shuttle payload specialists in February 1980.

Detroye was born January 14, 1955, and graduated from the US Air Force Academy in 1977. He left the MSE group in 1985, transferring to the Air Force manned spaceflight support group at the NASA Johnson Space Center.

In 1986 he resigned from the Air Force to work at JSC as a civilian flight controller.

Hamel, Michael

Air Force Major Michael A. Hamel was one of the first 13 manned spaceflight engineers chosen in February 1980. He trained as a possible payload specialist for a 1984 Shuttle mission which was cancelled, and left the MSE group in 1985.

Hamel was born December 24, 1950, and graduated from the US Air Force Academy in 1972.

Higbee, Terry

Major Terry A. Higbee, USAF, was a member of the first group of Department of Defense manned spaceflight engineers from 1980 to 1984. He never flew in space.

Higbee was born December 3, 1949, and joined the Air Force in 1972. He has a PhD.

Physical problems forced him to leave the MSE program in 1984. He is currently based at the Pentagon.

Holder, Livingston

Captain Livingston L. Holder, Jr., US Air Force, was a member of the second group of Department of Defense manned spaceflight engineers chosen in January 1983. He left the MSE group in 1985 without making a space flight, though he remains at Space Division in Los Angeles.

Holder, the only black in the MSE group, was born September 29, 1956, and graduated from the US Air Force Academy in 1978. He has a master's degree and served as a Titan 34D flight controller prior to joining the MSE program.

James, Larry

Air Force Captain Larry D. James is one of the 14 Department of Defense manned spaceflight engineers chosen in January 1983.

James was born August 8, 1956, and graduated from the US Air Force Academy in 1978. He is stationed at Space Division in Los Angeles and is a potential payload specialist for a future military Shuttle crew.

Jones, Charles

Air Force Major Charles E. Jones is one of the 14 manned spaceflight engineers chosen by the USAF in January 1983. He is eligible for assignment as a payload specialist on a future military Shuttle mission.

Jones was born November 8, 1952, and graduated from the US Air Force Academy in 1974. He has a master's degree and was stationed at Space Division in Los Angeles prior to becoming an MSE.

Joseph, Daryl

Major Daryl J. Joseph, US Air Force, was a member of the first group of Department of Defense manned spaceflight engineers from 1980 to 1985. In 1984 he trained briefly as a potential payload specialist for a military Shuttle mission which was cancelled.

Joseph was born December 12, 1949, and graduated from the Air Force Academy in 1971. He has a master's degree.

Lacomb, Maureen

Captain Maureen C. Lacomb is one of the Air Force manned spaceflight engineers selected in January 1983. She is currently assigned to Space Division in Los Angeles and is a candidate to be a Department of Defense payload specialist on future Shuttle missions.

Lacomb was born November 16, 1956 and joined the Air Force in 1978.

Lydon, Malcolm

Major Malcolm W. Lydon, USAF, was one of the first 13 Department of Defense manned spaceflight engineers chosen in February 1980. He left the MSE program in 1985 without flying in space.

An electrical engineer, Lydon was born June 3, 1946, and joined the Air Force in 1968. He remains at Space Division in Los Angeles.

Mantz, Michael

Air Force Major Michael R. Mantz is one of the fourteen Department of Defense manned spaceflight engineers who began training in January 1983 as potential Shuttle payload specialists.

Mantz was born February 16, 1953, and graduated from the Air Force Academy in 1976. He has a master's degree.

Odle, Randy

Captain Randy T. Odle was scheduled to serve as backup Department of Defense payload specialist for the first manned Shuttle launch from Vandenberg Air Force Base, California. This mission, delayed indefinitely because of the explosion of the Shuttle Challenger in January 1986, was to have carried the Teal Ruby satellite and a package of DOD scientific experiments.

Odle was originally chosen as one of two prime payload specialists, but was replaced by Air Force Undersecretary Edward Aldridge prior to the public announcement in August 1985.

Odle was born September 8, 1951, and entered the US Air Force via a civilian appointment. He has a master's degree. He joined the MSE program in January 1983.

Pailes, William

Major Bill Pailes of the US Air Force served as Department of Defense payload specialist for Shuttle Mission 51-J in October 1985. Pailes supervised the deployment of a classified DOD payload, rumored to be two Defense Satellite Communications Systems (DSCS) satellites. The four-day Mission 51-J was also the first flight of the orbiter Atlantis.

Pailes was born June 26, 1952, in Hackensack, New Jersey, but grew up in Kinelon. As a teenager he never thought for a moment that he would fly in space. He wanted to be a civil engineer, a bridge builder, but when he earned an appointment to the US Air Force Academy he received his BS in computer science (1974). In 1981 he received an MS in that field from Texas A&M University.

With his computer background and "non-standard vision" (he has color blindness), Pailes still thought he would become anything but an Air Force pilot, but he was assigned to flight school at Williams AFB, Arizona, and from December 1975 to July 1980 served as an HC-130 pilot with the Air Force Rescue Service at Royal AFB in Woodbridge, England. Following a year in graduate school he managed development of mini-computer software at Scott AFB, Illinois, where he read about the manned spaceflight engineer program in the *Air Force Times.* He applied and, in January 1983, was selected.

Pailes and the other thirteen members of the second MSE group were told they had a fifty percent chance of flying in space, a promise that would be impossible to fulfill after the explosion of the Shuttle Challenger. Like the members of the first MSE group chosen in 1980, the new payload specialists underwent extensive training on Shuttle systems, but spent most of their time acting as payload integration specialists—taking part in the design, purchase, construction and development of military satellites and experiments for the Shuttle. In October 1984 Pailes was assigned to the crew for Mission 51-J, though it was not publicly revealed until the following August.

Since his flight Pailes continues to work with the MSE group at Space Division in Los Angeles, though he expects to return to operational flying in 1987. He is currently head of the MSE program.

Lieutenant Colonel Pailes is married to the former Brenda Burleson.

Payton, Gary

US Air Force manned spaceflight engineer Gary E. Payton served as payload specialist of Shuttle Mission 51-C in January 1985, supervising the deployment of a classified military satellite which was placed in geosynchronous orbit by an inertial upper stage. The three-day flight of Mission 51-C was shortened by a day because of weather problems at its prime landing site, the NASA Kennedy Space Center in Florida.

Payton was born June 20, 1948, in Rock Island, Illinois. He attended Bradley University in Peoria for one year, then entered the US Air Force Academy at Colorado Springs, graduating in 1971 with a BS in astronautical engineering. He went on to earn an MS in astronautical and aeronautical engineering from Purdue University in 1972.

After completing pilot training in 1973, Payton served as a flight instructor at Craig Air Force Base, Alabama. In 1976 he became a spacecraft test controller at Cape Canaveral and remained in that job until selected for the first group of manned spaceflight engineers in 1980.

Payton has logged approximately 1100 hours of flying time in the T-37, T-38 and T-39 aircraft.

As one of the first 13 Department of Defense Shuttle payload specialists, Payton underwent a course of training that familiarized him with Shuttle systems, including use of the remote manipulator arm and underwater simulations of extra-vehicular activity. In May 1983 he was selected as the DOD payload specialist assigned to STS-10, then scheduled for November of that year. But continuing problems with the Air Force inertial upper stage forced the cancellation or postponement of Payton's secret payload.

When he finally rode the Shuttle Challenger into orbit on January 25, 1985, Payton became the first participant in a DOD manned space program to actually make a flight, over twenty-two years after the DOD chose its first potential space travelers, the X-20 pilots.

Since his space flight Lieutenant Colonel Payton has assumed new duties at the Air Force Space Division in Los Angeles.

He is married to the former Sue C. Campbell. They have a daughter, Courtney.

Puz, Craig

Captain Craig A. Puz, USAF, is in training as a future military Shuttle payload specialist at Space Division in Los Angeles. He was chosen with the second group of Department of Defense manned spaceflight engineers in January 1983.

Puz was born June 24, 1954, and attended the Air Force Academy, graduating in 1976.

Rij, Jerry

Air Force Major Jerry J. Rij was one of the first 13 Department of Defense manned spaceflight engineers selected as potential Shuttle payload specialists in February 1980. He left the MSE group in 1985.

Rij was born February 23, 1950, and joined the Air Force in 1972. He has a master's degree.

Roberts, Katherine

Captain Katherine E. Roberts, US Air Force, was a member of the second group of Department of Defense manned spaceflight engineers chosen in January 1983. She left the MSE program in 1985.

Roberts was born June 25, 1954, and joined the Air Force in 1976. She remains at Space Division in Los Angeles as a payload integration officer.

Sefchek, Paul

Major Paul A. Sefchek, US Air Force, was a member of the first group of Department of Defense manned spaceflight engineers chosen in February 1980. After five years of training he left the program without flying in space.

Sefchek was born July 7, 1946, and joined the Air Force in 1968. He is currently a systems project officer at Space Division in Los Angeles.

Sponable, Jess

Captain Jess M. Sponable, US Air Force, was selected for the second group of Department of Defense manned spaceflight engineers in January 1983. He left the MSE group in 1985 without flying in space, though he remains at Space Division in Los Angeles and is eligible for assignment as a military payload specialist on a future Shuttle crew.

Sponable was born November 29, 1953, and attended the US Air Force Academy, graduating in 1978.

Sundberg, Eric

Air Force Lieutenant Colonel Eric E. Sundberg was one of the first 13 Department of Defense manned spaceflight engineers who began training as potential Shuttle payload specialists in February 1980. Sundberg left the program in 1984 without flying in space.

He was born April 10, 1945, joined the Air Force in 1967, and is currently based at Air Force Space Command at Peterson AFB, Colorado.

Thompson, William

Captain William D. Thompson, USAF, was a member of the second group of Department of Defense manned spaceflight engineers from January 1983 to March 1985. He left the program without making a spaceflight.

Thompson was born January 14, 1956, and graduated from the Air Force Academy in 1978.

He remains at Space Division in Los Angeles.

Vidrine, David

David Vidrine came within a single phone call of becoming first manned spaceflight engineer to make a Shuttle flight. He was training as a payload specialist for Mission 41-C, the Shuttle flight that retrieved and repaired the ailing Solar Max satellite, in 1984, when a last-minute decision took him off the crew.

Vidrine, a Navy Commander, left the MSE program, of which he was director, shortly thereafter.

David Matthew Vidrine was born November 21, 1943, in Ville Platte, Louisiana. He moved with his family to Lafayette in 1955 and graduated from high school there in 1961.

Growing up, Vidrine was interested in aviation, and following the launch of Sputnik in October 1957, in space exploration. He was a reader of science fiction as well, particularly the works of Arthur C. Clarke. He attended South West Louisiana University in Lafayette, intending to major in aeronautical engineering, but found that it wasn't offered and settled for mechanical engineering instead. He would later earn two master's degrees from the US Naval Postgraduate School, one in aeronautics, the other in engineering.

Vidrine joined the US Navy aviation cadet program in February 1964 and entered pilot training. About two-thirds of the way through the program he switched to navigator training, a move he later regretted, in spite of the fact that he believed it saved him from being shot down over North Vietnam, as were many of his classmates.

Stationed at McGuire Air Force Base, Vidrine did one tour in Southeast Asia, flying C-130 cargo planes. Returning to the US, he was an instructor at Pensacola for two years, then a P-3 crewman at Jacksonville for another two years. From 1972 to 1975 he was in Monterey, California, attending the US Naval Postgraduate School.

Between 1975 and 1980 Vidrine was assigned to the US Navy Space Project, first at the Air Force Space Division in Los Angeles, then in Washington D.C. He was selected for the Manned Spaceflight Engineer program in February 1980, and commuted between Washington and Los Angeles for most of the year.

As an MSE, Vidrine became thoroughly familiar with Space Shuttle systems and operations, with a wide variety of military satellites and research payloads, and with NASA centers, including the Marshall Spaceflight Center in Alabama, where MSEs donned spacesuits and took part in EVA simulations in the huge water tank. In November 1983 Vidrine was named director of manned spaceflight, the head of the MSE program.

Since leaving the program and retiring from the Navy Vidrine has worked for TRW Space Systems in Los Angeles. He is single and has two daughters.

Watterson, John

Major John Brett Watterson, USAF, was to have been one of the Department of Defense payload specialists on the first Space Shuttle launched from Vandenberg Air Force Base, California. That flight, originally designated Mission 62-A and scheduled for launch in July 1986, was postponed indefinitely by the explosion of the Shuttle Challenger in January 1986.

Watterson was born September 10, 1949, in Garden City, New York, but grew up in Littleton, Colorado, where he graduated from high school in 1967. He attended Virginia Military Institute, receiving a BS in physics in 1971. He later earned an MS in engineering physics (1976) from the Air Force Institute of Technology at Wright-Patterson AFB, Ohio.

Entering active duty with the Air Force, Watterson served at Korat Royal Thai AFB, Thailand, from 1972 to 1973, then spent three years with the Foreign Technology Division at Wright-Patterson. From 1976 to 1980 he was a systems engineer at the Air Force Space Division in

Los Angeles. In 1980 he was chosen as one of the first 13 DOD manned spaceflight engineers and worked on national security payloads as an MSE until 1984. After leaving the MSE group he continued to be involved in potential Shuttle payloads, including the Space Test Program of DOD scientific experiments, and remained eligible for assignment to a Shuttle mission. He was announced as one of the Mission 62-A payload specialists in August 1985.

Watterson and his wife, Teri, have a son, Travis.

Wright, Keith

Major Keith C. Wright, US Air Force, served as backup payload specialist for Shuttle Mission 51-C in January 1985. During that flight a secret Department of Defense satellite was place in geosynchronous orbit.

Wright was born August 31, 1947, and joined the Air Force in 1969. He has a master's degree and was selected for the first group of manned spaceflight engineers in 1980. He left the MSE program in 1985.

Yeakel, Glenn

Air Force Captain Glenn Scott Yeakel is one of the 14 Department of Defense manned spaceflight engineers chosen in January 1983. He remains with the MSE group and is eligible for assignment as a payload specialist on a future military Shuttle mission.

Yeakel was born May 28, 1956, and graduated from the Air Force Academy in 1978. He has a master's degree, and prior to joining the MSE program was stationed at Wright-Patterson Air Force Base, Ohio.

USAF X-15 Pilots

The X-15 was a rocket-powered aircraft built by North American Aviation for joint NASA, US Air Force and US Navy research into flight at high speeds and altitudes. On 199 flights between June 1959 and October 1968 the X-15 ultimately achieved a top speed of 4520 miles per hour (Mach 6.7) and an altitude of 354,200 (66.8 miles).

Fourteen pilots were directly involved with the X-15, although only twelve actually flew the vehicles (there were three). There was no formal selection process, since everyone chosen was already a qualified test pilot.

For example, Scott Crossfield and Alvin White were the prime and backup North American Aviation test pilots and became involved with the project first. Air Force Captains Iven Kincheloe (prime pilot) and Robert White (backup) were assigned to the X-15 in 1957. When Kincheloe was killed in an accident before flying the rocket plane, White became the prime Air Force pilot and Captain Robert Rushworth became his backup. The first NASA pilots were Joseph Walker and Neil Armstrong. Lieutenant Commander Forrest Peterson represented the Navy.

Walker and Armstrong were eventually replaced by NASA pilots Jack McKay (1960), Milton Thompson (1963), and Bill Dana (1965). White and Rushworth were succeeded by Captain Joe Engle (1963), Captain Pete Knight (1964), and Major Michael Adams (1966).

The X-15 was not considered a spacecraft by its designers, though it operated at an altitude where conditions were little different from those encountered by orbiting vehicles. By the early 1960s, however, the US Air Force had decided that flights over 50 miles were space flights and created a special Astronaut Rating to honor those who did. And the Federation Astronautique Internationale (FAI), the international record-keeping body, recognizes flights over 100 kilometers or 62 miles as space flights.

Thirteen different X-15 flights, by Walker, White, Rushworth, Engle, McKay, Dana, Knight and Adams, qualified according to the Air Force, though only White, Rushworth, Engle, Knight and Adams received Astronaut Wings. Civilians Walker, McKay and Dana were not eligible. Two X-15 flights by Joe Walker qualified by FAI rules. (See Appendix 3)

USAF X-15 Pilot Biographies

Adams, Michael

Major Michael Adams, USAF, left the Manned Orbiting Laboratory program to fly the X-15 rocket plane. On November 15, 1967, on his seventh X-15 flight, Adams pushed the aircraft to an altitude of 266,000 feet, 50.4 statute miles, where it went off course and ultimately broke apart. Adams was killed, the only direct fatality of the X-15 program.

Michael James Adams was born May 5, 1930, in Sacramento, California. He graduated from Sacramento Junior College in 1950 and joined the Air Force. Following flight training he flew 49 combat missions in Korea as an F-86 pilot. He later served at bases in Louisiana and France before returning to school to complete his education, earning a bachelor of science degree in aeronautical engineering from Oklahoma University in 1958. He did eighteen months of graduate work at the Massachusetts Institute of Technology.

Adams attended the Air Force Test Pilot School at Edwards AFB in 1962 (earning the Honts Trophy as outstanding student) and the Aerospace Research Pilot School in 1963. His commander at ARPS, Colonel Chuck Yeager, described him as a pilot "good enough to name his own assignment, NASA or Air Force." He chose to remain with the Air Force and was selected as one of the first eight pilots for the Manned Orbiting Laboratory program in November 1965. He left MOL for the X-15 program on July 20, 1966.

On his fatal flight Adams qualified for the USAF Astronaut Rating, given to pilots who reach altitudes greater than 50 statute miles.

Adams was survived by his wife, Frieda, and three children, Michael Jr., Brent and Liese.

Armstrong, Neil

See entry under **NASA Astronauts**.

Crossfield, Scott

A. Scott Crossfield was the first pilot of the X-15 rocket research plane and made 14 flights in it between June 1959 and December 1960. More significantly, perhaps, Crossfield played an important role in the development of the X-15, first as a consultant to North American Aviation, the builders of the rocket plane, then as its prime test pilot.

Albert Scott Crossfield was born October 2, 1921, in Berkeley, California, but grew up in Wilmington, south of Los Angeles, where his father was in the oil business. Childhood bouts with pneumonia and rheumatic fever left young Scott bed–ridden for long periods of time during which he began to read about pilots and airplanes. When he recovered he took up a paper route that serviced the Wilmington Airport, where 13-year-old Scott made a deal with a pilot there: flying lessons in exchange for free delivery. Shortly thereafter, Crossfield's family moved to a farm in Washington State, where Crossfield graduated from Boistfort High School in 1939. He managed to continue his flying lessons at nearby Chehalis Airport.

Crossfield entered the University of Washington in September 1940, intending to study aeronautical engineering, and also found a job at the Boeing aircraft plant, which lasted until he joined the Navy following Pearl Harbor. He completed military pilot training, then served as a flying and gunnery instructor. He was assigned to the aircraft carrier Langley, headed for combat over Japan, when the war ended.

After the war Crossfield returned to the University of Washington, receiving a BS in aeronautical engineering in 1949 and an MS in aeronautical engineering the following year. He joined NACA in 1950 as a pilot at Edwards Air Force Base, California.

For the next five years Crossfield flew high speed jets and rocket planes for NACA, including the X-1, D-558 II Skyrocket, X-4, X-5, XF-92A, and the F-100. In 1953 he became the first pilot to fly twice the speed of sound.

Crossfield left NACA in December 1955 to join North American Aviation. He remained with the company as director of test and quality assurance until 1967. He was later employed by Eastern Airlines as director of research and development, and since 1977 has been a member of the staff of the Committee on Science and Technology, US House of Representatives.

He is the author of an autobiography, *Always Another Dawn* (1960).

Crossfield is married with six children. He lives in Herndon, Virginia.

Dana, William

NASA test pilot Bill Dana made 16 flights in the X-15 rocket plane, including two that exceeded fifty miles in altitude, qualifying him as a space traveler. On November 1, 1966, Dana piloted X-15 #3 to an altitude of 306,900 feet, 58 miles above the surface of the Earth. A second flight on August 21, 1968, in X-15 #1 reached 267,500 feet, or almost 51 miles in altitude.

William Harvey Dana was born November 3, 1930, in Pasadena, California. He attended the US Military Academy at West Point, graduating with a bachelor of science degree in 1952, and elected to serve in the US Air Force. He later earned an MS in aeronautical engineering from the University of Southern California (1958).

Dana served in the Air Force as a fighter pilot from 1952 to 1956. After completing graduate work at USC he went to work for NASA as a research and test pilot at the Dryden Flight Center at Edwards Air Force Base, California. In addition to work on the X-15 program, which he began in 1965, Dana flew all of the lifting body aircraft NASA and the US Air Force developed as precursors to the Space Shuttle, including the M2-F1, M2-F2, M2-F3, HL-10, X-24A and X-24B. On September 23, 1975, Dana was the pilot for the last rocket-powered flight of the X-24B, ending the series of rocket flights that had begun with the X-1 in 1947.

Dana is currently a project pilot on the Advanced Fighter Technology Program at Dryden. He and his wife, Judy, have four children and live in Tehachapi, California.

Engle, Joe

See entry under **NASA Astronauts**.

Kincheloe, Iven

Captain Iven Kincheloe was the original US Air Force project pilot for the X-15, chosen in September 1957. On July 26, 1958, he took off from Edwards Air Force Base to act as chase pilot during the test flight of an F-104. The engine on Kincheloe's F-104 flamed out during takeoff. He tried to eject at low altitude but was killed.

On September 7, 1956, Kincheloe had piloted the X-2 rocket plane to a record altitude of 126,200 feet, becoming famous as the "first man in space." In the next two years, while undergoing strenuous medical tests to prepare him for X-15 flights, Kincheloe placed well ahead of his contemporaries, who included Neil Armstrong. Tom Wolfe, in *The Right Stuff*, described Kincheloe as "a test pilot from out of a dream, blond, handsome, powerful, bright, supremely ambitious and yet popular with all who worked with him, including other pilots. There was no ceiling on his future in the Air Force." Many space officials considered him a shoo-in to be the first man on the Moon, though his height of six feet one inch might have kept him out of the Apollo program, had he lived.

Iven Carl Kincheloe, Jr., was born July 2, 1928, in Detroit, Michigan, but grew up on a farm in Cassopolis. He got interested in aviation as a teenager and took flying lessons, soloing at the age of fourteen. Following graduation from high school in Dowagiac, Michigan, he entered Purdue University, where he received a BS in aeronautical engineering in 1949.

An Air Force ROTC student, Kincheloe underwent pilot training in Texas, Arizona and Illinois. He flew almost 100 combat missions in Korea in F-86s, shooting down ten enemy aircraft to become a double ace. Returning to the US, he was a gunnery instructor at Nellis AFB, Nevada, then attended the British Empire Test Pilot School at Farnborough, England. Following graduation in December 1954, he was assigned to Edwards AFB as a test pilot.

He was survived by his wife, Dorothy, and a son, Sam. A biography, *First of the Spacemen* by James J. Haggerty, Jr., was published in 1960.

The Society of Experimental Test Pilots named its yearly trophy after Kincheloe.

Knight, William

Pete Knight set a world speed record by piloting an X-15 rocket plane to Mach 6.7, 4520 miles per hour, on October 3, 1967. That record for winged aircraft stood until the flight of STS-1, the first Space Shuttle mission, in April 1981. Two weeks after setting the speed record, on October 17, Knight flew an X-15 to an altitude of 280,500 feet, over 53 miles above the Earth, earning US Air Force astronaut wings.

In all, Knight made sixteen of the 199 X-15 flights. He was scheduled to pilot number 200 but the flight was postponed five different times, the last time, on December 20, 1968, because of snow. NASA's Paul Bikle, director of the X-15 program, knowing that NASA would not fund further flights past December, and noting that only one of the three X-15 aircraft still functioned, concluded that "someone up there is trying to tell us something," and canceled the flight.

Knight had previously trained as a pilot for the US Air Force X-20 Dyna-Soar program.

William J. "Pete" Knight was born November 18, 1929, in Noblesville, Indiana. He attended Butler and Purdue Universities, then joined the US Air Force in 1952. He completed his BS in aeronautical engineering at the Air Force Institute of Technology in 1958.

Following flight training Knight served as a fighter pilot, becoming briefly famous in 1954 when he won the Allison Jet Trophy race at the National Air Show in Dayton, Ohio. He entered the Air Force Test Pilot School at Edwards Air Force Base in 1958 and remained at the center as a test pilot. Ultimately he would log over 6000 hours of flying time in more than 100 different types of aircraft.

In 1969 Knight began a tour of duty in Vietnam, flying 253 combat missions in the F-100. When he returned to the US he served at Wright-Patterson AFB, Ohio, as test director for the new F-15 fighter and later directed weapons development for ten different fighters. He later became vice commander of the Air Force Flight Test Center at Edwards, and retired as a colonel in October 1982.

Knight had remained active as an F-15 test pilot until his retirement, and continues to fly. In June 1983 he was injured in the crash of an ultralight vehicle near Lancaster, California, but recovered.

He had intended to return to his native Indiana to pursue a political career, but remained in California, and in April 1984 was elected to the city council of Palmdale.

Knight has three sons, William, David and Stephen.

McKay, John

Jack McKay was a NASA test pilot who flew the X-15 rocket research plane on 29 flights between September 1960 and October 1966. During one of his early X-15 flights, on November 9, 1962, McKay was forced to crash land at Mud Lake near Edwards Air Force Base. The rocket plane flipped over, seriously injuring McKay, and though he recovered and flew the X-15 again, complications from this accident eventually caused his death at Lancaster, California, on April 27, 1975.

He made one flight, on September 28, 1965, in which he reached an altitude of 295,600 feet, qualifying him for the title of astronaut. As a civilian NASA employee, however, he was not eligible for Air Force astronaut wings.

McKay was born December 8, 1922, in Portsmouth, Virginia, where his father, a Navy officer, was based. He grew up in the West Indies and had no formal schooling between third and seventh grades. Returning to Virginia, he completed high school and also learned to fly, soloing at the age of 18. While continuing his education at Virginia Polytechnic Institute, he also went to work for the National Advisory Committee on Aeronautics (NACA), NASA's forerunner, in 1940, as a model builder at Langley Field, Virginia.

When World War II broke out McKay joined the Navy and eventually qualified as a fighter pilot. He flew combat missions against Japan from the carrier USS Hornet. After the war he returned to Virginia Polytechnic Institute, graduating with a BS in aeronautical engineering in 1950.

McKay went to work for NACA in 1951 as a test pilot at Edwards Air Force Base in California. For the next twenty years he flew the newest jets and rocket planes in existence: the X-1B, the X-1E, the D-558 Skyrocket, the X-4 and the X-5, in addition to the X-15. He retired in 1971.

He is survived by his wife, Shirley, and eight children, Sherry, Jim, Joanne, John, Milton, Mark, Charlie and Suzie.

Peterson, Forrest

Forrest Peterson was the only US Navy pilot to fly the X-15. Between September 1960 and January 1962 he made five flights in the rocket plane, ultimately reaching an altitude of 101,800 feet.

He went on to a distinguished career in naval aviation, including a tour as captain of the carrier USS Enterprise. His last assignment was vice chief of naval operations for air at the Pentagon.

Forrest Silas Peterson was born May 16, 1922, in Holdrege, Nebraska. He attended the US Naval Academy, graduating in 1944. He would later earn a BS in aerospace engineering from the US Naval Postgraduate School (1952) and an MS in engineering from Princeton University (1953).

Peterson served aboard a destroyer in the Pacific 1945, then underwent pilot training at Pensacola, Florida, beginning in January 1946. He graduated in June 1947 and later flew combat missions in Korea. He attended the Navy Test Pilot School at Patuxent River, Maryland (where he was first in his class) prior to joining the X-15 program in 1958.

After leaving the X-15 project in 1962 he held a variety of positions, becoming executive officer and later captain of the Enterprise, serving as commander of the 6th Fleet's Carrier Group Two, and working at several jobs in the Pentagon. He retired from the Navy in May 1980.

Vice Admiral Peterson is married with three children.

Rushworth, Robert

Air Force Major Bob Rushworth made 34 flights in the X-15 rocket plane, more than any other test pilot, and earned USAF astronaut wings on June 27, 1963, when he flew X-15 #3 to an altitude of 285,000 feet, or 55 miles.

Robert A. Rushworth was born October 9, 1924, in Madison, Maine, where he graduated from high school in 1942. He attended Hebron Academy for a year, and in June 1943 enlisted in the US Army. He entered the aviation cadet program and became a pilot, winning his wings in September 1944.

Assigned to the 12th Combat Cargo Squadron in the China-Burma-India theater of operations, he flew C-47 Skytrain and C-46 Commando transports on combat missions, including many over the Himalayas. Returning to the States, he left active duty in January 1946 and entered the University of Maine, where he received a BS in mechanical engineering in 1951.

Recalled to the Air Force in February 1951, Rushworth became an F-80C Shooting Star pilot. In August 1953 he was enrolled in the Air Force Institute of Technology at Wright-Patterson AFB, Ohio, where he earned an MS in aeronautical engineering in 1954. He remained at Wright-Pat for two more years as a test pilot, then was sent to Edwards AFB, California.

He graduated from the Experimental Test Pilot School there in January 1957 and for the next ten years flew aircraft and rocket planes at Edwards, including the F-101, TF-102, F-104, F-106 and X-15. He won a Distinguished Flying Cross for landing an X-15 safely after its landing gear extended prematurely.

Rushworth left Edwards in 1966 to attend the National War College, then became an F-4 Phantom pilot and served in Viet Nam, flying 189 combat missions. Returning to the US in 1969, he served as director of several test programs at Wright-Pat (1969-73), inspector general for the Air Force Systems Command (1973-74), commander of the flight test center at Edwards (1974-75), commander of the test center at Kirtland AFB, New Mexico (1975-76), and vice commander of the Aeronautical Systems Division at Wright-Pat (1976-81).

He logged over 6500 hours of flying time in 50 different types of aircraft.

Major General Rushworth is now retired. He was married to the former Joyce Butler, who died in April 1980. Rushworth has a daughter, Cheri.

Thompson, Milton

NASA test pilot Milton Thompson was one of the six pilots chosen in 1962 to fly the Air Force X-20 Dyna-Soar spaceplane, which was never built. He later made 14 flights in the X-15 rocket plane.

He became the first person to fly a "lifting body" aircraft, a wingless vehicle which gets lift from its shape, on August 16, 1963, when he flew the plywood, powerless M2-Fl. Lifting body aircraft served as precursors to the Space Shuttle and all future aerospace planes.

Milton O. Thompson was born May 4, 1926, in Crookston, Minnesota. He joined the US Navy during World War II and served as a combat pilot in China and Japan. Returning to the States after the war, he enrolled at the University of Washington, where in 1953 he received a BS in engineering.

He joined NASA as a test pilot in 1956 and, among other assignments, flew as F-104 chase pilot for X-15 flights (he was forced to eject during one of these flights) and tested a rudimentary "space kite," the Parasev, an abortive design to return early manned spacecraft on land rather than water by using a steerable, delta-shaped parachute. He was involved in tests of remotely piloted research vehicles.

Thompson became director of research projects at Dryden Flight Center in the fall of 1966 and is currently chief engineer for that facility.

The father of five children, he lives in Lancaster, California.

Walker, Joseph

Joe Walker, aside from Chuck Yeager the best-known pilot of the rocket plane era at Edwards Air Force Base, made 25 flights in the X-15 between March 1960 and August 1963. He established a world speed record of 4104 miles per hour in the X-15, and on three different occasions piloted the rocket plane to an altitude greater than 50 miles, including his final X-15 flight on August 22, 1963, which reached 354,300 feet, an altitude of almost 67 miles. In fact, two of Walker's X-15 flights exceeded 62 miles altitude and qualified as space flights according to the International Aeronautical Federation (FAI).

Walker was killed in a mid-air collision between his F-104 Starfighter and the XB-70 on June 8, 1966.

Joseph Albert Walker was born February 20, 1921, in Washington, Pennsylvania, and grew up on a farm there. He attended Washington and Jefferson College, graduating in 1942 with a BS in physics.

He enrolled in the civilian pilot training program in 1941 and, after graduation from college, entered the Army Air Corps. He flew P-38s in combat over North Africa and Italy during World War II. Returning to the US in 1945, he left the Army and went to work for the National Advisory Committee on Aeronautics (NACA) as a physicist at its Lewis Laboratory in Cleveland. NACA, the forerunner of NASA, soon transferred Walker to research flying, and in 1951 he moved to the NASA test facility at Edwards Air Force Base, California.

For the next fifteen years Walker flew the hottest airplanes and rocket planes in the world, serving as project pilot on the D-558, X-1, X-3 (which he considered the "worst" plane he ever flew), X-4 and X-5. He also served as research pilot on the B-47, F-100, F-101, F-102 and F-104. In addition to becoming the prime NASA pilot for the X-15, Walker also helped develop the lunar landing training vehicle, the so-called "flying bedstead," which his X-15 backup, Neil Armstrong, would later use to rehearse his landing on the Moon.

Like Yeager, who was famous for his "Aw, shucks" approach to test flying, Walker affected a casual, fatalistic attitude, claiming that for pilots in trouble, the only option was to "put yourself in the hands of a supernatural power." He was honored by his fellow test pilots with the Robert J. Collier Trophy, the Harmon International Trophy for Aviators, the Iven Kincheloe Award and the Octave Chanute Award, all in 1961. He was a charter member of the Society of Experimental Test Pilots.

Walker was survived by his wife, Grace, and four children, Thomas, James, Joseph, and Elizabeth.

White, Alvin

Al White is the veteran corporate test pilot who was Scott Crossfield's backup for the X-15 rocket plane project. An employee of North American Aviation, White went through all the difficult training and physical conditioning that Crossfield did, but never flew the X-15. He did fly chase planes for many X-15 flights, however.

Alvin Swauger White was born December 9, 1918, in Berkeley, California, where he grew up. As a student at the University of California in 1940 he enrolled in the civilian pilot training program, which was designed to provide the military with a pool of pilots in the case of war. When World War II began, White joined the Army Air Corps, first as an instructor. He flew combat missions beginning in 1944.

Returning to the US in 1946, White left the Army and returned to Cal, where he received a BS in mechanical engineering in 1947. He tried the general contracting business for a while, but disliked it and rejoined the Air Force. He attended the Test Pilot School in 1951 and was a military test pilot until 1954.

In that year he went to work for North American Aviation in Los Angeles and was involved in the X-15 and in XB-70 Valkyrie supersonic bomber programs. On June 8, 1966, White was the pilot of an XB-70A when a chase plane piloted by former X-15 pilot Joe Walker collided with it. Walker was killed instantly. The huge XB-70, its vertical fins gone and its wings damaged, began to tumble out of the sky. White managed to eject; his co-pilot was killed.

White left North American shortly thereafter to become manager of flight operations research and development for TWA. In 1969 he formed Al White & Associates, an Irvine, California, aviation consulting firm.

Divorced from his third wife, White, the father of three, lives in Auburn, California.

White, Robert

Bob White was the first person to pilot an X-15 to an altitude greater than 50 miles, thus winning US Air Force astronaut wings. On July 17, 1962, White flew X-15 number three to 314,750 feet, more than 59 miles high, in the first unofficial "space flight" of the X-15 program.

Several years later the Federation Aeronautique International (FAI), the world aviation record-keeping body, would define a space flight as any flight which exceeded an altitude of 100 kilometers, or 62 miles. White's flight, therefore, did not qualify (though two other X-15 flights did); nevertheless, he was the first to pilot a winged rocket plane in near-space. The previous November he had also become the first pilot to fly six times the speed of sound. These accomplishments earned him a profile in *Life* magazine, which at that time was heavily involved in the promotion of the NASA Mercury astronauts. Tom Wolfe in *The Right Stuff* (1979) describes White as the epitome of the "blue suit" Air Force test pilot, unconcerned with and perhaps even uncooperative when it came to public relations, interested only in being the best pilot.

Robert Michael White was born July 6, 1924, in New York City, where he grew up. He joined the US Army Air Corps in November 1942 at the age of 18, and became a pilot in February 1944.

During World War II he flew P-51s with the 355th Fighter Group in Europe. In February 1945, on his fifty-second combat mission, he was shot down over Germany, captured, and imprisoned until released that April. He returned to the US later that year and enrolled at New York University. He received a BS in electrical engineering from that institution in 1951.

He was recalled to active duty in May 1951 and served at Mitchel AFB, New York, with the 40th Fighter Squadron based near Tokyo, Japan, and as an engineer at the Rome Air Development Center in New York before going to Edwards AFB in California to enter the test pilot school in June 1954. He stayed at Edwards for nine years.

Between October 1963 and May 1967 White served as an operations officer and squadron commander in Germany and attended George Washington University, where he earned an MS in business administration (1966). He also worked on the F-111 program at Wright-Patterson AFB, Ohio.

In 1967 and 1968 he did a tour of duty in Vietnam, flying 70 combat missions in the F-105. He returned to Wright-Patterson in June 1968, and two years later was named commander of the Flight Test Center at Edwards. While at Edwards he completed the Naval Test Parachutist course.

White left Edwards in November 1972 to become commandant of the ROTC at Maxwell AFB, Alabama, then chief of staff of the 4th Allied Tactical Air Force in Europe (1975). He retired on February 1, 1981.

Major General White and his wife, Doris, have four children, Gregory, Pamela, Maureen and Dennis.

USAF X-20 Dyna-Soar Pilots

In November 1959, following three years of feasibility studies, the US Air Force selected Boeing Aircraft as the prime contractor for a manned glider which would be launched into orbit by a Titan rocket, returning to earth at Edwards AFB, California. Known originally as Dyna-Soar (a contraction of "dynamic soaring"), the spaceplane was formally known as the X-20.

Six pilots were chosen on September 19, 1962, to train for orbital flights which would begin in 1966: Air Force Major James Wood, Air Force Captains Albert Crews, Henry Gordon, Pete Knight and Russell Rogers, and civilian Milton Thompson of NASA.

The pilots trained at Edwards AFB, California, and at Wright-Patterson AFB, Ohio, until December 1963, when the X-20 was canceled in favor of a new Air Force space program, the Manned Orbiting Laboratory.

A winged spacecraft would not fly in space until the launch of the Shuttle Columbia in April 1981.

USAF X-20 Dyna-Soar Pilot Biographies

Crews, Albert

See entry under **Manned Orbiting Laboratory**.

Gordon, Henry

Henry Gordon was chosen in September 1962 to train for the first manned space flights in the US Air Force X-20 Dyna-Soar program. Dyna-Soar was canceled in December 1963, three years before scheduled flights were to begin.

Henry Charles Gordon was born December 23, 1925, in Valparaiso, Indiana, but grew up in Gary, where he graduated from Emerson High School in 1943. He immediately joined the Army Air Corps and served until the end of World War II. He then returned to Indiana to attend Purdue University, where he received a BS in aeronautical engineering in 1950.

Recalled to active duty in 1951, Gordon flew 100 combat missions in Korea. He returned to the US in 1952 and served as a pilot at several air force bases until entering the USAF Test Pilot School at Edwards AFB in 1957. He remained at Edwards as a test pilot until being chosen for the X-20 program. When it was canceled he served as a pilot, including a tour at Hill AFB, Utah, until his retirement in 1975.

Gordon and his wife, Leonor, have four children, Lee, Barbara, Nina and William.

Knight, William

See entry under **X-15 Pilots**.

Rogers, Russell

Russell Rogers was one of the six pilots who trained for the US Air Force X-20 Dyna-Soar program from September 1962 to December 1963. After returning to operational flying for the Air Force, Major Rogers died in the explosion of his F-105 fighter near Kadena Air Force Base, Okinawa, on September 13, 1967.

Russell Lee Rogers was born April 12, 1928, in Lawrence, Kansas. He joined the Air Force, became a fighter pilot and flew combat missions in Korea, then went back to college, receiving a BS in aeronautical engineering from the University of Colorado in 1958.

He attended the USAF Test Pilot School at Edwards AFB, California, in 1958, and remained at Edwards as a test pilot until being assigned to the X-20.

He was survived by his wife and four children.

Thompson, Milton

See entry under **X-15 Pilots**.

Wood, James

James Wood was one of the six pilots who trained for possible space flights aboard the X-20 Dyna-Soar from 1962 to 1963. When that program was canceled, he went on to become the first military pilot to fly the F-111 swing-wing fighter bomber and ultimately served as commander of test operations at Edwards Air Force Base.

James Wayne Wood was born August 9, 1924, in Paragould, Arkansas, but grew up in Pueblo, Colorado. He joined the Army Air Corps in 1943, becoming an aviation cadet, and became a B-17 bomber pilot. He flew ten missions over France and Germany during World War II. After the war he became a fighter pilot and flew 100 combat missions in Korea in the F-80 Shooting Star. Returning to the US from Korea he served as a gunnery instructor, then attended the Air Force Institute of Technology at Wright-Patterson AFB, Ohio, where he received a BS in aero-mechanical engineering in 1954.

He arrived at Edwards in August 1956 to attend the Test Pilot School, and after completion of that course remained at the center for the next nine years as a test pilot, working on the X-20, the F-111, F-102, F-104 and F-5 programs. In 1967 he attended the Air War College at Maxwell AFB Alabama and headed a test unit developing a guided bomb at Eglin AFB, Florida.

Wood flew 34 combat missions in Vietnam, his third war, from 1968 to 1969 as an F-4 Phantom pilot based in Thailand and Saigon. He returned to the US for a two-year tour planning test programs for the new F-15 Eagle fighter at Wright-Patterson, then was assigned again to Edwards, where he became commander for test operations, supervising over 1200 military and civilian pilots, engineers, researchers and support personnel.

As a pilot Wood logged over 6000 hours of flying time in 35 different types of aircraft.

Colonel Wood has retired from the Air Force. He is currently employed by Flight Systems, Inc., of Newport Beach, California.

He and his wife, Virginia, have a son, James II.

The USAF Manned Orbiting Laboratory

The Air Force's second venture into manned spaceflight was the Manned Orbiting Laboratory, better known as MOL. Developed beginning in 1963, and announced in August 1965, MOL was a proposed series of five or more two-man flights in polar orbit, scheduled to begin in late 1968. Air Force astronauts would use surplus Gemini spacecraft (called Gemini-B or Blue Gemini) attached to a new, cylindrical laboratory, with the whole complex launched aboard a Titan III rocket from Vandenberg Air Force Base in California. The missions, which were to last up to 30 days, were to involve military reconaissance.

The Air Force announced that it would select and train 20 astronauts, designated "aerospace research pilots," and chose the first eight men on November 12, 1965. A second group of five followed on June 30, 1966, and a third and final group of four was announced on June 30, 1967. (A fourth group was to have been selected in 1969.) Qualifications for MOL required that each man had to

- Be a qualified military pilot
- Be a graduate of the Aerospace Research Pilot School
- Be a serving military officer recommended by a commanding officer
- Be a US citizen by birth.

It is interesting to note that one of the third group of MOL pilots, Major Robert Lawrence, was the only black American chosen for any kind of astronaut training until 1978.

Budgetary problems (made worse by the costs of the Vietnam War) eventually cut the number of planned flights to four and postponed the first manned mission until 1972. (One unmanned test of a MOL/Gemini-B took place in November 1966.) When it became apparent to the Air Force that MOL would essentially be duplicating the effort of the NASA Skylab program, and that unmanned reconaissance satellites had developed to the point where manned presence in space was unnecessary, MOL was canceled in June 1969.

Seven MOL pilots became space travelers, however. Air Force Majors Karol Bobko, Charles Fullerton, Henry Hartsfield and Donald Peterson, Marine Major Robert Overmyer, and Navy Lieutenant Commanders Robert Crippen and Richard Truly, were accepted by NASA as astronauts on August 13, 1969. An eighth MOL pilot, Lieutenant Colonel Al Crews, also joined NASA, though not as an astronaut.

USAF Manned Orbiting Laboratory Pilot Biographies

Abrahamson, James

James Abrahamson trained for two years as a potential military astronaut in the USAF Manned Orbiting Laboratory only to see that program canceled in June 1969 before any flights could be made.

Nevertheless, Abrahamson became one of the most important figures in both civilian and military space programs when he served as NASA Associate Administrator for Space Transportation Systems—in effect, the man in charge of the Space Shuttle—during its difficult orbital flight tests and first operational flights from 1981 to 1984.

General Abrahamson is currently head of the Strategic Defense Initiative Organization (SDIO), also known as "Star Wars."

James Alan Abrahamson was born May 19, 1933, in Williston, North Dakota, but grew up in Inglewood, California. He attended the Masschusetts Institute of Technology, receiving a BS in aeronautical engineering in 1955, and the University of Oklahoma, where he earned an MS in aerospace engineering (1961).

Entering active service with the Air Force in 1955, Abrahamson underwent pilot training, then served as an instructor at Bryan AFB, Texas, until 1959. After completing graduate work at Oklahoma, he spent three years at the Air Force Space Division in Los Angeles as a systems project officer on the Vela nuclear detection satellite. He did a tour as a combat pilot in Vietnam, then attended the Air Force Aerospace Research Pilot School at Edwards AFB, graduating in 1967.

Major Abrahamson was one of the four pilots assigned to MOL in June 1967. When that program was canceled, Abrahamson, who was five months too old to transfer to NASA as an astronaut, was assigned to staff of the National Aeronautics and Space Council. When the Council was dissolved in 1971, he became director of the Maverick missile program, commander of the 495th Test Wing at Wright-Patterson AFB, Ohio, and, from 1974 to 1976, inspector general for the Air Force Systems Command. He later supervised the development of the F-16 fighter.

Abrahamson has two children. His wife, Barbara, was killed in a plane crash in California in December 1985.

Adams, Michael

See entry under **X-15 Pilots**.

Bobko, Karol

See entry under **NASA Astronauts**.

Crews, Albert

Air Force pilot Al Crews had the bad luck to be selected for two military manned space programs that were canceled before he could fly in space. He was one of the six pilots chosen for the X-20 Dyna-Soar spaceplane project in September 1962. When the Manned Orbiting Laboratory project began in 1963, X-20 was canceled. Crews was one of the first eight pilots assigned to MOL in November 1965, but that project, too, was cancelled, in June 1969.

All of the fourteen pilots still assigned to MOL requested transfers the NASA astronaut group, but only seven, those who were still 36 years old or younger, were accepted. Crews, who was 40, did transfer to the NASA Johnson Space Center, where he joined the flight crew operations directorate as a pilot. He is currently technical assistant for operations there.

Albert Hanlin Crews, Jr., was born March 23, 1929, in El Dorado, Arkansas. He received a BS in chemical engineering from the University of South West Louisiana in 1950, and later earned an MS in aeronautical engineering from the Air Force Institute of Technology (1959).

Crews joined the US Air Force in 1950 and became a jet pilot two years later. For the next five years he served with the Air Defense Command, including one posting to Wheelus AFB, Tripoli, Libya. Following further academic work at the Air Force Institute of Technology Crews was assigned to the Test Pilot School at Edwards AFB, graduating in 1960. He remained at Edwards as a test pilot and was also a member of the second group of pilots to attend the new Aerospace Research Pilot School (1962). Between his assignments to X-20 and MOL he taught lifting body landing and zoom maneuvering at the Test Pilot School, and also served as a crewman for a series of simulated lunar landing missions conducted at Martin Marietta in Baltimore, Maryland.

Crews retired from active Air Force duty as a colonel. He and his wife Grace have three daughters, Gail, Marina and Kellee.

Crippen, Robert

See entry under **NASA Astronauts**.

Finley, John

Lieutenant John L. Finley, USN, was one of the first eight pilots selected for the USAF Manned Orbiting Laboratory Program in November 1965. He remained with MOL until April 1968, when he was reassigned to the Navy at his own request.

John Lawrence Finley was born December 22, 1935, in Winchester, Massachusetts. He attended the US Naval Academy at Annapolis, graduating with a bachelor of science degree in 1957.

After completing pilot training Finley served for four years aboard the USS Ticonderoga flying F-8 aircraft. In 1964 he entered the Air Force Aerospace Research Pilot School at Edwards AFB, California, and was an instructor there when selected for the MOL program.

After returning to the Navy Finley served in the Department's Bureau of Personnel, as commander of attack carrier Air Wing 5 in San Francisco, as commander of the Naval Schools Command, and aboard the USS Kawishiwi. He retired from the Navy as a captain in May 1980, and is now employed by the Federal Express Corporation.

Finley and his wife, Florence, have two daughters, Vickie and Cindy.

Fullerton, Charles See entry under **NASA Astronauts**.

Hartsfield, Henry See entry under **NASA Astronauts**.

Herres, Robert

Lieutenant Colonel Robert Herres, USAF, was one of the four pilots chosen for the Manned Orbiting Laboratory in June 1967. He trained for orbital flights for two years until MOL was canceled in June 1969.

Like fellow MOL pilot James Abrahamson, Herres later became a high-ranking official in military space programs. Until December 1986 General Herres was commander of NORAD and the new US Space Command, based at Peterson AFB, Colorado.

He is currently vice chief of staff for the US Air Force at the Pentagon.

Robert Tralles Herres was born December 1, 1932, in Denver, Colorado. He attended the US Naval Academy, graduating in 1953 with a bachelor of science degree. He later earned an MS in electrical engineering from the USAF Institute of Technology and an MS in public administration from George Washington University.

After graduation from Annapolis, Herres elected to serve in the Air Force. He underwent flight training and became an interceptor pilot and electronics officer. He attended the Air Force Test Pilot School at Edwards AFB, California, in 1966.

Since the cancellation of MOL, Herres has commanded Air Force wings in Michigan and Thailand and served as director of Command, Control and Communications Systems for the Joint Chiefs of Staff.

He is married with three children.

Lawrence, Robert

Major Robert H. Lawrence, Jr., became the first black American chosen for spaceflight training when he was one of four pilots assigned to the Manned Orbiting Laboratory Program in June 1967.

Lawrence was killed in the crash of an F-104 jet at Edwards AFB, California, on December 8, 1967. Had he lived he would have been eligible for transfer to NASA as an astronaut in August 1969, and might have gone into space aboard the Shuttle.

Robert Henry Lawrence, Jr., was born October 2, 1935, in Chicago, Illinois. He graduated from Englewood High School there, then went on to Bradley University, where he received a BS degree in chemistry in 1956. In 1965 he received a PhD in nuclear chemistry from Ohio State University.

An ROTC student, Lawrence joined the Air Force in 1956. Following pilot training in Missouri he was stationed in West Germany as a fighter pilot and instructor, returning to the US in 1961. He entered the Air Force Institute of Technology at Wright-Patterson AFB, Ohio, which led to his PhD, and became a nuclear research officer at Kirtland AFB, New Mexico. When selected for the MOL program he had just graduated from the Air Force Aerospace Research Pilot School.

All MOL pilots, even those who had attended the Aerospace Research Pilot School, were enrolled in a six-month course at Edwards that included "booming and zooming," flying zero-G arcs or simulating very high-speed spacecraft landings in a modified F-104. It was while "zooming" that Lawrence crashed, ejecting too low for his parachute to open. Another pilot with him, Major Harvey Royer, ejected and survived.

Lawrence was survived by his wife, Barbara, and a son, Tracy.

Lawyer, Richard

Captain Richard Lawyer, USAF, was one of the eight pilots chosen for the Manned Orbiting Laboratory Program in November 1965. He remained with MOL until its cancellation in June 1969.

Richard Earl Lawyer was born November 8, 1932, in Los Angeles, growing up in Inglewood. He attended the University of California at Berkeley, receiving a BS in aeronautical engineering in 1955.

An ROTC student at Cal, Lawyer entered the Air Force in 1955 and underwent pilot training. From 1956 to 1963 he served with the Tactical Air Command, including 30 months stationed on Okinawa, and also served a brief tour in Vietnam as an airborne forward air controller in an L-19 aircraft. He attended the Air Force Test Pilot School at Edwards AFB in 1963, and the Aerospace Research Pilot School in 1964. He was an instructor at ARPS when selected for MOL.

After the cancellation of MOL Lawyer returned to active duty in the Air Force, eventually becoming deputy commander of operations at the Tactical Air War Center, Eglin AFB, Florida. He retired as a colonel in 1983.

Lawyer and his wife, Betty, have three children, Timothy, James and Lisa.

Macleay, Lachlan

Captain "Mac" Macleay was one of the first eight pilots chosen for the USAF Manned Orbiting Laboratory Program in November 1965. He remained with MOL until its cancellation in June 1969, when he transferred to other Air Force duties.

Lachlan Macleay was born June 13, 1931, in St. Louis, Missouri, but grew up in Kirkwood. He graduated from high school in Redlands, California, in 1949. He then attended the US Navy Academy at Annapolis, graduating with a BS degree in 1954, when he elected to serve in the Air Force.

After pilot training Macleay served as a flight instructor at Moody AFB in Valdosta, Georgia. In August 1960 he entered the Air Force Test Pilot School at Edwards AFB, and remained at Edwards for a year as a U-2 test pilot. In 1961 and 1962 he served as an adviser to the Republic of Korea air force, then returned to Edwards to attend the new Aerospace Research Pilot School.

Macleay retired from the USAF with the rank of colonel on June 1, 1978.

He and his wife, Beverly, have three children, Lachlan Jr., Douglas and Carol Anne.

Neubeck, Gregory

Captain Greg Neubeck was one of the first eight pilots chosen for the USAF Manned Orbiting Laboratory Program in November 1965. He

trained for 30-day earth orbital flights in MOL until the program was canceled in June 1969.

Francis Gregory Neubeck was born April 11, 1932, in Washington, D.C. He attended the US Naval Academy at Annapolis, graduating with a bachelor of science degree in 1955.

He elected to serve in the Air Force and became a pilot, serving as a flight instructor and later working on the development of weapons systems for jet fighters at Eglin AFB, Florida. He attended the USAF Test Pilot School at Edwards AFB, California, in 1960 and the Aerospace Research Pilot School in 1962. His classmates at ARPS included future NASA astronauts Michael Collins and Joe Engle.

After the cancellation of MOL Neubeck returned to USAF duty and was vice commander of the Tactical Air War Center at Eglin just prior to his retirement as a colonel in 1982. He is currently an engineering consultant in Florida.

He and his wife, Margaret, have a son, Gregory.

Overmyer, Robert

See entry under **NASA Astronauts**.

Peterson, Donald

See entry under **NASA Astronauts**.

Taylor, James

Captain James Taylor, USAF, was one of the first eight pilots chosen for the Manned Orbiting Laboratory Program in November 1965. He remained with MOL, training for proposed 30-day earth orbital spaceflights, until the program was canceled in June 1969.

Taylor became an instructor at the USAF Aerospace Research Pilot School at Edwards AFB, and was killed in the crash of a T-38 jet there on September 4, 1970.

James Martin Taylor was born November 27, 1930, in Stamps, Arkansas. He received an associate of arts degree from Southern State University in 1950 and joined the Air Force as an enlisted man the next year. He became an aviation cadet in 1952 and earned his pilot's wings in 1953, then served with the Air Defense Command. He returned to school, earning a BS in electrical engineering from the University of Michigan in 1959.

After serving as a flight test engineer for bombers and cargo aircraft, Taylor entered the Air Force Test Pilot School at Edwards AFB in 1963. The next year he attended the Aerospace Research Pilot School. He was project pilot for the F-106 when selected for MOL.

He was survived by his wife, Jacquelyn, and three children, Lisa Ann, Gregory and Mark.

Truly, Richard

See entry under **NASA Astronauts**.

Pioneers of the American Space Program

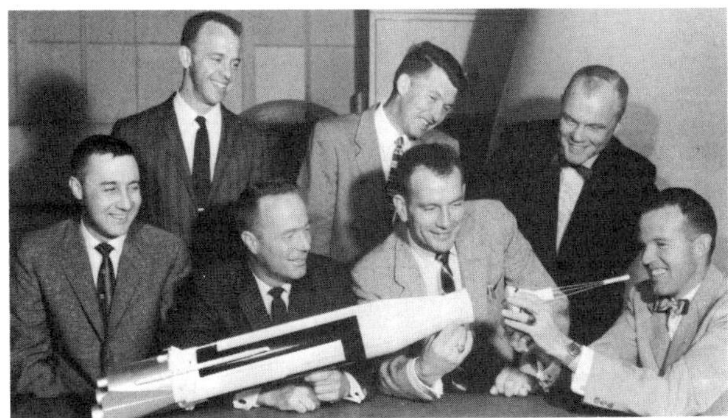

The "Mercury 7," the first NASA astronauts, selected in April 1959. Back row (left to right), Shepard, Schirra, Glenn; front row, Grissom, Carpenter, Slayton, Cooper.

Young (left) and Collins, the crew of Gemini 10, with a model of the Titan II booster. Gemini 10 was the first craft to dock in space with two separate targets.

White (left), Grissom, and Chaffee, the crew of Apollo 1. All were killed in flight simulation exercises at the launch pad on January 27, 1967.

Aldrin (left) and Lovell, the crew of Gemini 12, in a mock-up of the Gemini spacecraft.

Lovell (left), Anders, and Borman, the crew of Apollo 8, the first astronauts to orbit the moon.

Armstrong (left), Collins, and Aldrin, the crew of Apollo 11. Armstrong and Aldrin were the first to walk on the moon.

Roosa (left), Shepard, and Mitchell, the crew of Apollo 14, the first manned lunar landing following the Apollo 13 abort. Shepard was the only Mercury astronaut to reach the moon.

Schmitt (left, standing), Evans (right, standing), and Cernan, the crew of Apollo 17, the last manned lunar landing mission, pictured in a mock-up of the lunar roving vehicle.

Kerwin (left), Conrad, and Weitz, the crew of Skylab 2, the first American space station mission.

Conrad (left), Gordon, and Bean, the crew of Apollo 12, the second manned lunar landing, in front of a mock-up of the Apollo lunar module.

Ride (left), Fabian, Crippen, Thagard, and Hauck, the crew of the seventh Shuttle mission. Ride became the first American woman in space.

Brandenstein (left), Gardner, Truly, Thornton, and Bluford, the crew of the eighth Shuttle mission. Bluford was the first black American space traveler.

Stewart (left), Brand, McNair, Gibson, and McCandless, the crew of Shuttle Mission 41-B. Stewart and McCandless, in EVA suits, became the first astronauts to use maneuvering backpacks in space.

Crippen (left), Hart, van Hoften, Nelson, and Scobee, the crew of Shuttle Mission 41-C, which performed the first rescue and repair of an orbiting satellite.

Gardner (left), Walker, Fisher, Allen, and Hauck (sitting), the crew of Shuttle Mission 51-A, which retrieved two ailing satellites and returned them to earth.

Lucid, Nagel, Fabian, Al-Saud, Baudry (standing, left to right), and Brandenstein (left, kneeling) and Creighton, the crew of Shuttle Mission 51-G, the first tri-national crew.

Onizuka, McAuliffe, Jarvis, and Resnik (standing, left to right) and Smith, Scobee, and McNair (sitting, left to right), the crew of Shuttle Mission 51-L. All were killed during the explosion of the Shuttle Challenger seconds after launch on January 28, 1986.

The first group of Air Force manned spaceflight engineers, selected February 1980. Front row (left to right), Vidrine, Payton, Lydon, Joseph, Sundberg, Hamel. Back row (left to right), Sefchek, Rij, Wright, Detroye, Watterson, Higbee, Casserino.

Pioneers of the Soviet Space Program

May 1961 group portrait of 16 of the first 20 Soviet cosmonauts, with training officials. Front row (left to right), Popovich, Gorbatko, Khrunov, Gagarin, chief designer Korolev, Korolev's daughter Nina and Popovich's daughter Natasha, training chief Karpov, parachute instructor Nikitin, and medical chief Fyodorov; second row, Leonov, Nikolayev, Rafikov, Zaikin, Volynov, Titov, Nelyubov, Bykovsky, and Shonin; third row, Filatyev, Anikeyev, Belyayev; missing: Varlamov and Kartashov, who had left the group by May 1961; Bondarenko, deceased; and Komarov.

Feokistov (left), Komarov, and Yegorov, the world's first space crew, following the safe landing of their craft, the first Voskhod.

Alexei Leonov, pilot of Voskohd 2 and the world's first space walker, in his EVA spacesuit.

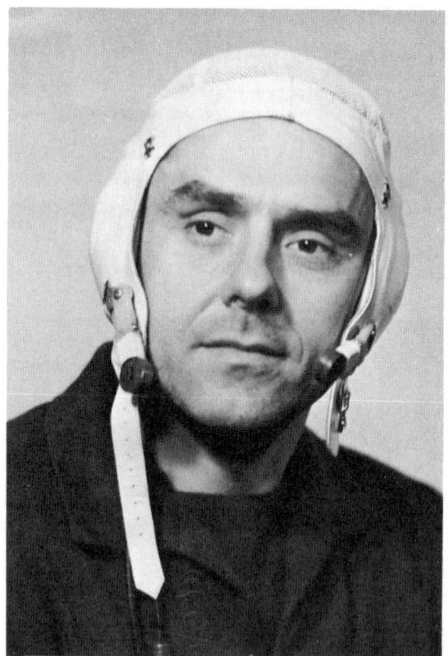

Vladimir Komarov, commander of Soyuz 1, the first Soviet cosmonaut to make two space flights; he was killed when Soyuz 1 crashed on returning to earth.

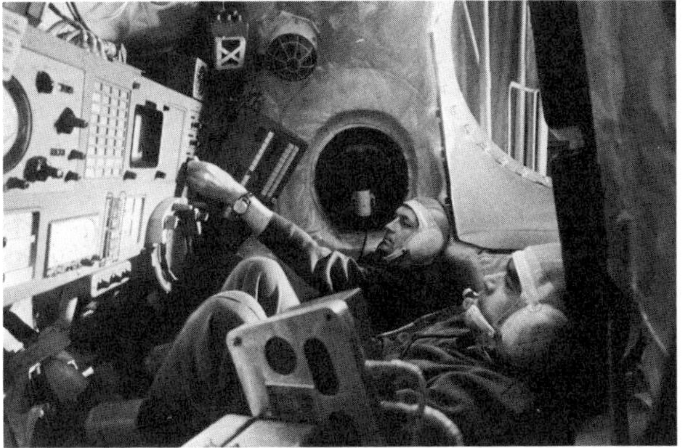

Sevastyanov (left) and Nikolayev, the crew of Soyuz 9, which set the 18-day space endurance record for the first decade of manned space flight.

Soviet cosmonaut Gubarev (left) and Czech pilot Remek, of Soyuz 28, the first international space crew.

Ivanchenkov (bottom) and Kovalenok, the crew of Soyuz 29. They were the fourth of 16 different Soviet crews to inhabit the Salyut 6 space station.

Demin (left) and Sarafanov, the crew of Soyuz 15. Demin was the first grandfather in space.

Vietnamese pilot Pham Tuan (left) and Soviet commander Gorbatko, the crew of Soyuz 37. Tuan became the first Asian in space.

Soviet commander Romanenko (left) and Cuban pilot Tamayo-Mendez, the crew of Soyuz 38. Tamayo-Mendez was the first black space traveler.

Berezovoy (left) and Lebedev, the crew of Soyuz T-5, pictured in the Soyuz T simulator. They spent seven months in space aboard Salyut 7, setting the endurance record for the second decade of manned space flight.

Soviet flight engineer Ivanchenkov (left), French pilot Chretien, and Soviet commander Dzhanibekov, the crew of Soyuz T-6. Chretien was the first Westerner to go into space aboard a Soviet spacecraft.

Savitskaya (left), Popov, and Serebrov, the crew of Soyuz T-7. Savitskaya was the second woman space traveler, 19 years after Tereshkova.

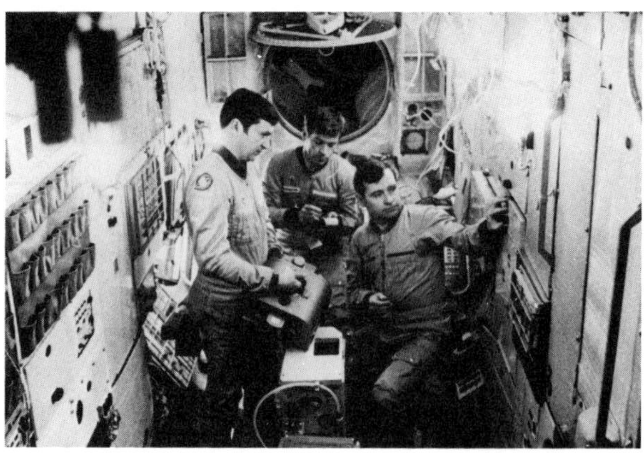

Titov (left), Serebrov, and Strekalov, the crew of Soyuz T-8, pictured in the Salyut mock-up at the cosmonaut training center. Their planned eight-month visit to the Salyut 7/Kosmos 1443 complex was aborted after two days because of failed rendezvous radar.

Atkov (left), Solovyov, and Kizim, the crew of Soyuz T-10, world space endurance record holders in the first 25 years for their 10-month stay aboard Salyut 7 in 1984.

Grechko (left), Volkov, and Vasyutin, the crew of Soyuz T-14, the first space "relief" crew.

PART 2 *Soviet Space Travelers*

The Soviet Cosmonaut Team

Rex Hall

The idea of sending men into space was more acceptable in the Soviet Union than it was for many years in the United States. The pioneering theorist, Konstantin Tsiolkovsky, had been honored by the young Soviet government, and early rocket experimenters, including a test pilot named Sergei Korolev, were given financial support. Nevertheless, the USSR did not start its manned space program until November 1958, when a unit of the design bureau headed by Korolev was authorized to construct a satellite capable of supporting a man in space. A few months later, in early 1959, just weeks before America's Mercury astronauts were introduced to the world, Mstislav V. Keldysh of the USSR Academy of Sciences chaired the first meeting to discuss the selection of space travelers.

Like the Americans, the Soviets also wondered where their space travelers—cosmonauts—would be found. Would they be engineers? Submarine crewmen, used to isolation and cramped quarters? Mountain-climbers? Or pilots? The faction supporting the choice of pilots won out. Korolev, the chief designer of the intercontinental ballistic missile which was used to launch Sputnik and all later Soviet manned spacecraft, said: "The fighter pilot is the all-arounder we require. He flies in the stratosphere in a single-seat, high-speed aircraft. He is a pilot, navigator and radio operator . . ." (*Our Gagarin*, 1981).

Beginning in August 1959, teams of military doctors began to visit air bases from the Urals to the Far East, interviewing young pilots for a program involving "aircraft of a completely new type." One pilot, 24-year-old Georgy Shonin, recalled:

> I immediately cooled off. A lot of pilots were then being transferred to helicopter units, and these did not at that time enjoy any great popularity among us. "I'm a fighter pilot, I specially chose a flying school where I would be taught to fly jet fighters, and you—" "No, no! You don't understand," the older of the two reassured me, having guessed what I was worried about. "What we're talking about are long-distance flights, flights on rockets, flights around the earth." (*Our Gagarin*)

Shonin reported that his "mouth dropped open in surprise." He volunteered for the new program, as did 3000 other pilots. That number was quickly cut to 102 who not only passed the initial physical examinations, but demonstrated "a fundamental desire" to fly in space. These candidates underwent rigorous medical and psychological screening at the Central Aviation Research Hospital in Moscow. By February 25, 1960, twenty young pilots had been selected. They were presented to Marshal Konstantin Vershinin, commander in chief of the Soviet air force, on March 7, and one week later began training at a military barracks at Khodynskoye Airport in downtown Moscow. The overall head of the cosmonaut program was Lieutenant General Nikolai Kamanin, a hero of the Great Patriotic War. Training was directed by Lieutenant Colonel Yevgeny Karpov, a specialist in aerospace medicine.

The Gagarin Group

The selection criteria for the first cosmonaut group required that candidates

- Be under thirty years of age
- Be less than 170 cm (5′7″) tall
- Weigh less than 70 kg (154 lbs)

(There were exceptions among the finalists: Major Pavel Belyayev was 35 and Captain Vladimir Komarov was 33. Shonin was taller than 5′7″.) In addition, all finalists were military officers who had graduated from Higher Air Force Schools (the educational equivalent of American junior colleges). Several had attended or graduated from air force acadamies as well. Fifteen were Party members and five belonged to the Komsomol, the Party youth organization.

Contrary to widespread belief, none of the first cosmonauts was a test pilot, though Komarov had performed engineering test work on new aircraft equipment. The most experienced pilot had logged only 900 hours of flying time, while another had logged as little as 250. Only one pilot, Captain Pavel Popovich, who had also earned the Order of the Red Star, had flown the high-performance MiG-19. The others had been limited to the slower MiG-15 and MiG-17.

During the early weeks of training the cosmonauts spent three days in classroom study concentrating on aviation medicine and three days in physical training. They found this demoralizing, so Korolev, Kamanin and Karpov added lectures on astronomy, aerospace medicine and physics by a number of experts, including future cosmonauts Vitaly Sevastyanov and Oleg Makarov, the famous rocket designer Mikhail Tikhonravov, and pilots Ivan Dzyuba and Mark Gallai. As time went on the academic load increased with the addition of radio and electrical engineering, spacecraft telemetry, and guidance systems as subjects.

By July the cosmonaut team had moved from the airport to a new site near the village of Shchelkovo, 24 miles northeast of Moscow. A training center for cosmonauts, including residences for their families and others involved in the manned program, was under construction. It would be called *Zvezdni gorodok*, literally "stellar village," more commonly called Star Town. By 1986 Star Town had a population of several thousand.

In contrast to the American astronauts (whose exploits were closely followed by their secret competitors in the Soviet Union), the cosmonauts' physical conditioning was extensive, planned and monitored. Medical control of the cosmonauts by space program doctors continues to this day.

The cosmonauts also had to undergo an intensive course of parachute training designed to make them experts in a matter of weeks. Senior Lieutenant Valery Bykovsky, veteran of dozens of parachute jumps and already rated an instructor, was exempt (and was given the job of testing the so-called chamber of silence). The other 19, most of them having made just five mandatory jumps early in their air force careers, had to make over 40 jumps in the next six weeks, each one of increasing complexity in a program directed by world record holder Lieutenant Colonel Nikolai Nikitin. Parachute training was essential for the first cosmonauts, since that was how one returned to Earth from a Vostok spacecraft, but space doctors discovered that parachuting gave cosmonauts experience with weightlessness and also with stress, and such training continues today.

By the end of May six of the young pilots were selected for accelerated training in the new Vostok simulator, under the direction of Colonel Gallai. They were Senior Lieutenants Yuri Gagarin, Anatoly Kartashov, Andrian Nikolayev, Gherman Titov and Valentin Varlamov and Captain Popovich.

Kartashov had a bad reaction to centrifuge testing, which began in early July, and was dropped from the program. His replacement among the six was Senior Lieutenant Grigori Nelyubov. On July 24, 1960, Varlamov cracked a vertebra in his neck while diving into a lake near Star Town. He was hospitalized for a month and discharged, but was not allowed to return to space training.

In early May the group had suffered its first casualty when Captain Komarov was hospitalized for a hernia operation. Unlike Varlamov and Kartashov, however, Komarov was able to return to the cosmonaut group.

The most serious blow of all occurred on March 23, 1961, when Senior Lieutenant Valentin Vasilyevich Bondarenko, 24, burned to death in a fire that raced through a pressure chamber in which he was conducting tests. Bondarenko was the first space traveler, Soviet or American, to die in an accident. The tragedy occurred just three weeks before Gagarin became the first person in space, and just one day before the six finalists departed for their first visit to the Baikonur spacecraft launch center in Kazakhstan.

In September 1961 all of the remaining members of the March 1960 group, with the exceptions of Belyayev and Komarov, were enrolled at the Zhukovsky Air Force Engineering Academy in Moscow. Eleven would eventually graduate in February 1968.

Women Cosmonauts

The publicity surrounding the day-long Vostok 2 flight of cosmonaut Gherman Titov encouraged hundreds of Soviet citizens, many of them women, to write to the space center asking to join the cosmonaut team. Soviet officials, who were considering sending a woman into space, reviewed these letters and used them as a starting place in the eventual recruitment of four women. They reported to Star Town in early March 1962.

All four of the women were veteran parachutists: Valentina Tereshkova is the only one officially identified, but the others were probably Tatyana Torchillova, Valentina Panomayevna, and Irina Umravlenya. The cover story they were to tell their families was that they had been chosen to join a special parachuting team. One of the women, Torchillova, had also learned to fly in a sporting club. The new cosmonauts were commissioned as junior lieutenants in the Soviet air force and given instruction to qualify them as passengers in MiG-15 trainers. Following the flight by Valentina Tereshkova in June 1963, all four were sent to the Zhukovsky Academy, graduating in 1969.

In spite of having sent the first women into space, Soviet officials disbanded the program, ostensibly out of concern for the effect of cosmonaut training on women and their families. As recently as 1980 cosmonaut chief Vladimir Shatalov insisted that "we just had no moral right to subject the 'better half' of mankind to such (physical) loads."

Nevertheless, in the summer of 1980 four woman cosmonauts were selected, two of them to train for a Soyuz T/Salyut 7 mission in 1982: Svetlana Savitskaya, a well-known sport and test pilot and engineer Irina Pronina.

The remaining two women selectees were joined by six others in 1984 (some of them are probably scientists and part of that group, for which see below), bringing to ten the total number of women currently enrolled in the cosmonaut team.

The Shatalov Group

In March 1962, at the same time the women cosmonauts were beginning their training, Soviet officials prepared to recruit a new cosmonaut group. The new cosmonauts were older on the average (the age limit was raised to 40) and included not only pilots but also military engineers. More significantly, all pilots and engineers had already graduated from either a military academy or a civilian university. Fourteen officers reported to Star Town on January 11, 1963. The senior pilot was Major Vladimir A. Shatalov, 35, an air force inspector, and the senior engineer was Major Lev S. Demin, 36, a professor at the Zhukovsky Academy. Other pilots included Anatoly Filipchenko, Alexei Gubarev and Georgy Dobrovolsky. Engineers included Yuri Artyukhin and Vitaly Zholobov. There are several others who have never been identified, rumored names including Kukhlin, a Fyodor N., and one man known only as T., who was dropped for medical reasons in the first year.

One member of the group, Dobrovolsky, was killed in the Soyuz 11 accident in 1971.

A year later an additional pilot joined this group, veteran test pilot and Hero of the Soviet Union Colonel Georgy T. Beregovoy, 42. Beregovoy was a personal friend of chief designer Korolev who thought his age prevented him from becoming a cosmonaut. Soviet doctors, with the experience of six space flights by that time, had concluded that age was no barrier: anyone who could pass the horrific tests devised by the State Medical Commission was eligible. Beregovoy joined the team in February 1964.

Doctors and Engineers

The changing eligibility requirements allowed Korolev to temporarily add a young physician, Boris Yegorov, to the cosmonaut team in 1963. (Korolev wanted to send him into space for a whole week on Vostok 7.) When plans for that flight were scrapped, Yegorov, who was working with the medical staff at the cosmonaut training center, simply returned to his everyday work.

One of Korolev's deputies, engineer Konstantin Feoktistov, had lobbied for a relaxation of the military pilots-only requirement as early as September 1961, subjecting himself to the Medicial Commission and passing. When plans were finalized in the spring of 1964 for the world's first three-man spacecraft, the Voskhod, Feoktistov wrested a promise from Korolev that he would be included in the crew. He was told on June 11, 1964, that he could begin training. Yegorov and two other doctors (one of them was Vasily Lazarev) had already started. A second engineer, still unidentified, trained with Feoktistov briefly.

This was not a formal or permanent cosmonaut group. Lazarev was considered nothing more than a reserve, and the engineer and doctor alternates were dropped from active training six weeks before the launch of Voskhod. Feoktistov and Yegorov returned to their other careers as soon as the flight was over.

The Klimuk Group: November 1965 and May 1967

In March and April 1965, the State Commission began to select more cosmonauts. These pilots and engineers were even less experienced than the members of the Gagarin group. Twenty men were chosen, reporting to Star Town in October and November 1965. The oldest pilot was just 24; the engineers, who required more schooling, were all 26. Apparently the intent was to take a large number of men and train them specifically for cosmonaut careers. There were still almost two dozen active senior men, so the new arrivals could not expect to make flights for five or six years, which would give them time to complete the two-year basic training course, to perform technical assignments such as serving as capcoms, and to attend test pilot schools or the Red Banner (later named for Yuri Gagarin) Air Force Academy.

The confirmed members of this group are pilots Pyotr Klimuk (the first to go into space, in 1973), Gennady Sarafanov, Vyacheslav Zudov and Leonid Kizim. The engineers included Valery Rozhdestvensky and Yuri Glazkov. Three trainees identified in a 1968 NBC television film were Rostislav Bogdashevsky, Yuri Vovkin and Andrei Korneyev. Other names associated with the selection include Alik Cherkashin, Boris Olesyuk, and Valery Illarionov. As of April 1986 at least one pilot, Kizim, was still making flights, and several other members, including engineers, remained eligible for assignment to cosmonaut crews.

Naturally, several trainees dropped out during the basic course. In May 1967, several replacements—men who had passed the examinations two years earlier, but had been placed "in reserve"—arrived at Star Town. These included Vladimir Kovalenok, Vladimir Lyakhov and Yuri Malyshev.

Flight Engineers: 1966-78

Korolev had always intended to add his engineers to cosmonaut crews as soon as it was possible, and in May 1964, just as Feoktistov was included in the Voskhod crew, announced as much to his staff. He was inundated with over 500 applications. Serious screening and medical tests did not begin until May 1966, not until the multi-seat Soyuz was ready to fly.

Eight engineers were invited to join the cosmonaut group: Alexei Yeliseyev, Georgy Grechko, Oleg Makarov, Valery Kubasov, Vladislav Volkov, Sergei Anokhin, Nikolai Rukavishnikov and Vitaly Sevastyanov. Most were in their early thirties: Anokhin, the dramatic exception, was 56! (Like Beregovoy, he was already an honored test pilot and engineer, a colonel in the air force, who had worked closely with Korolev for years.) Grechko had helped design the Luna unmanned probe. Makarov worked on Vostok and Voskhod. Makarov and Sevastyanov had taught the early cosmonauts, and Sevastyanov sat on the State Commission which approved crews for flights.

Yeliseyev, Kubasov, Volkov and Grechko began training immediately in August 1966 for the first Soyuz flights, though Grechko broke his back in a parachute jump in October, sidelining himself for a year. Makarov, Sevastyanov and Rukavishnikov reported later, due to other assignments. Anokhin's active involvement lasted only a few weeks. Apparently his age made it difficult for him to keep up.

The State Commission screened candidates from the Korolev bureau again in June 1966, though those who passed—including Valentin Lebedev, Vladimir Aksenov, Gennady Strekalov and Valery Ryumin—were not asked to report for cosmonaut training until 1972 and 1973. One young engineer, Anatoly Zykov, died in a glider crash in 1969 after passing the examinations but prior to joining the cosmonaut group.

A third screening took place in 1967 for engineers who were involved in the new Salyut space station program. Only two men are known to have entered cosmonaut training (early in 1969) from this selection: Viktor Patsayev and Vladimir Vetrov. One future cosmonaut, Alexandr Alexandrov, was rejected at this time.

At least two more Korolev engineers, Boris Andreyev and Alexandr Ivanchenkov, commenced cosmonaut training in May 1970, along with the fourth major group of young pilots. Unlike the engineers who preceeded them, who were directly involved in the design of Soyuz and Salyut vehicles and required little technical training, Andreyev and Ivanchenkov were computer specialists who needed to undergo the two-year basic course of instruction.

A major new group of engineers was screened in 1975 and reported in December 1978. Among them, and there were probably at least fifteen, are Savinykh, Alexandrov, Solovyev, Serebrov and Volk. Volk is unique in that he was not employed in the Korolev bureau, but in the Tupolev aircraft bureau, where he was an experienced civilian test pilot.

As of April 1986, twenty-one aerospace engineers were known to have entered the cosmonaut program, though the actual number selected was probably closer to forty.

Test Pilots: 1966

The first cosmonaut with a test pilot background was Beregovoy, who was a late addition to the 1963 group. One may speculate that his performance encouraged Korolev and the other program managers to recruit more, since several other pilots with similar backgrounds were enrolled in the cosmonaut team in the next couple of years: Vasily Lazarev, a physician and pilot who had tested space suits and other equipment; Sergei Anokhin; and others, possibly including pilot Vasily Ivanov, who trained cosmonauts.

Only Beregovoy and Lazarev ever flew in

space and the total number of test pilots selected is not known, but it was probably not more than six. Gagarin's diary reveals that in 1966, not long after Korolev's death, the cosmonaut spoke with Tikhonravov, who was apparently very enthusiastic about recruiting test pilots for the space program. Gagarin agreed that test pilots were a welcome addition, but wondered if officials were making full use of the cosmonauts already in the program.

Pilots: 1970, 1976 and 1982

The selection criteria for pilot cosmonauts seem to have stabilized for the State Commission examinations in late 1969. In addition to passing medical, psychological and political tests, pilot candidates must be between the ages of 24 and 30. Most have worked as flight instructors. New cosmonauts were enrolled in the Gagarin Air Force Academy following completion of the two-year basic course of instruction, if duties permitted.

The May 1970 group, whose training was directed by Colonel Boris Volynov, consisted of at least eight pilots, among them Romanenko, Dzhanibekov, Popov, and Berezovoy.

Another, larger group, numbering about 20 pilots, reported in February 1976. Only three members of this selection, V. Titov, Vasyutin and A. Volkov, have flown in space, though many others remain on flight status. In addition to further education at the Gagarin Academy, these pilots were also given test pilot training after entering the space program.

A third new pilot group, size unknown, began training in 1982 under the direction of Colonel Yuri Malyshev.

Doctors and Scientists

The first physician in space was Boris Yegorov, on Voskhod 1 in October 1964. Vasily Lazarev, a pilot who also had medical training, made two Soyuz flights (one of them aborted) in 1973 and 1975. But it was not until 1977 that a group of physicians was recruited into the cosmonaut team. Only one has flown in space so far, Dr. Oleg Atkov, a cardiologist who had helped develop heart-monitoring systems for use on Salyut space stations. There are at least five or six of these physicians in the cosmonaut group, including Atkov's backup, Dr. Valery Polyakov.

Scientists, on the other hand, were not recruited for the space program until 1984. (Earlier Soviet space travelers such as Feoktistov, often referred to as scientists, were actually aerospace engineers.) These specialists in biology, astronomy, and physics will be eligible for flights on the Mir space station beginning in 1986.

Guest Cosmonauts

Between December 1976 and September 1985, 24 cosmonauts from nations other than the USSR were trained at Star Town. See Part III for details. Two French spationauts are to begin training in October 1986 for a Mir mission in 1988, to be followed by two more Bulgarian cosmonauts.

Summary

Group I (Gagarin), March 1960.	20
Women Cosmonauts, March 1962	4
Group II (Shatalov), January 1963	15
Voskhod Cosmonauts, 1964	5
Group III (Klimuk), November 1965/May 1967	25*
Group IV (Engineers) 1966/1978	40*
Group V (Pilots-Engineers) May 1970	10*
Group VI (Pilots) February 1976	20*
International Cosmonauts, 1976/1985	24
Group VII (Physicians) 1977	6*
Group VIII (Women Cosmonauts) 1980	4
Group IX (Pilots) 1982	10*
Group X (Scientists) 1984	12*
Total career cosmonauts	136*
Total temporary cosmonauts	30
Total trained, 1960-85	168

* indicates approximate numbers. Roman numerals signify groups of career cosmonauts.

Although this is an approximation, it fits known totals from Soviet sources. (During the 1981 celebrations commemorating the 20th anniversary of the flight of Gagarin, about 135 cosmonauts were in attendance, according to European journalists present. At least seventeen of the 160-plus who had undergone training were dead.)

1986

Soviet cosmonauts are based at the Gagarin Cosmonaut Training Center, part of Star Town, a complex of laboratories, classrooms, simulators, apartments and office buildings twenty-five miles northeast of Moscow. Star Town has 3000 inhabitants, most of them officials of the space program and their families. It is here that the ninety or so military officers who have become cosmonauts live. (Civilian cosmonauts retain residences in Moscow.) Unlike American astronauts, who are officially "loaned" to the space program by their parent service and usually leave after several years, an assignment to the cosmonaut group is considered permanent. Academic dropouts are employed elsewhere in the space program; the families of those who were killed in training or space-related accidents remain in the community of Star Town. Only one resignation has ever been reported.

Georgy Beregovoy, now a lieutenant general, is head of the Cosmonaut Training Center at Star Town. His deputies include Major General Andrian Nikolayvev, Major General Alexei Leonov, Major General Pavel Popovich, and Major General Pyotr Klimuk. Other inactive cosmonauts have assumed administrative jobs in the space program.

Soviet Cosmonaut Biographies

Aksenov, Vladimir

Vladimir Aksenov made two Soyuz flights, including the first manned flight of the new Soyuz T transport, Soyuz T-2, in June 1980. The Soyuz T carried a new onboard computer which unfortunately malfunctioned during rendezvous and docking with the Salyut 6 space station. Aksenov and commander Yuri Malyshev were able to dock manually with Salyut 6. They returned to earth after four days.

In September 1976 Aksenov was flight engineer aboard Soyuz 22, an eight-day mission dedicated to earth resources using the German-built MKF-6 multi-spectral cameras.

Aksenov has logged twelve days in space.

Vladimir Viktorovich Aksenov was born February 1, 1935, in the village of Giblitsy in the Ryazan district of the USSR. After graduation from secondary school he attended the Kasimov Industrial School and the Mytishchi Engineering School, graduating in 1955. While at Mytishchi he also took flying lessons and in 1955 entered the Chuguyev Higher Air Force School, intending to become a pilot. But he left in January 1957 to become an engineer with the Korolev spacecraft design bureau, working on the first Sputnik.

From 1957 to 1973 Aksenov was a senior engineer at the Korolev bureau, becoming head of the testing department. His work put him in close contact with Soviet cosmonauts such as Valery Bykovsky, his future Soyuz 22 commander. Aksenov participated in weightless flights aboard aircraft, EVA training, and emergency splashdown exercises. He also continued his studies, attending the All-Union Polytechnic Institute, earning his degree in 1963. He had joined the Party in 1959.

Aksenov applied for the cosmonaut team as early as 1964, but was asked by Korolev to wait. He finally began training in 1973. Following his flight on Soyuz T-2 he helped train cosmonauts for the Soviet-French mission in 1982 and for the Soviet-Indian mission in 1984.

Aksenov is the author of *The Hard Road* (1982), a biography of engineer-test pilot Sergei Anokhin. He and his wife, Marina, an engineer, have two sons, Valery and Sergei.

Alexandrov, Alexandr

Alexandr Alexandrov was part of the most dramatic space flight in the history of the Soviet space program.

On June 27, 1983, Alexandrov and commander Vladimir Lyakhov were launched into space aboard Soyuz T-9 for a planned four-month stay operating Salyut 7 and a special "add-on" module called Kosmos 1443. They were replacements for the crew of Titov, Strekalov and Serebrov, whose attempt two months earlier to reach the Salyut 7/Kosmos 1443 orbital complex had been aborted.

Alexandrov and Lyakhov docked successfully with the orbital complex on June 29. On July 25 the station was struck by a micrometeorite,

which left a noticeable crater in one of the windows. More serious was an accident which occurred on September 9, when the complex was being refueled by the unmanned Progress cargo vessel: a pipe line burst, leaking fuel and damaging Salyut's control systems. Lyakhov and Alexandrov took refuge in their Soyuz until ground controllers could be sure the complex was still safe.

Salyut 7 was still habitable, but it was damaged. Soviet program managers developed repair procedures and trained cosmonauts Vladimir Titov and Gennady Strekalov to carry them out. Unfortunately, the attempt to launch Titov and Strekalov on September 26 was disastrous: a fire broke out at the base of their launch vehicle seconds before ignition and they were forced to escape from the pad. Alexandrov and Lyakhov were left in a difficult situation (some Western observers reported that the men were "marooned") because the Soyuz spacecraft had already been in orbit for more than one hundred days, the limit for safe operations. Nevertheless, a new cargo ship, Progress 18, was launched to the complex; it carried materials for repairing Salyut. Alexandrov performed two completely unrehearsed spacewalks on November 1 and 3, and he and Lyakhov returned safely to Earth three weeks later.

Alexandrov has logged approximately 150 days in space, including 3 hours, 45 minutes of EVA.

Alexandr Pavlovich Alexandrov was born February 20, 1943 in Moscow. His father was a military officer. As a boy, "Sasha" Alexandrov grew interested in rockets and kept a scrapbook about GIRD, the early Soviet rocket study group. Alexandrov attended the same primary school as future cosmonaut Valery Ryumin.

After graduation from secondary school in 1961, Alexandrov entered the Serpukhov Military-Technical school, hoping to become an air force pilot. Physical problems prevented that and he served out his military obligation as a soldier, probably in the Strategic Rocket Forces.

Demobilized in August 1964, Alexandrov joined the Korolev spacecraft design bureau, working under the direction of propulsion specialist Boris Raushenbakh on the Voskhod spacecraft. Alexandrov says that he found the March 1965 "spacewalk" of cosmonaut Alexei Leonov inspiring. He began to think of applying for the cosmonaut group himself.

Soviet chief designer Korolev had recruited young engineers from his design bureau into the cosmonaut team in 1964 and 1966, and when a new opportunity arose in 1967, Alexandrov applied and went before the strict State Medical Commission. But Alexandrov's inability to tolerate high G-loads on the centrifuge prevented his selection.

Undaunted, Alexandrov continued his work at the design bureau in the training of cosmonaut teams, a job which required him to travel all over the USSR. He studied nights at the Bauman Technical School and obtained his degree in 1969. He joined the Communist party of the Soviet Union in 1970. He also became a parachutist and pilot.

In 1976 he was transferred to the flight control center near Moscow and became a ground controller for Soyuz and Salyut missions. One of the missions he worked on was the 175-day Soyuz 32/Salyut 6 flight of Vladimir Lyakhov, his future space partner, and Valery Ryumin, his former schoolmate. Just prior to this, in December 1978, Alexandrov had applied a second time for admission to the cosmonaut group and been accepted. His first assignments were as backup flight engineer for Soyuz T-5 in 1982 and Soyuz T-8 in 1983. He has since served as backup flight engineer for Soyuz T-13 and T-15.

Alexandrov met his wife, Natalia, while both were working at the spacecraft design bureau, and she was on duty at the flight control center when he was in space. They have a son, Sergei.

Andreyev, Boris

Boris Andreyev was the backup flight engineer for the Soviet-American Soyuz 19 misssion in July 1975. He was trained as a possible replacement for cosmonaut Valery Kubasov, should he have been unable to make the flight.

Andreyev's cosmonaut career ended two years later when a back injury suffered during a parachuting mishap disqualified him. He had been training for a long-duration flight aboard Salyut 6.

Boris Dmitryevich Andreyev was born October 6, 1940, in Moscow. After completing secondary school he attended the Bauman Higher Technical School, graduating in 1965. He was known as a good athlete and was also active in the student scientific society.

After graduation Andreyev went to work at the Korolev spacecraft design bureau, at first as an engineer, later as head of a data-processing department involved with automatic spacecraft control systems. During this time he learned to speak English and, in 1969, joined the Party.

He became a cosmonaut in May 1970 and three years later was assigned to the training group for the Apollo-Soyuz Test Project. During the two-year course of training Andreyev made several trips to the United States.

Boris Andreyev is now a computer specialist at the Korolev bureau and is actively involved in Soviet space flights. He was a capcom for Soyuz 32/Salyut 6 in 1979.

He is married to a fellow Bauman school graduate, Tamara Vasilyevna, who is also an engineer, and they have a son, Dmitri, and a daughter, Tatyana.

Anikeyev, Ivan

Ivan Nikolayevich Anikeyev was one of the first Soviet cosmonauts selected in March 1960. He was dismissed from the program in late 1961 for disciplinary reasons.

According to fellow cosmonaut Georgy Shonin, Anikeyev was, like Shonin, from the Ukraine and became a naval air force pilot. He probably attended the Yeisk Higher Air Force School.

After leaving the space program Anikeyev served in the air force reserves as a pilot. He is now retired and lives in the city of Bezhetsky, in the Kalinin region.

Anokhin, Sergei

Colonel Sergei Nikolayevich Anokhin is the oldest person ever selected for cosmonaut training. In May 1966, when he was already 56 years old, he joined a group of seven aerospace engineers selected for future space flights aboard the Soyuz spacecraft.

According to cosmonaut Valery Kubasov, another member of that group, the small, thin Anokhin worked hard to endure the physical training required of cosmonauts, and was not above using trickery to even the odds in sporting events. His application had the blessing of chief designer Korolev and drew attention from Defense Minister Ustinov, but the State Medical Commission ultimately ended the experiment.

Anokhin continued to work with the engineer cosmonauts, serving

as flight instructor for those who became pilots. He also became head of the International Astronautical Federation office in Moscow and remained "commissioner" of space records until 1984.

He died on April 15, 1986.

Anokhin was born in Moscow in 1910 to the family of a civil servant. At the age of 17 he went to work on a railroad gang, but after eight years entered the Vishuyu School for glider pilots in the Crimea. He began to work as an airplane and glider test pilot and in 1940 set a series of records for glider altitude, distance and flight duration.

When the Great Patriotic War began, Anokhin commanded a squadron in the Soviet air force. He saw action on the Byelorussian Front and fought in support of partisans.

He became a Party member in 1943.

In that same year he became chief test pilot for projects that included the first Soviet jet plane. He continued to work as a pilot and test pilot for many years, until in 1964 chief spacecraft designer Korolev asked him to head the flight methods section of his construction bureau, training cosmonauts for flights on Voskhod, Soyuz and Salyut.

Cosmonaut Vladimir Aksenov published a biography of Anokhin, *The Hard Way*, in 1982.

Artyukhin, Yuri

Yuri Artyukhin was a member of the first successful Soviet space station crew, spending two weeks aboard Salyut 3 in 1974.

The USSR's previous two Salyut missions had seen technical problems which either prevented cosmonauts from going aboard the stations once they had docked or, in the case of Salyut 2, kept the crews from being launched in the first place. The three cosmonauts of Soyuz 11 who did manage to get aboard Salyut 1 in June 1971 were killed on returning to Earth.

Artyukhin, the flight engineer of Soyuz 14, and commander Pavel Popovich, were launched to Salyut 3 on July 3, 1974, docking and boarding the station two days later. Their two-week mission was conservative and largely uneventful, consisting of medical experiments and Earth surface observations, many of them of a military nature. (Western observers later concluded that Salyut 3 was the first of the "military" Salyut missions, operating in low Earth orbit and crewed solely by military officers whose communications with mission control were encrypted.) Artyukhin and Popovich returned to Earth on July 19, 1974.

Yuri Petrovich Artyukhin was born July 22, 1940, in Pershutino, a village near Moscow. His father was an air force bombadier who died in the Great Patriotic War. Artyukhin himself applied for military service as soon as he was of age, entering the Balashov Higher Air Force School at 17, hoping to emulate his father. But medical problems washed him out of flight school. He remained in the Soviet air force, however, enrolling in the Serpukhov Air Force Technical School. He became a specialist in military communications systems and served in that capacity in a number of air force units before being sent to the Zhukovsky Air Force Engineering Academy for advanced study.

He graduated from Zhukovsky in 1958 and remained at the Academy as a researcher before joining the cosmonaut group in January 1963. He had become a Party member in 1957.

Like other military engineer-cosmonauts, Artyukhin worked at the Yangel and Korolev spacecraft design bureaus. He also served as a capcom aboard tracking vessels based at sea during Soviet manned flights such as the "troika" flights of October 1969, the 19-day Soyuz 9 mission in June 1970, and the first two missions to Salyut 1 in 1971. In the autumn of 1973 he was named flight engineer of the Soyuz 14 crew.

Following his space flight Artyukhin worked as a flight controller for other Soviet manned flights, including the Salyut 5 missions in 1976.

Colonel Artyukhin and his wife, Nina, an employee of the "Nauka" ("Science") Publishing House, have two sons, Sergei and Vladimir.

Atkov, Oleg

Oleg Atkov was the third Soviet medical doctor assigned to a cosmonaut crew, but the first to spend more than two days in space. During 237 days in the unique environment of Salyut 7, Atkov had the unprecedented opportunity to study the effects of space travel on himself and fellow cosmonauts Leonid Kizim and Vladimir Solovyov. That mission, Soyuz T-10, lasted from February to October 1984 and was the longest manned space flight in history.

Oleg Yuriyevich Atkov was born May 9, 1949, in the town of Khvorostyanka in the Kuybyshev district of the USSR. In 1973 he graduated from the Sechenov First Moscow Medical Institute, the same school that cosmonaut Boris Yegorov, the first doctor in space, attended. From 1973 to 1977 Atkov was an intern and student at the All-Union Cardiological Center of the USSR Academy of Sciences specializing in ultrasound as a method of detecting heart disease. While at the Center he took part in preflight and postflight physical examinations of cosmonauts. He joined the Party in 1977.

Atkov was admitted to the cosmonaut team in 1977 with a group of medical specialists. During his training he designed a portable ultrasound cardiograph for use on the Soyuz T-5 flight in 1982.

Atkov and his wife, Yevgania, have a daughter, Katya.

Belyayev, Pavel

Pavel Belyayev commanded the space flight during which fellow cosmonaut Alexei Leonov took the world's first walk in space. It was March 18, 1965, and Belyayev acted as live television commentator to a Soviet audience as his co-pilot floated free outside the Voskhod 2 spacecraft for ten minutes. "Man has stepped out into open space!" Belyayev announced.

The Voskhod 2 flight lasted only a day. Because of a failure in the automatic guidance system, Belyayev was forced to make a manual reentry. He and Leonov landed far off course in the mountains near Perm and spent two cold days and nights in the wilderness, chasing away wolves, before being reached by rescue teams and returned to Moscow for a triumphant welcome.

Pavel Ivanovich Belyayev was born June 26, 1925, in the village of Chelishchevo in the Volgoda region. As a teenager he worked in a factory in Kamensk-Uralsk, then, at the age of 18, joined the Soviet army. He graduated from the Yeisk Higher Air Force School in 1945 and as a fighter pilot saw action against the Japanese during the last days of the War.

A military pilot second class and, since 1949, a Party member, Belyayev served with various air force units in the Far East before being sent to the Red Banner Air Force Academy near Moscow in 1956. He graduated in 1959 and was serving as a squadron commander for a naval air unit when he was selected for the cosmonaut team in March 1960.

Major Belyayev was the oldest and most experienced pilot among the cosmonauts and he became the first commander of the group, though a variety of physical ailments prevented him from becoming one of the first to make a space flight. He suffered a badly broken ankle during a parachute jump in August 1961 and spent a year recuperating, then supervised the selection and training of a new group of pilot and engineer cosmonauts who came to Star Town in January 1963.

In April 1964 he was chosen to command the spacewalk mission, which became Voskhod 2. After that flight, his only trip into space, Belyayev supervised the training of another group of new cosmonauts chosen in May 1967 and trained intensively himself for a circumlunar Soyuz flight scheduled for December 1968. He would have been the first man to circle the moon, several weeks before America's Apollo 8 astronauts, but technical problems prevented the flight.

Belyayev's failing health caused him to be hospitalized in December 1969. During surgery for an ulcer he developed peritonitis and died on January 10, 1970. He was survived by his wife, Tatyana, and two daughters, Irina and Ludmilla.

Beregovoy, Georgy

Georgy Beregovoy became the first Soviet test pilot to go into space when he flew aboard Soyuz 3 in October 1968. Soyuz 3 ended an 18-month hiatus in Soviet manned flights caused by the Soyuz 1 accident, which killed cosmonaut Vladimir Komarov. The 47-year-old Beregovoy, at that time also the oldest person to make a space flight, spent four days testing the re-designed vehicle and rendezvousing with the unmanned Soyuz 2. A planned docking had to be scrubbed, but the mission was considered a success.

Following his only flight, Beregovoy gave up active space training and in 1972 was appointed director of the Gagarin Cosmonaut Training Center, a post he still holds today.

Georgy Timofeyevich Beregovoy was born April 15, 1921, in the village of Fyodorovka in the Donbass region of the Ukraine. The Donbass is a land of iron and coal mines and steel mills and at age 17 Beregovoy was working in a plant in Yenakievo. But he had built model airplanes as a boy and became an amateur pilot, so he joined the air force, attending the Lugansk flight school and becoming a pilot in 1941. He graduated just in time for the Great Patriotic War and went from school directly to the front.

From 1941 to 1945 Beregovoy flew 185 combat missions against the Nazis in a division commanded by Major General Nikolai Kamanin, who would become the first chief of cosmonaut training. Most of these missions were low-flying support of infantry and tank assaults and Beregovoy was shot down several times. He always managed to return to his own lines and in 1944 earned his first Hero of the Soviet Union medal. He had become a Party member in 1943.

After the War Beregovoy graduated from a test pilot school and served in that capacity from 1946 until becoming a cosmonaut. One of his projects was the "all-weather interceptor." He attended the Red Banner Air Force Academy from 1953 to 1956.

Beregovoy's selection as a cosmonaut was almost an accident. He was interested in flying in space but assumed that his age—he was 40 when Gagarin flew—prevented it. He was already an honored Hero, a full colonel, and overqualified for the cosmonaut group. Nevertheless, his testing work brought him into contact with chief designer Korolev, who encouraged Beregovoy to take the cosmonaut medical tests. Beregovoy passed and arrived at Star Town in February 1964, joining the group of cosmonaut-candidates who had arrived the previous January.

Beregovoy's first assignment was as backup commander for a planned two week-long Voskhod 3 mission scheduled for early 1966. When those plans were scrapped, Beregovoy moved over to the Soyuz program, and was Komarov's backup on the tragic Soyuz 1.

Lieutenant General Beregovoy is the chief spokesman for the cosmonaut group and is frequently interviewed by journalists. He is also politically active as a member of the Supreme Soviet. He has published two autobiographies, *Angle of Attack* (1971) and *The Sky Begins on Earth* (1976), and several other books.

He and his wife, Lydia, have two grown children, a daughter, Ludmilla, and a son, Viktor.

Berezovoy, Anatoly

Anatoly Berezovoy commanded the first flight to Salyut 7, the seven-month Soyuz T-5 mission. He and engineer Valentin Lebedev were launched May 13, 1982, planning to remain in space for six months, with a possible extension. After docking with Salyut 7 on May 14, they activated the station, a process that took several days, and deployed an amateur radio satellite called Iskra 2, before settling down to a routine of Earth surface observations and space manufacturing. In June the expedition cosmonauts were host to three visitors, the crew of Soyuz T-6, which included French spationaut Jean-Loup Chretien. In August a second crew of three visited Salyut 7; this crew included Svetlana Savitskaya, the second woman in space.

By early December Berezovoy and Lebedev had taken over 20,000 pictures of the Earth's surface and had manufactured electronic crystals in a special factory. They had apparently survived their seven month mission in good physical condition as they prepared to return to Earth in Soyuz T-7, which had been left for their use by the August visitors.

Berezovoy and Lebedev's greatest challenge was the recovery following their landing in snowy Kazakhstan. They came down at night in unexpected fog and low clouds and rolled down a hillside. The first rescue helicopter attempting to reach them crash-landed and its commander had to "talk down" the second. Eventually the cosmonauts were rescued from their frigid spacecraft and given shelter in a rugged all-terrain vehicle. When they returned to the launch complex at Baikonur the next morning they were unable to walk without assistance. Within days, however, both men had recovered.

Berezovoy has logged over 211 days in space, including 2.5 hours of EVA.

Anatoly Nikolayevich Berezovoy was born April 11, 1942, in the settlement of Znem in the Adigei region of the USSR. As a teenager he took a job as a lathe operator at the Neftemash factory in the city of Novocherkassk, but soon joined the army. From 1961 to 1965 he attended the Kacha Higher Air Force School near Volgograd, then served in the air force as a fighter pilot. He joined the Party in 1966.

Berezovoy was admitted to the cosmonaut group in May 1970 and completed the basic training course two years later. He commenced a four-year course of study at the Yuri Gagarin Air Force Academy in 1973 and soon joined the military Salyut training group. By the time of his 33rd birthday, he later wrote, he was sure he would never fly in space. (Apparently he had been assigned to the fourth cosmonaut crew training for two Salyut 5 flights.) But the Soyuz 23 abort in October

1976 caused Soviet officials to make a third flight to Salyut 5, Soyuz 24, and Berezovoy, serving as backup commander for this mission, thus put himself first in line for Salyut 7.

Following Soyuz T-5 Berezovoy was named backup commander for the Soviet-Indian Soyuz T-11 flight, eventually launched in April 1984.

Colonel Berezovoy and his wife, Lydia, have a daughter, Tatyana.

Bondarenko, Valentin

Valentin Vasilyevich Bondarenko, a senior lieutenant in the Soviet air force, was killed in a fire that engulfed a pressure chamber on March 23, 1961, just three weeks before the flight of Yuri Gagarin. He was the first space traveler to die in training.

Bondarenko was completing ten days of experiments in the chamber, where, like others in the cosmonaut group, he had been subjected to isolation and silence. The atmospheric pressure inside the chamber was reduced, requiring a higher oxygen content. Following a medical examination, Bondarenko removed the sensors and cleaned himself with a piece of cotton dipped in alcohol. Without thinking, he tossed the cotton aside. It landed on a hot plate and ignited, quickly turning the oxygen-rich chamber into an inferno. Before the chamber could be opened, a process which took several minutes, Bondarenko had been burned over ninety percent of his body. He was taken to the Botkin Hospital not far away, where he died eight hours later.

According to one account, the cosmonaut who accompanied Bondarenko to the hospital was Gagarin. The next day, on March 24, Gagarin and the other cosmonauts left Moscow for their first visit to the Baikonur space center.

Bondarenko was the youngest of the Soviet cosmonauts. He was born in 1936 in the Ukrainian city of Kharkov. He had attended a higher air force school and served briefly as a military jet pilot prior to entering the space program in March 1960.

He was survived by his wife, Anya, and a son, Alexandr.

Bykovsky, Valery

Valery Bykovsky set a space duration record by spending five days aboard Vostok 5 in June 1963. That flight remains the longest space mission ever flown by a single astronaut or cosmonaut. Bykovsky later commanded Soyuz 22, a scientific mission, in 1976 and Soyuz 31, an Interkosmos flight by German researcher Sigmund Jaehn, in 1978.

He has logged almost 21 days in space.

Valery Fyodorovich Bykovsky was born August 2, 1934, in Pavlovsky-Posad, a suburb of Moscow. While still in secondary school he joined a flying club and became a pilot. At the age of 18 he entered the Kacha Higher Air Force School, graduating in 1955, then served in the air force as an interceptor pilot and parachute instructor. He became a cosmonaut in March 1960.

During the first months of cosmonaut training Bykovsky earned the Order of the Red Star for testing the isolation chamber. He was one of the finalists for the first manned flight flown by Gagarin in April 1961, and was backup to Andrian Nikolayev on the Vostok 3 flight in August 1962.

Following his record-breaking flight Bykovsky was involved with training for the first spacewalk, by Alexei Leonov in March 1965, then was named commander of the Soyuz 2 mission scheduled for launch on

April 24, 1967. Bykovsky and fellow cosmonauts Alexei Yeliseyev and Yevgeny Khrunov were to rendezvous and dock with Soyuz 1, carrying Vladimir Komarov and launched a day earlier. Yeliseyev and Khrunov were to make a spacewalk to Soyuz 1 and return to Earth aboard that spacecraft. It was hoped that this demonstration of rendezvous and docking procedures and of a new spacesuit would give the Soviet space program experience required for manned lunar landings. But Soyuz 1 developed technical problems during its first hours of flight. The launch of Soyuz 2 was canceled, and when Komarov was killed trying to land Soyuz 1, the whole manned program was suspended.

When Soyuz flights were ready to resume, Bykovsky was training as backup to Pavel Belyayev for a manned circumlunar flight which was ready for launch in December 1968. For unknown reasons, it, too, was cancelled, and in the wake of America's Apollo 8 voyage around the Moon a few weeks later, so was the whole Soviet manned lunar landing program. Bykovsky became a supervisor at the Gagarin Cosmonaut Training Center while preparing for Salyut mission. He was backup commander to Soyuz 13 in December 1973, training director for Apollo-Soyuz, and, finally, in 1976, was named to command his second space mission. He was also backup commander for Soyuz 37 in 1979.

Since 1978 Colonel Bykovsky has been a training official at the cosmonaut center.

He and his wife, Valentina, have two sons, Valeri and Sergei.

Demin, Lev

Lev Demin was the flight engineer aboard the Soyuz 15 mission to Salyut 3 in August 1974. He and commander Gennady Sarafanov were testing an automatic rendezvous and docking system prior to linking up with the Salyut for a month-long mission. The system failed, forcing Demin and Sarafanov to make an early return to Earth.

Lev Stepanovich Demin was born January 11, 1926, in Moscow. When the Great Patriotic War began he was a lathe operator in a drilling machine plant. He wanted to join a military school and was accepted, but only temporarily: his lack of proper mathematical training and the German advance on Moscow (which forced the school to relocate to Siberia) ended his schooling for the time being. Demin tried to join a flying club with the idea of becoming an air force pilot, but failed in this as well. He wound up working in a defense plant for the duration.

When the war ended he was finally able to complete ground training at the Moscow Air School, where one of his classmates was future cosmonaut Vladimir Komarov, but no sooner got his certificate of proficiency than he saw his school disbanded. Undaunted, he applied to the Borisoglebsk Air Force School, only to face another rejection, this time from the school's medical commission, for his nearsightedness.

Demin elected to remain in the air force, entering instead a technical school where he specialized in communications technology, eventually becoming commander of a radio platoon. In 1949 he entered the Zhukovsky Air Force Engineering Academy, graduating in 1956. He joined the Party that same year. Demin remained at Zhukovsky as a professor while pursuing his doctorate in systems analysis. His old friend Vladimir Komarov was one of his students. It was Komarov, a member of the 1960 cosmonaut group, who encouraged Demin to apply for the second cosmonaut recruitment, which had begun in March 1962. Demin was hesitant at first: he was completing his doctoral thesis, he was older than Komarov and other cosmonauts, and the selection process was in its final phase. Nevertheless, Demin went before the medical commission and passed, and joined the cosmonaut team with fellow "flight engineers" Artyukhin and Zholobov in January 1963. He finished his thesis that same month.

Demin worked on Soyuz and Salyut systems at the Korolev and Yangel design bureaus from 1965 until assigned to train for a Salyut mission in 1972. The Soyuz 15 flight on August 24-26, 1974, was his only space flight. He retired in 1978.

Demin's wife, Zinaida, works at Star Town. They have a grown son, Sergei, and a daughter, Natasha, who in turn had a son, Vladimir, making Demin the first grandfather in space.

Dobrovolsky, Georgy

Georgy Dobrovolsky commanded the first space station flight in history when he and two fellow cosmonauts spent 23 days aboard Salyut 1 in June 1971. The mission ended in tragedy when Dobrovolsky, Vladislav Volkov and Viktor Patsayev were killed during their return to Earth on June 30, 1971.

Georgy Timofeyevich Dobrovolsky was born June 1, 1928, in the Black Sea port city of Odessa. During the German occupation of Odessa he was arrested by the Nazis for illegal possession of firearms and sentenced to 25 years at hard labor, but escaped from jail.

As a boy Dobrovolsky dreamed of becoming a sailor, but failed to win admittance to a naval school, so he joined the air force and attended a prep school for pilots in 1945. In 1950 he graduated from the Chuguyev Higher Air Force School and became a naval aviator. He joined the Party in 1954. From 1955 to 1961 he took correspondence courses at the Red Banner Air Force Academy and was serving as a deputy squadron commander and parachuting instructor in a naval unit when chosen for the January 1963 cosmonaut group.

A witty man, Dobrovolsky became popular in the group for playing Grandfather Winter at the cosmonaut New Year's celebration. His first work as a cosmonaut saw him spending hours in various test chambers. From 1967 to 1969 he was a capcom for manned Soyuz missions, and also trained in the Soviet lunar program. He joined the Salyut cosmonaut group in 1970.

Lieutenant Colonel Dobrovolsky is buried in the Kremlin Wall. He is survived by his wife, Ludmilla, a mathematics teacher, and daughters Maria and Natasha.

A USSR Academy of Sciences space tracking vessel was named for him in 1978, and he is the subject of a biography, *The Flight Continues* (1977).

Dzhanibekov, Vladimir

Vladimir Dzhanibekov is the most experienced and successful Soviet cosmonaut of the era of manned flight, taking part in five different missions between 1978 and 1985 and participating in the dramatic repair of the Salyut 7 space station.

At a time when close to one out of four Soviet docking flights failed or suffered some difficulty, Dzhanibekov commanded five successes without a failure. It was his demonstrated skill at rendezvous that caused Soviet program managers to choose him to pilot Soyuz T-13 to a linkup with the dead Salyut 7 station in June 1985.

Salyut 7 had been in operation since its launch in April 1982, with seven cosmonaut crews spending as much as nine months at a time

aboard it. But the station suffered a fuel leak in 1983 which damaged it; repaired by one crew, it suffered repeated power shortages all through 1984. And by early 1985 it was adrift in space, unreponsive to commands from the ground.

Sending a manned crew to repair a dead station was not an attractive idea. The highly automated Soyuz T docking procedures depend on range and radar data from the target station. Without that data, the cosmonaut crew is flying "by the seat of its pants." In March 1985 Dzhanibekov and flight engineer Viktor Savinykh were chosen to attempt this tricky maneuver.

Launched on June 6, 1985, Dzhanibekov and Savinykh spent two days—one more than normal—chasing Salyut 7 around the Earth, eventually making a successful docking. Going aboard the station, they found it cold and lifeless. They were forced to rely on their Soyuz T-13 systems for support, even for radio contact with the ground. But within days they had made repairs to the Salyut 7 power systems, using the supplies they had brought and materials shipped to them aboard a Progress tanker. They performed a 6.5-hour spacewalk on August 2 to install new solar panels. By mid-September Salyut 7 was habitable again, and a new, long-term crew was launched to occupy it. Savinykh remained aboard while Dzhanibekov returned to Earth in the exchange Soyuz on September 27.

Vladimir Alexandrovich Dzhanibekov was born May 13, 1942, in the city of Iskander in Tashkent of the Uzbek republic of the USSR. Dzhanibekov was not his original name; he adopted the Uzbek name of his wife's family at marriage.

Dzhanibekov intended to become a physicist and after graduation from secondary school attended Leningrad University for one year. But he had always wanted to fly—even at LGU he had intended to join an aeroclub—and ultimately he decided to enlist in the air force. In 1961 he entered the Yeisk Higher Air Force School, graduating in 1965. He served as an instructor pilot in the Soviet air force before joining the cosmonaut team in May 1970. He became a Party member that same year.

After completing basic cosmonaut training, Major Dzhanibekov was given a challenging assignment. In May 1973 he was one of eight Soviet cosmonauts assigned to the training group for the Apollo-Soyuz Test Project, the joint Soviet-American space flight. During the next two years "Johnny" was a frequent visitor to NASA's Johnson Space Center in Houston and became well known to American astronauts. When the Soviet ASTP vehicle Soyuz 19 was launched on July 15, 1975, Dzhanibekov served as backup commander to Alexei Leonov.

Following ASTP Dzhanibekov joined the group of cosmonauts training for long duration missions aboard Salyut 6. His first space flight, however, only last eight days. He and engineer Oleg Makarov aboard Soyuz 27 docked with Salyut 6 in January 1978 and performed the first exchange of space vehicles, returning to Earth in Soyuz 26 and leaving Soyuz 27 for the use of expedition cosmonauts Yuri Romanenko and Georgy Grechko. Dzhanibekov then trained for flights in the Interkosmos program, during which guest cosmonauts from Eastern European nations went into space. Dzhanibekov was backup commander for the Soviet-Hungarian flight in 1980 and commanded the Soviet-Mongolian team in March 1981, when he spent another week aboard Salyut 6.

Dzhanibekov was again assigned to an expedition crew, this time for a planned eight-month mission aboard Salyut 7, but again found himself called upon to fill in: Yuri Malyshev, commander of the Soviet-French team, had to be replaced for health reasons, and recommended Dzhanibekov as his replacement. In June 1982 Dzhanibekov commanded Soyuz T-6 and spent eight more days in space with crewmates Alexandr Ivanchenkov and France's Jean-Loup Chretien. It was during

Soyuz T-6 that Dzhanibekov had a chance to demonstrate his docking skills. The Soyuz rendezvous computer failed during final approach to Salyut and Dzhanibekov made the docking manually. Chretien was later to describe the situation as "serious," praising Dzhanibekov for his calm piloting.

Dzhanibekov's fourth space flight, unusual for a Soviet cosmonaut, came in July 1984, a two-week visit to Salyut 7 and its resident crew of Kizim, Solovyov and Atkov with crewmates Svetlana Savitskaya and Igor Volk. Savitskaya and Dzhanibekov made a spacewalk in an attempt to repair Salyut-7's troubled power system, which would fail completely within a few months, bringing Dzhanibekov back to space for a fifth time.

In addition to his cosmonaut career Dzhanibekov is a deputy in the Uzbek Soviet.

Major General Dzhanibekov and his wife, Lilia, have two daughters, Olga and Inna.

Feoktistov, Konstantin

Konstantin Feoktistov was a member of the world's first space crew, one of three cosmonauts sent into space for a single day aboard Voskhod 1 in October 1964.

For Feoktistov, it was the culmination of a dream of many years. He was a 38-year-old senior engineer at the Korolev spacecraft design bureau and, after Korolev himself, the person most responsible for the design of the Vostok spacecraft, in which Yuri Gagarin made the world's first manned flight in 1961.

Feoktistov was a lecturer to the early cosmonauts but had ambivalent feelings about them: he had suggested for years that engineers would be the best candidates for space travel, only to find himself "filled with despair" when young air force pilots were selected instead. Feoktistov perservered, however, arranging to have himself put through the strenuous cosmonaut medical tests in the autumn of 1961. The State Commission approved him for spaceflight in early 1962, but an opportunity did not present itself until two years later.

Konstantin Petrovich Feoktistov was born February 7, 1926, in the city of Voronezh. At an early age he became interested in astronomy and spaceflight and at ten years old was making plans for the exploration of the Moon. But the Great Patriotic War forced him to postpone his dreams, and almost killed him. Feoktistov became a scout for a partisan unit when the Nazis occupied the Voronezh region. In 1942 the 16-year-old Feoktistov was captured by the Nazis, shot and left for dead. The next year, after recuperating from his wounds, he entered the Bauman Higher Technical School in Moscow. He graduated in 1949, then worked as an industrial engineer at a plant in Zlatonst.

In 1955 the USSR began a program aimed at the construction of long-range missiles and earth satellites, and Feoktistov, who had recently completed graduate work for a candidate of technical sciences degree, went to work here. He was involved in the Sputnik program and in all phases of the development of manned space vehicles. By the time of his flight he was head of his own group of young engineers, known as Korolev's "kindergarten," which included future cosmonauts Makarov and Sevastyanov.

Following his flight Feoktistov returned to his work at the Korolev bureau and also completed his doctoral thesis. He visited the Paris Air Show in 1967 and met American astronauts David Scott and Michael Collins.

From 1967 on he was actively involved in the design of the Salyut space station, the Soyuz T transport and the Progress supply vehicle.

He was a flight director for Salyut missions in the summer of 1975, and at age 55 trained for a possible second manned flight aboard Soyuz T-3 in 1980, but physical problems forced him to step aside.

Feoktistov continues to be one of the spokesmen for the Soviet space program and is the author of numerous technical works, and of two popular books, *On Spaceflight* (1982) and *Seven Steps to the Stars* (1984), in which he discusses manned missions to the planet Mars.

He and his wife, Galina, have four children.

Filatyev, Valentin

Valentin Ignatyevich Filatyev was a member of the first cosmonaut group selected in March 1960. He was a friend and colleague of Pavel Belyayev, the senior member of the group in age and military service, but Filatyev's appearance made him look older, so he was dubbed "Ded" ("Gramps") by the other pilots.

Filatyev never made a space flight. In 1961 was dismissed from the cosmonaut team for disciplinary reasons.

Prior to becoming a military pilot Filatyev had attended a school for teachers, and following service in the national air defense force, he settled in the city of Orel and became an educator. He is now retired.

Filipchenko, Anatoly

Anatoly Filipchenko commanded two successful Soyuz missions. Soyuz 7 in October 1969 was one of three Soviet manned craft in orbit at a single time. Soyuz 16 in December 1974 was a full-scale dress rehearsal for the Apollo-Soyuz Test Project.

Filipchenko has logged approximately 11 days in space.

Anatoly Vasilyevich Filipchenko was born February 26, 1928, in the town of Davydovka, Voronezh district, but raised in the city of Ostrogozhsk. His father had joined the Party as early as 1918 and served with distinction in both the Russian Civil War and the Great Patriotic War. As a 15-year-old during the War Filipchenko worked as a lathe operator in a munitions factory, but he was interested in flying and attended an air force preparatory school in Voronezh, then the Chuguyev Higher Air Force School, graduating in 1950. He served successively as a pilot, flight commander, deputy squadron commander, instructor, and inspector while also attending the Red Banner Air Force Academy. He joined the Party in 1952.

Filipchenko was one of 15 cosmonauts who began training in January 1963. As a cosmonaut Filipchenko took a test pilot course and worked on the Voskhod flights. In June 1968 he joined the cosmonaut group training for Soyuz missions and was backup commander for Soyuz 4 and later for Soyuz 9. From 1970 to 1973 he trained for a Salyut flight, but was assigned instead to the Apollo-Soyuz Test Project.

Since 1976 Major General Filipchenko has been a training official at Star Town and from 1979 to 1985 was Head of the Federation of Cosmonautics. He is also the author of a book, *Safe Orbits* (1978).

Filipchenko and his wife, Elizaveta, have two sons, Alexandr and Igor.

Gagarin, Yuri

Yuri Gagarin became the first person to make a space flight when he rode a Vostok spacecraft on a single orbit of the Earth on the morning of Wednesday, April 12, 1961.

It was a cloudless spring day at the Baikonur launch center on the arid steppes of Kazakhstan when the 24 rocket engines of the first stage of the R-7 rocket ignited. "*Poyekhali*!" Gagarin said as the rocket rose. "Here we go!" Within minutes he was in space reporting that he felt fine, that the Vostok was functioning. "I can see the Earth's horizon," he said, describing sights no human had ever seen. "It has a very beautiful sort of halo, a rainbow. . . ." He passed over the Pacific Ocean and over America (and thought of Alan Shepard, who Gagarin had believed would be the first to go into space). Over Africa the Vostok retrorockets fired, nudging the spacecraft out of orbit. After the fiery re-entry, Gagarin ejected as planned from Vostok and parachuted safely to a field on a collective farm near Saratov.

Gagarin's flight lasted one hour and forty-eight minutes. Tragically, Gagarin was killed in a plane crash while training for a second space flight on March 27, 1968.

Yuri Alexeyevich Gagarin was born March 9, 1934, in the village of Klushino in the Gzhatsk region of Smolensk, west of Moscow. His father was a carpenter, and the Gagarin family lived under German occupation for several years during the Great Patriotic War. After graduating from secondary school in 1949 Gagarin attended the Lyubertsy Agricultural Machinery School for two years followed by the Saratov Industrial Technical School. But while studying to become a factory worker Gagarin joined an amateur pilot's club and learned to fly. One of his instructors recommended him for air force duty and Gagarin entered the Orenburg Air Force School in 1955.

After graduation in November 1957 Gagarin was offered the chance to be an instructor at Orenburg, but he opted instead for service with the Northern Fleet. For two years he was a pilot based north of the Arctic Circle until volunteering for the cosmonaut group in October 1959. The following March, after months of medical, psychological and political testing, Gagarin was one of 20 young pilots who reported to the Frunze Central Airport in Moscow to begin training for manned flights into space. Gagarin also joined the Party that year.

Gagarin quickly established himself as one of the candidates for the first flight and in late March 1961 was advised by Lieutenant-General Nikolai Kamanin, the director of cosmonaut training, that he would be the pilot of the first Vostok. A meeting of the State Commission for Space Flight on April 8, 1961, confirmed the appointment.

Following his historic flight Gagarin spent many days and weeks making public appearances and trips, visiting Czechoslovakia, Britain, and Canada. He found it difficult to devote time to his career as an active pilot and cosmonaut and so found himself in administrative jobs. He was, in fact, named commander of the cosmonaut team in August 1961, a post he held until 1964, when he was promoted to deputy director of the Cosmonaut Training Center. In these posts he directed the training of the first women cosmonauts (who arrived at Star Town in March 1962) and acted as capcom for the twin flights of Vostok 3 and 4, Voskhod 1 and Voskhod 2. He was also active politically as a delegate to Party congresses in 1961 and 1966.

In 1966 Gagarin was finally able to devote himself to space training again. He was named backup commander for one of the two Soyuz missions scheduled for April 1967. When Soyuz 1 ended tragically, killing cosmonaut Vladimir Komarov, Gagarin remained active. He was assigned as backup pilot for Soyuz 3 and had just completed studies at the Zhukovsky Air Force Engineering Academy at the time of his death. Killed with him was his flying instructor, Colonel Vladimir Seregin.

Gagarin was survived by his wife, Valentina, and two daughters, Yelena and Galina.

Gagarin has been the subject of several biographies published around the world, including *Orbits of a Life* by Oleg Nudenko (1971), *My Brother Yuri* by Valentin Gagarin (1973), *It Couldn't Have Been Otherwise* by Pavel Popovich and Vasily Lesnikov (1980), *108 Minutes and an Entire Life* by his wife, Valentina (1981), *Words about a Son* by his mother, Anna (1983), and *Gagarin* by V. Stepanov (1986). His autobiographies include *My Road to Space* (1961) and *Flame* (1968). Gagarin also co-authored several technical works, including *Survival in Space* (1969).

A crater on the far side of the Moon, a Soviet space tracking vessel, the Red Banner (Order of Kutuzov) Air Force Academy, the Cosmonaut Training Center and his former hometown of Gzhatsk have all been named for Yuri Gagarin, the "first citizen" of space travel.

Glazkov, Yuri

Yuri Glazkov spent 19 days in space aboard Soyuz 23 and Salyut 5 in February 1977. He and commander Viktor Gorbatko made the first major repairs to an orbiting Soviet space station, replacing the entire air supply of Salyut 5. The station's first occupants, cosmonauts Volynov and Zholobov, had been forced to cut short their mission because of impurities in that air supply. Glazkov and Gorbatko successfully completed a short mission of military reconaissance and Earth resources studies.

Yuri Nikolayevich Glazkov was born in Moscow on October 2, 1939. He attended the Kharkhov Higher Air Force Engineering School, graduating in 1962, then served as a flight engineer in the Soviet air force. He joined the cosmonaut group in November 1965 and became a member of the Party in 1966.

During his cosmonaut training Glazkov became a pilot and an expert parachutist, eventually earning an instructor's rating in parachuting. He also did graduate work in aerospace engineering with emphasis on EVA and received his candidate of technical sciences degree in that subject in 1974.

His space-related work took him to several tracking stations and ships, where he acted as capcom for the Soyuz 6/7/8 missions in October 1969, for Salyut 3 flights in 1974 and Salyut 4 flights in 1975. He was also involved in Salyut medical tests.

During the Soyuz trio flights he became friends with pilot Viktor Gorbatko, and he and Gorbatko were teamed for Salyut training in December 1972. They were backups to the Soyuz 23 cosmonauts in October 1976.

Following his space flight Glazkov took part in the training of other space crews, notably those involving French and Indian cosmonauts. He has also written a technical book on EVA titled *Outside Orbiting Spacecraft* (1977) and a general book on space exploration, *The World around Us* (1986).

Colonel Glazkov and his wife have two daughters.

Gorbatko, Viktor

A member of the first group of Soviet cosmonauts, Viktor Gorbatko overcame two medical disqualifications which threatened his career and eventually took part in three successful space flights, including a 17-day mission aboard Salyut 5 in 1977, and the joint Soviet-Vietnamese flight in 1980.

Viktor Vasilyevich Gorbatko was born December 3, 1934, in the village of Ventsy-Zarya near Krasnodar, but grew up in the Kuban region, which was occupied by the Nazis during the Great Patriotic War. After completing secondary school he entered the Soviet army and was sent to the Baltic army pilot school for ground training. From 1953 to 1956 he attended the Bataisk Higher Air Force School, graduating as a jet pilot. One of his classmates at Bataisk was future cosmonaut Yevgeny Khrunov. Gorbatko and Khrunov served together in the same air force unit until cosmonaut selection in March 1960. Gorbatko joined the Party in 1959. From 1961 to 1968 he attended the Zhukovsky Air Force Engineering Academy.

As a member of the cosmonaut team, Gorbatko was assigned to be backup commander for Pavel Belyayev on the Voskhod 2 flight in March 1965. Cosmonaut Alexei Leonov took man's first walk in space on that flight. But a routine medical examination showed Gorbatko to have an irregular heartbeat and he was hospitalized for six weeks, losing his position. He trained as part of the ill-fated Soyuz 1/Soyuz 2 team, and was preparing for another Soyuz mission in 1969 when he broke his ankle during a parachute jump. He wrote later that he was afraid he would be dropped from the flight crew and the space program, but he recovered in time.

Gorbatko first went into space aboard Soyuz 7 on October 12, 1969. Soyuz 7 was the second of three manned Soyuz spacecraft launched in a period of three days for simultaneous maneuvers over the space of a week. Soyuz 7 was intended to dock with Soyuz 8, but technical problems prevented it.

After Soyuz 7 Gorbatko worked as capcom for other manned flights such as Soyuz 9 in 1970, and began training for a Salyut mission in 1972. In 1976 he was backup commander for Soyuz 23, and in February 1977 commanded Soyuz 24. During this flight Gorbatko and flight engineer Yuri Glazkov went aboard Salyut 5 and spent 17 days performing earth observations and medical experiments.

Later that year Gorbatko joined the group of Soviet commanders for Interkosmos missions, joint flights with cosmonauts from other nations. He was backup commander for the Soviet-East German flight in 1978, and went into space for the third time with Vietnamese cosmonaut Pham Tuan in July 1980.

Major General Gorbatko is now retired from active space training, though still active in political affairs. He is president of the USSR-Mongolia Friendship Society and also president of the USSR Parachute Jumping Federation.

He and his wife, Valentina, a doctor, have two daughters, Irina and Marina.

Grechko, Georgy

Georgy Grechko became the first Soviet cosmonaut to make a space walk to repair a manned spacecraft, and the first to perform an impromptu space rescue.

On December 20, 1977, flight engineer Grechko and mission commander Yuri Romanenko were in the second week of a planned 90-day mission aboard the Salyut 6 space station. They were not the intended crew members: the previous cosmonaut crew had accidentally rammed its Soyuz 25 vehicle into the the Salyut 6 docking mechanism, preventing them from going aboard the station. Their replacements, launched aboard Soyuz 26 on December 10, 1977, docked their spacecraft at the aft or secondary adaptor and moved into the station. But in order for Salyut 6 to be resupplied it was necessary for both docking adaptors to be functional. Grechko, in fact, was included in the crew specifically to

inspect and repair the forward adaptor. In the course of the one hour, 28-minute spacewalk Grechko concluded that the Soyuz 25 accident had not damaged the adaptor, thus salvaging the billion-ruble station and clearing the way for a full four years of operation.

The EVA almost ended tragically, however, when Romanenko, who had neglected to fasten his safety line, suddenly floated out of the Salyut 6 airlock. It was only Grechko's quick reflex in grabbing the trailing line that saved Romanenko's life.

This unlikely hero was, by training and profession, an aerospace engineer. Georgy Mikhailovich Grechko was born in Leningrad on May 25, 1931, though he spent much of his teens in the Urals, where his family was evacuated during the Great Patriotic War. After the War, Grechko attended the Leningrad Institute of Mechanics, graduating with honors in 1955. His specialty, unusual at the time, was computers.

Grechko went immediately to work in Sergei Korolev's rocket and spacecraft design bureau and was one of those engineers who calculated—often by hand—trajectories for the first Sputnik. By 1964 Grechko was head of his own team of spacecraft designers. He received the Lenin Prize for this work, which resulted in the Luna series of space probes. Luna 9 was the first unmanned spacecraft to softland on the Moon.

The flight of fellow Korolev engineer Konstantin Feoktistov aboard the first Voskhod in 1964 prompted Grechko to apply for the cosmonaut team. He passed the Medical Commission in 1964, but did not start to train until the summer of 1966. His cosmonaut career almost ended that October, when he broke his back in a parachuting accident. He was sidelined for a year. When he returned to active training he was logically included in a group of ten cosmonauts who were training for possible Soviet manned flights to the Moon. As that flight seemed less and less likely by early 1969, Grechko was transferred to the Soyuz Earth orbital program, serving as backup cosmonaut researcher for Soyuz 7 that October, and backup flight engineer for Soyuz 9 in June 1970 and Soyuz 12 in September 1973.

Grechko's first flight was Soyuz 17 on January 11, 1975. He and commander Alexei Gubarev made rendezvous and docked with the Salyut 4 station the next day, and spent thirty days in space performing medical experiments and a host of astronomical observations. It was the longest Soviet manned space flight to that date.

Soviet engineer cosmonauts continue to work at the spacecraft design bureau between flight assignments and Grechko was no exception, becoming heavily involved in the planned Salyut 6 series of missions. In June 1977 he was assigned to fly a Salyut 6 mission as commander of an Interkosmos crew. Before he could make that flight, however, the Soyuz 25 abort occured, and as an experienced cosmonaut who was intimately familiar with the Salyut 6 docking mechanism, Grechko was included in the replacement crew. It was ironic because Grechko had said that he did not particularly enjoy long space flights; it was later learned that he was ill for much of his 30-day mission.

But Grechko and Romanenko spent 90 days aboard Salyut 6, shattering the five-year-old record of 84 days held by America's Skylab 4 astronauts. They were host to two visiting crews, including one composed of Grechko's Soyuz 17 comrade Gubarev and the first of the Interkosmos pilots, Czech Vladimir Remek. (Grechko's father died during the mission, a fact which commander Romanenko withheld from him until their return to earth.) The mission was a complete success.

Grechko continued to work on the Salyut 6 missions in a support role, sometimes as capcom. He trained as backup flight engineer for the joint Soviet-Indian mission in 1984, and made his third spaceflight aboard Soyuz T-14 in September 1985, when he spent eight days aboard the recently repaired Salyut 7, raising his total time in space to 134 days.

Grechko is a short, stocky, jovial man. He joked during his last space flight that he had lost eleven pounds so that more supplies could be carried. He and his wife, Nina, who is also an engineer, live in Moscow, with their sons Alexei and Mikhail.

Gubarev, Alexei

Alexei Gubarev commanded successful space missions in 1975 and in 1978, including a month-long stay aboard Salyut 4, and the world's first multi-national crew.

Gubarev and flight engineer Georgy Grechko were launched January 11, 1975, aboard Soyuz 17 and docked with Salyut 4 the next day. For the next four weeks they performed observations of the sun and medical experiments in what was, to that time, the Soviet Union's longest and most successful space mission.

In March 1978 Gubarev was commander of Soyuz 28. With him on that flight was Captain Vladimir Remek, a Czechoslovakian pilot and the first person to travel into space who was not Soviet or American. Gubarev and Remek docked with Salyut 6 during their eight-day mission.

Gubarev has logged 37 days in space.

Alexei Alexandrovich Gubarev was born March 29, 1931, in the Kuybyshev region near the Volga River. He attended the Yeisk Higher Air Force School and after graduation in 1952 served in the Pacific Fleet. In December 1952 he flew combat missions in Korea in support of Chinese and North Korean units. He attended the Red Banner Air Force Academy from 1957 to 1959, and joined the Party in 1957. At the time of his selection as a cosmonaut he was commander of a naval air squadron with the Black Sea Fleet.

Gubarev became a cosmonaut in January 1963 and served in several support assignments, including capcom for Voskhod and Soyuz missions, before joining the Salyut training group in 1971. He was backup commander for Soyuz 12 in 1973.

Major General Gubarev is the author, with Vladimir Remek, of *International Orbit* (1983).

Gubarev and his wife, Nadizhda, have a son, Vladimir, and a daughter, Olga.

Illarionov, Valery

Valery Illarionov is a pilot cosmonaut who served as capcom for the Apollo-Soyuz Test Project at the NASA Johnson Space Center in Houston in July 1975. He has not flown in space.

Valery Vasilyevich Illarionov was born July 2, 1939, in Moscow. He served as an air force pilot and joined the cosmonaut group in 1965. He worked in the ground support team for Apollo-Soyuz, then began training for a long duration flight to Salyut 6. He had been chosen as backup commander for Soyuz 35, scheduled for launch in April 1980, when physical problems forced him to drop out.

He remains at Star Town as an instructor and equipment tester.

Ivanchenkov, Alexandr

Alexandr Ivanchenkov was flight engineer on two Soyuz flights, including a 140-day expedition aboard the Salyut 6 space station in 1978. During that flight, Soyuz 29, he and commander Vladimir Kovalenok broke the previous record of 96 days in space established by the crew of Soyuz 26. They performed the usual experiments in space manufacturing and Earth resources observations but, more importantly, were able to establish health maintenance and exercise routines which were of great value to later Salyut crews. (Both men were able to walk away from their Soyuz upon landing on Earth, in contrast to the Soyuz 26 cosmonauts.) They also learned valuable lessons about the effectiveness of their ground training when it was put to use in weightlessness. (They found that the procedures they had rehearsed on the ground to unload the Progress robot tankers were "useless" in space.)

Ivanchenkov and Kovalenok also conducted a spacewalk lasting just over 2 hours on June 29, 1978.

In June 1982 Ivanchenkov visited Salyut 7 for a week as a member of the Soyuz T-6 crew, which included French spationaut Jean-Loup Chretien.

Alexandr Sergeyevich Ivanchenkov was born September 28, 1940, in Ivanteyevka near Moscow. His father was killed in the Great Patriotic War when Sasha was just two years old. Ivanchenkov graduated from secondary school with a gold medal in 1958 and was admitted to the Moscow Aviation Institute, where he studied engineering and computer science. Upon graduation from MAI in 1964 he went to work at the Korolev spacecraft design bureau. While he was working at the bureau he learned to fly; his teacher was Colonel Sergei Anokhin, who had trained briefly as a cosmonaut.

Ivanchenkov joined the Party in 1972.

He was admitted to the cosmonaut group in May 1970 with another engineer and computer specialist, Boris Andreyev, and several young pilots. Three years later, after completing his preliminary training, Ivanchenkov, who is fluent in German and English, was assigned as a backup flight engineer for the Apollo-Soyuz Test Project. He made several trips to the United States for training and served on the backup crew for Soyuz 16, the ASTP dress rehearsal flown in December 1974.

Ivanchenkov and Yuri Romanenko trained as a Salyut expedition crew from late 1975 to October 1977, when they were reassigned in a shuffle of cosmonaut assignments following the Soyuz 25 abort. Ivanchenkov and Vladimir Kovalenok were backups for Soyuz 26 and Soyuz 27, and Ivanchenkov later served as backup flight engineer for Soyuz T-3 in 1980.

Since his second flight Ivanchenkov has returned to the Korolev bureau to work on the design and development of the Salyut-7 and Mir space stations. He remains a candidate for future flights.

Ivanchenkov and his wife, Rimma, a physician, have a daughter, Tatyana. They live in Moscow.

Kartashov, Anatoly

Anatoly Yakovlevich Kartashov was one of the first twenty Soviet cosmonauts who began training in March 1960. A highly regarded pilot, within two months he had earned a place among the six early finalists for the first manned space flight. However, when centrifuge tests began in July 1960, Kartashov developed pinpoint hermorrhaging along his spine. The super-cautious doctors grounded him in spite of a personal appeal by Yuri Gagarin, who said Kartashov "is the best among us. He will be the first man in space."

Kartashov later served as a pilot in the Soviet Far East, then became a test pilot based in Kiev. He is now retired.

Khrunov, Yevgeny

Yevgeny Khrunov became the first person to transfer from one manned spacecraft to another when he took a walk in space from Soyuz 5 to Soyuz 4 on January 15, 1969. Khrunov and fellow cosmonaut Alexei Yeliseyev completed the historic transfer in one hour.

Following their daring transfer to Soyuz 4, piloted by Lieutenant Colonel Vladimir Shatalov, Khrunov and Yeliseyev returned to Earth aboard that spacecraft, having spent forty-eight hours in space.

Yevgeny Vasilyevich Khrunov was born September 10, 1933, in the village of Prudy in the Tula region, south of Moscow. He attended the Kashina agricultural technical school but a newfound interest in flying caused him to join the Soviet air force in 1953. After graduation from the Serov Higher Air Force School in Bataisk in 1956, he served with future cosmonaut Viktor Gorbatko (who was one of his Bataisk schoolmates as well) in an air force squadron. He became a member of the Communist Party of the Soviet Union in 1959.

Chosen as one of the first cosmonauts in 1960, Khrunov was as a capcom during the flight of Yuri Gagarin. In the summer of 1963 he began to train for the world's first spacewalk, which was performed by Alexei Leonov in March 1965. Khrunov was his backup.

Trained for the Soyuz 2 mission, which was canceled because of the death of cosmonaut Vladimir Komarov aboard Soyuz 1, Khrunov finally went into space aboard Soyuz 5 on January 15, 1969. With him were crew commander Boris Volynov and flight engineer Yeliseyev.

Following his space flight, Khrunov returned to the Zhukovsky Military Engineering Academy, which he attended from 1961 to 1968, to perform graduate work, eventually earning a candidate's degree. In 1976 he also graduated from the Lenin Military-Political Academy. He was a training director for the Salyut 3 cosmonaut teams from 1972 to 1974, and was named backup commander of the joint Soviet-Cuban Soyuz 38 mission in 1980. This should have meant a second flight for Khrunov in 1981, but he is reported to have declined the assignment.

Khrunov has published several books, including textbooks on astronautics such as *Man as an Operator in Open Space*, (1976) about extra-vehicular activity; a science fiction novel, *The Way to Mars* (1979); and an autobiography, *The Conquest of Weightlessness* (1976). He is also the subject of a book, *Cosmonaut, Son of the Land of Tula* (1970).

Colonel Khrunov and his wife, Svetlana, have a son, Valery.

Kizim, Leonid

Leonid Kizim commanded the world's longest manned spaceflight, in which he and two fellow cosmonauts spent 237 days in space from February to November 1984, and in 1986 became the world space endurance champion when he spent an additional 125 days aboard the Salyut 7 and Mir stations as commander of Soyuz T-15.

Kizim and Vladimir Solovyov, a flight engineer, and Oleg Atkov, a cardiologist, were launched aboard Soyuz T-10 on February 8, 1984, and docked with the Salyut 7 station the next day. For the next eight months they performed experiments in space medicine, made astronomical observations, took detailed photographs of the Earth's surface, and tested space manufacturing techniques. They were host to two teams of visiting cosmonauts, one of which included Indian pilot Rakesh Sharma.

Kizim and Solovyov performed a record six different spacewalks, most of them aimed at repairing the Salyut's main rocket engines, which had been badly damaged in a refueling accident the previous year.

The long spaceflight meant that Kizim was in space when his daughter Galina was born on May 24, 1984. When the Soyuz T-12 cosmonauts visited the space station in July, they brought Kizim videotapes of the little girl.

The three cosmonauts returned to Earth on October 1, 1984, in frail physical condition (Kizim had trouble walking for several days after landing), but within three weeks they were back to normal and Soviet space doctors were predicting that manned flights lasting a year or longer were possible.

As a further step toward a permanent manned presence in space, Soviet program managers launched what was described as a "third generation" station, called *Mir* (Peace), on February 19, 1986. Mir outwardly resembled Salyut 7, but its interior had been re-designed to provide more comfortable accommodations for as many as six cosmonauts. Scientific and engineering experiments that occupied volume inside Salyut were moved to add-on vehicles, which could be attached to Mir's special five-port docking module.

In late 1985 Kizim and Solovyov were chosen for the difficult double task of activating the new station and continuing operations with the still-functioning Salyut 7.

The Soyuz T-15 launch on March 13, 1986, was, in a break with past Soviet practice, announced publicly in advance, and televised live. Two days later Kizim and Solovyov reached Mir and transferred to it.

Since Mir and Salyut 7 were in almost identical orbits, it was possible for the two cosmonauts, once their initial work aboard Mir was complete, to re-board Soyuz T-15, separate it, and transfer to Salyut 7. This, the first maneuver of its kind in space history, took place on May 5, 1986, and required 28 hours.

While aboard Salyut 7, Kizim and Solovyov took two additional spacewalks, constructing a 50-foot tower in addition to retrieving scientific experiments abandoned by the previous occupants, cosmonauts Vasyutin, Savinykh and Volkov.

Kizim and Solovyov used Soyuz T-15 to return to Mir on June 25 and June 26, and landed back on Earth on July 16.

Soyuz T-15 was Leonid Kizim's third space flight. In addition to Soyuz T-10, in November and December 1980 he commanded a crew of three Soyuz T-3 cosmonauts who performed repairs on the Salyut 6 station, which at that time had been in operation for three years.

Kizim has spent almost 376 days in space, and has logged over 31 hours of EVA time.

Leonid Denisovich Kizim was born August 5, 1941, in the city of Krasny Liman in the Donetsk region of the Ukraine. At the age of 18 he was enrolled in the Chernigov Lenin Komsomol Higher Air Force School and graduated as a pilot in 1963. For the next two years he served as an air force pilot in the Caucasus before being invited to join the cosmonaut team.

He became a Party member in 1966.

Kizim was one of 20 young pilots and flight engineers who began cosmonaut training in November 1965. In 1967 he completed the basic course and was assigned to test pilot work, flying ten different types of aircraft and earning a Test Pilot 3rd Class rating. In October 1969 he was a support cosmonaut for the Soyuz 6, 7, and 8 missions. From 1971 to 1975 he attended the Yuri Gagarin Red Banner Air Force Academy.

In 1976 he joined a group of cosmonauts helping in the development of an advanced Soyuz spacecraft, eventually known as the Soyuz T (for Transport). He served as backup commander for Soyuz T-2, the first manned flight of the new vehicle. After his first spaceflight he served as backup commander for the Soviet-French Soyuz T-6 mission in 1982, and for the aborted Soyuz T-10-1 in September 1983.

Colonel Kizim lives with his wife, Galina, and their two children in Star Town.

Klimuk, Pyotr

Pyotr Klimuk commanded three manned space flights before he was 36, the age when many cosmonauts are making their first.

As commander of Soyuz 13 in December 1973, Klimuk and engineer Valentin Lebedev flew an eight-day astronomical mission using the Orion observatory (which had been developed for use in Salyut space stations) to observe the comet Kahoutek.

From May to July 1975, Klimuk and Vitaly Sevastyanov occupied the Salyut 4 space station. Their Soyuz 18 mission lasted a total of 63 days, a Soviet record. Most of the cosmonauts' time was devoted to studies of the Earth's surface; they took over 2000 photographs of suspected ore deposits and other features. They also used a special telescope to photograph the Sun. The mission was not without its challenges: the Salyut environmental system allowed the station's internal humidity to rise to uncomfortable levels, fogging the windows and causing green mold to grow on the walls.

Klimuk's third flight came as commander of Soyuz 31 in July 1978. With him on that eight-day Interksomos mission, which docked with Salyut 6, was Polish researcher Miroslaw Hermaszewski.

Klimuk has logged almost 79 days in space.

Pyotr Ilyich Klimuk was born July 10, 1942, in the city of Komarovka, near Brest in Byelorussia. His father was killed in the Great Patriotic War. At the age of 18 Klimuk entered the military, attending the Chernigov Higher Air Force School from 1960 to 1964, then served as a fighter pilot. He joined the Party in 1963.

In March 1965 Klimuk and dozens of other young military pilots and engineers were invited to take medical examinations for the cosmonaut team. Those who passed reported to Star Town in October and November of that year.

Soviet space program managers were recruiting their third cosmonaut group with their third set of qualifications. The most recent selectees, the January 1963 cosmonauts, were all graduates of military academies who had held commands or research posts and averaged 30 years of age. The Klimuk group, as it came to be known, eventually consisted of 20 pilots and engineers who averaged 24 years of age and had no academy training or command experience. The intent was to train bright young men specifically for spaceflight and not for war.

After completing the two-year basic training course Klimuk was immediately assigned to the Soviet lunar program. When that program was shelved in 1969 he transferred to the new Salyut cosmonaut group, making three flights in the next nine years. While working as an active cosmonaut Klimuk graduated from the Gagarin Red Banner Air Force Academy in 1977 and from the Lenin Military Political Academy in 1984.

Since 1978 Major General Klimuk has been the deputy director of the Gagarin Cosmonaut Training Center for political affairs. He has been a member of the Supreme Soviet (1980-82) and a member of the Central Committee of the Communist Party. He has also published an autobiography, *Next to the Stars* (1979).

Klimuk and his wife, Liliya, a physican, have a son, Mikhail, and a daughter, Natasha.

Komarov, Vladimir

Vladimir Komarov was the first person to die in space. The tragedy occurred on April 24, 1967, during the return to Earth of Soyuz 1, which had been launched the day before.

Soyuz 1 was a highly ambitious mission, intended to be the first manned test of a brand-new spacecraft which was designed to take Soviet cosmonauts to the Moon. Soyuz 1, piloted by Komarov, was to dock in space with Soyuz 2, crewed by cosmonauts Bykovsky, Yeliseyev and Khrunov, at which time Khrunov and Yeliseyev would transfer from one vehicle to the other by spacewalk.

But Soyuz 1 developed guidance problems during its first few hours in orbit, making the spacecraft difficult to orient. In addition, one of the two solar panels aboard the spacecraft failed to deploy, depriving Soyuz 1 of much of its power. The Soyuz 2 launch was canceled and flight controllers tried to return Komarov safely to Earth, something which would normally occur on the sixteenth orbit. The situation was apparently so serious that Komarov's family and Soviet Premier Kosygin were rushed to mission control at Yevpatoria in the Crimea.

Only on their third try—orbit eighteen—were controllers successful in getting Soyuz 1 into a proper orientation for re-entry. But problems forced Komarov to use a "ballistic" re-entry mode, in which the spacecraft spins like a bullet, rather than the normal mode. Fighting unusually high G-forces, with a damaged guidance system, Komarov was unable to stop Soyuz 1 from spinning, and when its parachutes deployed the lines fouled, preventing the chutes from opening. Komarov's struggles were heard by Americans at a listening post in Norway right up to the moment Soyuz 1 crashed at several hundred miles an hour to the Orenburg steppe, 25 miles from the settlement of Novoorsk. Komarov was killed instantly.

Vladimir Mikhailovich Komarov was born in Moscow on March 16, 1927. He attended a prep school for potential air force pilots from 1942 to 1945, then went on to the Borisoglebsk Higher Air Force School and, finally, to the Bataisk Higher Air Force School, from which he graduated in 1949. He served in units of the Soviet air force as a pilot and instructor pilot and became a member of the Party in 1952. From 1954 to 1959 he attended the Zhukovsky Military Engineering Academy and had embarked on a career as a tester of aircraft equipment when he was invited to try out for the cosmonaut team.

Selected for the first group in 1960, Komarov quickly became known for his intelligence and piloting skills, and also for his bad luck. He had to undergo a hernia operation on May 15, 1960, that came close to ending his cosmonaut career before it really started. He spent six months recuperating and trying to keep up with his studies. In 1962, after he was named as backup to cosmonaut Pavel Popovich for Vostok 4, a medical examination showed that Komarov had an irregular heartbeat, a condition very similar to the one which grounded American astronaut Donald Slayton for ten years. Komarov had to submit to dozens of tests by a variety of cardiologists before he was allowed to continue his cosmonaut career.

But in April 1964, when Soviet Chief Designer Korolev needed a pilot for the world's first space "team," it was Komarov who was selected, and on October 16, 1964, he went into space aboard Voskhod 1. With him were an engineer from the Korolev design bureau, Konstantin Feoktistov, and a young aerospace physician, Boris Yegorov. They returned safely to Earth after twenty-four hours.

Komarov, who had been the chief cosmonaut member of the Soyuz design team, returned to his work on that spacecraft in September of 1966, and was named to command its maiden flight. He was the first Soviet cosmonaut to make two space flights.

Komarov left a widow, Valentina, who still works as a librarian at Star Town, a son, Zhena, and a daughter, Irina. He was the subject of a biography, *Tester of Spaceships*, written by his close friend and fellow cosmonaut Vasily Lazarev (in collaboration with Mikhail Rebrov), published in 1976.

A Soviet space tracking vessel was later named for Komarov, as was the Yeisk Higher Air Force School.

Kovalenok, Vladimir

Vladimir Kovalenok made three visits to the Salyut 6 space station between 1977 and 1981, two of them for long-duration missions.

He was commander of Soyuz 25, launched October 9, 1977, for a planned 90-day stay aboard Salyut 6, a mission which would have included activation of the station. But technical problems forced the docking to be cancelled and Kovalenok and flight engineer Valery Ryumin returned to Earth after only two days.

Kovalenok's next visit, as commander of Soyuz 29 with flight engineer Alexandr Ivanchenkov, was much more successful. The two cosmonauts occupied Salyut 6 from June 16, 1978, until November 2, 1978, spending over 139 days in space, a record at the time. During their mission they hosted visits from two Interkosmos crews and three Progress supply vehicles while carrying out space manufacturing and Earth resources work. Kovalenok and Ivanchenkov also performed an EVA of two hours and five minutes on June 29, 1978.

Following the repair of Salyut 6 by three other cosmonauts in late 1980, Kovalenok and flight engineer Viktor Savinykh were launched March 13, 1981, aboard Soyuz T-4. During their 75 days in space they were visited by two more Interkosmos crews.

On his three flights Kovalenok has logged over 216 days in space, including two hours of EVA time.

Vladimir Vasilyevich Kovalenok was born March 3, 1942, in the town of Beloye in the Minsk district of Byelorussia. He attended the Balashov Higher Air Force School from 1959 to 1963 and served as a crew commander flying An–24 transport planes in the Soviet air force, logging over 1600 hours of flying time. He also became a parachute instructor. He joined the Party in 1962.

Kovalenok applied for the 1965 cosmonaut selection and was accepted, but placed in a reserve group. While waiting to start cosmonaut training he flew search aircraft for returning space vehicles. He became a cosmonaut in May 1967.

Kovalenok joined the Salyut training group in 1972 and was backup commander to Soyuz 18 in 1975. He was also backup commander to Soyuz 26, Soyuz 27 and Soyuz 35. At the same time he was actively training for Salyut missions he graduated from the Gagarin Red Banner Air Force Academy in 1976.

Since his space flights Colonel Kovalenok has been politically active as a deputy in the Supreme Soviet of the Byelorussian Soviet Socialist Republic. He attended the International Astronautical Federation congress in Munich in 1979. In 1986 he was reported to be chief of a technical division at the Baikonov Cosmodrome.

Kovalenok and his wife, Nina, have a daughter, Inessa, and a son, Vladimir.

Kubasov, Valery

Valery Kubasov became the world's first space construction worker when, as flight engineer of Soyuz 6 in October 1969, he operated a prototype welding unit that may one day be used in the assembly of orbiting space stations. The Vulcan unit, as it was called, remained in the orbit module of Soyuz 6 and was operated by remote control by Kubasov, who remained inside the re-entry module with commander Georgy Shonin. It was the single highlight of a space flight whose original goals are still obscure: the simultaneous flight of three manned Soyuz spacecraft, 6, 7, and 8, carrying seven cosmonauts, for one week. Indications are that Soyuz 7 and Soyuz 8 were to have docked, but technical problems prevented it.

Kubasov later served as flight engineer for the least obscure mission in the history of the Soviet space program, the Soviet half of the Apollo-Soyuz Test Project. For six days Kubasov and commander Alexei Leonov orbited the Earth in Soyuz 19, remaining docked with the American Apollo spacecraft for two of those days. It was the culmination of a two-year training and public relations program which saw astronauts and cosmonauts exchanging visits to each other's space centers.

On his third space flight Kubasov served as commander with Hungarian pilot Bertalan Farkas as cosmonaut-researcher. This Interkosmos mission lasted eight days, during which Kubasov and Farkas visited cosmonauts Popov and Ryumin aboard the Salyut-6 space station.

Kubasov has spent almost 19 days in space.

Valery Nikolayevich Kubasov was born January 7, 1935, in Vyazniki, a city northeast of Moscow. His father was a mechanic and Kubasov grew up around machines. His aptitude for mathematics and excellent grades in secondary school earned him admittance to the Moscow Aviation Institute in 1952. He didn't even have to take the entrance exams. Upon graduation in 1958, Kubasov, now an aerospace engineer, immediately went to work at the Korolev spacecraft design bureau. At first he was involved in ballistics, the calculation of spacecraft trajectories, but he later went to work under Mikhail Tikhonravov, Korolev's chief deputy, on the Voskhod spacecraft.

He joined the Party in 1968.

Kubasov was one of the young engineers in Korolev's "kindergarten" who deluged the chief designer with applications for cosmonaut training the moment they found out, in the spring of 1964, that Konstantin Feoktistov, one of their chiefs, was to be included in the first Voskhod crew. Kubasov was told to wait, finally beginning space training in the summer of 1966 with seven other engineers. He was chosen as a backup crewman for the proposed dual flight of Soyuz 1 and Soyuz

2 scheduled for April 1967, working with Yuri Gagarin and Viktor Gorbatko on techniques for walking in space from one docked Soyuz to another. Soyuz 2 was not launched, however, owing to problems that arose early in the Soyuz 1 mission, and the death of cosmonaut Vladimir Komarov at the end of that flight forced an 18-month suspension of Soviet manned launches. When they resumed, Kubasov remained as backup for Soyuz 4.

Following Soyuz 6, Kubasov served as backup for the 19-day Soyuz 9 flight of cosmonauts Nikolayev and Sevastyanov in 1970, then trained for a 60-day visit to the new Salyut space station. But the first crew sent to Salyut failed to go aboard the station. Kubasov, commander Alexei Leonov and a still-unidentified military research engineer then prepared for a shorter, 30-day mission, only to see that disappear when Kubasov developed a lung ailment which removed him from flight status. Their replacements, Georgy Dobrovolsky, Vladislav Volkov and Viktor Patsayev, spent 24 days aboard Salyut, but were killed during a re-entry accident. According to one report, Leonov visited Kubasov in the hospital and broke the news to him that the others had died in their spacecraft.

As soon as Kubasov regained his health, he and Leonov trained as a two-man team for Salyut missions in 1972 and 1973 which could not be launched because of Salyut failures. Following the second of these, in May 1973, they were assigned to Apollo-Soyuz. Neither of them spoke English but, as cosmonaut chief Vladimir Shatalov pointed out to them, they had two years and two months in which to learn.

During his encounters with American astronauts Kubasov rarely spoke, in marked contrast to the ebullient Leonov. Soviet reporters also describe Kubasov as reserved.

After Apollo-Soyuz, Kubasov trained for a flight to Salyut 6, serving first as backup commander for the joint Soviet-Polish Soyuz 30 in 1978. He continues to work at Star Town (he helped train the French spationauts Chretien and Baudry) and at the spacecraft design bureau and remains eligible for future space flights.

He is the author of several technical papers and of a memoir, *To Touch Space* (1984).

Kubasov and his wife, Ludmilla, who is also an aerospace engineer, have a daughter, Katya, and a son, Dmitri.

Lazarev, Vasily

Vasily Lazarev is a test pilot and physician who had the bad luck to command the Soviet Union's first launch abort.

Lazarev and flight engineer Oleg Makarov, who had trained together for five years, were launched toward the orbiting Salyut 4 space station on April 5, 1975, for a planned 60 day mission. In September 1973 these same two cosmonauts had flown the two-day Soyuz 12 mission, which requalified the Soviet spacecraft for manned flight following the Soyuz 11 disaster. This new, long-duration mission would set a Soviet space record and, with the presence of a veteran aerospace physician, would provide new insights into human adaptability to weightlessness.

But just minutes after launch from the Baikonur Cosmodrome, at a height of about 90 miles—the point where the Soyuz launcher drops its second stage and continues to orbit using the single third stage engine—a malfunction occurred. The explosive bolts that should have separated the stages failed. The third stage engine ignited with the massive second stage still attached, and the whole vehicle began to tumble out of control. Ground controllers had no choice but to separate the Soyuz from the errant rocket. Lazarev and Makarov endured a painful 18-G re-entry that landed them on a mountainside near the Soviet-Chinese border. Their "flight" lasted just 22 minutes—the shortest in Soviet space history—and was later known as the April 5th Anomaly, and finally as Soyuz 18-1.

It is thought that Lazarev, who was 47 at the time of Soyuz 18-1, suffered injuries during the re-entry that made him ineligible for future missions, though on one occasion he did serve as a backup cosmonaut.

During his two flights he logged less than 48 hours in space.

Vasily Grigoryevich Lazarev was born February 23, 1928, in the village of Poroshino in the Altai Krai mountains of Soviet Siberia. He grew up in the city of Sverdlovsk and attended the medical institute there from 1948 to 1951, intending to become a surgeon. During his final year he switched his field of study to aerospace medicine and transferred to the Saratov Medical Institute, where he received his degree in 1952. He then spent two years at the Chuguyev Higher Air Force School becoming a military pilot. He joined the Party in 1956.

Lazarev served initially as an air force flight surgeon but later became involved in testing new equipment for aircraft. He took part in a series of flights in Volga-class high-altitude balloons, during which test subjects wearing prototype pressure suits were carried to altitudes of twenty miles, from which they parachuted to Earth. He joined the team of specialists at the Korolev design bureau testing equipment to be used in manned spacecraft. Lazarev became close friends with one of the other engineers, Vladimir Komarov.

Lazarev applied for the cosmonaut team three times, in 1959, 1962 and 1964 before finally earning admittance. For several weeks in the summer of 1964 he was a "reserve" for the two teams training for the first Voskhod flight, but he did not become a cosmonaut until 1966. He immediately joined the Soyuz training group—he worked on Soyuz 1 with his old friend Vladimir Komarov—and was backup commander for Soyuz 9 in 1970. He began training for Salyut flights in 1971.

Since 1976 Lazarev has supervised the training of cosmonauts from countries other than the USSR. He has co-authored a biography of cosmonaut Vladimir Komarov, *Spacecraft Test Pilot* (1976).

For several months in 1980, at the age of 52, he came out of retirement to act as backup commander for the Soyuz T-3/Salyut 6 mission.

He and his wife, Luiza, have a son, Alexandr, a military pilot.

Lebedev, Valentin

Valentin Lebedev was flight engineer aboard the Soyuz T-5 mission to Salyut 7 in 1982. Lebedev and commander Anatoly Berezovoy spent seven months in space, performing a variety of technical and scientific work, deploying two student satellites, and playing host to visitors who included French spationaut Jean-Loup Chretien and the second woman space traveler, Svetlana Savistkaya.

In excerpts from his diary, published in Soviet newspapers after his return to Earth, Lebedev was frank about the experience of such a long mission, discussing the joy with which he and Berezovoy greeted the Soyuz T-7 crew (understandably, they weren't quite so relaxed about the Soyuz T-6 visit, which included a Westerner) and the nervousness they felt before a spacewalk. He also wrote candidly that while he and Berezovoy both thought they knew each other well before the flight, they were wrong. Both men were nitpickers and worriers and occasionally got on each other's nerves. Both cosmonauts have since suggested that space teams should consist of people with opposite personality traits.

Lebedev was in an earlier space crew, that of Soyuz 13 in December 1973. He and commander Pyotr Klimuk spent eight days in orbit using the Orion observatory to do astronomical studies of Comet Kahoutek.

He has logged over 219 days in space and 2.5 hours of EVA.

Valentin Vitalyevich Lebedev was born April 14, 1942, in Moscow. After completing secondary school in 1958, Lebedev, who was fascinated by aviation, attended the Orenburg air force school, the same one which trained Yuri Gagarin to be a pilot, for a year. In 1960 he enrolled in the Moscow Aviation Institute, graduating six years later as an aerospace engineer, when he went to work in the Korolev spacecraft design bureau.

There he acted as a test engineer for new spacecraft systems, served on search-and-rescue teams, and prepared flight documentation for use by cosmonauts. He also took pilot instruction from former cosmonaut Sergei Anokhin and became qualified in jets and helicopters.

He joined the Party in 1971.

Lebedev applied for cosmonaut training while he was still a student at MAI, and again as soon as he went to work for the Korolev bureau in 1966. He was eventually allowed to take the physical examinations, and was admitted to the cosmonaut group in 1972, where he was immediately assigned to a team training for scientific Soyuz missions, those not flown to Salyut space stations. When two different Salyuts failed to reach orbit in the spring of 1973, Lebedev was teamed with pilot Klimuk from the Salyut group in order to fly astronomical experiments which would have been on those stations. Following Soyuz 13 Lebedev completed work on a candidate of technical sciences degree (1974).

Later that year he began to train for a long-duration flight aboard Salyut 6. He was preparing for the Soyuz 35 launch in March 1980 when he injured his knee while jumping on a trampoline. (Lebedev is chairman of the USSR Federation of Acrobatics.) Forced to undergo surgery, he had to give up his place on the Soyuz 35 crew. He was assigned to the very next long duration mission, Soyuz T-5.

Lebedev continues to work at the spacecraft design bureau and remains a candidate for future flights. He is also head of a group at MAI working on the massive Baikal-Amur Railway.

He and his wife, Ludmilla, an engineer, have a son, Vitaly. They live in Moscow.

Leonov, Alexei

Alexei Leonov became the first man to walk in space when he floated outside the spacecraft Voskhod 2 for ten minutes on March 18, 1965.

It was during the second orbit of the Voskhod 2 flight, just as the spacecraft approached the Soviet Union, that Leonov, clad in a white pressure suit and wearing a backpack which would supply him with oxygen, crawled into a cylindrical airlock that had been inflated on the side of Voskhod. Commander Pavel Belyayev closed the inner hatch behind Leonov and, moments later, after the air had been bled out of the airlock, Leonov, secured by a safety line, opened the outer hatch and uncovered a movie camera. Then he pushed himself away from the spacecraft, stretching the lifeline to its 17.5-foot limit, and pulled himself back. Inside Voskhod, Belyayev heard scraping noises as Leonov's feet contacted the spacecraft.

Minutes later Leonov was back inside Voskhod 2, after a nervous moment when he discovered that his pressure suit was so rigid he could not bend enough to get inside the airlock. He quickly solved the problem by bleeding some of the air out of his suit.

Leonov and Belyayev were to experience further unplanned adventure. The next day, as ground controllers prepared to fire the Voskhod retrorockets and return the craft to Earth, the cosmonauts noticed that their ship was facing the wrong direction. Belyayev activated the manual control system and fired the retrorockets on the next orbit.

The delay, however, meant that Voskhod 2 did not land in the prime recovery area, but in the snowy Ural mountains near the city of Perm. Though they were able to make radio contact with rescue teams, the cosmonauts were forced to spend a cold night in the wilderness.

Leonov, a gifted athlete and pilot who had also trained himself to be a painter, was later chosen to command the Soviet crew for the Apollo-Soyuz Test Project. During this weeklong mission in July 1975, Leonov and flight engineer Valery Kubasov spent two days docked with three American astronauts aboard an Apollo spacecraft.

During two flights Leonov has logged approximately seven days in space.

Alexei Arkhipovich Leonov was born May 30, 1934, in the village of Listvyanka in the Altai region of Siberia. He came from a large family and decided to become a pilot after one of his older brothers became an air force mechanic. First he attended the Kremenchug prep school for pilots, then the Chuguyev Higher Air Force school in the Ukraine, graduating in 1957. He served as a jet pilot with a unit based in East Germany and was a student at the Zhukovsky Air Force Engineering Academy in October 1959 when selections began for the manned space program.

Of the first twenty Soviet cosmonauts, who began training in March 1960, Leonov was the least senior in rank, a fact which subjected him to some good-natured teasing. But his quick wit and cheerful temperament won him many friends, and according to at least one published report he was an early candidate to make the world's first flight into space, until concern over the Vostok hatch and ejection seat encouraged program managers to choose cosmonauts Gagarin and Titov, who were several inches shorter than Leonov. Nevertheless, Leonov was actively involved in Gagarin's flight, acting as assistant capcom.

In early 1963 Leonov's space career and his life almost came to an end when his car skidded off an icy road near Moscow and plunged into a lake. Leonov managed to pull his wife and his driver from the icy water, and by that summer he was training to take the world's first walk in space.

After Voskhod 2 Leonov was named deputy commander of the cosmonaut team, supervising EVA training for the planned Soyuz 1/Soyuz 2 space walk and serving as launch capcom for that ill-fated mission. He also completed studies at the Zhukovsky Academy and was involved for two years in the Soviet manned lunar landing program. When that effort was shelved in 1969 he began to train for a long duration mission aboard a Salyut space station.

In the spring of 1971 Leonov, flight engineer Valery Kubasov and a still-unnamed research engineer were preparing to make the second visit to Salyut 1 when the first visit was aborted after only two days. Before Leonov's crew could be launched as replacements, however, Kubasov developed a lung ailment, forcing space program managers to turn to a third crew, Dobrovolsky, Volkov and Patsayev, who spent 24 days aboard Salyut 1 but died returning to Earth.

In May 1973 Leonov and Kubasov were assigned to the Apollo-Soyuz Test Project, becoming frequent visitors to the United States (where Leonov impressed American astronauts with his charm and humor) and hosting visits by their NASA counterparts.

Since Apollo-Soyuz Major General Leonov has served as deputy director of the Gagarin Cosmonaut Center as chief of international or guest cosmonauts. In 1985 he and Kubasov traveled to the United States for the ten-year anniversary commemoration of the Apollo-Soyuz Test Project.

Leonov has published three art books, *Wait for Us, Stars* (1967), *Stellar Roads* (1977) and *Life Among the Stars* (1981), all in collaboration with artist Andrei Sokolov. He remains the editor and chief designer of the cosmonaut group newspaper *Neptune*, which is now called *Apogee*. He has also co-authored a screenplay, *Star System* (1979).

He and his wife, Svetlana, a teacher, have two daughters, Viktoria and Oksana.

Lyakhov, Vladimir

Vladimir Lyakhov commanded two difficult long-duration flights aboard Salyut space stations in 1979 and in 1983.

Launched into space aboard Soyuz 32 in February 1979, Lyakhov and flight engineer Valery Ryumin performed experiments in radio astronomy, Earth resources, and space manufacturing on Salyut-6 while establishing a new endurance record of 175 days. According to Ryumin's diary, the flight was especially difficult psychologically because the cosmonauts had no visitors. One relief crew was forced to return to Earth before docking in April, and a second flight planned for July was postponed.

Lyakhov's second long stay in space was equally challenging. He and flight engineer Alexandr Alexandrov docked their Soyuz T-9 spacecraft with the Salyut 7 space station on June 28, 1983, for a mission scheduled to last two months. A fuel leak aboard Salyut forced the cosmonauts to curtail many of their scientific studies, which lengthened the mission, and then on September 26 a manned resupply craft was forced to abort at launch. Lyakhov and Alexandrov were left aboard Salyut 7 with a Soyuz T-9 vehicle that was close to exceeding its safe design lifetime. Nevertheless, after performing repairs—including emergency EVAs—on the station, Lyakhov and Alexandrov returned safely to Earth on November 23, 1983.

Lyakhov has spent over 354 days in space.

Vladimir Afanaseyevich Lyakhov was born July 20, 1941, in Antratsit in the Voroshilovgrad region of the Ukraine. At the age of 19 he enrolled in the Kharkov Higher Air Force School, graduating in 1964, then served as an air force pilot based on Sakhalin Island in the Far East. He became a Party member in 1963.

Lyakhov applied for the November 1965 cosmonaut group but was placed in reserve, finally reporting in May 1967. During his early years as a cosmonaut he qualified as a test pilot third class and attended the Gagarin Red Banner Air Force Academy. In 1975 he was assigned to the Salyut cosmonaut group and was backup commander to Soyuz 29. Later assignments included backup commander for the Soviet-Mongolian flight in 1980, and for Soyuz T-5 and Soyuz T-8.

Colonel Lyakhov's wife, Zinaida, is an economist. They have a son and a daughter.

Makarov, Oleg

Oleg Makarov was the flight engineer for four Soviet space flights between 1973 and 1980, twice visiting the Salyut 6 station he had helped design.

Makarov's first flight was Soyuz 12 in September 1973, the first Soviet manned mission in the wake of the Soyuz 11 tragedy which killed three cosmonauts. Following the accident the Soyuz command module had been re-designed to allow two cosmonauts to wear pressure suits, if necessary, during launch and re-entry. Weight and volume limitations had made it impossible for Soyuz to carry three cosmonauts with suits, so cosmonauts from Soyuz 1 through Soyuz 11 had not worn them. Makarov and commander Vasily Lazarev, who had been training for a long duration mission aboard a Salyut station, only to see it postponed when their 1973 Salyut failed to reach orbit, returned safely to Earth after just two days.

On April 5, 1975, Makarov and Lazarev were launched aboard Soyuz 18 for a planned 60-day mission aboard Salyut 4, which had been occupied for 30 days by cosmonauts Alexei Gubarev and Georgy Grechko. But only minutes into the flight problems developed with the Soyuz booster. The Soyuz command module containing Makarov and Lazarev was separated from the booster and plunged back to Earth, eventually coming to rest on a Siberian mountainside near the Chinese border. The emergency re-entry profile forced the cosmonauts to endure as many as 18 Gs, twice the normal load, and may have caused injuries. Certainly Lazarev never flew in space again.

Makarov did, twice, with better luck. He was aboard Soyuz 27 in January 1978, a weeklong flight during which he and commander Vladimir Dzhanibekov docked with the Salyut 6 station, swapping vehicles with the Soyuz 26 crew of Yuri Romanenko and Georgy Grechko, who were in the first month of a planned three-month mission. It was a rehearsal for future operations that permitted cosmonauts to remain aboard Salyut stations for missions lasting nine months.

In November 1980 Makarov returned to Salyut 6 as a member of the Soyuz T-3 crew. The three-man crew of Makarov, Leonid Kizim and Gennady Strekalov overhauled several systems inside Salyut 6 during their 13 days in space, permitting Salyut 6 to be occupied in early 1981 for another long duration mission.

Oleg Grigoryevich Makarov was born January 6, 1933, in Udomlia in the Kalinin region near Moscow. As a boy he became interested in space travel rather than airplanes, and earned admittance to the Bauman Higher Technical School in Moscow, planning to become a rocket scientist. His timing was perfect: upon graduation in 1957 he immediately went to work in Sergei Korolev's spacecraft design bureau and was involved in the development of Vostok, the world's first manned spaceship. He also lectured to the cosmonaut group. In 1961 he joined the Party.

He played an important role in the preparations for Voskhod-1 during 1964. One of the Voskhod crewmen was Makarov's friend and former boss, engineer Konstantin Feoktistov. As soon as Makarov learned that Feoktistov had been chosen to fly in space he applied himself, and two years later, during which he helped design the new Soyuz spacecraft, Makarov joined the cosmonaut team.

From 1966 to 1969 Makarov was involved in the Soviet manned lunar program. Had such a flight actually occurred, Makarov might have been one of the first cosmonauts to walk on the Moon. But the program was put on hiatus in early 1969 and Makarov began to train for a mission aboard a Salyut space station. In 1970 he was teamed with test pilot and physician Vasily Lazarev.

In addition to his four space flights, Makarov was a backup for Soyuz T-2 in 1980. Between active flight training he continued to work at the spacecraft bureau and is now a senior engineer.

In 1981 he earned his candidate of technical sciences degree and published a futuristic work, *The Sails of Stellar Brigantines*, written in collaboration with Grigory Nemetsky.

Makarov and his wife, Valentina, who is employed in a design office, have two sons, Leonid and Konstantin.

Malyshev, Yuri

Yuri Malyshev commanded the first manned test flight of a redesigned Soyuz spacecraft, Soyuz T-2 in June 1980. Malyshev and flight engineer Vladimir Aksenov made a successful rendezvous and docking with the orbiting Salyut 6 space station in spite of the failure of the new Soyuz T guidance computer. They returned to Earth after four days.

Four years later Malyshev commanded his second flight, Soyuz T-ll, which also carried Indian pilot Rakesh Sharma into space, spending a week aboard Salyut 7.

Yuri Vasilyevich Malyshev was born August 27, 1941, in Nikolayevsk, a city near Volgograd, then known as Stalingrad. The Great Patriotic War had begun and Stalingrad and environs were the sight of a long siege, so Malyshev's early years were very difficult. He did not see his father, a soldier, until he was almost four years old.

Malyshev originally enrolled in the Kacha Higher Air Force School in Volgograd, but transferred to the Kharkov School, graduating in 1963. He served as a fighter-bomber pilot flying MiG-17s and MiG-21s until joining the cosmonaut group in May 1967. He became a Party member in 1964.

Malyshev was one of several pilots originally screened and approved in March 1965, but whose enrollment in the space program was postponed for eighteen months because only twenty could be trained at a time. He finally reported to Star Town just weeks after the death of cosmonaut Vladimir Komarov in the Soyuz 1 accident, while Komarov's colleagues and friends, including Pavel Belyayev, Malyshev's new boss, were still in a state of shock. Training proceeded, however, and by 1969 Malyshev had completed the basic course. He was then sent to test pilot school, earning a Test Pilot Third Class rating, and after that, to the Gagarin Air Force Academy, graduating in 1977.

In 1976 Malyshev served as backup commander to the Soyuz 22 Earth resources mission flown by Valery Bykovsky and Vladimir Aksenov. Malyshev and Aksenov worked together in the new Soyuz T program.

Following his first flight Malyshev was chosen to command Soyuz T-6, the Soviet-French mission, and trained with flight engineer Alexandr Ivanchenkov and French spationaut Jean-Loup Chretien for many months. In January 1982, six months prior to the scheduled launch, Soviet officials announced that Malyshev had been replaced by Vladimir Dzhanibekov because of health problems, but it was later learned that Malyshev and Chretien were not getting along. Malyshev spent 1982 supervising the training of a new cosmonaut group, then assumed command of the Soviet-Indian prime crew.

Colonel Malyshev is married and the father of a son and a daughter.

Nelyubov, Grigori

Grigori Grigoryevich Nelyubov was one of the most talented pilots in the first group of Soviet cosmonauts but never flew in space.

Nelyubov was a navy pilot who served the with Black Sea Fleet prior to becoming a cosmonaut in March 1960. By the end of the first year of training he had become one of the six finalists for the first manned flight.

According to memoirs by fellow cosmonauts Shonin and Popovich and a stunningly frank account in *Izvestia* by journalist Yaroslav Golovanov in 1986, Nelyubov was brilliant, witty and a good athlete in addition to being competitive, outspoken, and arrogant. He tried to set an endurance record in the heat chamber, for example, and criticized some training programs to chief designer Korolev himself. He was also quite open about his desire to be the first man in space. Nevertheless, he was one of the best pilots in the group. As Popovich wrote, "His flying made us forgive the defects in his character."

Nelyubov was the second backup to Gagarin on the first Vostok flight and accompanied him to the launch pad that day. He had been chosen as number one backup to Popovich for the Vostok 4 flight planned for 1962, but earned a dismissal from the cosmonaut team.

Some time after Titov's flight in August 1961, Nelyubov and fellow cosmonauts Ivan Anikeyev and Valentin Filatyev got into an altercation with militia at a railway depot. (Rumors have persisted for years that some heretofore unidentified Soviet cosmonauts were dropped from the program because of a drunken brawl.) Nelyubov arrogantly threatened to go over the head of the arresting officers if they dared to make a report. The directors of the cosmonaut center were called and a deal was struck: the report would not be made, but Nelyubov would have to apologize to the officers. Nelyubov refused. The report wound up on the desk of General Kamanin, the head of the cosmonaut team. Furious, he fired Nelyubov, Anikeyev and Filatyev.

Nelyubov, as might be expected, was sent to the Far East to serve as an interceptor pilot. It was very difficult for him to see not only his comrades from the "first six" going into space—Nikolayev, Popovich, Bykovsky—but also others who had not rated as highly as he had, such as Komarov. He would tell people that he had been a cosmonaut, a backup to the famous Gagarin, no less, but was not often believed. On February 18, 1966, while drunk, he was hit by a train and killed on a railroad bridge at Ippolitovka in the Far East.

Nikolayev, Andrian

Andrian Nikolayev set endurance records on both of his flights into space. He was the pilot of Vostok 3 in August 1962, spending four days in space. At that time the American record totaled nine hours. In 1970 Nikolayev commanded the Soyuz 9 mission; he and flight engineer Vitaly Sevastyanov spent almost 18 days in space.

Nikolayev was a logical choice for these early space marathons because of his incredible stamina. During the diabolical medical testing before and after joining the cosmonaut group he consistently surprised Soviet doctors with his ability to endure silence, isolation, and temperature extremes. Yuri Gagarin said of Nikolayev, "He is the most unflappable man in a crisis I know."

Andrian Grigoryevich Nikolayev was born September 5, 1929, in the village of Shorshely in the Chuvash republic of the USSR. His father was a farmer and his older brother a lumberjack, so Nikolayev followed the family tradition, attending the Marinsky-Posad Forestry Institute. From December 1947 until he was drafted into the army in 1950 he was a lumberjack and the foreman of a logging operation.

As a soldier Nikolayev was first trained as an aircraft gunner and radio operator, but soon earned a chance to become a pilot. He graduated from the Chernigov Higher Air Force School in 1954 and served in the Moscow military district. He joined the Party in 1957.

Nikolayev became a cosmonaut in March 1960 and was backup to Gherman Titov on Vostok 2 in 1961. Between his flights in 1962 and

1970 he served as commander of the cosmonaut team and graduated from the Zhukovsky Air Force Engineering Academy. Since 1970 he has been a training official, flight controller and deputy director at the Gagarin Cosmonaut Training Center. He visited the United States in 1970 and met several American astronauts. He has also authored several books, including the autobiographies *Meeting in Orbit* (1966) and *Space, a Road without End* (1974, 1979).

Major General Nikolayev was married to Valentina Tereshkova, the first woman in space, from 1963 to 1982. They have a daughter, Yelena.

Patsayev, Viktor

Viktor Patsayev was the test-engineer of the cosmonaut crew that became the first in history to board an orbiting station, and which spent a record 24 days in space. The mission, Soyuz 11/Salyut 1, ended tragically on June 30, 1971, when cosmonauts Patsayev, Dobrovolsky and Volkov were killed on returning to Earth.

Viktor Patsayev was born June 19, 1933, in the city of Aktyubinsk in Kazakhstan. His father was killed in October 1941 in the defense of Moscow. He grew up with his mother and sister in Aktyubinsk and, after 1946, other cities. Always interested in science and space, Patsayev attended the Penza Industrial Institute, graduating in 1955. For the next few years he worked at the Central Aerological Observatory on studies of the atmosphere, then, following the first Sputnik launches in 1957-58, he obtained a job in the Korolev spacecraft design bureau.

As an engineer at the bureau, Patsayev became close friends with future cosmonaut Vladislav Volkov. Both of them were members of a flying club, and both were members of the recovery teams for manned spaceflights. Volkov was admitted to the cosmonaut team in 1966, but Patsayev, who was deeply involved in the design of the Salyut space station, had to wait three more years.

He became a Party member in 1968 and earned his candidate's degree in 1971.

Patsayev left a widow, Vera, a researcher, and two children, Dmitri and Svetlana. In 1974 Vera Patsayeva published a book, *Salyut in Orbit*, dealing with her husband's space mission.

Polyakov, Valery

Valery Polyakov was identified in 1986 as the backup cosmonaut-researcher to Oleg Atkov on the long duration Soyuz T-10 mission aboard Salyut 7 in 1984.

Polyakov is reported to be a physician who, like Atkov, studied at the All-Union Cardiological Institute prior to entering cosmonaut training in 1977.

Popov, Leonid

Leonid Popov has commanded three Soyuz missions, including a record 185-day aboard the Salyut 6 space station in 1980. During their six months in space, Popov and flight engineer Valery Ryumin hosted four different visiting crews, including cosmonauts from Hungary, Vietnam and Cuba, in addition to carrying out extensive observations of the Earth, materials processing and medical experiments.

Popov later commanded Soyuz 40, during which he and Rumanian cosmonaut Dumitru Prunariu visited Salyut 6, and Soyuz T-7, whose crew included woman cosmonaut Svetlana Savitskaya. During this third flight Popov visited Salyut 7.

He has spent 200 days in space.

Leonid Ivanovich Popov was born August 31, 1945, in the city of Alexandria in the Kirovgrad region of the USSR. At the age of 15 he left school to work as an industrial electrician, but two years later joined the Soviet air force. He attended the Chernigov Lenin Komsomol Higher Air Force School, graduating as a pilot in 1968. For the next two years he served as a MiG-19 pilot at a base in Azerbaijan.

He became a Party member in 1971.

Popov joined the cosmonaut group in May 1970 and underwent the basic training course. He then attended the Gagarin Air Force Academy, and upon graduation in 1976 was assigned to his first flight crew, serving as backup commander for the Soyuz 22 mission. He joined the group of cosmonauts working on the Salyut 6 project and served as backup commander for Soyuz 32 in 1979.

Since his last flight in August 1982 he has been politically active as a deputy to the Supreme Soviet. He remains on flight status and served as backup commander for the daring Soyuz T-13 mission which repaired and rescued the Salyut 7 space station in 1985.

Colonel Popov and his wife, Valentina, have a son, Alexei, and a daughter, Yelena.

Popovich, Pavel

Pavel Popovich took part in the world's first "group" space flight when his Vostok 4 spacecraft was launched into orbit on August 12, 1962, one day after Vostok 3 carrying cosmonaut Andrian Nikolayev. Popovich and Nikolayev passed within five miles of each other during their joint mission. Both cosmonauts returned to Earth on August 14, 1962.

Pavel Romanovich Popovich was born October 5, 1930, in Uzin, a town near Kiev in the Ukraine. Uzin was occupied by the Nazis during the Great Patriotic War and Popovich's early teens were very difficult. He worked in a factory while completing his schooling, then earned entry to the Magnitogorsk Industrial Polytechnic, where he overcame a language barrier—Popovich grew up speaking Ukrainian, not Russian—and graduated as a building technician.

But while at trade school he had also joined an aeroclub, becoming a pilot, and his new-found love for flying caused him to join the air force. He attended the Kacha Air Force College from 1951 to 1954, then served in the Arctic with a fighter squadron. During his service in the Arctic he won the coveted Order of the Red Star for a still-undisclosed government assignment. He became a Party member in 1957.

Popovich was the first young pilot to join the cosmonaut group in March 1960, and served as unofficial greeter and quartermaster for the other arrivals. His outgoing personality and love of singing made him popular; the other pilots chose him as their Party secretary. He also earned selection as one of the finalists for the first manned flight made by Gagarin. It was Popovich who was capcom for Gagarin's launch.

After his Vostok 4 flight Popovich graduated from the Zhukovsky Air Force Engineering Academy and trained in the Soviet manned lunar program. He made a second space flight in July 1974 as commander of Soyuz 14, which docked with the Salyut 3 orbiting space station. Popovich and flight engineer Yuri Artyukhin spent 16 days in space performing Earth observations and medical experiments.

Popovich later acted as a flight controller for the Salyut 5 missions in 1976, and completed work on a candidate's thesis. He has also written three books: an autobiography titled *Takeoff in the Morning* (1974); a biography of Yuri Gagarin, *It Couldn't Have Been Otherwise* (1980); and another memoir, *Testing in Space and on Earth* (1982). He is active in Ukrainian politics as well.

Since 1978, Major General Popovich has been deputy director of the Gagarin Cosmonaut Training Center. He is married to test pilot-engineer Marina Lavrentyevna Popovicha, herself a colonel in the Soviet air force, and they have two daughters, Natasha and Oxana.

Pronina, Irina

Irina Pronina was identified in 1986 as backup to Svetlana Savitskaya for the Soyuz T-7 mission in 1982 and the Soyuz T-12 mission in 1984.

Pronina is reported to be an engineer born in 1952 and entered the cosmonaut training program in 1980. She is likely to fly on a future Soyuz TM mission.

Rafikov, Mars

Mars Zakirovich Rafikov was one of the first Soviet cosmonauts whose training began in March 1960. He resigned from the program in early 1962.

Rafikov was a Tatar from Soviet Central Asia, and apparently quite a character. When the members of the first cosmonaut group were asked for a "peer rating," a written evaluation of each member to select the one who should be sent into space first, Rafikov named himself. "I should be sent, although I know that they will not send me. But my first name is 'cosmic' and this would sound good."

After leaving the space program Rafikov served as a fighter pilot in the Caucasus, then left the air force altogether, eventually settling with his family in Alma-Ata, where he worked for a home construction collective.

Romanenko, Yuri

Yuri Romanenko commanded the record-breaking Soyuz 26/Salyut 6 mission in 1977 and 1978. He and flight engineer Georgy Grechko activated the Salyut 6 station and lived aboard it for 96 days, eclipsing the

previous American record of 84 days, set by the third Skylab crew in 1974.

Their flight did more than just break an American a record—it demonstrated a new and more flexible Soviet approach to manned space flight. For example, two-man cosmonaut teams for long duration missions are carefully screened and monitored during months of training to ensure that they are compatible and comfortable with each other's working habits. Romanenko and Grechko were thrown together just six weeks before launch, because suspected technical problems with the main Salyut docking port had prevented the original 90-day expedition crew of Kovalenok and Ryumin from reaching the station. Grechko, a Salyut engineer as well as a cosmonaut, was a specialist in that docking system and was the logical choice to make repairs to it. He was assigned to the flight in spite of the fact that he had already flown one 30-day mission and hadn't liked it.

The two cosmonauts got along quite well. Grechko saved Romanenko's life during a spacewalk on December 20, 1977, when Romanenko, who had failed to attach his safety line, drifted out of the Salyut airlock. Grechko grabbed him and pulled him back to safety. A month later Romanenko was told that Grechko's father had died on Earth and faced a difficult decision: to tell Grechko now, a third of the way through the mission, when the effect of the news would be unpredictable, or to wait. Romanenko waited until they had returned to Earth.

Romanenko and Grechko were the first cosmonauts to be resupplied by robot tanker spacecraft and were host to two visiting cosmonaut crews, including Czech cosmonaut Vladimir Remek. Their flight was successful even though both cosmonauts skimped on their exercise program and found their readaptation to Earth's gravity to be more prolonged and painful as a result.

Romanenko later commanded Soyuz 38, an eight-day Interkosmos mission during which he and Cuban cosmonaut Arnaldo Tamayo-Mendez visited Salyut 6.

Yuri Viktorovich Romanenko was born August 1, 1944, in the Koltubanovsky settlement in the Orenburg region of the USSR. As a secondary school student he became interested in math and physics, and built model airplanes. After spending a year working in construction he joined the Soviet air force, attending the Chernigov Lenin Komsomol Higher Air Force School. He graduated as a pilot-engineer in 1966 and spent the next four years at Chernigov as a flight instructor.

He became a Party member in 1965.

Romanenko was enrolled in the cosmonaut group along with Vladimir Dzhanibekov, Leonid Popov and others in May 1970. Upon completion of the basic training course, Romanenko and Dzhanibekov were assigned as backup commanders for the Apollo-Soyuz Test Project, and from May 1973 to July 1975 made several trips to the United States and, in turn, played host to American astronauts who visited Star Town. Romanenko had to learn English as well. Teamed with flight engineer Alexandr Ivanchenkov, Romanenko served as backup commander for Soyuz 16, the ASTP dress rehearsal flown in December 1974.

At the end of 1975 Romanenko and Ivanchenkov began training for a long-duration Salyut 6 mission together. They were backups to Kovalenok and Ryumin for Soyuz 25, and found themselves re-assigned to different crews in the subsequent shuffle. Romanenko later served as backup commander for Soyuz 33, the flight of Bulgarian cosmonaut Georgy Ivanov in April 1979 and in the same capacity for the flight of Rumanian cosmonaut Dumitru Prunariu in May 1981. In late 1981 and 1982 he trained for a Salyut 7 mission as the backup commander for Soyuz T-7, but health problems forced him to step aside.

He attended the Gagarin Air Force Academy from 1975 to 1980.

Colonel Romanenko and his wife, Alevtina, a voice teacher, have two sons, Roman and Artem.

Rozhdestvensky, Valery

Valery Rozhdestvensky took part in one of the most spectacular and dangerous landings in the history of manned space flight. On October 24, 1976, he was flight engineer aboard Soyuz 23 when he and commander Vyacheslav Zudov made the first splashdown in the Soviet space program, coming down in the middle of Lake Tengiz during a snowstorm in the dark.

It was a fitting end, perhaps, to an aborted space flight. Rozhdestvensky and Zudov had been launched on October 23, 1976, for a planned month-long mission aboard Salyut 5. During their approach to the space station, however, the Soyuz guidance system failed and the docking was called off. Mission rules dictated a swift return to Earth, resulting in the cold, late-night splashdown.

Rescue craft were able to reach Soyuz 23 and divers attached a flotation collar to the craft, but it could not be towed to shore until dawn, many hours later. Rozhdestvensky and Zudov spent a cold and one may assume seasick night in the bobbing command module. They recovered, but neither has flown in space again.

Ironically, Rozhdestvensky had once commanded a team of deep sea divers in the Soviet navy.

Valery Ilyich Rozhdestvensky was born on February 13, 1939, in Leningrad and graduated from the F. E. Dzherzhinsky Higher Naval Engineering School in 1961. He served in the navy with the rescue service of the Baltic Fleet prior to joining the cosmonaut group in November 1965. He became a Party member in 1961.

As a cosmonaut Rozhdestvensky transferred to the air force and became an expert parachutist and pilot. He studied aerospace medicine and wrote articles on the subject (under a pen name) for *Red Star*, the Soviet army newspaper. In 1968 he began working as a specialist in guidance and telemetry, taking part in several manned flights as a ground controller based at mission control in Yevpatoriya in the Crimea. He joined the Salyut training group in 1972 and was backup flight engineer for Soyuz 21 in 1976.

He was senior capcom at mission control in the Kaliningrad mission control center during the Salyut 6 missions from 1977 to 1981. During Salyut 7 missions he has worked as a flight controller.

Rozhdestvensky is married; his wife, Svetlana, is a systems specialist working at Star Town. They have daughter, Tanya.

Rukavishnikov, Nikolai

Nikolai Rukavishnikov is the hard-luck engineer-cosmonaut whose three attempts to complete a flight aboard a Salyut space station have all failed.

Rukavishnikov was the cosmonaut-researcher of the Soyuz 10 crew, launched April 23, 1971, for a planned 30-day mission aboard Salyut 1. It would have been the world's first space station mission, but though Soyuz 10 and its three cosmonauts were able to dock with the station, technical problems prevented them from going aboard the station, and they were forced to make an emergency return to Earth.

Rukavishnikov's second encounter with Salyut was even more dangerous. On April 10, 1979, he and Bulgarian cosmonaut Georgy Ivanov

were launche'd aboard Soyuz 33 for an eight-day stay aboard Salyut 6. But during their final approach to the station on April 12 their main maneuvering engines failed, threatening to strand them in space. The cosmonauts were forced to use backup equipment to get home, landing in darkness after enduring unusually high G-loads during re-entry.

By October 1982, when Rukavishnikov began to train as part of a USSR-Indian team for a Salyut 7 flight, the other cosmonauts were joking that each Salyut was equipped with an "anti-Rukavishnikov" device. (He had also been assigned to a Salyut crew in 1973, but Salyut itself had failed to reach orbit.) Sure enough, in March 1984, just weeks before launch, Rukavishnikov caught a bad cold which forced him off the flight crew.

Rukavishnikov did make one very successful flight aboard Soyuz 16 in December 1984. This six-day mission was a full-scale dress rehearsal for the Apollo-Soyuz mission in 1975. On his three flights Rukavishniov has spent ten days in space.

Nikolai Nikolayevich Rukavishnikov was born September 18, 1932, in the city of Tomsk in western Siberia. As a child he traveled all over the Soviet Union with his parents, who were both surveying and building new railways. He attended the Moscow Institute of Engineering and Physics, graduating in 1957, and immediately went to work in Korolev's spacecraft design bureau. His early field of work was in automatic controls for spacecraft. Later he headed a team of scientists who developed Earth and solar physics experiments.

Rukavishnikov was selected for cosmonaut training in May 1966 and reported to Star Town the following January. He trained in the Soviet manned lunar program, then served as a backup cosmonaut-researcher for Soyuz 7 in 1969 before being assigned to the Salyut cosmonaut group. He was also the backup commander for Soyuz 28 in 1978.

Rukavishnikov has been described as an outgoing and humorous man and is a favorite of Soviet space journalists. He speaks fluent English and would be a candidate for a future Soviet-American space flight. Currently he is head of the Soviet Federation of Cosmonautics.

His wife, Nina, is a technician. They have a son, Vladimir.

Ryumin, Valery

Between February 1979 and October 1980 Valery Ryumin spent almost one year in space during two visits to Salyut 6. With 361 days, 21 hours and 34 minutes logged on three different flights, Ryumin was, until 1986, the undisputed world space endurance record-holder.

But where early Soviet candidates for long duration space flights were selected for their unusual endurance, Ryumin's record was set by accident. As flight engineer of Soyuz 25, launched October 9, 1977, Ryumin was trained for a planned 90-day mission that would involve activation of the newly launched Salyut 6 station, medical experiments, and tests of new systems which would allow a Salyut to be refueled and resupplied by robot tanker vehicles. But Soyuz 25 failed to link up with Salyut 6 because of a mechanical failure in its docking mechanism and just 48 hours after launch Ryumin and commander Vladimir Kovalenok were back on Earth. To make matters worse, early indications were that the docking failure might have been crew error: they were the first cosmonauts not named Heroes of the Soviet Union after a flight.

But in the ensuing shuffle Kovalenok was assigned to a new Salyut 6 crew and Ryumin to another. On February 25, 1979, Ryumin and pilot Vladimir Lyakhov were sent into space aboard Soyuz 32. By this time cosmonauts had made successful "expeditions" aboard Salyut 6 of 96 days and 139 days, increasing the duration of their stays by about a month with each mission. Ryumin and Lyakhov were to attempt to spend 6 months in a living space approximately 25 feet long and 10 feet wide.

Ryumin, who would later publish frank diaries of his two long visits to Salyut 6, thought of a quote from the American writer O. Henry: "If you want to encourage the craft of murder, all you have to do is lock up two men for two months in an 18- by 20-foot room." But he and Lyakhov got along well during their months of confinement. They were kept busy with astronomical observations using a radiotelescope, with space manufacturing, and with repairs to equipment aboard Salyut 6, which had outlived its original 18-month design life. One major disappointment for the cosmonauts was the lack of visitors. On April 12, 1979, as Ryumin and Lyakhov watched from Salyut, the first guests, Soviet commander Nikolai Rukavishnikov and Bulgarian researcher Georgy Ivanov, suffered a major engine failure aboard their Soyuz 33 craft and were forced to make an emergency return to Earth without going aboard the station. Ryumin knew that the subsequent investigation would postpone a Soviet-Hungarian flight scheduled for July.

On August 15, near the end of the mission, Ryumin made a daring spacewalk to cut away the radio-telescope, which had snagged as it was jettisoned from the outside of Salyut 6. Four days later, after 175 days in space, the cosmonauts were back on Earth. Their physical condition was better than expected, but not as good as it would have been if Ryumin had fully carried out his exercise program, something he would correct on his next flight.

Ryumin went on leave, then, in early 1980, took up his new job, supervising the training of the next Salyut 6 expedition crew, pilot Leonid Popov and engineer Valentin Lebedev, who had been backups to Lyakhov and Ryumin. But just weeks before the planned launch in April Lebedev broke his knee while working out on a trampoline. Soviet flight director Alexei Yeliseyev, an ex-cosmonaut, wanted to replace Lebedev with his backup, Gennady Strekalov, and asked Ryumin to fill in for Strekalov in the thankless and time-consuming backup role. Ryumin suggested instead that he be sent in Lebedev's place. He was already more familiar with Salyut 6 than Strekalov could be, and there might be some medical value in having him fly again. After consulting with doctors, Yeliseyev agreed, and on April 9, 1980, Ryumin and Popov were launched aboard Soyuz 35.

Ryumin's second expedition went more smoothly. He was able to adapt to life aboard Salyut 6 more quickly, and his experience helped Popov, who was on his first flight, to be more productive. The cosmonauts were more faithful to their exercise regime than earlier crews, which made their eventual re-adaptation to Earth shorter and easier. The psychological burden of isolation was not nearly as great, since Ryumin and Popov were visited by four different crews, including guest cosmonauts from Hungary, Vietnam and Cuba. The mission ended on October 11, 1980.

Valery Viktorovich Ryumin was born August 16, 1939, in Komsomolsk-on-Amur in eastern Siberia. His father was a construction worker on the railroad being built there. Intending to become a metallurgical engineer, Ryumin attended a technical school in Kaliningrad, then was drafted into the army, where he became a tank commander in the Transcaucasus military district. Demobilized in 1961, he enrolled in the Moscow Forestry Institute's department of computer science, graduating in 1966.

For the next seven years Ryumin was an engineer in the Korolev spacecraft design bureau and played a major role in the development of the Salyut space station. He joined the Party in 1972. In 1973, when Salyut specialists were recruited into the cosmonaut group, Ryumin was one of those accepted, in spite of the fact that he was considered too tall for the cramped quarters of most spacecraft.

One of his projects as a cosmonaut was the design of astronomical experiments for upcoming Salyut 4 missions. This work often took him to the famous Crimean Observatory, where he met pilot-cosmonaut Vladimir Kovalenok. During the Salyut 4 and Apollo-Soyuz flights of 1975 Ryumin was a capcom based aboard the tracking ship Academician Sergei Korolev. At the end of that year he was named to the first Salyut 6 crew with Kovalenok.

After his third space flight Ryumin served as assistant flight director for Soyuz T-4, the last expedition to Salyut 6, which was commanded by Kovalenok. He was involved in the design of the new Salyut 7 station, and ultimately succeeded Alexei Yeliseyev as chief flight director for all missions to Salyut 7, a job which also makes him one of the more visible spokesmen for the Soviet space program.

Asked recently if he would ever go into space again, Ryumin replied that he thought not, but added nevertheless that his old space suit was still available.

Ryumin and his wife, Lydia, an engineer, live in Moscow with their son, Vladimir, and daughter, Vika.

Sarafanov, Gennady

Gennady Sarafanov's only space flight was the aborted Soyuz 15 in August 1974. Sarafanov and flight engineer Lev Demin were launched into space on August 26, 1974, for a scheduled month-long mission aboard Salyut 3. But during the final approach to the space station the Soyuz guidance system failed and Sarafanov and Demin returned to earth.

Gennady Vasilyevich Sarafanov was born January 1, 1942, in the village of Sinenkiye near Saratov. At the age of 17 he joined the Soviet army, transferring to the air force after one year. He attended the Balashov Higher Air Force School, graduating in 1964, then served as a fighter pilot in the Guards Regiment prior to joining the cosmonaut group in November 1965. He became a Party member in 1963.

After completing his basic cosmonaut training in 1967, Sarafanov served the usual apprenticeship in support of other flight crews and their missions, and eventually earned his assignment to the Salyut training group in 1972. Following his only flight in 1974 he attended the Gagarin Air Force Academy until 1980. Since then he has been a training official at the cosmonaut center.

Colonel Sarafanov and his wife, Tamara, have a son, Alexei, and a daughter, Katya, and live in Star Town.

Savinykh, Viktor

Viktor Savinykh took part in one of the most daring Soviet space flights ever, the rescue of the Salyut 7 space station in the summer of 1985.

Salyut 7 had been launched in April 1982 and designed to operate for two years as home to three long-duration crews of cosmonauts, who would successively spend seven, eight and nine months in orbit. Since this station's predecessor, Salyut 6, had doubled its intended lifetime, allowing for several "bonus" missions, Soviet planners were optimistic

that Salyut 7 would, in fact, operate for three to four years, until the new Mir station was ready. But a fuel leak in August 1983, which occurred when cosmonauts Lyakhov and Alexandrov were on board, severely damaged the station. The 1984 expedition crew of Kizim, Solovyov and Atkov were able to repair the damage done by the leak in a series of spacewalks, but just weeks after they left Salyut 7 in November 1984 the station suffered a massive electrical failure that allowed it to drift out of control, its solar panels useless.

Savinykh had been training as flight engineer for the crew of the 1985 expedition. When contact with Salyut 7 was lost in the closing days of 1984, Soviet space officials devised a clever plan to rendezvous with the dead vehicle (a difficult task for the Soviet Soyuz T spacecraft, which depends on response from its target for accurate maneuvering), go aboard it, and restore it to life. Savinykh was chosen to join four-time space veteran Vladimir Dzhanibekov as the rescue team, and they were launched aboard Soyuz T-13 on June 6, 1985. Two days later, taking an extra day to approach Salyut 7, they docked.

When the two cosmonauts opened the connecting hatch they found a dead space station. Dzhanibekov wrote later, "There was complete silence in the docking chamber. We remained in semi-darkness, the portholes half-covered with blinds. Only the rays of the flashlight picked out specks of dust hanging motionless in the air." Moving inside the station, to the central work station, they found complete darkness (the shades were drawn) and a smell like that of a "stagnant machine shop." It was also cold; the windows had a layer of frost on the inside.

Savinykh and Dzhanibekov went to work trying to connect the solar panels to the batteries they normally charged. Within two days they had succeeded in bypassing the ruined circuit panel (which was the source of the original failure) and began to charge up the batteries. The cosmonauts' exhaled carbon dioxide built up, since the station's air circulating system had shut down, giving them headaches and making the repairs even more difficult. (Salyut 7 was so dead that the cosmonauts had to communicate with mission control through the radios on their Soyuz.) But within two weeks they were ready to receive a supply of spare parts and fuel from a Progress robot tanker, which arrived on June 23. Progress was followed on July 21 by the Kosmos-1669 supply ship, which carried new EVA spacesuits to replace those ruined by the freezing temperatures aboard the station. On August 2 Savinykh and Dzhanibekov conducted a five-hour EVA to install a third solar panel and dust collectors designed by French scientists for the study of Halley's Comet.

On September 18, Soyuz T-14 arrived, crewed by cosmonauts Vladimir Vasyutin, Georgy Grechko and Alexandr Volkov. Vasyutin and Volkov had been members of the 1985 expedition crew with Savinykh. Seven days later, Dzhanibekov and Grechko left Salyut 7 in the Soyuz T-13 spacecraft, having taken part in the first "handover" of space teams in history.

Savinykh, Vasyutin and Volkov settled down for a winter of work with the Kosmos-1686 laboratory module, which was docked to the station on October 2, and for observations of Halley's Comet. But by mid-November Vasyutin had developed an infection which resisted treatment. Reluctantly, but with proper concern for Vasyutin's health, the crew left Salyut-7, landing on Earth on November 21.

Soyuz T-13 was Savinykh's second trip into space. In 1981 he and Vladimir Kovalenok spent 74 days aboard Salyut 6, where they were visited by cosmonauts from Mongolia and Rumania. Savinykh has spent almost 243 days in space.

Viktor Petrovich Savinykh was born March 7, 1940, in the village of Berezkiny in the Kirov region of the USSR. After completing secondary school he attended the Perm Institute of Railroads and was working on the Sverdlovsk railway when he was drafted. From 1961 to 1963 he served in the Soviet army as a topographer. When he was demobilized he went to Moscow to attend the Institute of Geodetic Engineering, Aerial Photogaphy and Cartography, where he specialized in the design of optical geodetic equipment.

He became a Party member in 1963.

In 1969 he joined the Korolev spacecraft design bureau, originally working on optical instruments for Soyuz, Progress and Salyut spacecraft. Eventually he became a flight controller and planner, working with future space partner Kovalenok on Salyut 4 in 1975.

Savinykh was one of several engineers and test pilots admitted to the cosmonaut group in December 1978. He was immediately assigned to the team of cosmonauts training for flights on the new Soyuz T vehicle and served as backup cosmonaut-researcher for Soyuz T-3 in late 1980. Between flights he served as backup flight engineer for Soyuz T-7, Soyuz T-10 and Soyuz T-12.

He is the author of memoir, *The Earth Waits and Hopes* (1983).

Savinykh and his wife, Lilia, an instructor at the Moscow Forestry Institute, have a daughter, Valentina. They live in Moscow.

Savitskaya, Svetlana

In August 1982, nineteen years after Valentina Tereshkova's pioneering flight, Svetlana Savitskaya became the second woman to fly in space. She and fellow cosmonauts Leonid Popov and Alexandr Serebrov were sent into space in Soyuz T-7 and joined two other cosmonauts aboard the Salyut 7 space station.

Savitskaya made a second space flight in July 1984, during which she became the first woman to walk in space.

On her two flights Savitskaya has logged a total of 20 days in space and 3 and a half hours in EVA.

Svetlana Yevgenyevna Savitskaya was born August 8, 1948, in Moscow. Her father is Air Marshal of the Soviet Union Yevgeny Savitsky, chief of National Air Defense. While attending the DOSAAF Central Aerotechnical School as a teenager she became a parachutist and a pilot, then attended the Moscow Aviation Institute from 1966 to 1972, graduating with a degree in aeronautical engineering. She became a Party member in 1975.

In 1970 she traveled to Great Britain for the 6th World Aerobatics Championship and returned to the USSR as the world champion in all-around flying. She then went to work with the Yakovlev aircraft design bureau, where she became a test pilot (her chief examiner was future fellow cosmonaut Igor Volk) and established many speed records for Soviet planes. She also earned a master of sport rating with 500 parachute jumps.

Savitskaya joined the cosmonaut team in 1980. She is currently one of ten women cosmonauts and is expected to make a third space flight in the future, this time as a spacecraft commander.

Savitskaya's husband, Viktor Khatosky, is an engineer and pilot with the Ilyushin design bureau. They have a son, born in 1986.

Serebrov, Alexandr

Alexandr Serebrov was aboard two successive space missions in 1982 and 1983.

As flight engineer on Soyuz T-7 in August 1982, Serebrov was part

of the crew that included cosmonaut Svetlana Savitskaya, the second woman to go into space. Serebrov, Savitskaya and commander Leonid Popov rendezvoused and docked with the Salyut 7 space station and spent a week as guests of cosmonauts Berezovoy and Lebedev.

Serebrov's primary training involved "add-on" free-flying modules to the Salyut, and it was for a planned eight-month mission aboard a combined Salyut 7/Star module complex that he was sent into space on Soyuz T-8 with commander Vladimir Titov and flight engineer Gennady Strekalov. But Soyuz T-8 suffered the loss of its rendezvous radar during its first day in space and was forced to return to Earth without reaching the space complex. Since then Serebrov continues to train for another mission. Fluent in English, he visited the Paris Air Show in 1985 and discussed the Soviet Union's planned space shuttle program with Western journalists there.

Serebrov was born February 14, 1944, in Moscow, and attended the Moscow Physical-Technical Institute, earning his degree in 1967. He remained at the Institute as a graduate student and researcher until earning his candidate of technical sciences degree in physics in 1976, at which point he went to work in the Petrov spacecraft design bureau. He joined the Party in 1976 as well. Serebrov became a cosmonaut in December 1978.

He and his wife, Yekaterina, have two children.

Sevastyanov, Vitaly

Vitaly Sevastyanov is an engineer-cosmonaut who took part in two different long duration space missions.

During the first, in June 1970 he spent a record 18 days in space aboard Soyuz 9, a difficult experience which left Sevastyanov and commander Andrian Nikolayev so weak at its end that they had to be carried from their spacecraft.

By the time Sevastyanov made his second flight, Soyuz 18 in May 1975, a new program of exercise and medical supervision and the roomier quarters aboard Salyut 4 allowed the cosmonaut to endure 63 days in space with happier results. Sevastyanov and commander Pyotr Klimuk were able to walk away from Soyuz 18 on landing. They had carried out a number of scientific experiments, including observing the Sun with a solar telescope, while struggling with the space station's troubled environmental system, which raised the humidity inside Salyut 4 to the point where mold was starting to form on the walls.

Sevastyanov has spent 81 days in space.

Vitaly Ivanovich Sevastyanov was born July 8, 1935, in Krasno-Uralsk, a village near the city of Sverdlovsk, but grew up in Sochi, a resort on the Black Sea, where during school holidays he worked as a deckhand on boats. He attended the Moscow Aviation Institute, studying to become an aeronautical engineer, and on graduation in 1959 went to work in Korolev's spacecraft design bureau.

At the Korolev bureau Sevastyanov was a member of the team that created the Vostok spacecraft. He was also a lecturer to the cosmonauts and sat on the review board which approved cosmonauts for space flight assignments. He did graduate work at MAI, receiving his candidate's degree in 1965, and he joined the Party in 1963.

Sevastyanov was invited to join the cosmonaut team in May 1966 and started training in January 1967. He first worked in the Soviet manned lunar program group, then was named backup flight engineer for the three Soyuz missions flown in October 1969. From 1971 to 1975 he was a member of the Salyut cosmonaut group, and since that time has been a Salyut flight controller and, more recently, head of his own group in the Korolev design bureau.

Sevastyanov is President of the Soviet Chess Federation (during Soyuz 9 he played a game from orbit with fellow cosmonaut Viktor Gorbatko, who was at mission control), a member of the journalist's union of the USSR and has been the host of a popular television series. He has traveled to many foreign countries and has made two visits to the US.

Sevastyanov and his wife, Alevtina, a journalist, have a daughter, Natasha. They live in Moscow.

Shatalov, Vladimir

Vladimir Shatalov commanded three Soyuz flights between 1969 and 1971, including the first rendezvous and docking between Soviet manned spacecraft, and went on to become chief of the cosmonaut training program.

Shatalov's first space flight began on January 14, 1969, when he was launched alone aboard Soyuz 4. The next day cosmonauts Boris Volynov, Alexei Yeliseyev and Yevgeny Khrunov were put into space aboard Soyuz 5. Shatalov gave chase, and on January 16 made a successful rendezvous and docking with the three-man vehicle. Yeliseyev and Khrunov donned pressure suits and made a space walk from Soyuz 5 to Soyuz 4, returning to Earth with Shatalov on January 17.

In October of that same year Shatalov served as commander of Soyuz 8, the "flagship" of a trio of Soyuz vehicles that were launched on successive days. Soyuz 8 was the last of the three sent into space. Shatalov and flight engineer Yeliseyev apparently planned to rendezvous and dock with Soyuz 7 and its three-man crew, but were unable to do so. The original purpose of this "troika" flight is still not clear: the crew of Soyuz 6 performed an experiment in space welding, but the other two vehicles merely carried out simple maneuvers and observations.

Shatalov's third flight, the most ambitious, was also troubled. On April 23, 1971, Shatalov, Yeliseyev, and research-engineer Nikolai Rukavishnikov were sent into orbit aboard Soyuz 10 intending to dock with the Salyut 1 space station for a 30-day mission. When they linked up with Salyut on April 25 the cosmonauts were unable to open the hatch between the two vehicles. They backed away from the station after only 5.5 hours and returned to Earth.

Shatalov logged approximately ten days in space during his three flights.

Vladimir Alexandrovich Shatalov was born December 8, 1927, in the city of Petropavlovsk in Kazakhstan, but moved to Leningrad with his family at the age of 2. His father was a railroad mechanic and engineer in aviation and in communications whose experiences during the Great Patriotic War convinced young Vladimir that he should become a soldier. He attended the Lipetsk prep school for military pilots until 1946, then the Kacha Higher Air Force School, graduating in 1949.

In the next thirteen years Shatalov advanced through the ranks of the air force, from squadron leader to deputy regimental commander to pilot-instructor to, finally, air force inspector. He earned admittance to the Red Banner (later named for Yuri Gagarin) Air Force Academy in 1953, the same year that he joined the Party. In March 1962 he was training to become a military test pilot when he learned that a new cosmonaut group was being selected, one whose members were required to be Academy graduates with command experience. The age limit was raised to 40 and engineers were recruited along with pilots. This was a change from the requirements for the first group, who were mostly junior pilots aged 25 to 27. Shatalov applied, was accepted, and reported to Star Town on January 11, 1963.

Some cosmonaut memoirs report a certain amount of tension between the two groups. By January 1963 the original group of 20 pilots had lost 6 men for a variety of medical and academic reasons, and 11 of the remaining 14 (including space veterans Gagarin, Titov, Nikolayev and Popovich) had been sent to the Zhukovsky Air Force Engineering Academy for further study. The younger men viewed the new arrivals with suspicion, fearing that they were being replaced and that their chances of ever going into space were disappearing. One sign of the difference between the two groups was that the younger pilots were forbidden to fly jets without instructors. This rule, when applied to the 1963 men, was quickly discarded, since men like Shatalov had already served as instructors, logging hundreds of hours of flying time.

It was Yuri Gagarin, the commander of the cosmonaut team, who acted as peacemaker between the two groups, reassuring the younger men that they would eventually fly in space, while making it clear that the senior pilots and engineers were going to play an important role in the next few years. As the obvious leader of the new group, Shatalov immediately became involved in the support of the Vostok 5 and Vostok 6 flights in June 1963 and in the Voskhod missions of 1964 and 1965.

In the spring of 1965 Shatalov and a late addition to the 1963 group, a 44-year-old test pilot named Georgy Beregovoy, were chosen as one of two cosmonaut teams training for a two-week-long Voskhod 3 mission. At the same time work was proceeding on an entirely new spacecraft called Soyuz, which was designed to take Soviet cosmonauts to the Moon, and when delays forced Voskhod 3 into 1966, it was canceled as redundant. Shatalov and Beregovoy immediately moved over to the Soyuz program, where Shatalov served as capcom for Soyuz 1, and had the difficult task of talking to the doomed Vladimir Komarov during his final, horrifying plunge to Earth.

When manned flights resumed with Soyuz 3 in October 1968, Shatalov served as Beregovoy's backup.

Following a second Soviet manned space fatality, the death of the three Soyuz 11 cosmonauts in June 1971, cosmonaut training chief Colonel-General Nikolai Kamanin was fired. In October 1971 a replacement was named: Major General Vladimir Shatalov. Chosen by Shatalov as director of the Gagarin Cosmonaut Training Center was Major General Georgy Beregovoy. The new chief flight director at mission control was Alexei Yeliseyev, who had flown with Shatalov on three different missions.

In 1972 Shatalov earned a candidate of technical sciences degree. He traveled to the United States several times between 1973 and 1975 with the Apollo-Soyuz cosmonauts. (He revealed to American astronauts that he came close to assigning himself to the flight with Yeliseyev.) In 1975 he was promoted to lieutenant general. Active in Party politics (from 1977 to 1980 he was deputy of the Supreme Soviet), he remains the director of all cosmonaut training and chief spokesman for the Soviet space program.

Shatalov has authored or co-authored several books on space flight, notably *Man and Space* (1979), and an autobiography, *The Hard Road to Space* (1977, 1979).

He and his wife, Muza, an agricultural scientist, have a son, Igor, and a daughter, Yelena.

Shonin, Georgy

Georgy Shonin commanded the Soyuz 6 flight in October 1969, when three Soviet manned spacecraft were in orbit at the same time. Aboard Shonin's vehicle cosmonaut Valery Kubasov performed the first demonstration of welding in space, a necessary step for the future construction of space stations. Shonin returned to Earth after spending six days in space.

Georgy Stepanovich Shonin was born August 3, 1935 in the city of Rovenki, in what is now the Voroshilovgrad section of the Ukraine. He attended the same Odessa pilot's prep school as fellow cosmonaut Georgy Dobrovolsky, and graduated from the Yeisk Higher Air Force School in 1957, joining the Party in the same year. His air force service took him to the Baltic, and later to the Northern Fleet, where he served in the same unit as Yuri Gagarin.

Shonin was a member of the first cosmonaut group which began training in March 1960. He almost washed out of space training when he had problems tolerating high-G loads on the centrifuge, but later adapted. From 1964 to 1966 he trained for a two-week-long Voskhod 3 mission, which was canceled before it could be flown. He served as backup commander for Soyuz 5 in January 1969.

Since his only space flight Shonin has served as a capcom for the Apollo-Soyuz Test Project (1975) and earned his candidate of technical sciences degree (1978). He is chief of a cosmonaut training unit at the Gagarin Center and is reportedly concentrating on development of the Soviet space shuttle.

Lieutenant General Shonin is the author of a memoir of the Gagarin group of cosmonauts titled *The Very First* (also published as *Space Pioneers*) (1977 and 1979). He and his wife, Lydia, have a son, Andrei, and a daughter, Nina.

Solovyov, Vladimir

Vladimir Solovyov was flight engineer aboard the world's longest manned space mission, Soyuz T-10/Salyut 7, which lasted from February 8 to October 1, 1984.

With Solovyov and commander Leonid Kizim was a cardiologist, Dr. Oleg Atkov, the first medical specialist to make a long duration flight in a Soviet spacecraft. Consequently many of the experiments aboard Salyut 7 dealt with the effects of weightlessness on human beings. Solovyov also performed numerous experiments in space manufacturing and made detailed observations of the Earth and stars.

His most interesting task was to act as an orbital repairman for Salyut 7's main rocket engines, which were badly damaged in a September 1983 accident. In six space walks totaling about 22 hours, Solovyov, working in a bulky pressure suit, replaced fuel lines in the delicate engine chamber, restoring it to use. (Ironically, Solovyov had helped design the Salyut propulsion system.) He also erected new solar panels on the outside of Salyut 7.

In March 1986, Solovyov went into space a second time, as flight engineer of Soyuz T-15. He and commander Kizim activated the new Mir space station, then, on May 5, transferred to the still-operating Salyut 7, where they retrieved experiments left by the previous cosmonaut crew and performed two more spacewalks, this time testing space construction techniques. Solovyov and Kizim returned to Mir on June 26, and landed back on Earth on July 16.

Solovyov has logged almost 352 days in space and 31 hours of EVA.

Vladimir Alexandrovich Solovyov was born November 11, 1946, in Moscow, and attended the Bauman Higher Technical School from 1964 to 1970, graduating as an aerospace engineer. He immediately went to work in the Korolev spacecraft design bureau, becoming an expert on space propulsion systems. He was a flight controller at Soviet mission control at Kaliningrad during Salyut 6 missions.

He became a Party member in 1977.

Solovyov joined the cosmonaut team with a group of fellow space engineers in December 1978. After basic training in Soyuz T and Salyut systems, he was assigned to the backup crew of the Soviet-French Soyuz T-6 mission in 1981. He later served as backup for Soyuz T-8 and Soyuz T-10-1 (the September 1983 aborted launch).

Between his two flights, Solovyov served as assistant flight director and was involved in the difficult repairs to the derelict Salyut 7 in the summer of 1985.

Solovyov and his wife, Yelena, a mechanical engineer, live in Moscow with their two children, Sergei and Maria.

Strekalov, Gennady

Gennady Strekalov served as flight engineer aboard three Soyuz T missions between 1980 and 1984. Late on the night of September 26, 1983 he was also involved in the USSR's first launch pad abort.

Strekalov and commander Vladimir Titov were to dock their Soyuz T-10 spacecraft with the Salyut 7 station occupied by cosmonauts Lyakhov and Alexandrov, who had been aboard it since late June. During a two-week mission Titov and Strekalov were to perform several spacewalks to add solar power cells to the already existing panels on the station. But ninety seconds before launch a fire broke out at the base of the Soyuz T-10 rocket and quickly spread up the side of the vehicle. Horrified flight controllers activated the escape rocket mounted on the nose of the spacecraft, pulling the the Soyuz T away from the booster before it exploded. Soyuz T-10 reached an altitude of several thousand feet, then dropped safely to the ground by emergency parachute.

On his first flight, Soyuz T-3 in November and December 1980, Strekalov joined Leonid Kizim and Oleg Makarov in forming the first 3-man Soviet space crew to fly in nine years. They visited the Salyut 6 space station, which had been in operation at that time for over three years, almost twice its design life, in order to perform needed repairs to its control systems. The flight lasted approximately 13 days.

Strekalov then trained for an eight-month expedition to Salyut 7 with cosmonauts Vladimir Titov and Alexandr Serebrov. But shortly after launch on April 20, 1983, the cosmonauts discovered that their Soyuz T-8's rendezvous radar had failed. They were unable to dock with the station and returned to Earth. With the launch failure five months later, the two unlucky cosmonauts had tried to reach Salyut 7 twice, and failed.

Strekalov's luck improved. In March 1984 he replaced the ailing Nikolai Rukavishnikov as flight engineer of Soyuz T-11, a Soviet-Indian mission, and spent eight days in space, most of them aboard Salyut 7, the next month.

It is ironic that both of Strekalov's scheduled visits to space stations failed to materialize, while his two successes came when he was a last-minute replacement (Konstantin Feoktistov was the original cosmonaut-researcher on Soyuz T-3).

He has spent almost 23 days in space.

Gennady Mikhailovich Strekalov was born October 28, 1940, in the Moscow suburb of Mytishchi. After completing secondary school he worked as an apprentice coppersmith in the factory where Sputnik 1 was built, and in 1959 enrolled in the Bauman Higher Technical School to study aerospace engineering. He graduated in 1965 and immediately went to work at the Korolev spacecraft design bureau, taking part in the design and development of Soyuz.

He became a Party member in 1972.

Strekalov joined the cosmonaut group in 1973 and spent several years working as a ground controller at the Kaliningrad Center, and on space tracking vessels. In 1976 he was one of the backup flight engineers for Soyuz 22, then he began to train for Salyut flights. He served as backup flight engineer for Soyuz 35 in 1980 prior to being added to the Soyuz T-3 crew, and was also a backup for Soyuz T-4 and for Soyuz T-5. He joined Titov and Serebrov as backup crewmen for Soyuz T-14 in 1985.

Strekalov and his wife, Lydia, have two daughters. They live in Moscow.

Tereshkova, Valentina

Valentina Tereshkova was the first woman space traveler. On June 16, 1963, the 26-year-old Tereshkova was launched into orbit aboard Vostok 6 and in the next three days circled the Earth 48 times, more than the six American astronauts combined. During her flight Tereshkova, using the call sign "Chaika" ("Seagull"), made television broadcasts to viewers in the Soviet Union, and also maintained regular radio contact with fellow cosmonaut Valery Bykovsky, whose Vostok 5 spacecraft was in orbit at the same time. The two spacecraft once passed within three miles of each other, and both returned to Earth on June 19, 1963.

Famed as a heroine of the women's movement in Soviet society, Tereshkova eventually went on to a career in politics. She married cosmonaut Andrian Nikolayev in a lavish state wedding (Soviet leader Nikita Khrushchev gave away the bride) in November 1963.

Valentina Vladimirovna Tereshkova was born March 6, 1937, in the village of Masslenikovo near Yaroslavl. Her parents worked on a collective farm, but her father was killed during the Great Patriotic War and Tereshkova's mother moved to the city, where Valentina went to work in a tire factory. At the age of 18 she joined her mother and sister, who had jobs at the Krasny Perekop textile mill. While working at the mill Tereshkova took a correspondence course from an industrial school and, more significantly, joined a club for parachutists, eventually making over 150 jumps.

In September 1961, shortly after the flight of cosmonaut Gherman Titov, Tereshkova, like hundreds of other young Soviet men and women, wrote a letter to the space center asking to join the cosmonaut team. Unknown to her, Soviet space officials were considering the selection of a group of women parachutists (there were very few women pilots) for cosmonaut training. In December 1961 Tereshkova was invited to Moscow for an interview and medical examinations, and the following March reported with three other women to Star Town. Valentina's mother and sister were told she had been selected for a special sky-diving team.

Most cosmonaut memoirs claim that the women were welcomed "like brothers" by the pilots, but other sources state that some of the men were not pleased by the new recruits, who apparently had little or no flying experience. Years later Tereshkova confided to an American in the Apollo-Soyuz project that the other cosmonauts avoided her "because I have invaded their little playground and because I am a woman."

Nevertheless, Tereshkova and the others were subjected to the same centrifuge rides and zero-G flights as the male cosmonauts. They were also commissioned as junior lieutenants in the Soviet air force. One of the women was a pilot, but Tereshkova and the others were not, and were given basic flight training by Colonel Vladimir Seregin, who would later die in the crash that also killed Yuri Gagarin. In May 1963 Tereshkova and Tatyana Torchillova were chosen to train for the Vostok 6 flight.

A number of rumors persist about Tereshkova and Vostok 6, primarily that she was originally the backup to Torchillova, stepping in at the last minute when the other woman failed the pre-flight physical. (The Vostok 6 mission was delayed a day, though high winds at the Baikonur launch center were blamed.) It has also been reported that Tereshkova was ill for most of her flight, though the official story is that Vostok 6's scheduled single day duration was extended after launch.

In the years following Vostok 6 Tereshkova made many public appearances and trips to other countries. She and Nikolayev had a daugther, Yelena. Tereshkova and the other women cosmonauts attended the Zhukovsky Air Force Engineering Academy, graduating in 1969. None of them ever trained for another space flight and new women cosmonauts were not selected until 1980.

Colonel Tereshkova later earned a candidate of technical sciences degree (1976).

Tereshkova had been a Komsomol organizer at the textile mill and joined the Party in 1962. She became a member of the Supreme Soviet in 1966 and, in 1971, a member of the Central Committee.

She has been the subject of at least one book-length biography, *This Is "Seagull!"* by Mitchell Sharpe (1975), and has published an autobiography.

Tereshkova and Nikolayev were divorced in 1982.

Titov, Gherman

Gherman Titov became the second human being to make an orbital space flight when he spent a record twenty-four hours in orbit aboard Vostok 2 in August 1961. With five weeks to go until his 26th birthday, Titov remains the youngest person to go into space.

Titov's flight, following, as it did, a single orbit by Yuri Gagarin and two suborbital flights by Americans Shepard and Grissom, was an electrifying world event, with the progress of the Vostok 2 reported hourly as it passed over the globe. Using his exuberant call sign—"Ya Orel!" or "This is Eagle!"—Titov was seen and heard on television, giving viewers a tour of his spacecraft and describing the sights he saw through his window.

What was not revealed at the time was that Titov was the first human to suffer from space adaptation syndrome—space sickness. He was hospitalized for a time following his flight and never made another space flight.

Gherman Stepanovich Titov was born on September 11, 1935, in the village of Verkhneye Zhilino in the Altai region of Siberia. His father was a schoolteacher and gave his son the name Gherman (Herman, unusual for a Russian) to honor his favorite Pushkin character. Young Gherman decided he wanted to become a pilot when his uncle, an aviator and war hero, paid the village a visit.

Titov entered the Kacha Higher Air Force School at Volgograd in 1953 and graduated in 1957. He was a pilot in the Leningrad military district when invited to apply for the cosmonaut group. On several occasions he came close to washing out, most notably when he rebelled at what he called "silly questions" during psychological testing. But he was selected and reported for training in March 1960.

In March 1961, after a year of training, Titov was one of six cosmonauts chosen as "finalists" for the first manned flight. It was an especially difficult time for Titov, who was recovering from the long illness and death of his infant son, Igor.

On the morning of April 12, 1961, Senior Lieutenant Titov, dressed in his orange pressure suit and space helmet, accompanied Yuri Gagarin to the launch pad at the Baikonur cosmodrome. Gagarin went aboard the Vostok spacecraft and Titov, his standby, returned to the cosmonaut quarters to wait for the launch. Shortly after Gagarin returned to Earth, Titov learned that he had been selected to make the next Soviet space flight, then planned to be three orbits. The proposed duration was later lengthened to seventeen orbits, or a full day.

Following his flight Titov attended the Zhukovsky Air Force Engineering Academy with other cosmonauts, graduating in 1968, and joined the editorial board of *Aviatsiya i kosmonavtika (Aviation and Spaceflight)*, the Soviet equivalent of the American trade journal *Aviation Week*. In 1964 and 1965, no longer actively training for space flights, he served as "chief cosmonaut." For many years in the late 1960s he was the most visible of the Soviet cosmonauts, frequently interviewed by Western journalists and contributor to many Soviet and Western publications.

Following graduation from Zhukovsky, Titov left the cosmonaut team and trained as a test pilot under well-known Soviet aviator Vladimir Ilyushin. From 1970 to 1972 he attended the K. E. Voroshilov Military Staff Academy. He returned to the space program, acting as a flight controller for the Salyut 3 mission in 1974. From 1975 to 1978 he commanded an aircraft testing program. He also was a member of the committee planning the 1980 Moscow Olympics.

Lieutenant General Titov currently holds a post in the Ministry of Defense.

He is the author of two books, *A Million Miles in Orbit* (1961) and *My Blue Planet* (1977). In addition, his autobiography, as told to journalists Wilfred Burchett and Anthony Purdy and written by Martin Caidin, was published as *I Am Eagle!* (1962).

Titov and his wife, Tamara, live in Moscow. They have two daughters, Tatyana and Galina.

Titov, Vladimir

Vladimir Titov is the unlucky young pilot-cosmonaut who commanded two aborted space flights within five months.

Titov was the commander of Soyuz T-8, launched April 20, 1983, with a crew of three cosmonauts on a planned eight-month mission aboard the Salyut 7 space station. But a failure in the Soyuz T rendezvous radar forced Titov to attempt a tricky manual docking with the station, an attempt which did not succeed. He and fellow cosmonauts Gennady Strekalov and Alexandr Serebrov returned to Earth. Titov later wrote an unusually candid account of the flight for the Soviet military newspaper *Red Star*.

Five months later, late in the evening of September 26, 1983, Titov and Strekalov were ready for launch on another mission to Salyut 7, this time to relieve the crew of Vladimir Lyakhov and Alexandr Alexandrov, who had been aboard the station for 64 days. Just seconds before engine ignition a fire broke out at the base of the Soyuz launch vehicle. Ground controllers activated the abort system and Titov and Strekalov's Soyuz T module was separated from the launcher by escape rockets. As the launch vehicle exploded, the module containing Titov and Strekalov landed safely three miles away. The cosmonauts were quickly rescued and described as "safe but unhappy."

Vladimir Georgyevich Titov was born January 1, 1947, in the city of Stretinsk in the Chita region of the USSR. In 1970 he graduated from the Chernigov Higher Air Force School and served in Siberia as a flight instructor and as a military pilot first class. He joined the Party in 1971.

Titov joined the cosmonaut group in February 1976, completing the basic training course a year later, and a test pilot course in 1978, when he was then assigned to the Salyut 6 support group. He was backup commander for the Soyuz 35 flight in 1980, for Soyuz T-4 in 1981, Soyuz T-5 in 1982, and Soyuz T-14 in 1985.

Colonel Titov and his wife, Alexandra, and daughter Marina live in Star Town. He is a distant relative of Gherman Titov, the second Soviet cosmonaut to orbit the Earth.

Varlamov, Valentin

Valentin Stepanovich Varlamov was one of the most promising members of the first class of Soviet cosmonauts selected in March 1960. All through the first weeks of academic training, Varlamov was the best at mastering the intricacies of physics and astronavigation. By May 1960 he had been designated as one of the six finalists who were to undergo accelerated training for the first manned Vostok flight.

On July 24, 1960, however, Varlamov dislocated a vertabra in his neck while diving into a lake near Star Town. Hospitalized for a month, he was not allowed to continue training for space flight for medical reasons.

Varlamov remained with the space program, however, serving in the control center during the launch of Gagarin on April 12, 1961. He later became an instructor in astronavigation at the training center and was close friends with members of the cosmonaut group.

He died in October 1980 of a cerebral hemorrhage.

Vasyutin, Vladimir

Vladimir Vasyutin was the commander of the Soyuz T-14 mission to Salyut 7 in September 1985. He had the bad luck to become the first space traveler to become so ill during a mission that the flight was aborted.

Vasyutin, flight engineer Georgy Grechko and researcher Alexandr Volkov were launched on September 17, 1985, and docked with Salyut 7 the next day. Already aboard the station were cosmonauts Vladimir Dzhanibekov and Viktor Savinykh, who had just completed a dramatic repair of a station which had been adrift and out of control. Savinykh had trained with Vasyutin for many years and the two of them, with Volkov, made up the original 1985 Salyut 7 expedition crew, so he remained on board when Grechko returned to Earth with Dzhanibekov on September 25. For the next three weeks operations aboard the station went smoothly. The cargo and laboratory module Kosmos 1686 docked with the Salyut 7/Soyuz T-14 complex on October 2, carrying materials the cosmonauts would need during their "winter" mission, which would include observations of Halley's Comet in March 1986.

But in mid-October Vasyutin developed an infection which resisted treatment by antibiotics. By early November he was fighting a temperature which rose to 104 degrees F. Eventually there was no choice for Soviet space officials: the cosmonauts had to return to Earth, and they did, on November 21. Vasyutin was hospitalized for almost a month.

He spent a total of 65 days in space.

Vladimir Vladimirovich Vasyutin was born March 8, 1952, in the city of Kharkhov in the Ukraine. In 1970 he entered the Kharkov Higher Air Force School, graduating in 1974, then served as a pilot-instructor there until he was admitted to the cosmonaut team in February 1976.

After completing the basic training course, Vasyutin joined the Salyut 7 training group. His first assignment was as backup commander to Soyuz T-7 in 1982, replacing Yuri Romanenko, who had failed a physical exam. He then served as backup commander for Soyuz T-9, Soyuz T-10, and Soyuz T-12 before making his first flight.

Colonel Vasyutin is married and the father of two children.

Vetrov, Vladimir

Vladimir Vetrov is an engineer-cosmonaut who played a support role on missions to Salyut 4 in 1975 and Salyut 6 in 1977-81. He was originally assigned to two backup crews (one of them was probably Soyuz 18) but had to step down for physical reasons.

He was reportedly selected for cosmonaut training in 1967.

Volk, Igor

Igor Volk is a former test pilot turned spacecraft flight engineer who spent 12 days in space aboard Soyuz T-12 and Salyut 7 in July 1984.

Igor Petrovich Volk was born April 12, 1937, in the city of Gottwald in the Kharkov region. At the age of 17, while living in the city of Kursk, he joined a flying club and became a pilot. He then attended the Kirovgrad Higher Air Force School, graduating in 1956, after which he served as a pilot in the Soviet air force. He left the service in 1963 to enter the Moscow Aviation Institute, earning a degree in 1969.

He joined the Party in 1964.

While attending MAI Volk became a civilian test pilot for the Tupolev design bureau. He was a chase pilot for flights of the Tu-144 supersonic airliner and also tested the MiG-21. In 1976, while chairing an examination board judging student test pilots, he gave a passing grade to Svetlana Savtiskaya, whom he would later accompany into space.

Volk logged 4700 hours of flying time, 2700 as a test pilot, qualifying him as a Test Pilot First Class and an Honored Test Pilot of the USSR, prior to becoming a cosmonaut in December 1978.

Volk was a capcom for flights to Salyut 6 from 1979 to 1981, then joined the Salyut 7 training group. He is reportedly involved in the development of the Soviet space shuttle.

He and his wife, Valentina, have two daughters, Marina and Irina.

Volkov, Alexandr

Alexandr Volkov was cosmonaut-researcher of the Soyuz T-14 crew, which was launched September 17, 1985, for a planned six-month mission aboard the recently repaired Salyut 7. Volkov, a specialist in "add-on" modules, supervised the operations of Kosmos-1686, a transport craft and laboratory which carried eight tons of cargo, scientific equipment and fuel to Salyut 7 on September 27, 1985. Before the new materials could be fully utilized however, commander Vladimir Vasyutin became ill, and when he failed to respond to treatment Soviet officials cut short the mission. Volkov, Vasyutin and flight engineer Viktor Savinykh returned to Earth on November 21, 1985.

Volkov has logged approximately 65 days in space.

Alexandr Alexandrovich Volkov was born May 27, 1948, in the city of Gorlovka in the Donetsk region of the Ukraine. His father, a tank driver during the Great Patriotic War, was a bus driver there. Volkov joined the army, attending the Kharkov Higher Air Force School and graduating in 1970. From 1970 to 1976 he served as an air force instructor pilot, primarily at the Kharkhov school. He joined the Party in 1973.

Volkov joined the cosmonaut group in February 1976. After completing the basic training course he attended a test pilot school, earning a Test Pilot 2nd Class rating in 1978. He then joined the Soyuz T and Salyut training group and worked in support of the Soyuz T-8 and Soyuz T-9 missions, which were the first to involve Salyut add-on modules.

In November 1984 Volkov, Vasyutin and Savinykh were assigned to be the next Salyut "expedition" (long duration) crew, but major technical problems aboard Salyut 7 during the winter of 1984-85 caused the station to drift uncontrollably. In March 1985 a special rescue crew was formed consisting of Savinykh and veteran pilot Vladimir Dzhanibekov. Volkov and Vasyutin were joined by engineer Georgy Grechko in a second crew which would take over for the repairmen, should they be successful. Grechko returned to Earth with Dzhanibekov and the original expedition crew remained in space.

Colonel Volkov and his wife, Anna, have two sons, Dima and Sergei.

Volkov, Vladislav

Vladislav Volkov was flight engineer of the Soyuz 11 crew, the first cosmonauts to occupy an orbiting Salyut station. Tragically, on June 30, 1971, after 24 days in space, Volkov and fellow cosmonauts Georgy Dobrovolsky and Viktor Patsayev were killed during their return to Earth.

In October 1969 Volkov was flight engineer aboard Soyuz 7, one of three manned Soyuz craft which were in orbit at the same time.

At the time of his death he had spent almost 29 days in space.

Vladislav Nikolayevich Volkov was born November 23, 1935, in Moscow. His father was an aircraft designer, his mother worked in an aircraft factory, and an uncle was a pilot and War hero, so naturally Volkov wanted to become a pilot. He enrolled in a local flying club and took lessons. His family, however, suggested that rather than join the air force he should first study aeronautical engineering. Volkov took the advice and attended the Moscow Aviation Institute, graduating in 1959.

Volkov immediately went to work at the Korolev spacecraft design bureau, becoming a member of a group of young engineers under Korolev's chief assistant, Konstantin Feoktistov, and known as the "kindergarten," who designed the Vostok and Voskhod command modules and gave lectures to the cosmonauts, who were their contemporaries. In May 1964 Volkov and the others learned that their boss, Feoktistov, was going into space aboard the first Voskhod when chief designer Korolev announced that engineers from the bureau would be included in future space crews. The next morning Korolev found dozens of applications on his desk, one of them from Volkov. Two years later, in May 1966, Volkov was one of eight engineers admitted to the cosmonaut team.

During his cosmonaut training Volkov became an expert parachutist and also qualified as a jet pilot. He was not one of the first engineers to be chosen for a Soyuz crew, something which he found frustrating, but he was patient, and earned an assignment of his own in 1968. In addition to two flights in space, he also served as backup flight engineer for Soyuz 10.

Shortly before his death Volkov completed an autobiography titled *Stepping into the Sky*, which was published in 1971.

He is survived by his wife, Ludmilla, an engineer, and four sons. One of the boys, Konstantin Volkov, later became a champion pole vaulter, setting a world record in 1984.

Volynov, Boris

Boris Volynov commanded one of the two manned spacecraft that were the first to dock in space.

Volynov was the commander of the three-man Soyuz 5, launched January 15, 1969, which made a successful rendezvous and docking with Soyuz 4, piloted by Vladimir Shatalov, the next day. Volynov's two comrades, Yevgeny Khrunov and Alexei Yeliseyev, then donned spacesuits and made a walk in space to Soyuz 4. Volynov returned to Earth alone on January 17.

He later commanded a 48-day flight aboard the Salyut 5 space station in July and August 1976.

Boris Valentinovich Volynov was born December 18, 1934, in Irkutsk, Siberia. His father died when he was very young and he and his mother, a physician, moved to the mining city of Prokopyevsk, where Boris grew up. He was interested in the exploits of Soviet aviators as a child and joined the air force as soon as he was of age. He attended the Kacha Higher Air Force School near Volgograd, graduating in 1956. Future cosmonaut Gherman Titov was a student there at the same time. Volynov then served in the air force until joining the cosmonaut group in March 1960.

Volynov's cosmonaut career was an exercise in patience: he was a backup for two of the early Vostok flights, to Pavel Popovich on Vostok 4 in 1962, and to Valery Bykovsky on Vostok 5 in 1963. He was commander of one of two teams training for the first flight of a space crew, Voskhod 1 in 1964, but found himself as nominal backup a third time when the compressed training schedule (four months from crew selection to planned launch) caused the two crews to be combined. With Georgy Shonin as pilot, he trained as commander for a two-week-long Voskhod 3 mission planned for 1966, only to see that mission canceled before it could be flown. Transferred to the Soyuz group, he was a backup for a fourth time (Soyuz 3) before finally making his first space flight.

After Soyuz 5 he directed the training of the May 1970 cosmonaut group and was backup commander to the Soyuz 14 mission in 1974. He has also worked as a Salyut 6 and Salyut 7 flight controller, and performed graduate work for a candidate of technical sciences degree awarded in 1980. Since 1982 he has been chief of the cosmonaut team, responsible for the training of all flight crews.

Volynov joined the Party in 1958 and graduated from the Zhukovsky Air Force Engineering Academy in 1968.

His wife, Tamara, whom he met and married in his Siberian hometown, is a metallurgical engineer. They have a son, Andrei, and a daughter, Tatyana.

Yegorov, Boris

Boris Yegorov was the first medical doctor to make a spaceflight, as a member of the crew of the first Voskhod in October 1964. During this one-day flight Yegorov observed his and his fellow cosmonauts' reactions to microgravity and drew blood samples.

Boris Borisovich Yegorov was born in Moscow November 26, 1937. His father was a member of the USSR Academy of Medical Sciences and at a young age Boris decided to become a medical researcher specializing in aerospace medicine. He attended the First Moscow Medical Institute and during his last year there began to take part in the psychological testing of military pilots who were candidate cosmonauts. The first subject he met was his future commander, Vladimir Komarov. Upon graduation from the Institute in 1961 Yegorov went to work full time in the aerospace medical group headed by Dr. Nikolai N. Gurovsky.

While working on the cosmonaut medical team Yegorov oversaw sessions in the so-called soundproof chamber by cosmonauts Titov, Leonov and Popovich. Since he had become an amateur parachutist, Yegorov was assigned to one of the recovery teams for Vostok 1, the first manned space flight, in April 1961. Shortly thereafter Yegorov applied to Gurovsky for permission to join the cosmonaut group himself, and two years later, when chief designer Korolev planned a week-long Vostok flight by a medical specialist, Yegorov trained as one of the candidates. But the flight was canceled and he returned to his work, only to be recalled to cosmonaut training in April of 1964.

After his Voskhod flight Yegorov returned to school and in 1967 earned his doctor of medical sciences degree from Humbolt University in East Berlin. He was involved in the 22-day flight of two dogs aboard Kosmos 110 in 1966, and in the Soyuz 9 and Salyut 1 long duration missions. He joined the Party in 1975.

Yegorov is currently a professor and the head of a laboratory at a research institute. He and his wife Eleanora, an ophthalmologist, have a son, Boris.

Yeliseyev, Alexei

Alexei Yeliseyev made three Soyuz flights in three years and later directed the USSR's most successful space missions.

A flight engineer, Yeliseyev was part of the Soyuz 5 crew launched in January 1969. Soyuz 5 docked with Soyuz 4, launched a day earlier, and Yeliseyev and fellow cosmonaut Yevgeny Khrunov transferred from one spacecraft to the other by spacewalk, only the second spacewalk in the Soviet space program. Yeliseyev and Khrunov returned to Earth in Soyuz 4.

Yeliseyev was engineer aboard Soyuz 8 in October of 1969, a six-day mission that saw three manned Soyuz spacecraft in orbit at the same time. Yeliseyev's third flight, intended to be a month-long mission aboard the first Salyut, ended prematurely when the cosmonaut crew, after successfully docking Soyuz 10 with the station, could not open the hatch and enter the station. They were forced to return to Earth after just two days.

Yeliseyev logged nine days in space on his three missions, including one hour of EVA.

After his retirement from active cosmonaut training, Yeliseyev was the flight director for manned missions to Salyut 6 from 1977 to 1981. It was this series of 18 manned Soyuz and Soyuz T flights and several unmanned missions which inaugurated a new era in Soviet space flight. Originally planned to last two years at most, Salyut 6 was in operation for almost four years, at the end of which the USSR held all manned space duration records. It was a major technical achievement and also a miracle in management terms, demonstrating a new flexibility and ability to work around problems that had until then eluded Soviet space officials.

Alexei Stanislovich Yeliseyev was born July 13, 1943, in the village of Zhizdra in the Kaluga district of the USSR. His mother was a chemist and Yeliseyev grew up with an interest in science and mathematics. He won admittance to the elite Bauman Higher Technical School in Moscow, where he was not only an outstanding student but twice USSR champion in fencing. Following graduation in 1957 he went to work in the Korolev design bureau as an engineer. He joined the Party in 1967.

Yeliseyev applied for the cosmonaut team in June 1964, as soon as he heard the engineers might be accepted, and finally began to train in May 1966. He was part of the Soyuz 2 crew, scheduled for launch in April 1967 on a docking and spacewalk mission. But Soyuz 1, the target ship, developed problems and then crashed on return to Earth, killing cosmonaut Vladimir Komarov. Soyuz 2 was never launched; two years later its mission was accomplished by Soyuz 4 and Soyuz 5.

After Soyuz 10 in 1971 Yeliseyev completed his doctorate and became a flight controller and director. He was in charge of the Apollo-Soyuz Test Project flights in 1974 and 1975 and of Salyut 5 in 1976 and 1977. Since 1981 he has been a professor at the Bauman Higher Technical School, and in January 1986 became rector (president) of that institution.

Yeliseyev and his wife, Larissa, have a daughter, Yelena.

Zaikin, Dmitri

Dmitri Alexeyevich Zaikin was one of the first Soviet cosmonauts selected in March 1960. He served as backup commander to Pavel Belyayev on Voskhod 2 in 1965, replacing Viktor Gorbatko, who had to step aside for medical reasons. In April 1968 he was training with engineer Vladislav Volkov for a future Soyuz mission when a medical exam revealed that he had an ulcer, medically disqualifying him.

Colonel Zaikin graduated from the Zhukovsky Air Force Engineering Academy in February 1968. He remains at the Gagarin Cosmonaut Training Center as a senior engineer.

Zholobov, Vitaly

Vitaly Zholobov was flight engineer aboard the Soyuz 21 long-duration mission in 1976. He and commander Boris Volynov were launched on

July 6 of that year to a rendezvous with the Salyut 5 space station for a planned sixty days in space. Among their subjects for study was the effect of weightlessness on plants and animals. A large portion of their time was also taken up with military-related Earth surveillance. The mission ended after only 48 days because the cosmonauts seemed to be suffering from psychological problems caused by isolation; Salyut 5 had also suffered malfunctions in its air purification system. Zholobov and Volynov returned safely to Earth on August 24, 1976.

Vitaly Mikhailovich Zholobov was born June 18, 1937, in the village of Zburyevka in the Kherson region of the Ukraine. His family moved to Azerbaijan when he was young, where his father became a ship's captain on the Caspian Sea. Zholobov attempted to emulate him by joining the Soviet navy at age 17. He was rejected because he was too small.

Zholobov attended the Azerbaijan Petrochemical Institute, graduating in 1959, and then served as an inflight aerial refueling specialist in the Soviet army. He was chosen as a cosmonaut flight engineer in January 1963.

As a cosmonaut-trainee Zholobov transferred from the army to the air force. He joined the Party in 1966. After completing basic cosmonaut training in 1965 he became part of the Soyuz and Salyut engineering team at the Yangel design bureau, specializing in flight dynamics. He also worked on Earth resources experiments. Assigned to a Salyut training group in 1972, he served as backup flight engineer to Artyukhin on Soyuz 14 in 1974. During that same year Zholobov received a degree from the Lenin Military-Political Academy.

Following his only space flight, Zholobov served as capcom for Soyuz-23 in 1977. He retired from active cosmonaut status in 1981.

Zholobov and his wife, Lilia, have a daughter, Yelena.

Zudov, Vyacheslav

Vyacheslav Zudov commanded the ill-fated Soyuz 23 mission in October 1976. Zudov and flight engineer Valery Rozhdestvensky were to have linked up with the orbiting Salyut 5 space station for a sixty-day mission, but technical problems prevented the docking and the cosmonauts were forced to make an emergency return to Earth.

They landed in the salt water Lake Tengiz, one of the few lakes in the primary spacecraft landing zone, late at night in the middle of a blizzard. It was the first and so far only splashdown by a Soviet manned spacecraft. Zudov and Rozhdestvensky were not rescued until the next morning.

Vyacheslav Dmitriyevich Zudov was born January 8, 1942, in the village of Bor, Gorky region, but grew up in the Moscow area. He joined the Soviet air force and attended the Balashov Higher Air Force School, graduating in 1963, in the same class with future cosmonaut Gennady Sarafanov. Zudov flew military transports prior to joining the cosmonaut team in November 1965. He became a Party member in 1963.

As a cosmonaut-trainee, Zudov learned to fly high performance jets and also became an expert parachutist. He served as capcom for Soyuz flights from 1967 to 1969. In 1972 he joined the Salyut training group and served as backup to his old classmate Sarafanov on Soyuz 15 in 1974, and to Boris Volynov on Soyuz 21 in 1976.

Since his only space flight Zudov has graduated from the Yuri Gagarin Air Force Academy and currently works at Star Town as a training official. He and his wife, Nina, an engineer, have two daughters, Lena and Natasha.

PART 3 *International Space Travelers*

International Space Programs and Travelers

Michael Cassutt

From 1961 to the present, only the Soviet Union and the United States have demonstrated the ability to put human beings into space, meaning that ninety percent of space travelers have been citizens of those two countries.

But beginning in the mid-1970s, following the joint Soviet-American Apollo-Soyuz Test Project (1975), both countries began to provide citizens of other nations with the chance to go into space as guests.

In September 1976, the Soviet Union announced that it was recruiting pilots and engineers from countries who were members of Interkosmos, the international space organization formed in April 1967, for flights aboard Soyuz and Salyut spacecraft. Two guest cosmonauts were chosen from each member nation. The cosmonauts were all military officers and many had already studied in the Soviet Union. The first six guests, from Czechoslovakia, Poland and East Germany, arrived at the Gagarin Cosmonaut Training Center (Star Town) in December 1976. Ten others, from Bulgaria, Hungary, Cuba, Mongolia and Rumania, arrived in April 1978. Vietnam, which joined Interkosmos in 1979, sent two pilots in July of that year.

The guest cosmonaut program was expanded to allow flights by French citizens (with the first pair arriving in September 1980 and a second pair to start in September 1986), Indians (September 1982), and Syrians (September 1985).

The first international space travelers on American spacecraft were selected by the European Space Agency for flights on Spacelab originally scheduled to begin in 1980. Over 2000 scientists and engineers applied to ESA and in December 1977, four semifinalists were chosen. The three finalists, Merbold, Nicollier and Ockels, were announced in May 1978.

In December 1982, West Germany selected two scientists to train for the German Spacelab, Dl. ESA/Spacelab 1 scientists Merbold and Ockels were assigned here as well.

As Shuttle launches became more frequent, NASA liberalized its criteria for payload specialist opportunities. Prior to 1982, only customers (nations or companies) buying half of a Shuttle payload, or who were flying an experiment which required the presence of a particular scientist or engineer, were allowed to provide a payload specialist. Beginning in 1984, NASA said, all "major" Shuttle customers could, for a fee (usually $80,000 to cover 100 hours of training) send someone into space with a payload.

International payload specialists were selected by Great Britain (4 in March 1984), France (its 2 Interkosmos veterans, April 1984), Saudi Arabia (2 in April 1985), Mexico (2 in July 1985), Indonesia (2 in October 1985), and India (2 in November 1985). In addition, Brazil and Australia were invited to select Shuttle payload specialists, though none have been announced.

With the increased opportunities for flight aboard the Shuttle, Soviet spacecraft, and the proposed French Hermes, several nations actually selected teams of career astronauts who became employees of various national space agencies.

Canada became the first. Its National Research Council in Ottawa received over four thousand applications for "Space Team Canada" in 1983. Six people were selected in December of that year.

The National Space Development Agency of Japan (NASDA) chose three scientists in August 1985 to train for dedicated Japanese Spacelab missions and other Shuttle flights.

The French space agency, CNES, selected seven new "spationauts" in September 1985.

West Germany's Federal Aerospace Research Establishment (DFVLR) was in the final stages of selection for six science astronauts at the time of the Shuttle Challenger disaster in January 1986. The announcement of the finalists and the start of their training was postponed.

Italy selected five astronauts in early 1986.

International Space Travelers A Chronology of First Flights

1978	Czechoslovakia
	Poland
	German Democratic Republic
1979	Bulgaria
1980	Hungary
	Republic of Viet Nam
	Cuba
1981	Mongolia
	Rumania
1982	France
1983	European Space Agency
1984	India
	Canada
1985	Saudi Arabia
	Federal Republic of Germany
	Mexico

International Space Traveler Biographies

Bulgaria

Alexandrov, Alexandr

Alexandr Alexandrov was the backup Bulgarian cosmonaut-researcher for the aborted Soyuz 33 mission in April 1979.

Alexandrov was born December 1, 1951, in Omourtag, in northern Bulgaria. He attended the Georgy Benkovsky Higher Air Force School near Dolna. Injured in a parachuting accident while at school, he spent several months recuperating, but nevertheless managed to keep up with his studies and graduated with his class in 1974. He joined the Bulgarian Communist party in 1972.

Trained as a flight engineer, Alexandrov served with the Bulgarian air force and earned a chance to attend the Yuri Gagarin Air Force Academy in Moscow, graduating in 1978. In that same year Lieutenant-Engineer Alexandrov and Major Georgy Ivanov were chosen to be Bulgaria's Interkosmos cosmonauts. They reported to Star Town in March 1978.

Captain Alexandrov returned to air force service in Bulgaria in 1979. He is unmarried.

Ivanov, Georgy

Georgy Ivanov became the first Bulgarian in space when he served as cosmonaut-researcher of Soyuz 33 in April 1979. Ivanov's flight, however, unlike those of the other Interkosmos cosmonauts, was aborted after two days when an engine failure aboard Soyuz prevented docking with the Salyut 6 space station. The engine problem forced Ivanov and Soviet commander Nikolai Rukavishnikov to use backup systems to return to Earth, subjecting the cosmonauts to high G-loads during a tricky nighttime landing.

Ivanov was born July 2, 1940, in Lovech, Bulgaria. He attended a technical secondary school, where he joined the DOSO, a junior civil defense organization, in which he became a parachutist and light aircraft pilot. He tried to join the air force, but failed the physical. A year later he was accepted, and enrolled in the Georgy Benkovsky air force college, graduating in 1964.

His lifelong dream was to be a fighter pilot and he found his first assignment after leaving school—teaching other students—frustrating. He persevered, however, and ultimately became a flight leader, then a squadron commander. He joined the Bulgarian Communist Party in 1968.

Ivanov passed the medical examinations for the cosmonaut team in 1976, but did not report to Star Town for training until March 1978.

Since returning to Bulgaria Ivanov has become a candidate for membership in the central committee of the Bulgarian Communist party.

He and his wife, Natalia, have a daughter, Ani.

Canada

Bondar, Roberta

Dr. Roberta Bondar is one of the six astronauts of Space Team Canada selected in December 1983. She is currently training as backup payload specialist to Robert Thirsk for a future Space Shuttle mission. She also heads the Life Sciences Subcommittee for Canada's participation in the NASA Space Station.

Roberta Lynn Bondar was born December 4, 1945, in Sault Ste. Marie, Ontario, where she attended primary and secondary schools. She earned several university degrees: a BS in zoology and agriculture from the University of Guelph (1968), MS in experimental pathology from the University of Western Ontario (1971), PhD in neurobiology from the University of Toronto (1974), and MD degree from McMaster University in 1977. She has been a Fellow of the Royal College of Physicians and Surgeons of Canada since 1981.

While still an undergraduate, Bondar began working for the Canadian Fisheries and Forestry Department, an association which lasted for six years. She also completed medical training at Toronto General Hospital and at Tufts New England Medical Center in Boston. Her specialization is neuro-ophthalmology. In 1982 she became assistant professor of medicine at McMaster University while also serving as director of the Multiple Sclerosis Clinic for the Hamilton-Wentworth Region. Since joining the Canadian space program she has been a part-time lecturer at the University of Ottawa and teaches at Ottawa General Hospital.

Bondar is a pilot and her hobbies include target shooting. She is unmarried.

Garneau, Marc

Marc Garneau became the first citizen of Canada to make a space flight when he was a payload specialist aboard Shuttle Mission 41-G in October 1984. During his eight days aboard the Shuttle Challenger Garneau worked on ten different experiments designed by Canadian scientists, including medical tests devoted to discovering the causes of space adaptation syndrome (SAS).

Garneau, a Commander in the Canadian Navy, was born February 23, 1949, in Quebec City, Quebec. He attended primary and secondary schools there and in London, England. In 1970 he received a bachelor of engineering physics degree from the Royal Military College of Kingston. He went on to earn a doctorate in electrical engineering from the Imperial College of Science and Technology, London, in 1973.

Garneau has a lifelong interest in the sea: in 1969 and 1970 he sailed across the Atlantic twice in a 59-foot yawl with 12 other people, including his brother Phillipe, a journalist who later interviewed him while Garneau was in space.

From 1974 until joining Space Team Canada in December 1983 Garneau served in the Canadian Navy in a number of posts. He was a combat systems engineer aboard HMCS Algonquin from 1974 to 1976, and the following year worked as an instructor at the Candian Forces Fleet School. He later served as a project engineer in naval weapons systems in Ottawa and Halifax.

In July 1983, while on vacation, Garneau saw a newspaper ad soliciting applicants for a team of Canadian astronauts. He applied and was selected, and in March 1984 was assigned to a Space Shuttle crew.

Garneau is married to the former Jacqueline Brown of London, England. They have twin sons, Yves and Simone, and live in Ottawa, where Garneau continues his work with Space Team Canada.

MacLean, Steven

Dr. Steve MacLean has been chosen to become Canada's second space traveler. In December 1985 he was named as payload specialist for a Shuttle mission then scheduled for 1987, during which he was to operate the space vision system designed by the Canadian National Research Council. The SVS, one of five Canadian experiments to travel with MacLean, is designed to test improvements in the use of the Shuttle's remote manipulator arm (also built in Canada).

Steven Glenwood MacLean was born December 14, 1954, in Ottawa, Canada, where he grew up. He attended York University, receiving a BS in honors physics in 1977, and a PhD in astrophysics in 1983.

MacLean was doing research in laser physics at Stanford University in California when selected for the Canadian astronaut group. He also has a background in sports, as a member of the Canadian National Gymnastics Team in 1976 and 1977.

He is unmarried.

Money, Ken

Dr. Ken Money, a physiologist and pilot, is one of the six astronauts of Space Team Canada. He is currently working on experiments concerning space adaptation syndrome.

Kenneth Money was born January 4, 1935, in Toronto, Ontario. He attended primary and secondary schools in Toronto and Noranda, Quebec, then attended the University of Toronto, where he received a BS in phsyiology and biochemistry (1958), an MS in physiology (1959), and a PhD in physiology (1961).

While he was still a college undergraduate Money earned Royal Canadian Air Force pilot's wings at the Advanced Flying School in Portage La Prairie, Manitoba, in 1957. He eventually logged over 4000 hours of flying time in T-33, F-86, C-45 and Otter aircraft as a member of the Canadian Forces Air Reserve. In 1972 he attended the National Defence College.

He also found time to represent Canada as a high-jumper in the 1956 Olympic Games in Melbourne, Australia, and in the 1958 British Empire and Commonwealth Games in Cardiff, Wales.

Since 1961 Money has been a scientist at the Defence and Civil Institute of Environmental Medicine, Department of National Defence in Toronto. His main area of research has been motion sickness and its effects on pilots. He has published over 80 scientific papers, and, as a result of a long association with NASA, has seen his experiments concerning motion sickness selected for several Spacelab missions.

Money is also associated with St. Michael's Hospital, Toronto, and with the University of Toronto.

He and his wife, Sheila, have a daughter, Laura Ann.

Thirsk, Robert

Dr. Bob Thirsk served as backup payload specialist to Commander Marc Garneau for Shuttle Mission 41-G in October 1984, during which Garneau became the first Canadian in space. Thirsk, a physician and engineer, has been chosen to be Canada's third space traveler.

Robert Brent Thirsk was born August 17, 1953, in New Westminster, British Columbia, attending primary and secondary schools there and in Alberta. He graduated from John Taylor Collegiate in Winnipeg, then received a BS in mechanical engineering from the University of Calgary (1976), an MS in mechanical engineering from the Massachusetts Institute of Technology (1978), and a doctor of medicine degree from McGill University (1982).

Thirsk was chief resident in family medicine at Queen Elizabeth Hospital in Montreal when chosen for the Canadian astronaut group in 1983. He had also done research in biomedical engineering.

He is married to Brenda Biasutti.

Tryggvason, Bjarni

Bjarni V. Tryggvason is one of the six astronauts chosen for Space Team Canada in December 1983. In December 1985 he was designated backup payload specialist to Steven MacLean for a Space Shuttle mission then scheduled for 1987.

Tryggvason was born September 21, 1945, in Reykjavik, Iceland, but grew up in Nova Scotia and British Columbia. He attended the University of British Columbia, receiving a BS in physics in 1972. He has done graduate work in aerodynamics and applied mathematics at the University of Western Ontario.

Beginning in 1972 Tryggvason worked as a meteorologist at the Atmospheric Environment Service in Toronto. Two years later he became a research associate at the University of Western Ontario, performing studies of the effects of wind on structures such as the Sears Tower in Chicago. He later did research at Kyoto University in Japan, at James Cook University of North Queensland in Australia, finally joining the National Research Council in 1982.

Tryggvason is also a pilot and instructor.

He and his wife, Lily-Anna, have a son, Michael.

Cuba

Lopez-Falcon, Jose

Jose Armando Lopez-Falcon was the backup cosmonaut-researcher for fellow Cuban Arnaldo Tamayo-Mendez during the Soyuz-38 flight in September 1980.

Lopez-Falcon was born February 8, 1950, in Havana, and was a captain in the Cuban air force when he began cosmonaut training in March 1978. He is married and the father of one child.

Tamayo-Mendez, Arnaldo

Arnaldo Tamayo-Mendez, a pilot in the Cuban air force, became the first Latin and the first black in space when he served as cosmonaut-researcher aboard Soyuz 38 in September 1980. He and Soviet commander Yuri Romanenko spent eight days in space, seven of them visiting cosmonauts Popov and Ryumin aboard the Salyut 6 space station.

Tamayo-Mendez was born January 29, 1942, in Guantanamo, Cuba. He was orphaned as a child and by the age of thirteen was working as a shoeshine boy. He later worked as an apprentice carpenter, then became an anti-Batista activist and rebel. After the Cuban Revolution in 1959, Tamayo-Mendez, then a soldier, was enrolled in the Rebeldi Technical Institute where he was first trained as an aviation technician prior to becoming a pilot.

He was sent to the Soviet Union in April 1961 to attend the Yeisk Higher Air Force School for a year. He returned to Cuba to serve in the Playa Giron Brigade as a flight instructor, then squadron leader, and finally as deputy wing commander. He also studied at the General Maximo Gomez Basic College of Revolutionary Armed Forces (1969-71).

He became a member of Cuba's Communist party in 1967.

Tamayo-Mendez was selected for cosmonaut training in 1976 and reported to Star Town in April 1978.

He and his wife, Maria, have two sons, Orlando and Arnaldo.

Czechoslovakia

Pelczak, Oldrich

Colonel Oldrich Pelczak was the backup cosmonaut-researcher for Vladimir Remek, the first citizen of a nation other than the Soviet Union or the United States to make a spaceflight.

Remek, from Czechoslovakia, was launched into space aboard Soyuz 28 in March 1978. He and Soviet commander Alexei Gubarev joined two other Soviet cosmonauts aboard the Salyut 6 space station as they broke the American-held space endurance record of 84 days. Pelczak supported his countryman's eight-day flight from Soviet mission control at Kaliningrad, near Moscow.

Pelczak was born November 2, 1943, in the city of Gottwaldow, Czechoslovakia. In 1962 he graduated from the Ukerske-Hradiste junior engineering college, then entered the Kosice Air Force College. From 1965 on he was a flight engineer in the Czech air force. He joined the Czechoslovakian Communist party in 1964.

Pelczak also spent several years in the Soviet Union as a student at the Yuri Gagarin (Red Banner) Air Force Academy, from which he graduated in 1972. He and Remek began training for space flight in December 1976.

Pelczak and his wife, Hana, have two children, Oldrich and Milos.

Remek, Vladimir

Vladimir Remek was the first citizen of a nation other than the US or the USSR to go into space. A pilot in the Czechoslovakian air force, the 29-year old Remek served as cosmonaut-researcher aboard Soyuz 28 in March 1978. He and Soviet commander Alexei Gubarev spent eight days in space, most of it aboard the Salyut 6 space station as visitors to cosmonauts Romanenko and Grechko. During the flight Remek supervised the operation of several Czech-designed scientific experiments.

Remek was born September 26, 1948, in the city of Ceske-Budejovice, Czechoslovakia. His father is a pilot who became a lieutenant general in the Czech air force. Remek finished secondary school (majoring in physics and mathematics) in 1966 and enrolled in the Kosice air force college, graduating in 1970. He became a member of the Czechoslovakian Communist party in 1968.

Beginning in 1970 he served as a jet pilot with the Czech air force. In 1972 he was sent to the USSR to attend the Gagarin Air Force Academy and had recently completed that program in 1976 when he was selected for Interkosmos training.

After leaving the Interkosmos program in 1978 Remek returned to his homeland, where he attended the Antonin Zapotsky Military Academy. He also published two books, *Above Our Planet Earth* and, with Gubarev, *International Orbit*.

Colonel Remek married actress Hana Davidova in 1979 and is now divorced. He has a daughter, Anna.

European Space Agency

Merbold, Ulf

German scientist Dr. Ulf Merbold was the first non-American to go into space on a US vehicle. He served as payload specialist on Spacelab 1/ STS-9, launched November 28, 1983. As a member of a crew of six, Merbold operated experiments in a variety of disciplines aboard the European-built Spacelab. The Shuttle Columbia returned to Earth at Edwards Air Force Base, California, on December 8, 1983.

In 1985 Merbold served as backup payload specialist for Spacelab D1, the German Spacelab, launched aboard Shuttle Mission 61-A.

Ulf Merbold was born in Greiz, Germany, on June 20, 1941. His father was killed in World War II, and Merbold grew up in Soviet East Germany until he fled to the West at the age of 19. His mother still lives in East Germany.

Merbold attended Stuttgart University, receiving a diploma in physics in 1968. While still a student he began working at the Max-Planck Gesellschaft in Stuttgart and later became a staff member there. One of his projects studied the irradiation damage inflicted on iron and vanadium by fast neutrons. This research led to Merbold's doctorate in science from Stuttgart University in 1976.

Merbold was a researcher at Max-Planck in 1978 when the European Space Agency selected him as a finalist for payload specialist aboard the Spacelab 1 mission, then planned for 1981. Merbold relocated to Huntsville, Alabama, home of the NASA Marshall Space Flight Center, to train for the mission while continuing his research.

Merbold is married and the father of two children. He has returned to Stuttgart and the Max-Planck Institute.

Nicollier, Claude

Claude Nicollier is a European Space Agency payload specialist who, under a special agreement between ESA and NASA, joined the May 1980 group of astronaut candidates for training to qualify him as a Shuttle mission specialist. He successfully completed the year-long training and evaluation course in July 1981 and was assigned as an astronaut on the Spacelab Earth Observation Mission, originally scheduled for the summer of 1986, but postponed because of the Shuttle Challenger disaster.

Nicollier was born September 2, 1944, in Vevey, Switzerland. He graduated from Gymnase de Lausanne (secondary school) in 1962, then received a BS in physics from the University of Lausanne in 1970. He later earned his MS in astrophysics from the University of Geneva in 1975.

Nicollier worked as a scientist with the Institute of Astronomy at Lausanne University and at the Geneva Observatory while also attending the Swiss Air Transport School and piloting DC-9s for Swissair. In 1976 he accepted a fellowship at the ESA Space Science Department at Noordwijk, the Netherlands, where he took part in the ASSESS-II Spacelab mission simulation. In July 1978 he was selected by ESA as one of three ESA Spacelab 1 payload specialists. He spent two years training for Spacelab 1 prior to transferring to the astronaut group.

Nicollier is a first lieutenant in the Swiss Air Force and has logged over 3100 hours of flying time, including 2000 hours in jets.

He and his wife, Susana, and children Maya and Marina live in Houston.

Ockels, Wubbo

Wubbo Ockels was a payload specialist aboard the Spacelab D1 (Deutschland 1), Space Shuttle Mission 61-A in October and November 1985. He and seven other astronauts performed experiments in life sciences and materials processing that were designed and controlled by the Federal German Aerospace Research Establishment (DFVLR).

The eight astronauts aboard Spacelab D1 were divided into two three-astronaut teams working in twelve-hour shifts. Ockels and mission commander Henry Hartsfield "floated" between shifts, working where and as much as each wanted, and during the flight Ockels had to be reminded by German mission control to make sure he got some sleep.

Ockels has logged approximately 169 hours in space flight.

Wubbo Ockels was born March 28, 1946, in Almelo, The Netherlands, though he grew up in Groningen. He received his doctorate in physics and mathematics from the University of Groningen in 1973 and finished his thesis in 1978.

From 1973 to 1978 Ockels was a researcher at the Nuclear Physics Accelerator Institute at Groningen, involved in designing computer software and detection devices for the particle accelerator there. He also taught.

In 1978 Ockels was chosen by the European Space Agency as one of three finalists for the Spacelab 1 mission. When Spacelab 1 was launched in November 1983 Ockels was the backup payload specialist for Dr. Ulf Merbold, and supported the flight from the mission control center at NASA's Marshall Space Center in Huntsville, Alabama.

In May 1980, under an agreement between NASA and the ESA, Ockels and fellow Spacelab payload specialist Claude Nicollier began astronaut training with 19 NASA candidates, successfully completing this course in August 1981.

Dr. Ockels, a Dutch citizen, and his wife, Joos, have two children, Geanneke and Martin.

Federal Republic of Germany

Furrer, Rheinhard

Dr. Rheinhard Furrer was a payload specialist aboard the Spacelab D1 (Deustchland 1), Space Shuttle Mission 61-A flight in October and November 1985. During this week-long flight Furrer and seven other astronauts performed 76 experiments, many of them involving the manufacturing of new metals in a weightless environment, and the study of human reactions to space flight.

The experiments aboard Spacelab D1 were controlled by the Federal German Aerospace Research Establishment (DFVLR), not NASA, as had been the case in three previous Spacelab missions.

Furrer has logged 169 hours in space.

Rheinhard Furrer was born in Worgl, Germany, on November 25, 1940. He attended secondary school at Kempten/Allgau, then studied physics at the Universities of Kiel and Berlin. He received a diploma in physics in 1969 and a doctorate in physics in 1972.

Furrer has been a researcher at the University of Stuttgart, at the Free University of Berlin, and a visiting scientist at the University of Chicago's Argonne National Laboratory. He also holds a commercial pilot rating. He was selected as a D1 payload specialist in December 1982.

Furrer is unmarried.

Messerschmid, Ernst

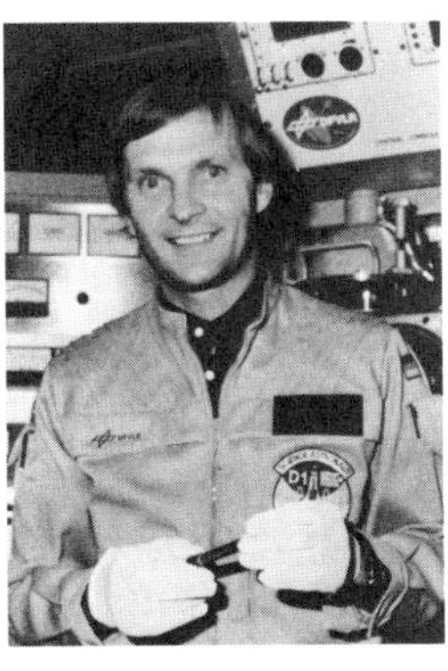

Dr. Ernst Messerschmid was a payload specialist aboard Spacelab D1 (Deustchland 1), Space Shuttle Mission 61-A, the first space flight to be controlled by a country other than the US or the USSR.

For seven days Messerschmid and seven fellow astronauts (D1 had a crew of eight, the largest sent into space in one vehicle) performed 76 different experiments, most of them concerning materials processing and life sciences. The flight was unique because the scientific payloads were directed from the mission control center of the DFVLR (Federal German Aerospace Research Establishment) at Oberpfaffenhoffen, near Munich, West Germany. The German control center was known as "D-Eins Munchen" during the flight, for which the DFVLR had paid NASA $75 million.

Messerschmid himself suffered mild symptoms of Space Adaptation Syndrome, one of the subjects he was sent into space to study. He also kept tabs on the adaptation to spaceflight of a fruit fly—named "Willi"—who escaped from one of the experiments.

At the end of the Dl mission Messerschmid had logged approximately 169 hours in space.

Ernst Willi Messerschmid was born May 21, 1945, in the city of Reutlingen, in what is now the Federal Republic of Germany. He passed the entrance examinations for the Technisches Gymnasium in Stuttgart in 1965, but was drafted and spent two years in the army. He studied physics at Tubingen and Bonn Universities, receiving his diploma in 1972 and his doctorate in 1976.

Messerschmid has been a scientist at the CERN high energy physics institute in Geneva and at the Brookhaven National Laboratory in New York. Since 1978 he has been with the DFVLR. He also lectures at Stuttgart University. He was selected as a Dl payload specialist in December 1982.

Messerschmid is married.

France

Baudry, Patrick

Patrick Baudry was the first French spationaut to fly aboard the American Space Shuttle, serving as payload specialist of Mission 51-G in May 1985. During that eight-day flight of the Shuttle Discovery, Baudry operated a specially designed French echocardiograph similar to the one flown aboard the Soviet Salyut 7 space station in 1982.

He has logged approximately 7 days, 2 hours in space.

Patrick Baudry was born March 6, 1946, in Douala, United Republic of Cameroon. In 1967 he entered the Ecole de l'Air (the French Air Force Academy), graduating two years later with a master's degree in aeronautical engineering.

He underwent pilot training at Salon-de-Provence and Tours in France, receiving his wings in 1970. For the next eight years he served as a fighter pilot with Squadron 1/11 "Roussillon," flying F-100s and Jaguars on missions in France and Africa. He entered the Empire Test Pilot School at Boscombe Down, England, in 1978, and won the Patuxent River Trophy as the highest-ranking student. In 1979 he was assigned to the flight test center at Bretigny-sur-Orge in France.

As a pilot he has logged over 4000 hours of flying time, including 3300 hours in jets, in over 100 different types of aircraft.

In June 1980 Baudry was one of two French Air Force pilots chosen by CNES, the French space agency, as "spationauts." For the next two years he trained at CNES and at Star Town near Moscow for a Soviet Soyuz/Salyut mission, serving as backup cosmonaut-researcher to Chretien at the launch in 1982. In April 1984 Baudry was chosen to be prime French payload specialist for an American Shuttle flight and came to the United States for training.

Following his Shuttle mission in 1985 Baudry returned to France to become chief test pilot for Hermes, the French-built space shuttle scheduled for launch in the mid-1990s.

Baudry speaks Russian and English and is known as a wine connoisseur. (He managed to take wine aboard his Shuttle flight.)

Colonel Baudry and his wife have a daughter, Melodie, and live in the Bordeaux region of France.

Chretien, Jean-Loup

Jean-Loup Chretien became the first Westerner to go into space aboard a Soviet spacecraft when he served as the Soyuz T–6 cosmonaut-researcher in June and July 1982. Chretien and Soviet cosmonauts Vladimir Dzhanibekov and Alexandr Ivanchenkov spent eight days in space, seven of them with cosmonauts Berezovoy and Lebedev aboard the Salyut 7 space station. During the mission Chretien supervised the operations of a French-built echocardiograph, a heart-monitoring system designed for use in space.

Chretien is also the leading candidate for a month-long visit by a French "spationaut" to the Soviet Mir space station in 1988.

He has logged approximately 7 days, 23 hours in space.

Jean-Loup Chretien was born August 20, 1938, in La Rochelle, France, and attended the Ecole de l'Air (the French Air Force Academy), graduating in 1961. He later earned a master's degree in aeronautical engineering.

Chretien underwent flight training and earned his wings in 1962.

For the next seven years he was a Mirage III fighter pilot with the 5th Fighter Squadron based in Orange, France. In 1970 he entered the test pilot school at Istres, becoming the chief test pilot for the Mirage Fl. At the time of his selection to be a French space traveler he was deputy chief of the South Air Defense Division.

He has logged over 6000 hours of flying time.

In June 1980 Chretien and Patrick Baudry, another French Air Force pilot, were chosen by CNES, the French space agency, to train for a flight on the Soviet Soyuz and Salyut spacecraft. In October 1980 they arrived at Star Town, the cosmonaut training center outside Moscow, where they lived and worked for the next eighteen months.

Though training went smoothly, there were problems: the French spationauts found themselves eating lunch in a section of the center's cafeteria that had been cordoned off. And the original Soviet commander, Yuri Malyshev, was replaced in early 1982, apparently because he insisted on treating veteran test pilot Chretien as nothing more than a passenger.

In 1984 and 1985 Chretien served as backup to Baudry during training for an American Shuttle flight, eventually flown as Mission 51-G in May 1985. The French pilots also had some problems with the American system, beginning on their first day at the Johnson Space Center, when they were left waiting at the entrance for hours.

Chretien speaks fluent Russian and English. He and his wife have four children, Jean-Baptiste, Oliver, Emmanuel, and Francois.

Clervoy, Jean-Francois

Jean-Francois Clervoy is one of the seven French spationauts selected in September 1985 for possible space flights aboard the Soviet Mir station, the American Shuttle, and the Hermes spaceplane.

Clervoy was born November 19, 1958, at Longueville, France. He attended a polytechnical school and studied avionics, and earned a degree from the National Higher School for Aeronautics and Space in 1983.

A private pilot who has also made over 155 parachute jumps, Clervoy is an engineer employed by CNES, the French space agency, at Toulouse.

In April 1986 he joined French space veteran Jean-Loup Chretien and pilot Michel Tognini in preliminary tests and training for a month-long flight by a French spationaut aboard the Mir space station in 1988.

Clervoy is unmarried.

Deshays, Claudie

Dr. Claudie Deshays is one of the seven French spationauts selected in September 1985 to train for flights aboard the Soviet Mir space station, the American Space Shuttle, and the French Hermes spacecraft. As one of four "experimenters" in the group she will be concerned primarily with scientific experiments.

Deshays was born May 13, 1957, in Creusot, France. She earned her doctorate in medicine (with honors) in 1981, specializing in biology and sports medicine. She performed further study in aviation medicine in 1983. Currently she is a professor of rheumatics at Cochin Hospital in Paris.

She is married.

Favier, Jean-Jacques

Dr. Jean-Jacques Favier, a physicist, was chosen in September 1985 as one of seven French spationauts who will participate in flights aboard Soviet, American and European spacecraft between 1988 and the mid-1990s. Favier is one of four "experimenters" (scientists) in the group.

Favier was born April 13, 1949, in Kehl, France. After completing secondary school in 1968 he entered the Grenoble Polytechnical Institute to study electrical engineering. He earned a degree in physics in 1972, a doctor of engineering in 1976 and a doctor of science in 1977.

Since 1976 he has been head of the physics group at the Nuclear Research Center in Grenoble.

Favier is married with three children.

Haignere, Jean-Pierre

Major Jean-Pierre Haignere of the French air force is one of the seven new spationauts selected in September 1985 to train for future flights aboard Soviet, American and French spacecraft.

Haignere was born May 19, 1948, in Paris and entered the French Air Academy in 1969, earning a diploma in engineering in 1971. He served as a fighter pilot and squadron leader in the French air force, then attended the Empire Test Pilot School at Boscombe Down, England, graduating in 1982. He is currently chief test pilot at the flight test center in Bretigny, France, and has logged over 3000 hours of flying time.

He is married with two children.

Patat, Frederic

Dr. Frederic Patat is one of the four "experimenters" (scientists) chosen with three "onboard engineers" as French spationauts in September 1985. Patat and the others will train for possible space flights aboard Soviet, American and French vehicles.

Patat was born June 24, 1958, in the city of Lyons, France. He attended a polytechnical school, and in 1981 earned a degree in acoustic physics from the University of Paris. He completed a doctorate in engineering in 1984.

He is currently a biophysicist at the Faculty of Medicine in Tours, France. He has been involved in the development of the echocardiograph experiment which has flown on the Soviet Salyut 7 space station and on the American Space Shuttle Discovery.

Patat is married.

Tognini, Michel

Major Michel Tognini of the French air force is one of seven spationauts selected in September 1985. Members of this group join space veteran

Jean-Loup Chretien in training for flights aboard Soviet, American and French spacecraft.

Tognini was born September 30, 1949, in Vincennes, France. He qualified as an air force engineer in 1973, then became a fighter pilot the following year. After serving in the air force, he attended the Empire Test Pilot School at Boscombe Down, England, graduating in 1982. He has logged over 3000 hours of flying time.

Tognini is currently deputy chief test pilot at the air base at Cazaux. In April 1986 he and Jean-Francois Clervoy were chosen semifinalists with Chretien for a flight aboard the Mir space station scheduled for 1988. In August 1986 CNES announced that Tognini was a finalist, with Chretien, and would soon commence cosmonaut training.

Tognini is married with two children.

Viso, Michel

Dr. Michel Viso, a veterinary surgeon and engineer, is one of the seven French spationauts chosen in September 1985. Viso, like the three other "experimenters" (scientists) and three "onboard engineers" chosen with him will train for flights into space on the American Space Shuttle, the Soviet Mir space station, and the French Hermes spaceplane.

Viso was born June 16, 1951, in Mauvezin, France. From 1971 to 1975 he attended the Maison Alfort Veterinary School, then practiced for three years. He taught from 1978 to 1980, when he joined the national Institute for Agronomical Studies, where he studied immunology and became a researcher in the pathology of viruses.

He is unmarried.

German Democratic Republic

Jaehn, Sigmund

Sigmund Jaehn became the first German in space when he served as cosmonaut-researcher of Soyuz 31 during an eight-day flight in August and September 1978. He and Soviet commander Valery Bykovsky visited cosmonauts Kovalenok and Ivanchenkov aboard Salyut 6, returning to Earth in their Soyuz 29 vehicle.

Jaehn was born February 13, 1937, in Rautenkranz in what later became East Germany (the German Democratic Republic). He grew up in a war-torn land in difficult circumstances. At the age of 13 he went to work as a printer. Five years later he joined the army, enrolling at the Franz Mering air force college, from which he graduated in 1958. He joined the German Socialist Unity party in 1956.

He served as a pilot, instructor and squadron commander until 1966, when his work earned him an appointment to the Gagarin Air Force Academy in the Soviet Union. Returning to Germany, he became an inspector for the general staff of the German air force. He was selected for cosmonaut training in December 1976.

Colonel Jaehn and his wife, Erika, have two daughters, Marina and Grit.

Kohllner, Eberhard

Colonel Eberhard Kohllner served as backup cosmonaut-researcher for Sigmund Jaehn, the first German in space. During the eight-day flight of Jaehn and Soviet cosmonaut Valery Bykovsky aboard Soyuz 31, Kohllner served as capcom and support crewman from mission control at Kaliningrad, near Moscow.

Kohllner was born September 29, 1939, in Strassfurt, Germany. In 1961 he graduated from the Franz Mering Air Force School and served as a pilot. He spent several years in the Soviet Union as a student at the Yuri Gagarin (Red Banner) Air Force Academy, graduating in 1970. In March 1978 he and Jaehn were selected for cosmonaut training.

Kohllner is married with two children.

Great Britain

Boyle, Tony

Lieutenant Colonel Tony Boyle, Royal Signals, was named in March 1984 as one of four British payload specialists for Space Shuttle missions. But a security breach in his former command in West Germany forced him to drop out of the space program in 1985.

Boyle was born in 1940 in Kidderminster. He attended the Army's Welbeck College and St. Catharine's College, Cambridge, where he earned a BA in mechanical sciences in 1965. He later added an MA in mechanical sciences.

He served as a military communications officer in the Far East and in Germany, and also held a position in the Ministry of Defense. He was commander of the 20th Armored Brigade Headquarters and Signals Squadron in West Germany prior to becoming an instructor at the Royal Military College of Science in Shrivenham, his post at the time he was chosen for space training.

Boyle and his wife, Ann, have three children, Andrew, Katie, and Jenny.

Farrimond, Richard

Major Richard A. Farrimond, Royal Corps of Signals, was chosen as the backup payload specialist for the American Shuttle mission during which the first Briton will fly in space.

Farrimond was added to the group of UK astronauts in the summer of 1985 when Lieutenant Colonel Tony Boyle, also of Signals, was recalled to other duties.

Farrimond was born September 15, 1947, in Birkenhead, Cheshire. His father is a retired army officer. He was educated at Clifton College, Bristol and Wellback College, then entered the Sandhurst military college, graduating in 1967.

From 1968 to 1982 he served at a variety of Signals posts in Germany, Northern Ireland, and Canada, and also did further study in telecommunications engineering at Kings College, Cambridge, and the Royal Military College of Science at Shrivenham. Since 1982 he has been commander of the 8th Infantry Brigade Headquarters and Signals Squadron in Northern Ireland.

Farrimond and his wife, Annette, have three sons, David, Andrew and Peter.

Holmes, Christopher

Christopher Holmes is one of the four British Shuttle astronauts chosen in March 1984. He was assigned as the backup payload specialist for the Skynet 4B satellite launch originally scheduled for 1988.

Holmes was born in London in 1950 and attended Queen Mary College there, earning an honors degree in physics in 1972. He has been employed by the Ministry of Defense since that time, as a procurement executive and satellite specialist in the field of military telecommunications. At the time of his selection for space training he was deputy project manager for Skynet 4.

Holmes is unmarried and lives in London.

Longhurst, Peter

Commander Peter Longhurst, Royal Navy, was originally scheduled to be Great Britain's second space traveler, accompanying the launch of the Skynet 4B military communications satellite. But the Shuttle Challenger explosion forced Britain to shift Skynet 4B to the European Arianne expendable launch vehicle.

It was widely rumored in London newspapers in 1983 that Longhurst, a specialist in the Skynet satellite, had already been chosen to be the first British astronaut. The publication of those rumors apparently roused the competing services to action. When the Ministry of Defense announced its astronauts, there were four: one from each of the services, and one civilian. Longhurst was named to be the second Briton in space in 1985.

Peter Longhurst was born in 1942 in Staines, Middlesex, though he spent much of his youth in Devon. He attended Ardling School and Dartmouth, then spent a year at sea as a midshipman. He graduated from the Royal Naval Engineering College at Manadon, earning a BS in electrical engineering. He then served in a series of Navy berths as a weapons engineer specialist on frigates and as a teacher. He joined the Skynet program in 1981 as the Ministry of Defense director of naval operational requirements.

Longhurst is unmarried and lives in London.

Wood, Nigel

Squadron Leader Nigel Wood, Royal Air Force, is scheduled to become Great Britain's first astronaut in 1989, when he supervises the launch of the Skynet 4A military communications satellite from the American Space Shuttle.

Wood was born in 1950 and educated at Brockenhurst Grammar School and Bristol University, where he received a BS with first class honors in aeronautical engineering. He joined the RAF in 1968 at the same time he entered Bristol, and earned his wings in 1972.

From 1974 to 1976 Wood was based in Germany, where in addition to regular duties as a Lightning pilot, he was part of the "Cobra Five" air demonstration team. He was then chosen for test pilot training and from 1976 to 1983 served at the French Istres center near Marseille, the RAF center in Farnborough, and the USAF Test Pilot School at Edwards AFB, California. At Edwards Wood observed six Shuttle landings.

At the time of his selection in March 1984 as a Shuttle payload specialist by the Ministry of Defense Wood was based at RAF Binbrook in Lincolnshire. He and his backup, Richard Farrimond, reported to the NASA Johnson Space Center in early February 1986, just one week after the explosion of the Shuttle Challenger.

Wood and his wife, Irene, and daughters Melanie and Katherine live at Church Crookham, Aldershot, England.

Hungary

Farkas, Bertalan

Bertalan Farkas was the cosmonaut-researcher aboard Soyuz 36 in May 1980, becoming the first citizen of Hungary to make a space flight. He and Soviet commander Valery Kubasov docked with the Salyut 6 space station, visiting cosmonauts Popov and Ryumin, during their eight-day flight. Kubasov and Farkas were originally to have flown in July of 1979, but the Soyuz 33 abort that April suspended new manned Soyuz launches for several months.

Farkas was born August 2, 1949, in Gyulahaza, Hungary. As a secondary school student he joined the Hungarian Defense Union, a junior civil defense organization, where he learned to parachute jump and eventually became a light plane pilot. Upon graduation from school he joined the air force, enrolling in the Gyorgy Kilian aeronautical engineering college.

He became an air force pilot in 1972 and served as an instructor with several units. He joined the Hungarian Socialist Workers party in 1976.

Farkas and his close friend Bela Magyari were chosen as Hungary's Interkosmos pilots in 1977, and reported to the cosmonaut training center at Star Town the following March.

Lieutenant Colonel Farkas and his wife, Aniko, have two children, Gabor and Aida.

Magyari, Bela

Bela Magyari is the Hungarian air force pilot who served as backup to Bertalan Farkas, the cosmonaut-researcher of Soyuz 36 in May 1980.

Magyari was born August 1949 in Kiskunfelegyhaza, Hungary. He graduated from the Gyorgy Kilian aeronautical engineering college in 1969 and served with the Hungarian air force prior to reporting to Star Town in the Soviet Union for cosmonaut training in March 1978.

He and Farkas have known each other since 1965.

Major Magyari and his wife, Marta, have a daughter, Greta.

India

Bhat, N. C.

Nagapath Chidambar Bhat is one of two Indian space scientists chosen in 1985 as future Shuttle payload specialists. Bhat and fellow Indian Radhakrishnan Nair were to have arrived in the US in 1986 to train for the launch of the Insat communications satellite later that year when the Shuttle Challenger exploded, indefinitely postponing all American manned space missions.

Bhat was born January 1, 1948, in North Kanara, Karnatka State, India. He earned a BS from Arts and Science College in Sirsi and a BE in mechanical engineering from Engineering College, Gulbarga, in 1970. He received an MS in mechanical engineering from the Indian Institute of Science at Bangalor in 1972.

Bhat joined ISRO, the Indian space agency, in July 1973, as a satellite engineer. He is currently stationed at the ISRO Satellite Center in Bangalore.

He and his wife, Sreelekha, have two children, a son, Viraj, and a daughter, Reevathi.

Malhotra, Ravish

Squadron Leader Ravish Malhotra of the Indian Air Force served as backup cosmonaut-researcher for Soyuz T-11 in April 1984, during which fellow pilot Rakesh Sharma became the first Indian in space.

Malhotra was born December 25, 1943, in Calcutta, and attended India's National Defense Academy. He joined the Indian air force, became a fighter pilot, and in 1974 attended the US Air Fôrce Test Pilot School at Edwards Air Force Base, California.

At the time of his selection as one of two Indian cosmonauts, Malhotra had logged 3400 hours of flying time.

He and his wife, Mira, have a son, Rohid, and a daughter, Rakhi.

Nair, Radhakrishnan

P. Radhakrishnan Nair is one of two Indian space scientists selected in 1985 to train as payload specialists for the launch of the Insat communications satellite from the American Space Shuttle. The Insat launch, originally scheduled for the fall of 1986, was indefinitely postponed following the explosion of the Shuttle Challenger.

Nair was born October 10, 1943, in Trivandum, Kerala State. He attended University College Trivandum, receiving a BS in physics and mathematics (1963) and an MS in physics (1965).

In April 1966 Nair went to work for ISRO, the Indian Space Research Organization, where he served as an engineer for several Indian satellite projects such as Rohini, ARYABHATA, and APPLE before becoming head of test and evaluation for launch vehicles and other projects at the Vikram Sarabhai Space Center in Trivandrum.

Nair and his wife, K. Rundrani Devi, have a daughter, Lakshmi, and a son, Gautham.

Sharma, Rakesh

Major Rakesh Sharma became the first citizen of India in space when he joined Soviet cosmonauts Yuri Malyshev and Gennady Strekalov aboard Soyuz T-11 in April 1984. Sharma, who acted as cosmonaut-researcher, spent eight days in space performing scientific experiments devised by Indian scientists. Sharma, Malyshev and Strekalov joined cosmonauts Kizim, Solovyov and Atkov for a week aboard the Salyut 7 space station.

Rakesh Sharma was born January 13, 1949, in Patiala, India. At the age of 15 he qualified for the Khadakvasla National Defence Academy while an undergraduate at the Nizam College in Hyderabad. Commissioned in 1970, he flew 21 combat missions in MiG-21s during the 1971 India-Pakistan conflict. He later attended a test pilot school.

Sharma and fellow Indian pilot Ravish Malhotra arrived at Star Town to begin cosmonaut training in September 1982.

He and his wife, Madhu, have a son, Kapil. A daughter, Mansi, is deceased.

Indonesia

Akbar, Taufic

Taufic Akbar, a telecommunications engineer, has been chosen as alternate Indonesia payload specialist for a Space Shuttle mission which is scheduled to launch his country's Palapa satellite. Akbar and the primary candidate, Dr. Pratiwi Sudarmono, arrived at the NASA Johnson Space Center in March 1986 to begin training.

Akbar was born January 8, 1951, in Medam, Indonesia. He attended the Bandung Institute of Technology, graduating with a telecommunications degree in 1975, and has since studied at Hughes Aircraft in the US and at the University of Concordia in Montreal, Canada. He is currently head of the national satellite program for Peruntel, the Indonesian government telecommunications company.

Sudarmono, Pratiwi

Dr. Pratiwi Sudarmono, a microbiologist, is scheduled to be Indonesia's first space traveler when she serves as payload specialist aboard a future Shuttle mission. She will accompany a Palapa communications satellite during her flight.

Sudarmono was born July 31, 1952, in Sanduko, Indonesia. She graduated from high school in Jakarta in 1971, then attended the University of Indonesia, receiving a medical degree in 1976 and a microbiology degree in 1980. She earned her PhD in genetic engineering and bio-technology from the University of Osaka in Japan.

She was one of four Indonesian finalists submitted to NASA in October 1985 for inclusion in the crew of Mission 61-M, originally scheduled for June 1986. The explosion of the Shuttle Challenger in January of that year forced a postponement.

Sudarmono is married and currently is a lecturer in microbiology at the University of Indonesia.

Japan

Doi, Takao

Dr. Takao Doi is one of three scientists selected in August 1985 by Japan's National Space Development Agency to train as payload specialists for a Japanese Shuttle/Spacelab mission. Spacelab J was originally scheduled for launch in January 1988, but was postponed following the Shuttle Challenger disaster.

Doi was born September 18, 1954, in Minamitama-Gun, Tokyo, Japan, and attended the University of Tokyo, where he received his BS (1978), MS (1980) and PhD (1983) in aeronautical engineering.

From 1983 to 1985 he served as a research associate with the Japanese Institute of Space and Astronautical Science, and since 1985 has been a spacecraft propulsion engineer at the NASA Lewis Research Center in Cleveland, Ohio.

Doi and his wife, Hitomi, live in North Olmsted, Ohio.

Mori, Mamoru

Dr. Mamoru Mori, a physicist, is one of three Japanese scientists selected in August 1985 to train for a space flight aboard Spacelab J (for Japan), then scheduled for January 1988. The explosion of the Shuttle Challenger in January 1986 forced an indefinite postponement of Spacelab J.

Mori was born January 29, 1948, in Yoichi-Machi, Hokkaido, and educated at Hokkaido University, where he received his BS (1970) and MS (1972) in physical science. He earned his PhD in 1976 at Flinders University in South Australia.

Since 1975 Mori has been on the faculty of Hokkaido University and is currently associate professor in the department of nuclear engineering there.

He and his wife, Akiko, have three sons, Ken, Taku and Yu-u, and live in Sapporo, Hokkaido.

Naito, Chiaki

Dr. Chiaki Naito, a surgeon, is one of three Japanese scientists training for the Shuttle/Spacelab J mission originally scheduled for January 1988. Following the explosion of the Shuttle Challenger in January 1986 and the subsequent suspension of all Shuttle launches, Spacelab J was postponed indefinitely.

Naito was born May 6, 1952, in Tokyo, where she grew up, and attended Keio University in that city. She received her MD degree in 1977 and worked for the next two years as a resident in general surgery at Keio University Hospital. Since 1979 she has been an instructor in the department of cardiovascular surgery at that institution.

She is unmarried and lives in Tokyo.

Mexico

Neri Vela, Rudolfo

Dr. Rudolfo Neri Vela became the first Mexican in space when he served as payload specialist aboard Shuttle Mission 61-B in November and December 1985. He accompanied the Mexican Morelos B communications satellite, which was deployed from the Shuttle Atlantis and later reached its position in synchronous orbit above Mexico. He also conducted four scientific experiments and served as a subject for medical tests during his six days and 21 hours in space.

Neri was born February 19, 1952, in Chilpancingo, Guerrero, Mexico. He attended the University of Mexico and received a BS in mechanical and electronic engineering in 1975. He entered the master's program in science (telecommunications) at the University of Essex, England, in 1975, and received his doctoral degree in electromagnetic radiation from the University of Birmingham, England, in 1979.

He has worked at the Institute of Electrical Research in Mexico, specializing in satellite communications systems, and was head of the Morelos Satellite program for the Mexican Ministry of Communications and Transportation. Currently he is a lecturer and researcher at the National University of Mexico.

Neri is single and lives in Mexico City.

Peralta y Fabi, Ricardo

Dr. Ricardo Peralta y Fabi was the backup payload specialist for Shuttle Mission 61-B in November and December 1985. During 61-B, Dr. Rudolfo Neri became the first Mexican space traveler.

Peralta was born August 15, 1950, in Mexico City. He attended the University of Illinois in Chicago, receiving a BS in aerospace engineering in 1973. He earned an MS in mechanical engineering from McGill University, Montreal, Canada, in 1975, and later received his PhD in mechanical engineering research from McGill in 1977.

Prior to 1978, Peralta did research in aerospace medicine at Illinois and McGill. He then spent a year working for the Mexican Petroleum Institute, and since 1979 has been with the National University of Mexico's Institute of Engineering as a professor and researcher. He developed several Get-Away Special experiments for flight on the Space Shuttle.

He is married with two sons, Ernesto and Emiliano, and lives in Mexico City.

Mongolia

Ganzorig, Maidarzhavin

M. Ganzorig was the backup cosmonaut-researcher for the Soviet-Mongolian Interkosmos mission, Soyuz 39, in March 1981. While his countryman J. Gurragcha and Soviet commander Vladimir Dzhanibekov spent a week aboard the Salyut 6 space station, Ganzorig worked in Kaliningrad mission control.

Ganzorig was born February 5, 1949, in the settlement of Tsetserleg in the Khangai region of Mongolia. In 1969 he was sent to the Soviet Union to attend the Order of Lenin Polytechnical Institute in Kiev, graduating in February 1975 as an engineer specializing in thermodynamics. For the next two years he worked as a surveyor in the capital city of Ulan-Bator.

In 1977 and 1978 he completed further studies at the Mongolian Academy of Sciences Physical-Technical Institute, then became an engineer with the Mongolian People's Army. That same year Captain Ganzorig was chosen as one of two Mongolian cosmonaut-researchers. He spent three years at the Yuri Gagarin Cosmonaut Training Center near Moscow, then returned to Mongolia.

He became a member of the Mongolian People's Revolutionary party in 1979.

He and his wife have two sons.

Gurragcha, Jugderdemidyn

Captain J. Gurragcha became the first Mongolian in space when he served as cosmonaut-researcher aboard Soyuz 39 in March 1981. Gurragcha and Soviet commander Vladimir Dzhanibekov spent eight days in space, seven of them with cosmonauts Kovalenok and Ivanchekov aboard Salyut 6.

The son of a shepherd, Gurragcha was born December 5, 1947, in the Gurvan-Bulak settlement in the Bulgan province of Mongolia. He attended the Ulan-Bator Agricultural Institute from 1966 to 1968, then was drafted into the army, where he served as a radio operator.

In 1971 Gurragcha was sent to an aviation engineering school in the Soviet Union, where he studied military communications. From 1973 to 1977 he attended the Zhukovsky Air Force Engineering Academy. He returned to Mongolia, where he was promptly selected for cosmonaut training.

Major General Gurragcha became a member of the Mongolian People's Revolutionary party in 1979.

He and his wife, Batmankh, have a son.

Poland

Hermaszewski, Miroslaw

Miroslaw Hermaszewski was the first citizen of Poland to make a space flight. In June 1978 he was cosmonaut-researcher aboard the Soyuz 30 spacecraft; he and Soviet commander Pyotr Klimuk spent eight days in space, most of them with cosmonauts Kovalenok and Ivanchenkov aboard the Salyut 6 space station. Like all Interkosmos space travelers, during his flight Hermaszewski operated several experiments created by Polish scientists in his country.

Hermaszewski was born September 15, 1941, in Lipniki, Poland. He grew interested in space and aviation at an early age, and by the time he was sixteen had enrolled in a flying club. In 1961 he was admitted to an air force college at Deblin and graduated in 1964. He joined the Polish Communist party in 1963.

He served as a fighter pilot and flight instructor in the Polish air force for several years, then attended the Karol Swierczewsky Military Staff Academy in Warsaw, graduating in 1971. He was commander of a regiment of flight instructors when selected for cosmonaut training in December 1976.

Since his space flight Colonel Hermaszewski has graduated from the Soviet Union's K. E. Voroshilov Military Staff Academy (1982).

He and his wife, Emilia, have two children, Miroslav and Emilia.

Jankowski, Zenon

Colonel Zenon Jankowski was the backup cosmonaut-researcher for Miroslaw Hermaszewski, the first Pole to go into space. During the 8-day flight of Hermaszewski and Soviet cosmonaut Pyotr Klimuk aboard Soyuz 30 in June 1978, Jankowski supported the flight from mission control at Kaliningrad, near Moscow.

Jankowski was born November 22, 1937, in Poznan, Poland, and entered the Polish Air Force in 1959. He attended an air force officer's school, served as a pilot, and later graduated from the Karol Swierczewski General Staff Academy. With Hermaszewski, he was selected for cosmonaut training from five finalists in March 1978.

Jankowski is married with one child.

Rumania

Dediu, Dumitru

Lieutenant Colonel Dumitru Dediu served as backup cosmonaut-researcher to fellow Rumanian Dumitru Prunariu for the Soyuz 40/Salyut 6 mission in May 1981.

Dediu was born in 1942 in the city of Galati. He attended the Vasily Alexandri school, where he excelled in mathematics and physics, then studied electronics at a military academy. He served as an engineer with the Rumanian air force and, like Prunariu, was selected for cosmonaut training in 1978.

Colonel Dediu and his wife, Veronica, have returned to Rumania.

Prunariu, Dumitru

Dumitru Prunariu became the first citizen of Rumania to go into space when he served as cosmonaut-researcher aboard Soyuz 40 in May 1981. Prunariu and Soviet commander Leonid Popov spent eight days in space, joining cosmonauts Kovalenok and Savinykh aboard the Salyut 6 space station for a week.

Dumitru Dorin Prunariu was born September 27, 1952, in Brashov, Rumania, and grew up there. As a teenager he built award-winning model airplanes and rockets. He attended the Bucharest Polytechnical Institute, graduating in 1976, and went to work as an aviation engineer. He became a member of the Rumanian Communist party in 1973.

Prunariu took flying lessons from a pilot in the Rumanian air force reserve who encouraged him to join the service, and in September 1977 the young engineer enrolled in a school for air force officers. Shortly after graduation he was chosen as a candidate to become Rumania's Interkosmos space traveler. Prunariu and fellow air force engineer Dumitru Dediu were selected in 1978 and reported to Star Town that April.

Since returning to Rumania in 1981, Major Prunariu has written a book about his experiences.

He and his wife, Crina, have two sons.

Saudi Arabia

Al-Bassam, Abdulmohsen

Major Abdulmohsen Hamad Al-Bassam of the Saudi Royal Air Force was the backup payload specialist for Shuttle Mission 51-G (June 17-24, 1985) during which Prince Sultan Al-Saud became the first Arab in space.

During the week-long flight Al-Bassam provided ground support from the Johnson Space Center, acting occasionally as capcom for his colleague in orbit.

Al-Bassam was born December 12, 1948, in the city of Onaizah, Saudi Arabia. His parents, Hamad Al-Bassam and Modawe Al-Saade, reside in eastern Saudi Arabia.

Al-Bassam graduated from high school in Damman in 1968 and then attended the King Faisal Air Academy in Riyadh, graduating with a bachelor of air science degree. He attended schools for military pilots at Randolph Air Force Base, Texas, and Williams Air Force Base, Arizona, while serving in the Saudi air force.

He has logged more than 2,600 hours of flying time, including over 1,000 hours as an instructor pilot.

Married, with a daughter and a son, Al-Bassam resides in Al-Khobar, eastern Saudi Arabia.

Al-Saud, Sultan

Prince Sultan ibn Salman al-Saud was the first Arab to go into space, spending one week in orbit aboard the Space Shuttle Discovery during Mission 51-G in June 1985.

Sultan's launch date of June 17, 1985, coincided with the last day of Ramadan, the Muslim holy month, and gave him the opportunity to be the first Muslim to see the setting of the Moon, which, according to Islamic law, would signal the end of Ramadan. Sultan did not see the Moon set that day, however. Nevertheless, he was able to successfully complete his primary tasks: performing scientific experiments designed by his country's University of Petroleum and Minerals in Dharan and observing the launch of the Arabsat 1-B communications satellite.

During his week in space Sultan was able to take his countrymen on a televised tour of the Discovery, remarking that the Shuttle was being "guided through the stars, just like our Bedoins used to navigate in the desert." Sultan carried with him an astrolabe, the ancient Arab instrument of celestial navigation.

Sultan was born June 27, 1956, in Riyadh, Saudi Arabia. His parents are His Royal Highness Prince Salman bin Abdul Aziz (the governor of Riyadh) and Sultana Al-Sudairy.

Sultan completed his elementary and secondary schooling in Saudi Arabia, then attended the University of Denver in Colorado, graduating with a bachelor of arts degree in mass communications. He became a commercial pilot and logged over 1,000 hours in jet aircraft and helicopters. He was employed as a researcher in the Saudi Ministry of Information from 1982-84, and also was Deputy Director in the Saudi Arabian Olympic Information Committee during the 1984 Olympiad in Los Angeles.

At the time of his selection to fly aboard the Shuttle Sultan was Acting Director of the Saudi Arabian Television Commercial Department.

Sultan is unmarried and since his space flight has joined the Saudi air force as a pilot with the rank of major.

Syria

Faris, Muhammed

Muhammed Ahmad Faris is one of two Syrian air force pilots who arrived at Star Town in September 1985 to train as a cosmonaut-researcher on a future Soviet space station mission.

Faris was born in 1951. He and his wife, Gind Akil, have a son, Kutaib, and a daughter, Gadil.

Habib, Munir

Munir Habib is one of two Syrian air force pilots who arrived at Star Town in September 1985 to train as a cosmonaut-researcher on a future Soviet space station mission.

Habib was born in 1953. He and his wife, Yumna, have two sons, Mdyan and Raid.

Viet Nam

Liem, Bui Thanh

Bui Thanh Liem served as backup to Pham Tuan, the first Vietnamese space traveler, during the Soyuz 37 mission in July 1980. While Tuan and Soviet commander Viktor Gorbatko spent 8 days aboard Salyut-6, Liem provided ground support from mission control in Kalinin.

Bui Thanh Liem was born June 30, 1949, in Hanoi, Vietnam, and in February 1966 enlisted in the Vietnamese air force. He was sent to the USSR for pilot training, returning in 1970, when he became an interceptor pilot with the Red Star regiment and flew in combat. He joined the Vietnamese Communist party in 1973.

In 1974 Liem was sent back to the Soviet Union to attend the Gagarin Air Force Academy, graduating in 1978. He was a staff officer in the Vietnamese Air Force when selected for cosmonaut training along with Pham Tuan in April 1979.

Major Bui Thanh Liem returned to Vietnam and operational flying in 1980. In September 1981 he was killed in a plane crash. He is survived by his wife and daughter.

Tuan, Pham

Vietnamese air force pilot Pham Tuan became the first Asian in space when he served as cosmonaut-researcher aboard Soyuz 37 in July 1980. Tuan and Soviet commander Viktor Gorbatko spent eight days in space, most of them aboard the Salyut 6 space station with cosmonauts Popov and Lebedev. Tuan also carried out Earth observations for scientists in his country.

Pham Tuan was born February 14, 1947, in the village of Quoc Tuan, Thai Binh province. He studied to be an engineer, but when the Vietnam War began he was drafted into the North Vietnamese army. He was sent to the Soviet Union for pilot school, graduating in May 1968. He joined the Vietnamese Communist party that same year.

Tuan flew air defense missions over North Vietnam with the Red Star Regiment. It is reported that on December 27, 1972, he shot down a US Air Force B-52 bomber over Hanoi. (The USAF denied that any bomber was shot down by a fighter during the war.) He later served as a regimental commander, and in 1977 was sent to the Soviet Union again to attend the Gagarin Air Force Academy. He was a student there when selected for cosmonaut training in April 1979, and following the conclusion of his cosmonaut career, graduated from the Academy (1982).

Tuan and his wife, an army medical officer, have a daughter.

Appendix 1 Chronological Log

1. Yuri Gagarin (USSR) — Vostok (1961)
2. Alan B. Shepard (USA) — MR-3 (1961)
3. Virgil I. Grissom (USA) — MR-4 (1961)
4. Gherman Titov (USSR) — Vostok 2 (1961)
5. John H. Glenn, Jr. (USA) — MA-6 (1962)
6. M. Scott Carpenter (USA) — MA-7 (1962)
7. Andrian Nikolayev (USSR) — Vostok 3 (1962)
8. Pavel Popovich (USSR) — Vostok 4 (1962)
9. Walter M. Schirra, Jr. (USA) — MA-8 (1962)
10. L. Gordon Cooper, Jr. (USA) — MA-9 (1963)
11. Valery Bykovsky (USSR) — Vostok 5 (1963)
12. Valentina Tereshkova (USSR) — Vostok 6 (1963)
13. Vladimir Komarov (USSR) — Voskhod (1964)
    Konstantin Feoktistov (USSR) — Voskhod (1964)
    Boris Yegorov (USSR) — Voskhod (1964)
16. Pavel Belyayev (USSR) — Voskhod 2 (1965)
    Alexei Leonov (USSR) — Voskhod 2 (1965)
18. John W. Young (USA) — Gemini 3 (1965)
19. James A. McDivitt (USA) — Gemini 4 (1965)
20. Edward H. White II (USA) — Gemini 4 (1965)
21. Charles Conrad, Jr. (USA) — Gemini 5 (1965)
22. Frank Borman (USA) — Gemini 7 (1965)
    James A. Lovell, Jr. (USA) — Gemini 7 (1965)
24. Thomas P. Stafford (USA) — Gemini 6A (1965)
25. Neil A. Armstrong (USA) — Gemini 8 (1966)
    David R. Scott (USA) — Gemini 8 (1966)
27. Eugene A. Cernan (USA) — Gemini 9A (1966)
28. Michael Collins (USA) — Gemini 10 (1966)
29. Richard F. Gordon, Jr. (USA) — Gemini 11 (1966)
30. Edwin E. Aldrin, Jr. (USA) — Gemini 12 (1966)
31. Donn F. Eisele (USA) — Apollo 7 (1968)
    R. Walter Cunningham (USA) — Apollo 7 (1968)
33. Georgy Beregovoy (USSR) — Soyuz 3 (1968)
34. William A. Anders (USA) — Apollo 8 (1968)
35. Vladimir Shatalov (USSR) — Soyuz 4 (1969)
36. Boris Volynov (USSR) — Soyuz 5 (1969)
    Alexei Yeliseyev (USSR) — Soyuz 5 (1969)
    Yevgeny Khrunov (USSR) — Soyuz 5 (1969)
39. Russell L. Schweickart (USA) — Apollo 9 (1969)
40. Georgy Shonin (USSR) — Soyuz 6 (1969)
    Valery Kubasov (USSR) — Soyuz 6 (1969)
42. Anatoly Filipchenko (USSR) — Soyuz 7 (1969)
    Vladislav Volkov (USSR) — Soyuz 7 (1969)
    Viktor Gorbatko (USSR) — Soyuz 7 (1969)
45. Alan L. Bean (USA) — Apollo 12 (1969)
46. John L. Swigert, Jr. (USA) — Apollo 13 (1970)
    Fred W. Haise, Jr. (USA) — Apollo 13 (1970)
48. Vitaly Sevastyanov (USSR) — Soyuz 9 (1970)
49. Stuart A. Roosa (USA) — Apollo 14 (1971)
    Edgar D. Mitchell (USA) — Apollo 14 (1971)
51. Nikolai Rukavishnikov (USSR) — Soyuz 10 (1971)
52. Georgy Dobrovolsky (USSR) — Soyuz 11 (1971)
    Viktor Patsayev (USSR) — Soyuz 11 (1971)
54. Alfred M. Worden (USA) — Apollo 15 (1971)
    James B. Irwin (USA) — Apollo 15 (1971)
56. Thomas K. Mattingly II (USA) — Apollo 16 (1972)
    Charles M. Duke, Jr. (USA) — Apollo 16 (1972)
58. Ronald E. Evans, Jr. (USA) — Apollo 17 (1972)
    Harrison H. Schmitt (USA) — Apollo 17 (1972)
60. Joseph P. Kerwin (USA) — Skylab 2 (1973)
    Paul J. Weitz (USA) — Skylab 2 (1973)
62. Owen K. Garriott (USA) — Skylab 3 (1973)
    Jack R. Lousma (USA) — Skylab 3 (1973)
64. Vasily Lazarev (USSR) — Soyuz 12 (1973)
    Oleg Makarov (USSR) — Soyuz 12 (1973)
66. Gerald P. Carr (USA) — Skylab 4 (1973-74)
    Edward G. Gibson (USA) — Skylab 4 (1973-74)
    William R. Pogue (USA) — Skylab 4 (1973-74)
69. Pyotr Klimuk (USSR) — Soyuz 13 (1973)
    Valentin Lebedev (USSR) — Soyuz 13 (1973)
71. Yuri Artyukhin (USSR) — Soyuz 14 (1974)

72.	Gennady Sarafanov (USSR)	Soyuz 15 (1974)
	Lev Demin (USSR)	Soyuz 15 (1974)
74.	Alexei Gubarev (USSR)	Soyuz 17 (1975)
	Georgy Grechko (USSR)	Soyuz 17 (1975)
76.	Vance D. Brand (USA)	ASTP (1975)
	Donald K. Slayton (USA)	ASTP (1975)
78.	Vitaly Zholobov (USSR)	Soyuz 21 (1976)
79.	Vladimir Aksenov (USSR)	Soyuz 22 (1976)
80.	Vyacheslav Zudov (USSR)	Soyuz 23 (1976)
	Valery Rozhdestvensky (USSR)	Soyuz 23 (1976)
82.	Yuri Glazkov (USSR)	Soyuz 24 (1977)
83.	Vladimir Kovalenok (USSR)	Soyuz 25 (1977)
	Valery Ryumin (USSR)	Soyuz 25 (1977)
85.	Yuri Romanenko (USSR)	Soyuz 26 (1977)
86.	Vladimir Dzhanibekov (USSR)	Soyuz 27 (1978)
87.	Vladimir Remek (Czech.)	Soyuz 28 (1978)
88.	Alexandr Ivanchenkov (USSR)	Soyuz 29 (1978)
89.	Miroslaw Hermaszewski (Pol.)	Soyuz 30 (1978)
90.	Sigmund Jaehn (GDR)	Soyuz 31 (1978)
91.	Vladimir Lyakhov (USSR)	Soyuz 32 (1979)
92.	Georgy Ivanov (Bulg.)	Soyuz 33 (1979)
93.	Leonid Popov (USSR)	Soyuz 35 (1980)
94.	Bertalan Farkas (Hun.)	Soyuz 36 (1980)
95.	Yuri Malyshev (USSR)	Soyuz T-2 (1980)
96.	Pham Tuan (RVN)	Soyuz 37 (1980)
97.	Arnaldo Tamayo-Mendez (Cuba)	Soyuz 38 (1980)
98.	Leonid Kizim (USSR)	Soyuz T-3 (1980)
99.	Gennady Strekalov (USSR)	Soyuz T-3 (1980)
100.	Viktor P. Savinykh (USSR)	Soyuz T-4 (1981)
101.	J. Gurragcha (Mon.)	Soyuz 39 (1981)
102.	Robert L. Crippen (USA)	STS-1 (1981)
103.	Dumitru Prunariu (Rum.)	Soyuz 40 (1981)
104.	Joe H. Engle (USA)	STS-2 (1981)
	Richard H. Truly (USA)	STS-2 (1981)
106.	C. Gordon Fullerton (USA)	STS-3 (1982)
107.	Anatoly Berezovoy (USSR)	Soyuz T-5 (1982)
108.	Henry Hartsfield, Jr. (USA)	STS-4 (1982)
109.	Jean-Loup Chretien (France)	Soyuz T-6 (1982)
110.	Alexandr Serebrov (USSR)	Soyuz T-7 (1982)
	Svetlana Savitskaya (USSR)	Soyuz T-7 (1982)
112.	Robert F. Overmyer (USA)	STS-5 (1982)
	Joseph P. Allen IV (USA)	STS-5 (1982)
	William B. Lenoir (USA)	STS-5 (1982)
115.	Karol J. Bobko (USA)	STS-6 (1983)
	Donald H. Peterson (USA)	STS-6 (1983)
	F. Story Musgrave (USA)	STS-6 (1983)
118.	Vladimir Titov (USSR)	Soyuz T-8 (1983)
119.	Frederick C. Hauck (USA)	STS-7 (1983)
	John M. Fabian (USA)	STS-7 (1983)
	Sally K. Ride (USA)	STS-7 (1983)
	Norman E. Thagard (USA)	STS-7 (1983)
123.	Alexandr Alexandrov (USSR)	Soyuz T-9 (1983)
124.	Daniel C. Brandenstein (USA)	STS-8 (1983)
	Dale A. Gardner (USA)	STS-8 (1983)
	Guion S. Bluford, Jr. (USA)	STS-8 (1983)
	William E. Thornton (USA)	STS-8 (1983)
128.	Brewster H. Shaw, Jr. (USA)	STS-9 (1983)
	Robert A. R. Parker (USA)	STS-9 (1983)
	Byron K. Lichtenberg (USA)	STS-9 (1983)
	Ulf Merbold (ESA/FRG)	STS-9 (1983)
132.	Robert L. Gibson (USA)	41-B (1984)
	Bruce McCandless II (USA)	41-B (1984)
	Ronald E. McNair (USA)	41-B (1984)
	Robert L. Stewart (USA)	41-B (1984)
136.	Vladimir Solovyov (USSR)	Soyuz T-10 (1984)
	Oleg Atkov (USSR)	Soyuz T-10 (1984)
138.	Rakesh Sharma (India)	Soyuz T-11 (1984)
139.	Francis R. Scobee (USA)	41-C (1984)
	Terry J. Hart (USA)	41-C (1984)
	George D. Nelson (USA)	41-C (1984)
	James D. A. van Hoften (USA)	41-C (1984)
143.	Igor Volk (USSR)	Soyuz T-12 (1984)
144.	Michael L. Coats (USA)	41-D (1984)
	Steven A. Hawley (USA)	41-D (1984)
	Richard M. Mullane (USA)	41-D (1984)
	Judith A. Resnik (USA)	41-D (1984)
	Charles D. Walker (USA)	41-D (1984)
149.	Jon A. McBride (USA)	41-G (1984)
	David C. Leestma (USA)	41-G (1984)
	Kathryn D. Sullivan (USA)	41-G (1984)
	Paul D. Scully-Power (USA)	41-G (1984)
	Marc Garneau (Canada)	41-G (1984)
154.	David M. Walker (USA)	51-A (1984)
	Anna L. Fisher (USA)	51-A (1984)
156.	Loren J. Shriver (USA)	51-C (1985)
	James F. Buchli (USA)	51-C (1985)
	Ellison S. Onizuka (USA)	51-C (1985)
	Gary E. Payton (USA)	51-C (1985)
160.	Donald E. Williams (USA)	51-D (1985)
	M. Rhea Seddon (USA)	51-D (1985)
	S. David Griggs (USA)	51-D (1985)
	Jeffrey A. Hoffman (USA)	51-D (1985)
	Jake Garn (USA)	51-D (1985)
165.	Frederick D. Gregory (USA)	51-B (1985)
	Don L. Lind (USA)	51-B (1985)
	Lodewijk van den Berg (USA)	51-B (1985)
	Taylor G. Wang (USA)	51-B (1985)
169.	John O. Creighton (USA)	51-G (1985)
	Shannon W. Lucid (USA)	51-G (1985)
	Steven R. Nagel (USA)	51-G (1985)
	Patrick Baudry (France)	51-G (1985)
	Sultan Al-Saud (Saudi Arabia)	51-G (1985)
174.	Roy D. Bridges (USA)	51-F (1985)
	Anthony W. England (USA)	51-F (1985)

	Karl G. Henize (USA)	51-F (1985)
	Loren W. Acton (USA)	51-F (1985)
	John-David F. Bartoe (USA)	51-F (1985)
179.	Richard O. Covey (USA)	51-I (1985)
	John M. Lounge (USA)	51-I (1985)
	William F. Fisher (USA)	51-I (1985)
182.	Vladimir Vasyutin (USSR)	Soyuz T-14 (1985)
	Alexandr Volkov (USSR)	Soyuz T-14 (1985)
184.	Ronald J. Grabe (USA)	51-J (1985)
	David C. Hilmers (USA)	51-J (1985)
	William A. Pailes (USA)	51-J (1985)
187.	Bonnie J. Dunbar (USA)	61-A (1985)
	Rheinhard Furrer (FRG)	61-A (1985)
	Ernst W. Messerschmid (FRG)	61-A (1985)
	Wubbo J. Ockels (ESA/Neth.)	61-A (1985)
191.	Bryan D. O'Connor (USA)	61-B (1985)
	Jerry L. Ross (USA)	61-B (1985)
	Mary L. Cleave (USA)	61-B (1985)
	Sherwood C. Spring (USA)	61-B (1985)
	Rudolfo Neri Vela (Mexico)	61-B (1985)
196.	Charles F. Bolden, Jr. (USA)	61-C (1986)
	Franklin Chang-Diaz (USA)	61-C (1986)
	Robert J. Cenker (USA)	61-C (1986)
	Bill Nelson (USA)	61-C (1986)

NOTE: This log does not include Mission 51-L crewmembers Michael J. Smith, Gregory K. Jarvis or Christa McAuliffe, who died before reaching space, nor does it include X-15 rocketplane pilots who reached altitudes greater than 50 miles. For the latter, see Appendix 3.

Appendix 2 Manned Space Flights, April 1961 to April 1986

MISSION refers to the official designation given to a particular space flight. As there are obvious numerical and sequential anomalies, some explanation is in order:

1. Unmanned test flights of Soviet Vostok and Voskhod spacecraft were identified as Kosmos satellites, eliminating any gaps in numbering. But several Soyuz missions have been flown unmanned: Soyuz 2 (1968), Soyuz 20 (1975), Soyuz 34 (1979), Soyuz T (1979), and Soyuz TM (1986).

2. Unmanned test flights in American manned space programs were usually included in the numerical sequence: Mercury-Redstone 3 (Alan Shepard) was preceded by two unmanned launches, Mercury-Atlas 6 (John Glenn) by five, Gemini-Titan 3 (Grissom and Young) by two.

3. Apollo missions were originally intended to have two designations. The first, a three-digit number such as Apollo-Saturn 202 or Apollo-Saturn 504, would identify a specific mission—manned or unmanned. (The 200 series referred to vehicles launched by Saturn 1B rockets, the 500 series to those launched by Saturn 5s.) Only manned Apollo flights would be designated Apollo 1, Apollo 2, etc. That is why the ill-fated Apollo 1, in which astronauts Grissom, White, and Chaffee were killed, is officially known as Apollo-Saturn 204—the fourth Apollo spacecraft launched aboard a Saturn 1B. (In fact, Apollo-Saturn 204 *was* launched in 1968. It carried the first unmanned lunar module and was designated Apollo 5. See below.)

When Apollo launches were resumed in November 1967, NASA jettisoned its original system and designated Apollo-Saturn 501, the first unmanned test of the Saturn 5 booster, as Apollo 4, the fourth flight of Apollo hardware after Apollo-Saturns 201, 202, and 203, which could be known as Apollos 1, 2, and 3 only retrospectively. The Apollo-Saturn 204 mentioned above became Apollo 5 and Apollo-Saturn 502 was Apollo 6. The first manned Apollo mission, number 205, was Apollo 7.

4. Although the three manned Skylab missions were officially known as Skylabs 2 through 4 (Skylab 1 was the unmanned station itself), some NASA documents — including the crews' mission patches—called them Skylab 1, 2, and 3.

5. The American spacecraft used in the Apollo-Soyuz Test Project has been variously known as "ASTP," "Apollo 18" and simply "Apollo." The mission designation was "ASTP," the call sign was simply "Apollo."

6. The first four Shuttle missions—later known as STS (Space Transportation System) 1 through 4—were originally to have been designation OFT (Orbital Flight Test) 1 through 4.

7. In 1983, following the cancellation of STS-10 and a re-shuffling of the Shuttle flight manifest which predicted a mission sequence of STS-11, STS-13, STS-12, STS-14, NASA adopted a new official designation system consisting of three elements: fiscal year (4,5,6, etc.), launch site (1 for Kennedy Space Center, 2 for Vandenberg AFB) and sequence (A,B,C, etc.), transforming STS-11 into Mission 41-B, STS-13 into Mission 41-C, and so on. Although some NASA documents continue to refer to, for example, STS 41-C, the true name is simply Mission followed by the three-part designation.

LAUNCH DATA are that given by the agency responsible. Soviet launch times are based on Moscow Time; actual launch time at the Baikonur Cosmodrome is plus-two hours. It is interesting to note that very few reported launch sites, Soviet or American, are accurate. The complex known as the Baikonur Cosmodrome is located 200 miles from the city of Baikonyr, Kazakhstan; its actual location was fictitiously altered by the USSR for many years. In addition, of American launches, only Mercury and Gemini flights were launched from Cape Canaveral—and from 1963 to 1973 Cape Canaveral was renamed Cape Kennedy. Apollo and Shuttle launches are from the NASA John F. Kennedy Space Center on Merrit lsland, Florida, which is *not* part of Cape Canaveral.

CREWS are given in the order used in original launch announcements, with these abbreviations for function:

CDR	Commander (Gemini) Command pilot
PLT	Pilot
PLT2	Second pilot (Voskhod 2 only)
SCI	Scientist (Voskhod 1 only)
DR	Doctor (Voskhod 1 only)
FE	Flight engineer
RE	Research engineer
TE	Test engineer
CR	Cosmonaut-researcher
CMP	Command module pilot
LMP	Lunar module pilot
DMP	Docking module pilot (ASTP only)
SP	Science pilot
MS	Mission specialist
PS	Payload specialist
SR PLT	Senior pilot

CALL SIGNS refer to the spacecraft names used in communications between ground controllers and cosmonauts or astronauts during the mission.

LANDING DATA are that given by official announcements, with all distances converted to statute miles.

DURATION is the time from liftoff to splashdown (American missions from Mercury through ASTP), liftoff to touchdown (Soviet missions), or liftoff to wheel stop (STS).

REMARKS note significant mission events, records, unusual orbits, inclinations, etc.

MISSION	LAUNCH DATA	CREW	CALL SIGN	LANDING DATA	DURATION	REMARKS
Vostok	April 12, 1961 0907 MT Baikonur	Sr. Lieutenant Yuri A. Gagarin, 27		April 12, 1961 1055 MT Near Smelovka, Saratov region	1 hour, 48 minutes	The world's first manned space flight. The only orbit ranged from 112 to 203 miles in altitude. Following re-entry, Gagarin ejected at 22,000 feet, as planned, landing in a pasture.
Mercury-Redstone 3	May 5, 1961 0934 EDT Cape Canaveral	Cmdr. Alan B. Shepard, Jr., USN, 37	"Freedom 7"	May 5, 1961 0949 EDT 303 miles downrange, recovered by USS Lake Champlain	15 minutes	Shepard became the first American in space, three weeks after Gagarin's flight, rocketing to an altitude of 125 miles.
Mercury-Redstone 4	July 21, 1961 0720 EDT Cape Canaveral	Capt. Virgil I. Grissom, USAF, 35	"Liberty Bell 7"	July 21, 1961 0736 EDT 302 miles downrange, recovered by USS Randolph	16 minutes	Grissom made the second US suborbital flight, reaching an altitude of 126 miles. The Liberty Bell 7 capsule sank before it could be recovered, though Grissom was rescued.
Vostok 2	August 6, 1961 0900 MT Baikonur	Captain Gherman S. Titov, 25	"Orel" ("Eagle")	August 7, 1961 1018 MT Saratov	25 hours, 18 minutes	Titov became the first to spend an entire day in space. His orbit ranged from 113 to 151 miles.
Mercury-Atlas 6	February 20, 1962 0948 EST Cape Canaveral	Lt. Col. John H. Glenn, Jr., USMC, 40	"Friendship 7"	February 20, 1962 1443 EST Atlantic Ocean, 40 miles from the USS Noa	4 hours, 55 minutes	Glenn made the United States' first manned orbital flight, circling the Earth three times in an orbit ranging from 100 to 162 miles at an inclination of 28 degrees.
Mercury-Atlas 7	May 24, 1962 0745 EDT Cape Canaveral	Lt. Cmdr. M. Scott Carpenter, USN, 36	"Aurora 7"	May 24, 1962 1241 EDT Atlantic Ocean, 260 miles from the USS Intrepid	4 hours, 56 minutes	Carpenter flew the second American manned orbital flight, completing three orbits. Attitude control problems caused Aurora 7 to overshoot its landing target by 260 miles and Carpenter and his spacecraft spent an hour in the water before being rescued.
Vostok 3	August 11, 1962 1130 MT Baikonur	Major Andrian G. Nikolayev, 32	"Sokol" ("Falcon")	August 15, 1962 0955 MT Kazakhstan	3 days, 22 hours, 22 minutes	First four-day flight and the first "group" flight with Vostok 4 carrying Popovich, launched a day later. Orbit: 112 to 145 miles.
Vostok 4	August 12, 1962 1102 MT Baikonur	Lt. Col. Pavel R. Popovich, 31	"Berkut" ("Golden Eagle")	August 15, 1962 0959 MT Kazkahstan	2 days, 22 hours, 57 minutes	The other half of the first space "group" flight. Vostok 4 closed to within five miles of Vostok 3. Popovich landed just six minutes after Nikolayev, but 190 miles away. Orbit: 111 to 147 miles.
Mercury-Atlas 8	October 3, 1962 0715 EDT Cape Canaveral	Lt. Cmdr. Walter M. Schirra, Jr., USN, 39	"Sigma 7"	October 3, 1962 1628 EDT Pacific Ocean, 4.5 miles from the USS Kearsarge	9 hours, 13 minutes	Schirra piloted a "textbook" engineer flight, doubling the duration for which Mercury was intended to operate.

MISSION	LAUNCH DATA	CREW	CALL SIGN	LANDING DATA	DURATION	REMARKS
Mercury-Atlas 9	May 15, 1963 0804 EDT Cape Canaveral	Maj. L. Gordon Cooper, Jr., USAF, 36	"Faith 7"	May 16, 1963 1824 EDT Pacific Ocean, 4 miles from the USS Kearsarge	34 hours, 20 minutes	Cooper piloted the longest, and last Mercury mission, spending a day and a half in orbit.
Vostok 5	June 14, 1963 1500 MT Baikonur	Lt. Col. Valery F. Bykovsky, 28	"Yastreb" ("Hawk")	June 19, 1963 1406 MT Kazakhstan	4 days, 23 hours, 6 minutes	Bykovsky set an endurance record, five days in space, that would last for two years. This was also the second group flight. Orbit: 99 to 146 miles.
Vostok 6	June 16, 1963 1230 MT Baikonur	Jr. Lt. Valentina V. Tereshkova, 27	"Chaika" ("Seagull")	June 19, 1963 1120 MT Kazakhstan	2 days, 22 hours, 50 minutes	First space flight by a woman and second group flight, though the 24-hour delay in the launch of Vostok 6 meant that it didn't get as close to Vostok 5 as did Vostok 3/Vostok 4. Orbit: 108 to 143 miles.
Voskhod	**October 12, 1964 1030 MT Baikonur**	**Col. Vladimir M. Komarov, 37 (CDR) Konstantin P. Feoktistov, 38 (SCI) Jr. Lieutenant Boris B. Yegorov, 27 (DR)**	"Rubin" ("Ruby")	October 13, 1964 1047 MT Kazakhstan	1 day, 17 minutes	First space crew, consisting of a pilot and two passengers. It was later disclosed that all three suffered from space sickness during their single day in space. They were the first space travelers to do without spacesuits and the first cosmonauts to land in their spacecraft. Orbit: 111 to 254 miles.
Voskhod 2	March 18, 1965 1000 MT Baikonur	Col. Pavel I. Belyayev, 39 (CDR) Lt. Col. Alexei A. Leonov, 30 (PLT2)	"Almaz" ("Diamond")	March 19, 1965 1202 MT Perm region	1 day, 2 hours, 2 minutes	Leonov became the first spacewalker, floating outside Voskhod 2 for 12 minutes. Belyayev also became the first Soviet cosmonaut to manually control his spacecraft, firing the retrorockets on the 17th orbit after the autopilot had failed. The delay forced the cosmonauts to land far from the prime recovery zone. Orbit: 107 by 308, a record altitude at the time.
Gemini-Titan 3	March 23, 1965 0924 EST Cape Kennedy	Maj. Virgil I. Grissom, USAF, 38 (CDR) Lt. Cmdr. John W. Young, USN, 34 (PLT)	"Molly Brown" "Gemini 3"	March 23, 1965 1417 EST Atlantic Ocean, 50 miles from the USS Intrepid	4 hours, 53 minutes	Gemini was the first true spaceship, carrying a computer for guidance and powered by rockets that enabled it to maneuver in space. From an initial orbit of 161 by 224 miles, Grissom and Young lowered Molly Brown to a 158 by 169 mile orbit, a vital step toward the eventual rendezvous and docking of vehicles in space.
Gemini-Titan 4	June 3, 1965 1016 EDT Cape Kennedy	Maj. James A. McDivitt, USAF, 37 (CDR) Maj. Edward H. White II, USAF, 35 (PLT)	"Gemini 4"	June 7, 1965 1212 EDT Atlantic Ocean, 40 miles from the USS Wasp	4 days, 1 hour, 56 minutes	McDivitt and White set an American space endurance record during their four days aboard Gemini 4. They failed to "station keep" with their Titan 2 booster, but White later made America's first spacewalk.

Gemini-Titan 5	August 21, 1965 0900 EDT Cape Kennedy	Lt. Col. L. Gordon Cooper, Jr., USAF, 38 (CDR) Lt. Cmdr. Charles Conrad, Jr., USN, 35 (PLT)	"Gemini 5"	August 29, 1965 0755 EDT Atlantic Ocean, 104 miles from the USS Lake Champlain	7 days, 22 hours, 55 minutes	Cooper and Conrad endured eight days, many of them drifting, in the cramped Gemini 5 spacecraft, giving America the world space endurance record for the first time, and proving that humans could survive in space long enough to travel to the Moon and back.
Gemini-Titan 7	December 4, 1965 1430 EST Cape Kennedy	Lt. Col. Frank Borman, USAF, 37 (CDR) Cmdr. James A. Lovell, Jr., USN, 37 (PLT)	"Gemini 7"	December 18, 1965 0905 EST Atlantic Ocean, 7 miles from the USS Wasp	13 days, 18 hours, 35 minutes	Borman and Lovell set a new space endurance record aboard Gemini 7 and participated in the first rendezvous between two manned spacecraft when visited by Gemini 6, carrying Schirra and Stafford, on December 15.
Gemini-Titan 6-A	December 15, 1965 0837 EST Cape Kennedy	Capt. Walter M. Schirra, Jr., USN, 41 (CDR) Maj. Thomas P. Stafford, USAF, 35 (PLT)	"Gemini 6"	December 16, 1965 1028 EST Atlantic Ocean, 8 miles from the USS Wasp	1 day, 1 hour, 51 minutes	Schirra and Stafford, frustrated in previous attempts to accomplish the first rendezvous and docking in space, guided Gemini 6 to within a few feet of Gemini 7 during their single day in space.
Gemini-Titan 8	March 16, 1966 1141 EST Cape Kennedy	Neil A. Armstrong, 35 (CDR) Maj. David R. Scott, USAF, 33 (PLT)	"Gemini 8"	March 16, 1966 2222 EST Pacific Ocean, 600 miles east of Japan, recovered by USS Mason	10 hours, 41 minutes	Armstrong and Scott guided Gemini 8 to the first docking with another spacecraft, an Agena, before being forced to abort the mission because of a stuck thruster on their Gemini. They made an emergency landing in the Pacific.
Gemini-Titan 9-A	June 3, 1966 0840 EDT Cape Kennedy	Lt. Col. Thomas P. Stafford, USAF, 35 (CDR) Lt. Cmdr. Eugene A. Cernan, USN, 32 (PLT)	"Gemini 9"	June 6, 1966 0900 EDT Atlantic Ocean, one-half mile from the USS Wasp	3 days, 20 minutes	Stafford and Cernan made rendezvous with the unmanned Augmented Target Docking Adaptor, but were unable to dock with the vehicle. Cernan's planned two-hour spacewalk using a maneuvering backpack was unsuccessful.
Gemini-Titan 10	July 18, 1966 1720 EDT Cape Kennedy	Cmdr. John W. Young, USN, 35 (CDR) Maj. Michael Collins, USAF, 35 (PLT)	"Gemini 10"	July 21, 1966 1607 EDT Atlantic Ocean, 4 miles from the USS Guadalcanal	2 days, 22 hours, 17 minutes	Young and Collins piloted Gemini 10 to rendezvous and docking with two different Agena targets, one of them left over from Gemini 8, and reached a record altitude of 468 miles. Collins performed two spacewalks.
Gemini-Titan 11	September 12, 1966 0942 EDT Cape Kennedy	Cmdr. Charles Conrad, Jr., USN, 36 (CDR) Lt. Cmdr. Richard F. Gordon, Jr., USN, 37 (PLT)	"Gemini 11"	September 15, 1966 0759 EDT Atlantic Ocean, 3 miles from the USS Guam	2 days, 23 hours, 17 minutes	Conrad and Gordon made rendezvous and docking with a target Agena, using it to raise their orbit to a new record altitude of 850 miles. Gordon made two spacewalks. The reentry and landing were flown on autopilot, another American first.
Gemini-Titan 12	November 11, 1966 1547 EST Cape Kennedy	Capt. James A. Lovell, Jr., USN, 38 (CDR) Maj. Edwin E. Aldrin, Jr., USAF, 36 (PLT)	"Gemini 12"	November 16, 1966 1421 EST Atlantic Ocean, 3 miles from the USS Wasp	3 days, 22 hours, 34 minutes	In this, the last flight in the Gemini series, Lovell and Aldrin again demonstrated rendezvous and docking techniques, including a final approach to the Agena using manual systems. Aldrin also completed three spacewalks totaling 5.5 hours.

MISSION	LAUNCH DATA	CREW	CALL SIGN	LANDING DATA	DURATION	REMARKS
Apollo-Saturn 204	January 27, 1967 1830 EST Kennedy Space Center, Pad 34	Lt. Col. Virgil I. Grissom, USAF, 40 (CDR) Lt. Col. Edward H. White II, USAF, 36 (SR PLT) Lt. Cmdr. Roger B. Chaffee, USN, 31 (PLT)	"Apollo 1"			Grissom, White and Chaffee, the crew for the first manned Apollo mission scheduled for launch February 14, 1967, were killed on the launch pad during a flight simulation when fire broke out in their spacecraft.
Soyuz 1	April 23, 1967 0325 MT Baikonur	Col. Vladimir M. Komarov, 40	"Rubin" ("Ruby")	April 24, 1967 0613 MT Orenburg	1 day, 2 hours, 48 minutes	Komarov was launched alone in this new spacecraft, to be joined on April 24 by Soyuz 2 and cosmonauts Bykovsky, Yeliseyev and Khrunov, with the latter two performing a spacewalk to Soyuz 1. Technical problems with Soyuz 1 canceled the second launch and forced Komarov to attempt a re-entry on the 18th orbit. Soyuz 1 crashed and he was killed. Initial orbit: 124 to 139 miles with a new inclination, 51.7 degrees.
Apollo-Saturn 7	October 11, 1968 1103 EDT Kennedy Space Center, Pad 34	Capt. Walter M. Schirra, Jr., USN, 45 (CDR) Maj. Donn F. Eisele, USAF, 38 (CMP) R. Walter Cunningham, 36 (LMP)	"Apollo 7"	October 22, 1968 0712 EDT Atlantic Ocean, recovered by USS Essex	10 days, 20 hours, 9 minutes	Schirra, Eisele and Cunningham piloted the first American manned flight since the Apollo 1 fire. They performed rendezvous exercises with the upper stage of Saturn IB launch vehicle during eleven days in space.
Soyuz 3	October 26, 1968 1134 MT Baikonur	Col. Georgy T. Beregovoy, 47	"Argon"	October 30, 1968 1025 MT Kazakhstan	3 days, 22 hours, 51 minutes	First manned flight of the re-designed Soyuz. Beregovoy made a rendezvous with the unmanned Soyuz 2, launched October 25, but failed to dock. Initial orbit: 109 to 127 at 51.7 inclination.
Apollo-Saturn 8	December 21, 1968 0751 EST Kennedy Space Center, Pad 39A	Col. Frank Borman, USAF, 40 (CDR) Capt. James A. Lovell, Jr., USN, 40 (CMP) Maj. William A. Anders, USAF, 35 (LMP)	"Apollo 8"	December 28, 1968 1051 EST Pacific Ocean, recovered by USS Yorktown	6 days, 3 hours	Borman, Lovell and Anders were launched aboard the Saturn 5, the most powerful rocket used in the first twenty-five years of manned flight, and became the first humans to reach the Moon. They made ten orbits of the Moon on December 24 and December 25, 1968.

Soyuz 4	January 14, 1969 1039 MT Baikonur	Lt. Col. Vladimir A. Shatalov, 41	"Amur"	January 17, 1969 1000 MT Kazakhstan	2 days, 23 hours, 21 minutes	Shatalov on Soyuz 4 was joined in orbit on January 15 by Soyuz 5 and cosmonauts Volynov, Yeliseyev and Khrunov. Shatalov piloted the rendezvous and docking on January 16. Yeliseyev and Khrunov performed a spacewalk to Soyuz 4 and returned to Earth in that vehicle. Initial orbit: 131 to 139 miles.
Soyuz 5	January 15, 1969 1014 MT Baikonur	Lt. Col. Boris V. Volynov, 34 (CDR) Alexei S. Yeliseyev, 34 (FE) Lt. Col. Yevgeny V. Khrunov, 35 (RE)	"Baikal"	January 18, 1969 1108 MT Kazakhstan	3 days, 54 minutes	Soyuz 5 served as the passive docking target for Soyuz 4. Khrunov and Yeliseyev transferred to the other spacecraft (total EVA time, 37 minutes) and Volynov returned to Earth alone. Initial orbit: 124 by 131.
Apollo-Saturn 9	March 3, 1969 1100 EST Kennedy Space Center, Pad 39A	Col. James A. McDivitt, USAF, 39 (CDR) Col. David R. Scott, USAF, 36 (CMP) Russell L. Schweickart, 33 (LMP)	"Apollo 9," "Gumdrop" and "Spider"	March 13, 1969 1201 EST Atlantic Ocean, recovered by USS Guadalcanal	10 days, 1 hour, 1 minute	McDivitt and Schweickart made the first manned test of the lunar module Spider while Scott remained aboard the command module Gumdrop. Schweickart also made a spacewalk testing the Apollo lunar spacesuit.
Apollo-Saturn 10	May 18, 1969 1249 EDT Kennedy Space Center, Pad 39B	Col. Thomas P. Stafford, USAF, 38 (CDR) Cmdr. John W. Young, USN, 38 (CMP) Cmdr. Eugene A. Cernan, USN, 35 (LMP)	"Apollo 10," "Charlie Brown" and "Snoopy"	May 26, 1969 1252 EDT Pacific Ocean, recovered by USS Princeton	8 days, 3 minutes	Stafford, Young and Cernan completed a full dress rehearsal for a lunar landing. Stafford and Cernan, aboard the LM Snoopy, came to within ten miles of the surface of the Moon.
Apollo-Saturn 11	July 16, 1969 0932 EDT Kennedy Space Center, Pad 39A	Neil A. Armstrong, 38 (CDR) Lt. Col. Michael Collins, 38 (CMP) Col. Edwin E. Aldrin, Jr., 39 (LMP)	"Apollo 11," "Columbia" and "Eagle"	July 24, 1969 1250 EDT Pacific Ocean, recovered by USS Hornet	8 days, 3 hours, 18 minutes	Armstrong and Aldrin made the historic first manned landing on the Moon in the LM Eagle on July 20, 1969. Collins remained in lunar orbit in the CM Columbia. Armstrong and Aldrin remained on the Moon for 20 hours and took a two-hour moonwalk.
Soyuz 6	October 11, 1969 1410 MT Baikonur	Lt. Col. Georgy S. Shonin, 34 (CDR) Valery N. Kubasov, 34 (FE)	"Antei" ("Anteus")	October 16, 1969 1253 MT Kazakhstan	4 days, 22 hours, 43 minutes	Soyuz 6 was the first of three Soviet manned vehicles launched on successive days, forming the first "space squadron." Kubasov performed the first space welding experiment.
Soyuz 7	October 12, 1969 1345 MT Baikonur	Lt. Col. Anatoly V. Filipchenko, 41 (CDR) Vladislav N. Volkov, 34, (FE) Lt. Col. Viktor V. Gorbatko, 34 (RE)	"Buran" ("Snowstorm")	October 17, 1969 1225 MT Kazakhstan	4 days, 22 hours, 40 minutes	The second element of the "space squadron." Soyuz 7 was intended to dock with Soyuz 8, launched on October 13, but did not, though the two spacecraft rendezvoused on October 15, closing to within 500 yards of each other. Initial orbit: 129 to 141 miles.

MISSION	LAUNCH DATA	CREW	CALL SIGN	LANDING DATA	DURATION	REMARKS
Soyuz 8	October 13, 1969 1329 MT Baikonur	Col. Vladimir A. Shatalov, 41 (CDR) Alexei S. Yeliseyev, 35 (FE)	"Granit" ("Granite")	October 18, 1969 1220 MT Kazakhstan	4 days, 22 hours, 51 minutes	Shatalov and Yeliseyev made their second flights in ten months. Intended to dock with Soyuz 7, Soyuz 8 only made rendezvous on October 15. Initial orbit: 128 to 139 miles.
Apollo-Saturn 12	November 14, 1969 1122 EST Kennedy Space Center, Pad 39A	Cmdr. Charles Conrad, Jr., USN, 39 (CDR) Cmdr. Richard F. Gordon, Jr., USN, 40 (CMP) Cmdr. Alan L. Bean, USN, 37 (LMP)	"Apollo 12," "Yankee Clipper" and "Intrepid"	November 24, 1969 1250 EDT Pacific Ocean, recovered by USS Hornet	10 days, 4 hours, 36 minutes	Conrad and Bean landed on the Moon's Ocean of Storms on November 18 just 300 yards from the unmanned Surveyor 3. The two astronauts took two moonwalks totaling 7.5 hours.
Apollo-Saturn 13	April 11, 1970 1413 EDT Kennedy Space Center, Pad 39A	Capt. James A. Lovell, Jr., USN, 42 (CDR) John L. Swigert, 38 (CMP) Fred W. Haise, Jr., 36 (LMP)	"Apollo 13," "Odyssey" and "Aquarius"	April 17, 1970 1218 EDT Pacific Ocean, recovered by USS Iwo Jima	5 days, 22 hours, 55 minutes	A planned third manned lunar landing (by Lovell and Haise near the crater Fra Mauro) was aborted by an explosion aboard the command module Odyssey on April 13. Lovell, Swigert and Haise used the lunar module Aquarius as a lifeboat during a loop around the Moon and a safe return to Earth.
Soyuz 9	June 1, 1970 2200 MT Baikonur	Col. Andrian G. Nikolayev, 40 (CDR) Vitaly I. Sevastyanov, 34 (FE)	"Sokol"	June 19, 1970 1501 MT Kazakhstan	17 days, 16 hours, 59 minutes	Nikolayev and Sevastyanov's 18-day flight set a new endurance record. However, the cosmonauts had to be carried from their spacecraft after landing.
Apollo-Saturn 14	January 31, 1971 1603 EDT Kennedy Space Center, Pad 39A	Capt. Alan B. Shepard, Jr., USN, 47 (CDR) Maj. Stuart A. Roosa, USAF, 37 (CMP) Cmdr. Edgar D. Mitchell, USN, 40 (LMP)	"Apollo 14," "Kitty Hawk" and "Antares"	February 9, 1971 1645 EDT Pacific Ocean, recovered by USS New Orleans	9 days, 42 minutes	Shepard and Mitchell landed the lunar module Antares at Fra Mauro on February 5 and performed two moonwalks totaling 9 hours.
Soyuz 10	April 23, 1971 0254 MT Baikonur	Col. Vladimir A. Shatalov, 43 (CDR) Alexei S. Yeliseyev, 36 (FE) Nikolai N. Rukavishnikov, 38 (TE)	"Granit"	April 25, 1971 0250 MT Kazakhstan	1 days, 23 hours, 46 minutes	Soyuz 10 was launched four days after Salyut, the first Soviet space station. Cosmonauts Shatalov, Yeliseyev and Rukavishnikov docked their spacecraft to the station on April 24, but were unable to enter. After 5.5 hours the two craft separated and the cosmonauts returned to Earth, aborting a planned 30 days in space. Initial orbit: 131 to 155 miles.

Soyuz 11	June 6, 1971 0755 MT Baikonur	Lt. Col. Georgy T. Dobrovolsky, 43 (CDR) Vladislav N. Volkov, 36 (FE) Viktor I. Patsayev, 37 (TE)	"Yantar" ("Amber")	June 30, 1971 0217 MT Kazakhstan	23 days, 18 hours, 22 minutes	The Soyuz 11 cosmonauts succeeded in docking with Salyut on June 7 and spent 23 days aboard the station. During their return to Earth on June 30, however, a valve in their Soyuz opened by mistake, causing their spacecraft to depressurize, and killing all three cosmonauts. Orbit at docking: 116 to 136 miles.
Apollo-Saturn 15	July 26, 1971 0934 EDT Kennedy Space Center, Pad 39A	Col. David R. Scott, USAF, 39 (CDR) Maj. Alfred M. Worden, USAF, 39 (CMP) Lt. Col. James B. Irwin, USAF, 41 (LMP)	"Apollo 15," "Endeavour" and "Falcon"	August 7, 1971 1646 EDT Pacific Ocean, recovered by USS Okinawa	12 days, 7 hours, 12 minutes	Scott and Irwin spent three days on the lunar surface near Hadley Rille, including almost 21 hours in moonwalks and excursions with the lunar rover. On the return to Earth, Worden took a spacewalk to recover materials from an experiment bay on the Endeavour's service module.
Apollo-Saturn 16	April 16, 1972 1254 EDT Kennedy Space Center, Pad 39A	Capt. John W. Young, USN, 41 (CDR) Lt. Cmdr. Thomas K. Mattingly II, USN, 36 (CMP) Lt. Col. Charles M. Duke, Jr., USAF, 36 (LMP)	"Apollo 16," "Casper" and "Orion"	April 27, 1972 1445 EDT Pacific Ocean, recovered by USS Ticonderoga	11 days, 1 hour, 51 minutes	Young and Duke landed the LM Orion near the crater Descartes for three days of exploration using a lunar rover. Problems with main engine of the CM Casper delayed the lunar landing, and shortened the flight by one day.
Apollo-Saturn 17	December 7, 1972 0033 EST Kennedy Space Center, Pad 39A	Capt. Eugene A. Cernan, USN, 38 (CDR) Cmdr. Ronald E. Evans, Jr., USN, 39 (CMP) Harrison H. Schmitt, 37 (LMP)	"Apollo 17," "Challenger" and "America"	December 19, 1972 1424 EST Pacific Ocean, recovered by USS Ticonderoga	12 days, 13 hours, 51 minutes	Following the first nighttime launch in the US space program, Cernan and geologist Schmitt landed the LM America near the Taurus mountains, spending the next three days exploring the lunar surface.
Skylab SL-2	May 25, 1973 0900 EDT Kennedy Space Center, Pad 39B	Capt. Charles Conrad, Jr., USN, 42 (CDR) Cmdr. Joseph P. Kerwin, USN, 41 (SP) Cmdr. Paul J. Weitz, USN, 41 (PLT)	"Skylab"	June 22, 1973 0950 EDT Pacific Ocean, recovered by USS Ticonderoga	28 days, 50 minutes	Conrad, Kerwin and Weitz boarded Skylab, America's first space station on May 26, and following repairs to the station (which had been damaged during launch on May 14), completed a successful 28-day mission.
Skylab SL-3	July 28, 1973 0711 EDT Kennedy Space Center, Pad 39B	Capt. Alan L. Bean, USN, 41 (CDR) Owen K. Garriott, 42 (SP) Maj. Jack R. Lousma, USMC, 37 (PLT)	"Skylab"	September 25, 1973 1819 EDT Pacific Ocean, recovered by USS New Orleans	59 days, 11 hours, 9 minutes	Bean, Garriott and Lousma made further repairs to Skylab and completed a two-month mission aboard the station.

MISSION	LAUNCH DATA	CREW	CALL SIGN	LANDING DATA	DURATION	REMARKS
Soyuz 12	September 27, 1973 1518 MT Baikonur	Lt. Col. Vasily G. Lazarev, 45 (CDR) Oleg G. Makarov, 40 (FE)	"Ural"	September 29, 1973 1434 MT Kazakhstan	1 day, 23 hours, 16 minutes	Following the Soyuz 11 accident, the Soyuz spacecraft was redesigned. Lazarev and Makarov tested its systems on a two-day mission, becoming the first cosmonauts since 1965 to wear spacesuits in flight.
Skylab SL-4	November 15, 1973 0901 EST Kennedy Space Center, Pad 39B	Lt. Col. Gerald P. Carr, USMC, 41 (CDR) Edward G. Gibson, 37 (SP) Lt. Col. William R. Pogue, USAF, 43 (PLT)	"Skylab"	February 8, 1974 1016 EST Pacific Ocean, recovered by USS New Orleans	84 days, 1 hour, 15 minutes	Carr, Gibson and Pogue set a world space endurance record by spending 84 days aboard Skylab in the most scientifically productive mission in the program.
Soyuz 13	December 18, 1973 1455 MT Baikonur	Maj. Pyotr I. Klimuk, 31 (CDR) Valentin V. Lebedev, 31 (FE)	"Kavkaz" ("Caucasus")	December 26, 1973 1150 MT Kazakhstan	7 days, 20 hours, 55 minutes	Soyuz 13 carried the Orion astrophysical observatory originally intended to be flown on Salyut space stations, but a series of Salyut failures prevented that. Klimuk and Lebedev observed Comet Kahoutek as did the Skylab astronauts. It was the first time that Soviet and American space travelers were in orbit simultaneously.
Soyuz 14	July 3, 1974 2151 MT Baikonur	Col. Pavel R. Popovich, 43 (CDR) Engineer-Lt. Col. Yuri P. Artyukhin, 43 (FE)	"Berkut"	July 19, 1974 1521 MT 88 miles SE of Dzhezhkagan, Kazakhstan	15 days, 17 hours, 30 minutes	Popovich and Artyukhin conducted the USSR's first successful space station mission, spending almost 14 days aboard Salyut 3 in a low earth orbit. They performed medical studies and military reconaissance. Orbit at docking on July 5 was 159 by 173 miles.
Soyuz 15	August 26, 1974 2258 MT Baikonur	Lt. Col. Gennady V. Sarafanov, 32 (CDR) Engineer-Col. Lev S. Demin, 48 (FE)	"Dunai" ("Danube")	August 28, 1974 2310 MT 30 miles NE of Tselinograd, Kazakh.	2 days, 12 minutes	Sarafanov and Demin were scheduled to spend a month aboard Salyut 3 but a failure in the guidance system of Soyuz 15 forced them to call off their docking on August 28 and return to Earth.
Soyuz 16	December 2, 1974 1240 MT Baikonur	Col. Anatoly V. Filipchenko, 46 (CDR) Nikolai N. Rukavishnikov, 42 (FE)	"Buran"	December 8, 1974 1104 MT 188 miles N of Dzhezhkagan	5 days, 22 hours, 24 minutes	Apollo-Soyuz backups Filipchenko and Rukavishnikov conducted a six-day dress rehearsal for the Soviet-American flight scheduled for the following July. NASA ground stations tracked Soyuz 16 after launch was announced.
Soyuz 17	January 11, 1975 0043 MT Baikonur	Lt. Col. Alexei A. Gubarev, 43 (CDR) Georgy M. Grechko, 43 (FE)	"Zenit" ("Zenith")	February 9, 1975 1403 MT 69 miles NE of Tselinograd	29 days, 13 hours, 20 minutes	Gubarev and Grechko conducted scientific experiments aboard Salyut 4, launched December 29, 1974. Docking took place on January 13 with Soyuz 17 in a corrected orbit of 183 by 221 miles.

Soyuz 18-1	April 5, 1975 unknown Baikonur	Col. Vasily G. Lazarev, 46 (CDR) Oleg G. Makarov, 42 (FE)	"Ural"	April 5, 1975 unknown Near Gorno-Altaisk, Siberia	22 minutes	Lazarev and Makarov were to have spent two months aboard Salyut 4, but saw the mission aborted when two stages of their booster rocket failed to separate. Soyuz reached an altitude of approximately 90 miles, then re-entered without reaching orbit.
Soyuz 18	May 24, 1975 1758 MT Baikonur	Lt. Col. Pyotr I. Klimuk, 33 (CDR) Vitaly I. Sevastyanov, 40 (FE)	"Kavkaz"	July 26, 1975 1718 MT 35 miles NE of Arkalyk, Kazakh.	62 days, 23 hours, 20 minutes	Klimuk and Sevastyanov, backups for Lazarev and Makarov, docked with Salyut 4 on May 26 and spent the next 61 days performing scientific experiments and making earth observations. Soyuz 18 was in orbit during Apollo-Soyuz.
Soyuz 19	July 15, 1975 1520 MT Baikonur	Col. Alexei A. Leonov, 41 (CDR) Valery N. Kubasov, 40 (FE)	"Soyuz"	July 21, 1975 1351 MT 34 miles NW of Arkalyk	5 days, 22 hours, 31 minutes	On July 17 cosmonauts Leonov and Kubasov docked with an American Apollo crewed by astronauts Stafford, Brand and Slayton. The spacecraft remained linked for two days, during which crewmen performed scientific experiments and made television broadcasts commemorating this first international space flight.
Apollo-Soyuz Test Project (ASTP)	July 15, 1975 1550 EDT Kennedy Space Center, Pad 39B	Brig. Gen. Thomas P. Stafford, USAF, 45 (CDR) Vance D. Brand, 43 (CMP) Donald K. Slayton, 51 (DMP)	"Apollo"	July 24, 1975 1718 EDT Pacific Ocean, recovered by USS New Orleans		American astronauts Stafford, Brand and Slayton linked up with Soviet Soyuz 19 and cosmonauts Leonov and Kubasov on July 17, spending two days in joint activities. The remainder of the mission was devoted to Earth observations and scientific experiments. A fuel leak during splashdown caused one of the astronauts to black out, but all were recovered safely.
Soyuz 21	July 6, 1976 1509 MT Baikonur	Col. Boris V: Volynov, 41 (CDR) Engineer-Lt. Col. Vitaly M. Zholobov, 39 (FE)	"Baikal"	August 24, 1976 2133 MT 125 miles SWS of Kokchetav, Kazakh.	49 days, 6 hours, 23 minutes	On July 7, Volynov and Zholobov linked up with Salyut 5, launched June 22, for a mission devoted to space manufacturing and military reconaissance. The cosmonauts returned to Earth three weeks early because of a problem with their Salyut's atmosphere.
Soyuz 22	September 15, 1976 1458 MT Baikonur	Col. Valery F. Bykovsky, 42 (CDR) Vladimir V. Aksenov, 41 (FE)	"Yastreb"	September 23, 1976 1042 MT 94 miles NW of Tselinograd	7 days, 21 hours, 52 minutes	Bykovsky and Aksenov flew the backup Apollo-Soyuz spacecraft on a mission devoted to observations of the Earth's surface with the East German-built MKF-6 camera. Soyuz 22 was the first Soviet manned flight since 1965 to have an orbital inclination of 65 degrees.
Soyuz 23	October 14, 1976 2040 MT Baikonur	Lt. Col. Vyacheslav D. Zudov, 34 (CDR) Eng.-Lt. Col. Valery I. Rozhdestvensky, 37 (FE)	"Rodon" ("Radon")	October 16, 1976 2047 MT Lake Tengiz, 122 miles SW of Tselinograd	2 days, 7 minutes	Zudov and Rozhdestvensky were to have spent at least two months aboard Salyut 5, following replacement of the station's contaminated atmosphere. But Soyuz guidance problems again canceled the docking. The cosmonauts made the Soviet Union's first "splashdown" on their return.

MISSION	LAUNCH DATA	CREW	CALL SIGN	LANDING DATA	DURATION	REMARKS
Soyuz 24	February 7, 1977 1912 MT Baikonur	Col. Viktor V. Gorbatko, 42 (CDR) Eng.-Lt. Col. Yuri N. Glazkov, 37 (FE)	"Terek"	February 25, 1977 1236 MT 23 miles NE of Arkalyk	17 days, 17 hours, 26 minutes	Gorbatko and Glazkov, backups for Soyuz 23, docked with Salyut 5 on February 8 for a relatively short mission to complete experiments begun by the Soyuz 21 cosmonauts and to load a special re-entry module.
Soyuz 25	October 9, 1977 0540 MT Baikonur	Lt. Col. Vladimir V. Kovalenok, 35 (CDR) Valery V. Ryumin, 38 (FE)	"Foton" ("Photon")	October 11, 1977 0626 MT 116 miles NW of Tselinograd	2 days, 46 minutes	Kovalenok and Ryumin were to have boarded Salyut 6, launched September 29, for a planned 90-day mission involving a visit by a second cosmonaut team and resupply by a robot tanker, the most ambitious Soviet space flight ever attempted. But a mechanical failure in the Salyut docking mechanism on October 11 prevented the cosmonauts from boarding the station and they returned to Earth that day.
Soyuz 26	December 10, 1977 0419 MT Baikonur	Lt. Col. Yuri V. Romanenko, 33 (CDR) Georgy M. Grechko, 46 (FE)	"Taimyr"	March 16, 1978 1419 MT 166 miles W of Tselinograd	96 days, 10 hours	Romanenko and Grechko set a space endurance record aboard Salyut 6, which they boarded on December 11. In addition to scientific and medical work, they performed the Soviet Union's first EVA since 1969 and were visited by two teams of cosmonauts. They were also resupplied by the Progress robot tanker. The cosmonauts returned to Earth in Soyuz 27.
Soyuz 27	January 10, 1978 1526 MT Baikonur	Lt. Col. Vladimir A. Dzhanibekov, 35 (CDR) Oleg G. Makarov, 44 (FE)	"Pamir"	January 16, 1978 1425 MT 194 miles W of Tselinograd	5 days, 22 hours, 59 minutes	Dzhanibekov and Makarov docked with Salyut 6, joining cosmonauts Romanenko and Grechko, on January 11. They swapped spacecraft with the expedition crew and returned to Earth in Soyuz 26.
Soyuz 28	March 2, 1978 1828 MT Baikonur	Col. Alexei A. Gubarev, 46 (CDR) Capt. Vladimir Remek, 29 (CR) [Czechoslovakia]	"Zenit"	March 10, 1978 1625 MT 194 miles W of Tselinograd	7 days, 22 hours, 17 minutes	Remek, the first non-Soviet, non-American space traveler, and Gubarev joined Romanenko and Grechko aboard Salyut 6 on March 3 for a week of experiments.
Soyuz 29	June 15, 1978 2317 MT Baikonur	Col. Vladimir V. Kovalenok, 36 (CDR) Alexandr S. Ivanchenkov, 37 (FE)	"Foton"	November 2, 1978 1405 MT 113 miles SE of Dzhezhkagan	139 days, 14 hours, 48 minutes	The second expedition crew to inhabit Salyut 6, Kovalenok and Ivanchenkov set a new endurance record. They were visited by two teams of guest cosmonauts and resupplied by three Progress tankers. The cosmonauts returned to Earth on Soyuz 31.
Soyuz 30	June 27, 1978 1827 MT Baikonur	Col. Pyotr I. Klimuk, 36 (CDR) Maj. Miroslaw Hermaszewski, 36 (CR) [Poland]	"Kavkaz"	July 5, 1978 1630 MT 188 miles W of Tselinograd	7 days, 22 hours, 3 minutes	Hermaszewski, the first Polish cosmonaut, and Klimuk spent a week with Kovalenok and Ivanchenkov aboard Salyut 6 beginning June 28.

Soyuz 31	August 26, 1978 1751 MT Baikonur	Col. Valery F. Bykovsky, 44 (CDR) Lt. Col. Sigmund Jaehn, 41 (CR) [German Dem. Rep.]	"Yastreb" ("Hawk")	September 3, 1978 1440 MT near Dzhezhkagan	7 days, 20 hours, 49 minutes	Jaehn, the first German space traveler, and commander Bykovsky joined Kovalenok and Ivanchenkov aboard Salyut 6 beginning August 27. The visitors returned to Earth in Soyuz 29.
Soyuz 32	February 25, 1979 1454 MT Baikonur	Lt. Col. Vladimir A. Lyakhov, 37 (CDR) Valery V. Ryumin, 39 (FE)	"Proton"	August 19, 1979 1530 MT 106 miles SE of Dzhezhkagan	175 days, 36 minutes	Lyakhov and Ryumin, the third Salyut 6 expedition crew, set another endurance record of almost six months in space. Their work included astronomical observations with the KT-10 radiotelescope and they also performed an unscheduled EVA. The cosmonauts did not have visitors during their mission, returning to Earth aboard Soyuz 34, which had been launched unmanned.
Soyuz 33	April 10, 1979 2024 MT Baikonur	Nikolai N. Rukavishnikov, 46 (CDR) Maj. Georgy Ivanov, 38 (CR) [Bulgaria]	"Saturn"	April 12, 1979 1935 MT 200 miles SE of Dzhezhkagan	1 day, 23 hours, 1 minute	Soyuz 33 suffered a major engine failure during final approach to Salyut 6 on April 12. Cosmonauts Rukavishnikov and Ivanov were forced to use a backup engine to return to Earth.
Soyuz 35	April 9, 1980 1638 MT Baikonur	Lt. Col. Leonid I. Popov, 34 (CDR) Valery V. Ryumin, 40 (FE)	"Dnepr"	October 11, 1980 1250 MT 113 miles SE of Dzhezhkagan	184 days, 20 hours, 12 minutes	The fourth expedition to Salyut 6 included Ryumin, a last-minute replacement. He and Popov were resupplied by four Progress tankers and visited by four different teams of cosmonauts during their six months. The cosmonauts returned to Earth in Soyuz 37.
Soyuz 36	May 26, 1980 2121 MT Baikonur	Valery N. Kubasov, 45 (CDR) Capt. Bertalan Farkas, 30 (CR) [Hungary]	"Orion"	June 3, 1980 1807 MT 88 miles SE of Dzhezhkagan	7 days, 20 hours, 46 minutes	Hungarian pilot Farkas and Soviet commander Kubasov joined Popov and Ryumin aboard Salyut 6 on May 27. The visitors returned to Earth a week later in Soyuz 35.
Soyuz T-2	June 5, 1980 1719 MT Baikonur	Lt. Col. Yuri V. Malyshev, 38 (CDR) Vladimir V. Aksenov, 45 (FE)	"Yupiter" ("Jupiter")	June 9, 1980 1539 MT 124 miles SE of Dzhezhkagan	3 days, 22 hours, 20 minutes	Malyshev and Aksenov made the first manned test flight of an improved Soyuz. The new guidance system failed on approach to Salyut 6, though the cosmonauts were able to dock manually. They spent three days with Popov and Ryumin before returning to Earth.
Soyuz 37	July 23, 1980 2133 MT Baikonur	Col. Viktor V. Gorbatko, 45 (CDR) Lt. Col. Pham Tuan, 33 (CR) [Vietnam]	"Terek"	July 31, 1980 1815 MT 112 miles SE of Dzhezhkagan	7 days, 20 hours, 42 minutes	Vietnamese pilot Tuan and Soviet commander Gorbatko docked with Salyut 6 on July 24. Among their tasks was a commemoration of the 1980 Moscow Summer Olympics. They returned to Earth in Soyuz 36.
Soyuz 38	September 18, 1980 2211 MT Baikonur	Col. Yuri V. Romanenko, 36 (CDR) Lt. Col. Arnaldo Tamayo Mendez, 38 (CR) [Cuba]	"Taimyr"	September 26, 1980 1854 MT 109 miles SE of Dzhezhkagan	7 days, 20 hours, 43 minutes	Cuban pilot Tamayo Mendez and Soviet commander Romanenko joined expedition cosmonauts Popov and Ryumin for a week aboard Salyut 6.

MISSION	LAUNCH DATA	CREW	CALL SIGN	LANDING DATA	DURATION	REMARKS
Soyuz T-3	November 27, 1980 1718 MT Baikonur	Lt. Col. Leonid D. Kizim, 39 (CDR) Oleg G. Makarov, 47 (FE) Gennady M. Strekalov, 40 (CR)	"Mayak" ("Lighthouse")	December 10, 1980 1226 MT 81 miles E of Dzhezhkagan	12 days, 19 hours, 8 minutes	The first three-man Soviet space crew since 1971 docked with the unoccupied Salyut 6 on November 28. For the next twelve days they performed repairs on the station to prepare it for a fifth expedition crew.
Soyuz T-4	March 12, 1981 2000 MT Baikonur	Col. Vladimir V. Kovalenok, 39 (CDR) Viktor P. Savinykh, 41 (FE)	"Foton"	May 26, 1981 1638 MT 78 miles E of Dzhezhkagan	74 days, 17 hours, 38 minutes	Kovalenok and Savinykh conducted a "bonus" mission aboard Salyut 6, which had already exceeded its designed lifetime. The cosmonauts were visited by two guest crews.
Soyuz 39	March 22, 1981 1759 MT Baikonur	Col. Vladimir A. Dzhanibekov, 39 (CDR) Eng.-Capt. Jugderdimidyn Gurragcha, 33 (CR) [Mongolia]	"Pamir"	March 30, 1981 1442 MT 106 miles SE of Dzhezhkagan	7 days, 20 hours, 43 minutes	Mongolian engineer Gurragcha and Soviet commander Dzhanibekov joined Kovalenok and Savinykh aboard Salyut 6 beginning on March 23.
STS-1	April 12, 1981 0700 EST Kennedy Space Center, Pad 39A	John W. Young, 50 (CDR) Capt. Robert L. Crippen, USN, 43 (PLT)	"Columbia"	April 14, 1981 1021 PST Edwards AFB, California	2 days, 6 hours, 21 minutes	Young and Crippen were launched on the 20th anniversary of Gagarin's flight aboard the first winged, reusable spacecraft, landing two days later on the lake bed at Edwards AFB.
Soyuz 40	May 14, 1981 2117 MT Baikonur	Col. Leonid I. Popov, 35 (CDR) Eng.-Sr. Lt. Dumitru D. Prunariu, 28 (CR) [Rumania]	"Dnepr"	May 22, 1981 1758 MT 141 miles SE of Dzhezhkagan	7 days, 20 hours, 38 minutes	Rumanian pilot Prunariu and Soviet commander Popov spent seven days aboard Salyut 6 beginning May 15. They were the last cosmonauts to fly in a Soyuz spacecraft.
STS-2	November 12, 1981 1010 EST Kennedy Space Center, Pad 39A	Col. Joe H. Engle, USAF, 49 (CDR) Capt. Richard H. Truly, USN, 44 (PLT)	"Columbia"	November 14, 1981 1323 PST Edwards AFB, California	2 days, 6 hours, 13 minutes	After several delays, Engle and Truly made the second flight aboard the reusable Shuttle Columbia, though technical problems shortened the mission from five to two days.
STS-3	March 22, 1982 1100 EST Kennedy Space Center, Pad 39A	Col. Jack R. Lousma, USMC, 46 (CDR) Col. C. Gordon Fullerton, USAF, 45 (PLT)	"Columbia"	March 30, 1982 0905 MST Northrup Strip, White Sands, New Mexico	8 days, 5 minutes	Lousma and Fullerton made the third Shuttle orbital flight test aboard Columbia, which carried an experiment packaged called OSS-1. The mission was extended by one day and landing was switched to backup site in New Mexico because of rains at Edwards AFB.

Soyuz T-5	May 13, 1982 1358 MT Baikonur	Lt. Col. Anatoly N. Berezovoy, 40 (CDR) Valentin V. Lebedev, 40 (FE)	"Elbrus"	December 10, 1982 2203 MT 119 miles E of Dzhezhkagan	211 days, 8 hours, 5 minutes	Berezovoy and Lebedev docked Soyuz T-5 to the new Salyut 7, which had been launched April 19, on May 14, for a mission scheduled to last four months, with possible extensions. Ultimately they spent seven months in space, hosting two teams of visiting cosmonauts, deploying a scientific satellite, performing spacewalks, in addition to other medical, engineering and scientific work. They returned to Earth in the middle of a raging blizzard aboard Soyuz T-7.
Soyuz T-6	June 24, 1982 2030 MT Baikonur	Col. Vladimir A. Dzhanibekov, 40 (CDR) Alexandr S. Ivanchenkov, 42 (FE) Lt. Col. Jean-Loup Chretien, 44 (CR) [France]	"Pamir"	July 2, 1982 1821 MT 41 miles SE of Arkalyk	7 days, 22 hours, 42 minutes	French test pilot Chretien became the first Westerner to go into space aboard a Soviet vehicle. He and fellow cosmonauts Dzhanibekov and Ivanchenkov spent a week with Berezovoy and Lebedev on Salyut 7 beginning June 25.
STS-4	June 27, 1982 1100 EDT Kennedy Space Center, Pad 39A	Capt. Thomas K. Mattingly II, USN, 46 (CDR) Henry W. Hartsfield, Jr., 48 (PLT)	"Columbia"	July 4, 1982 0909 PDT Edwards AFB, California	7 days, 1 hour, 10 minutes	Mattingly and Hartsfield completed the fourth and final Shuttle orbital flight test. Columbia carried a Department of Defense experiment and the first commercial experiment.
Soyuz T-7	August 19, 1982 2112 MT Baikonur	Col. Leonid I. Popov 36 (CDR) Alexandr A. Serebrov, 38 (FE) Svetlana Y. Savitskaya, 34 (CR)	"Dnepr"	August 27, 1982 2203 MT 44 miles SE of Arkalyk	7 days, 21 hours, 52 minutes	Savitskaya, a test and sport pilot, became the second woman in space. She and Popov and Serebrov joined cosmonauts Berezovoy and Lebedev for a week aboard Salyut 7, then returned to Earth on Soyuz T-5.
STS-5	November 11, 1982 0719 EST Kennedy Space Center, Pad 39A	Vance D. Brand, 51, (CDR) Col. Robert F. Overmyer, USMC, 46 (PLT) Joseph P. Allen IV, 45 (MSl) William B. Lenoir, 43 (MS2)	"Columbia"	November 16, 1982 0633 EST Edwards AFB, California	5 days, 2 hours, 14 minutes	First operational flight of the Space Shuttle, and the first manned spacecraft to carry four crew members. The astronauts deployed two commercial communications satellites.
STS-6	April 4, 1983 1330 EST Kennedy Space Center, Pad 39A	Paul J. Weitz, 50 (CDR) Col. Karol J. Bobko, USAF, 45 (PLT) F. Story Musgrave, 47 (MSl) Donald H. Peterson, 49 (MS2)	"Challenger"	April 9, 1983 1053 EST Edwards AFB, California	5 days, 25 minutes	First flight of the Shuttle Challenger. Musgrave and Peterson performed the first spacewalk in the Shuttle program, and the astronauts deployed the first TDRS communications satellite.

MISSION	LAUNCH DATA	CREW	CALL SIGN	LANDING DATA	DURATION	REMARKS
Soyuz T-8	April 20, 1983 1711 MT Baikonur	Lt. Col. Vladimir G. Titov, 36 (CDR) Gennady M. Strekalov, 42 (FE) Alexandr A. Serebrov, 39 (CR)	"Okean" ("Ocean")	April 22, 1983 1729 MT 38 miles SE of Arkalyk	2 days, 18 minutes	A planned eight month mission aboard the Salyut 7/Kosmos 1443 complex by cosmonauts Titov, Strekalov and Serebrov had to be aborted because of failed rendezvous radar on Soyuz T-8.
STS-7	June 18, 1983 0733 EDT Kennedy Space Center, Pad 39A	Capt. Robert L. Crippen, USN, 45 (CDR) Capt. Frederick H. Hauck, USN, 42 (PLT) Col. John M. Fabian, USAF, 44 (MSl) Sally K. Ride, 32 (MS2) Norman E. Thagard, 39 (MS3)	"Challenger"	June 24, 1983 0657 PDT Edwards AFB, California	6 days, 2 hours, 24 minutes	Ride became the first American woman to make a space flight as a member of this five-person crew which deployed two communications satellites as well as a retrievable satellite. A landing at Kennedy Space Center was canceled because of weather at the site.
Soyuz T-9	June 27, 1983 1312 MT Baikonur	Col. Vladimir A. Lyakhov, 41 (CDR) Alexandr P. Alexandrov, 40 (FE)	"Proton"	November 23, 1983 2258 MT 100 miles E of Dzhezhkagan	149 days, 9 hours, 46 minutes	Lyakhov and Alexandrov docked their Soyuz T-9 to the Salyut 7/Kosmos 1443 complex on June 28. During their five-month mission they operated the Star module—Kosmos 1443—and were resupplied by several Progress tankers. Salyut 7 suffered a massive fuel leak in August that almost disabled the station, forcing the cosmonauts to make two spacewalks to make repairs.
STS-8	August 30, 1983 0230 EDT Kennedy Space Center, Pad 39A	Capt. Richard H. Truly, USN, 45 (CDR) Cmdr. Daniel C. Brandenstein, USN, 40 (PLT) Lt. Col. Guion S. Bluford, Jr., USAF, 40 (MSl) Lt. Cmdr. Dale A. Gardner, USN, 34 (MS2) William E. Thornton, 54 (MS3)	"Challenger"	September 5, 1983 1240 PDT Edwards AFB, California	6 days, 1 hour, 9 minutes	First nighttime launch and landing in the Shuttle program. The astronauts deployed an Indian communications satellite. Bluford became the first black American in space.

Soyuz T-10-1	September 26, 1983 1136 MT Baikonur	Col. Vladimir G. Titov, 36 (CDR) Gennady M. Strekalov, 42 (FE)	"Okean"	Launch pad abort		Cosmonauts Titov and Strekalov were to have joined Lyakhov and Alexandrov aboard Salyut 7 in order to perform repair EVAs to the station and to provide the expedition cosmonauts with a fresh Soyuz T spacecraft. A fire broke out in their launch vehicle shortly before ignition; the Soyuz T capsule separated and the cosmonauts landed safely several miles away.
STS-9	November 28, 1983 1100 EST Kennedy Space Center, Pad 39A	John W. Young, 53 (CDR) Maj. Brewster H. Shaw, Jr., USAF, 38 (PLT) Owen K. Garriott, 53 (MSl) Robert A. R. Parker, 47 (MS2) Byron K. Lichtenberg, 35 (PS1) Ulf Merbold, 42 (PS2) [ESA]	"Columbia", "Spacelab"	December 8, 1983 1537 PST Edwards AFB, California	10 days, 7 hours, 47 minutes	First flight of the European Space Agency's Spacelab, after many delays. The four scientists in the crew conducted 72 different investigations in round-the-clock operations. The flight was extended by one day.
41-B	February 3, 1984 0800 EST Kennedy Space Center, Pad 39A	Vance D. Brand, 52 (CDR) Lt. Cmdr. Robert L. Gibson, USN, 37 (PLT) Ronald E. McNair, 33 (MSl) Lt. Col. Robert L. Stewart, USA, 41 (MS2) Capt. Bruce McCandless II, USN, 45 (MS3)	"Challenger"	February 11, 1984 0717 EST Kennedy Space Center, Florida	7 days, 23 hours, 17 minutes	McCandless made the first untethered spacewalk in history using the manned maneuvering unit (MMU). Two communications satellites deployed by the crew went into improper orbits, and were later recovered on Mission 51-A. The astronauts were the first to land at their launching site.
Soyuz T-10	February 8, 1984 1507 MT Baikonur	Col. Leonid D. Kizim, 42 (CDR) Vladimir A. Solovyov, 37 (FE) Oleg Y. Atkov, 34 (CR)	"Mayak"	October 2, 1984 1057 MT 91 miles SE of Dzhezhkagan	236 days, 22 hours, 50 minutes	Kizim, Solovyov and Atkov set a new space endurance record during their eight months aboard Salyut 7. Medical studies occupied most of their time—87 days—supervised by cardiologist Atkov. Kizim and Soloyov also made six EVAs. The crew was visited by two other cosmonaut teams and resupplied by five Progress tankers and logged over 3400 orbits, traveling almost 100 million miles.
Soyuz T-11	April 3, 1984 1709 MT Baikonur	Col. Yuri V. Malyshev, 42 (CDR) Gennady M. Strekalov, 43 (FE) Maj. Rakesh Sharma, 35 (CR) [India]	"Yupiter"	April 11, 1984 1450 MT 35 miles E of Arkalyk	7 days, 21 hours, 41 minutes	Sharma became the first citizen of India to make a spaceflight, spending a week aboard Salyut 7 with crewmates Malyshev and Strekalov visiting Kizim, Solovyov and Atkov. They returned to Earth in the Soyuz T-10 spacecraft.

MISSION	LAUNCH DATA	CREW	CALL SIGN	LANDING DATA	DURATION	REMARKS
41-C	April 6, 1984 0858 EST Kennedy Space Center, Pad 39A	Capt. Robert L. Crippen, USN, 46 (CDR) Francis R. Scobee, 44 (PLT) George D. Nelson, 33 (MSl) Terry J. Hart, 37 (MS2) James D. A. van Hoften, 39 (MS3)	"Challenger"	April 13, 1984 0538 PST Edwards AFB, California	6 days, 23 hours, 40 minutes	Nelson and van Hoften conducted the first capture, repair and redeployment of a satellite using MMUs. The astronauts also deployed the long duration exposure facility (LDEF).
Soyuz T-12	July 17, 1984 2141 MT Baikonur	Col. Vladimir A. Dzhanibekov, 42 (CDR) Svetlana Y. Savitskaya, 35 (FE) Igor P. Volk, 47 (CR)	"Pamir"	July 29, 1984 1655 MT 88 miles NE of Dzezhkagan	11 days, 19 hours, 14 minutes	Dzhanibekov, Savitskaya and Volk rendezvoused with Salyut 7 and Kizim, Soloyov and Atkov on July 13. Savitskaya became the first woman to make a spacewalk when, on July 25, she and Dzhanibekov spent 3.5 hours outside Salyut 7 testing space welding equipment. This was an unusually long (13 days instead of 8) resupply mission.
41-D	August 30, 1984 0841 EDT Kennedy Space Center, Pad 39A	Henry W. Hartsfield, Jr., 50 (CDR) Cmdr. Michael L. Coats, USN, 38 (PLT) Lt. Col. Richard M. Mullane, USAF, 38 (MSl) Steven A. Hawley, 33 (MS2) Judith A. Resnik, 35 (MS3) Charles D. Walker, 36 (PS)	"Discovery"	September 5, 1984 0637 PDT Edwards AFB, California	6 days, 56 minutes	First flight of the Shuttle Discovery, following many delays, including a launch pad abort on June 26. The crew included industrial payload specialist Charles Walker, who operated the Continuous Flow Electrophoresis Experiment. The astronauts deployed three communications satellites.
41-G	October 5, 1984 0703 EDT Kennedy Space Center, Pad 39A	Capt. Robert L. Crippen, USN, 46 (CDR) Cmdr. Jon A. McBride, USN, 41 (PLT) Lt. Cmdr. David C. Leestma, USN, 35 (MS1) Sally K. Ride, 33 (MS2)	"Challenger"	October 13, 1984 1226 EDT Kennedy Space Center, Florida	8 days, 5 hours, 23 minutes	First crew of seven. The astronauts deployed th Radiation Budget Satellite and conducted an EVA satellite refueling test, making Sullivan the first American woman to walk in space.

		Kathryn D. Sullivan, 32 (MS3) Paul D. Scully-Power, 40 (PSl) Cmdr. Marc Garneau, Navy, 35 (PS2) [Canada]				
51-A	November 8, 1984 0715 EST Kennedy Space Center, Pad 39A	Capt. Frederick H. Hauck, USN, 43 (CDR) Cmdr. David M. Walker, USN, 40 (PLT) Anna L. Fisher, 36 (MSl) Cmdr. Dale A. Gardner, USN, 36 (MS2) Joseph P. Allen IV, 47 (MS3)	"Discovery"	November 16, 1984 0700 EST Kennedy Space Center, Florida	7 days, 23 hours, 45 minutes	In this, the most spectacular of the Shuttle flights, astronauts Allen and Gardner used MMUs to retrieve two errant communications satellites, which were then returned to Earth. The crew members also launched two new satellites.
51-C	January 24, 1985 1440 EST Kennedy Space Center, Pad 39A	Capt. Thomas K. Mattingly II, USN, 48 (CDR) Lt. Col. Loren J. Shriver, USAF, 40 (PLT) Maj. Ellison S. Onizuka, USAF, 38 (MS1) Lt. Col. James F. Buchli, USMC, 39 (MS2) Maj. Gary E. Payton, USAF, 36 (PS)	"Discovery"	January 27, 1985 1623 EST Kennedy Space Center, Florida	3 days, 1 hour, 33 minutes	The first classified US Department of Defense Shuttle mission, 51-C reportedly deployed an electronic intelligence satellite. The mission was shortened by one day because of weather problems at KSC.
51-D	April 12, 1985 0859 PST Kennedy Space Center, Pad 39A	Col. Karol J. Bobko, USAF, 47 (CDR) Capt. Donald E. Williams, USN, 43 (PLT) M. Rhea Seddon, 37 (MSl) S. David Griggs, 45 (MS2) Jeffrey A. Hoffman, 40 (MS3) Charles D. Walker, 36 (PSl) Senator Jake Garn, 52 (PS2)	"Discovery"	April 19, 1985 0855 PST Kennedy Space Center, Pad 39A	6 days, 23 hours, 55 minutes	This oft-delayed flight successfully deployed one communications satellite but suffered failure with a second, which astronauts Hoffman, Griggs and Seddon attempted to repair, but could not.

MISSION	LAUNCH DATA	CREW	CALL SIGN	LANDING DATA	DURATION	REMARKS
51-B	April 29, 1985 1202 EST Kennedy Space Center, Pad 39A	Col. Robert F. Overmyer, USMC, 48 (CDR) Col. Frederick D. Gregory, USAF, 44 (PLT) William E. Thornton, 56 (MS1) Norman E. Thagard, 41 (MS2) Don L. Lind, 54 (MS3) Lodewijk van den Berg, 53 (PS1) Taylor G. Wang, 44 (PS2)	"Challenger," "Spacelab"	May 6, 1985 1211 EDT Edwards AFB, California	7 days, 8 minutes	Spacelab 3, the first operational Spacelab mission, carried five scientists who successfully operated 14 of 15 planned experiments.
Soyuz T-13	June 6, 1985 1040 MT Baikonur	Col. Vladimir A. Dzhanibekov, 43 (CDR) Viktor P. Savinykh, 45 (FE)	"Pamir"	September 26, 1985 1352 MT 138 miles NE of Dzhezhkagan	112 days, 3 hours, 12 minutes (Dzhanibekov) 8 days, 21 hours, 13 minutes (Grechko)	Veteran commander Dzhanibekov and flight engineer Savinykh docked with the dead Salyut 7 on June 8 and in days following performed repairs, restoring it to usefulness. They were resupplied by Progress 24 and Kosmos 1669 until the arrival of Soyuz T-14 and cosmonauts Vasyutin, Grechko and Volkov on September 18. Dzhanibekov and Grechko returned to Earth in Soyuz T-13.
51-G	June 17, 1985 0733 EDT Kennedy Space Center, Pad 39A	Capt. Daniel C. Brandenstein, USN, 42 (CDR) Cmdr. John 0. Creighton, USN 42 (PLT) Shannon W. Lucid, 42 (MSl) Lt. Col. Steven R. Nagel, USAF, 38 (MS2) Col. John M. Fabian, USAF, 46 (MS3) Lt. Col. Patrick Baudry, Air Force, 39 (PSl) [France] Sultan Salman Al-Saud, 29 (PS2) [Saudi Arabia]	"Discovery"	June 24, 1985 0912 EDT Edwards AFB, California	7 days, 1 hour, 39 minutes	This, the first tri-national space crew, deployed three communications satellites. Nagel became the lOOth American in space.

51-F	July 29, 1985 1700 EDT Kennedy Space Center, Florida	Col. C. Gordon Fullerton, USAF, 48 (CDR) Col. Roy D. Bridges, Jr., USAF, 42 (PLT) F. Story Musgrave, 49 (MSl) Anthony W. England, 43 (MS2) Karl G. Henize, 58 (MS3) Loren W. Acton, 49 (PSl) John-David F. Bartoe, 41 (PS2)	"Challenger," "Spacelab"	August 6, 1985 1545 EDT Edwards AFB, California	7 days, 22 hours, 45 minutes	Spacelab 2 carried experiments in life sciences, plasma physics, astronomy and solar physics, operated by five scientists, including 58-year-old Henize, the oldest person to make a space flight.
51-I	August 27, 1985 0658 EDT Kennedy Space Center, Pad 39A	Col. Joe H. Engle, USAF, 53 (CDR) Lt. Col. Richard O. Covey, USAF, 39 (PLT) James D. A. van Hoften, 41 (MSl) John M. Lounge, 39 (MS2) William F. Fisher, 39 (MS3)	"Discovery"	September 3, 1985 0916 EDT Edwards AFB, California	7 days, 2 hours, 18 minutes	The astronauts successfully deployed two communications satellites, then retrieved and repaired the ailing Leasat 3 (launched earlier aboard Mission 51-D) in spacewalks by van Hoften and Fisher.
Soyuz T-14	September 17, 1985 1639 MT Baikonur	Lt. Col. Vladimir V. Vasyutin, 33 (CDR) Georgy M. Grechko, 54 (FE) Lt. Col. Alexandr A. Volkov, 37 (CR)	"Cheget"	November 21, 1985 1331 MT 113 miles SE of Dzhezhkagan	64 days, 21 hours, 52 minutes (Vasyutin/Volkov) 168 days, 3 hours, 51 minutes (Savinykh)	Following the repair of Salyut 7 by Dzhanibekov and Savinykh, expedition cosmonauts Vasyutin and Volkov with veteran flight engineer Grechko arrived at the station on September 18, performing the first "relief" mission in space history. Vasyutin, Savinykh and Volkov were to have remained aboard Salyut 7 through March 1986, but had to return on November 21 because of Vasyutin's illness. They used the Kosmos 1686 laboratory module during the mission.
51-J	October 3, 1985 1115 EDT Kennedy Space Center, Pad 39A	Col. Karol J. Bobko, USAF, 47 (CDR) Lt. Col. Ronald J. Grabe, USAF, 40 (PLT) Maj. David C. Hilmers, USMC, 35 (MSl) Col. Robert L. Stewart, USA, 43 (MS2) Maj. William A. Pailes, USAF, 33 (PS)	"Atlantis"	October 7, 1985 1301 EDT Edwards AFB, California	4 days, 1 hour, 46 minutes	The first flight of the Shuttle Atlantis was the second "classified" Department of Defense Shuttle mission, deploying a pair of military communications satellites and setting a Shuttle altitude record of 320 nautical miles.

MISSION	LAUNCH DATA	CREW	CALL SIGN	LANDING DATA	DURATION	REMARKS
61-A	October 30, 1985 0600 EST Kennedy Space Center, Pad 39A	Henry W. Hartsfield, Jr., 51 (CDR) Col. Steven R. Nagel, USAF, 39 (PLT) Col. Guion S. Bluford, Jr., USAF, 42 (MSl) Col. James F. Buchli, USMC, 40 (MS2) Bonnie J. Dunbar, 36 (MS3) Rheinhard Furrer, 44 (PS1) [West Germany] Ernst Messerschmid, 40 (PS2) [West Germany] Wubbo Ockels, 39 (PS3) [ESA]	"Challenger," "Spacelab D1"	November 6, 1985 0645 EST Edwards AFB, California	7 days, 45 minutes	This Spacelab flight, D1, was controlled by the West German Federal Aerospace Research Establishment (DFVLR) and carried experiments devoted to materials processing, communications, and microgravity. It also carried the largest space crew in history.
61-B	November 26, 1985 1329 EST Kennedy Space Center, Pad 39A	Lt. Col. Brewster H. Shaw, Jr., USAF, 40 (CDR) Lt. Col. Bryan D. O'Connor, USMC, 39 (PLT) Maj. Jerry L. Ross, USAF, 37 (MS1) Mary L. Cleave, 38 (MS2) Lt. Col. Sherwood C. Spring, USA, 41 (MS3) Charles D. Walker, 37 (PSl) Rudolfo Neri Vela, 33 (PS2) [Mexico]	"Atlantis"	December 3, 1985 1633 EST Edwards AFB, California	6 days, 21 hours, 4 minutes	The crew of Mission 61-B deployed three communications satellites and also conducted spacewalks (by Ross and Spring) testing space construction techniques.
61-C	January 12, 1986 0655 EST Kennedy Space Center, Pad 39A	Cmdr. Robert L. Gibson, USN, 39 (CDR) Lt. Col. Charles F. Bolden, Jr., USMC, 39 (PLT) Franklin Chang-Diaz, 35 (MSl)	"Columbia"	January 18, 1986 0859 EST Edwards AFB, California	6 days, 2 hours, 6 minutes	Its launch delayed by weather and technical problems seven times, Mission 61-C suffered nagging failures throughout its duration, which was extended by one day to ensure a return to KSC. Weather problems still forced an Edwards landing.

		Steven A. Hawley, 34 (MS2) George D. Nelson, 35 (MS3) Robert J. Cenker, 37 (PSl) Congressman Bill Nelson, 43 (PS2)				
51-L	January 28, 1986 1138 EST Kennedy Space Center, Pad 39B	Francis R. Scobee, 46 (CDR) Cmdr. Michael J. Smith, USN, 40 (PLT) Lt. Col. Ellison S. Onizuka, USAF, 39 (MS1) Judith A. Resnik, 36 (MS2) Ronald E. McNair, 35 (MS3) Gregory K. Jarvis, 41 (PS1) Sharon Christa McAuliffe, 37 (PS2)	"Challenger"			This scheduled five-day Shuttle mission carrying teacher McAuliffe, the first private citizen in space, ended in tragedy when the Challenger disintegrated 75 seconds after launch, killing all seven crew members.
Soyuz T-15	March 13, 1986 1233 MT Baikonur	Col. Leonid D. Kizim, 44 (CDR) Vladimir A. Solovyov, 39 (FE)	"Mayak"	July 16, 1986 1634 MT 33 miles NE of Arkalyk	125 days, 4 hours, 1 minute	Space endurance record-holders Kizim and Solovyov were launched in the last Soyuz T vehicle to perform a difficult dual mission: to activate the new Mir space station, launched February 20, and to retrieve vital scientific experiments from Salyut 7. Kizim and Solovyov docked with Mir on March 15 and remained aboard until May 5, when they used Soyuz T-15 to transfer to Salyut 7. Aboard Salyut 7 they performed two spacewalks (May 28 and May 31), then returned to Mir on June 25 to complete their mission

Appendix 3 X-15 Space Flights

DATE	PILOT	ALTITUDE	VEHICLE	DATE	PILOT	ALTITUDE	VEHICLE
July 17, 1962	R.White	59.16 miles	#3	Sep. 28, 1965	McKay	56 miles	#3
Jan. 17, 1963	Walker	51 miles	#3	Oct. 14, 1965	Engle	50.17 miles	#1
June 27, 1963	Rushworth	55 miles	#3	Nov. 1, 1966	Dana	58 miles	#3
July 19, 1963	Walker	65.3 miles	#3	Oct. 17, 1967	Knight	53.4 miles	#3
Aug. 22, 1963	Walker	66.75 miles	#3	Nov. 15, 1967	Adams	50.4 miles	#3*
June 29, 1965	Engle	53.14 miles	#3	Aug. 21, 1968	Dana	50.7 miles	#1
Aug. 10, 1965	Engle	51.7 miles	#3				

*Pilot killed

Index

Boldface numbers indicate main biographical entries. Photo essays are identified by the following abbreviations: CP-NASA Crew Patches; PASP-Pioneers of the American Space Program; PSSP-Pioneers of the Soviet Space Program.

The Author

Michael Cassutt has been interested in space flight and collecting books and materials on the subject since the first Gemini missions in 1965. (He was eleven at the time.) The interest has persisted through his careers as a professional broadcaster (including a stint as a CBS network television programmer) and as a writer. He has published several articles about astronauts and cosmonauts in magazines such as *Space World, Future Life, L-5 News,* and *Spaceflight*.

In addition, he is also the author of a novel, *The Star Country*, published in 1986, and of several short stories.

His major work these days is for television, most recently as a member of the staff of "The Twilight Zone." He has written for other series, such as "Simon and Simon," "Alice," and, at the moment, "Max Headroom."

He lives in Los Angeles with his wife, Cynthia, and son, Ryan.

Contributors

David J. Shayler, Fellow of the British Interplanetary Society, has written about American astronauts for many books and magazines. Founder of Astro Information Service, he lives in England.

Rex Hall has written about Soviet cosmonauts for the *Journal of the British Interplanetary Society* and other publications. He lives in London.